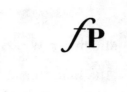

Also by Ian Wilson

The
BLOOD
and the
SHROUD

*New Evidence That the
World's Most Sacred Relic Is Real*

IAN WILSON

THE FREE PRESS

NEW YORK   LONDON   TORONTO

SYDNEY   SINGAPORE

THE FREE PRESS
A Division of Simon & Schuster Inc.
1230 Avenue of the Americas
New York, NY 10020

First published in Great Britain in 1998 by Orion Publishing Group Ltd.

THE FREE PRESS and colophon are trademarks
of Simon & Schuster Inc.

Manufactured in the United States of America

10   9   8   7   6   5   4   3

Library of Congress Cataloging-in-Publication Data is available.

ISBN 0–684–85359–0

Contents

Contents

Illustrations

Author's Preface

Whenever I have given talks on the Turin Shroud, those introducing me have often very kindly described me as an expert on the subject. Whatever impression this book may give to the contrary, I want immediately to disown any such label. And not because of any false modesty.

It is over forty years since I first learned of the Shroud and thirty years since I first actively began to study it. When, nearly twenty years ago, I wrote *The Turin Shroud* as my first ever book, although I tried to treat the subject as objectively as possible, my personal belief in its genuineness was obvious to all. Then, nearly ten years ago, following the highly publicised radiocarbon-dating tests that I had been among the loudest in calling for, the Shroud was very publicly declared a fake. In the eyes of most of the world, I had got it wrong. In the metaphor of this book, my blood had been spilled ...

It might have been very much easier if only I could have gracefully accepted this and got on with the rest of my life. As Judith, my wife for some thirty years, will attest, I am not overly stubborn about admitting to my mistakes. Also, I have long been conscious of the dangers of getting too 'wrapped up' in any one subject, for which reason as a full-time writer I mostly diverted after 1978 to other unrelated topics with the exception of one short 'interim' book in 1986.

But to admit that you have got something wrong, you must first genuinely believe that you made a mistake. And for me, Shroud-wise, that has been, and remains, my greatest difficulty. For although in many respects I feel more confused and ignorant about the subject today than I did when I first learned of it back in 1955 (hence my sincere disavowal of the label 'expert'), even so I cannot 'see' the Shroud as a forgery. Nor does my confusion derive solely from those who claim it on the strength of the carbon dating. Even among those who have upheld the Shroud's authenticity there comes a babble of conflicting ideas and theories, that certainly represents no source of comfort.

Now while, when you feel ignorant of a subject, the best advice is to keep quiet about it, that option closed for me when some flagrantly unworthy books were written in the immediate aftermath of the carbon dating; and again, when the Catholic Church decreed two fresh rounds of showings of the Shroud, for 1998 and 2000, during which the Shroud 'debate' will inevitably be fuelled again. Accordingly, I have assembled this book as my best assessment of where the subject stands at present.

To this end, the prime task of this preface must be to convey my warmest thanks to the innumerable individuals in many fields who in recent years have directly and generously helped me with advice and information from their fields of expertise. In particular:

Art: Isabel Piczek of Los Angeles (for so strenuously keeping me informed of developments both in the USA and in Italy, also for innumerable kindnesses to my wife and me on our visits to her studio in Los Angeles)

Archaeology and Egyptology: Dr Rosalie David of the Manchester Museum, Manchester; Bill Meacham of Hong Kong; Dr Eugenia Nitowski of Utah; Dr Deirdre O'Sullivan of Leicester University; John Ray of Selwyn College, Cambridge

Chemistry: Dr Alan Adler of Western Connecticut State College

Genealogy and Heraldry: Noel Currer-Briggs

History: Professor Robert Drews of Vanderbilt University; Fr Maurus Green, OSB; Professor Richard Kaeuper of the University of Rochester and Dr Elspeth Kennedy (for their timely publication of Dr Kennedy's fine translation of Geoffrey de Charny's *Book of Chivalry*); Père A. M. Dubarle of St Joseph's Convent, Paris (for helpful correspondence and some fine historical articles); Robert Babinet; Professor Dan Scavone (for much friendship and helpful correspondence); Professor Gino Zaninotto of Rome

History of Art: D. Aldring of Norwich; Dr Robin Cormack, Courtauld Institute; Lennox Manton, for his insights on Cappadocian frescos

Jewish Studies: Victor Tunkel of Queen Mary College, University of London

Medicine: Professor Michael Blunt, formerly of the University of Sydney; Dr Robert Bucklin; Professor James Malcolm Cameron, formerly of the London Hospital; Dr Michael Straiton of Surrey; Dr Victor Webster of Australia; Dr Alan Whanger and his wife Mary

Microbiology: Dr Leoncio Garza-Valdès of the University of Texas at San

Antonio, also his wife Maria, for their kind hospitality to my wife and myself; Dr Thomas Loy of the University of Queensland (for much helpful discussion)

Microscopy and microanalysis: Professor Giovanni Riggi of Turin

Nuclear Physics: Dr Kitty Little, formerly of AERE Harwell; Marie-Claire van Oosterwyck-Gastuche of Aubignan, France

Numismatics: Dr David Massa; Mario Moroni; the British Museum Department of Coins and Medals

Photography and Photographic Technology: Professor Nicholas Allen of South Africa; Dr Allan Mills of the University of Leicester; Kevin Moran of North Carolina; Barrie Schwortz of Los Angeles

Physics: Dr John Jackson and his wife Rebecca on our visit to Colorado Springs

Textiles and Textile conservation: Professor Randall Bresee of the Department of Textiles, University of Tennessee; Jean Glover of the North West Museum and Art Gallery Service (UK); Sheila Landi, formerly of the Victoria and Albert Museum conservation department, London; Marc Mees of the church of St Gommaire, Lierre, Belgium; Gabriel Vial of the Textile Museum, Lyon; Dr John Peter Wild, Senior Lecturer in Archaeology, Manchester University.

Radiocarbon dating inevitably looms large among the issues dealt with in this book, and I am grateful to several of those prominent in this field for their kindnesses, in particular Professor Harry Gove of the University of Rochester; Professor Paul Damon of the University of Arizona, Professors Edward Hall and Michael Tite of the University of Oxford, Dr Sheridan Bowman of the British Museum, also Dr Robert Otlet formerly of the Low Level Measurements Laboratory, AERE Harwell, all of whom went out of their way to be helpful.

Also deserving of special mention is microanalyst Dr Walter McCrone of Chicago. However much he may figure in this book as the 'opposition', this should in no way diminish my gratitude to him for a friendly correspondence of twenty years' standing, also for his many kindnesses.

In recent years the subject of the Shroud has spawned a series of journals and newsletters that have served, and continue to serve, as an invaluable source of information, in which regard my special thanks are due to Dorothy Crispino for *Shroud Spectrum*; Gino Moretto for *Sindon*; Professoressa Emanuela Marinelli for *Collegamento Pro Sindone*; Fr Joseph Marino for *Shroud Sources*; Daniel Raffard de Brienne and André van

Cauwenberghe for the CIELT monthly Newsletter, followed more recently by the *Revue Internationale du Linceul de Turin*; Rex Morgan for Australia's *Shroud News*; and by no means least, Barrie Schwortz of Los Angeles for his absolutely excellent Internet site.

More general thanks are also due to Rodger and Connie Apple; Professor Bruno Barberis of Turin; Professor Ed Cherbonnier; Mayor Michel Continant of Lirey; Fr Kim Dreisbach; Miss Gresham Wells; Mark Guscin; Paul and Lois Maloney; Harold Nelson (particularly for his constant thoughtfulness sending me snippets of new information); Fr Francis O'Leary of Jospice International, Liverpool; film-maker Roel Oostra of Hilversum (for facilitating my revisit to Urfa in 1994); Turkish guide Mustafa Rastgeldi (for his helpfulness on that same occasion); Dr Thaddeus Trenn of the University of Toronto and many more.

Some of those who helped in the course of this book died before it could be completed. These included: geneticist Professor Jérôme Lejeune, who was most hospitable to my wife and me on our visit to his home in Paris in 1994; Italian-born American pastor Fr Peter Rinaldi, to whom I owe my first ever viewing of the Shroud in 1973, and who died in the very week of February 1993 that the Shroud was moved to the display case in which it came so close to destruction; also Manchester textile specialist John Tyrer. All of these lived long enough to receive the news of the Shroud's radiocarbon dating yet to be unfazed by it.

On the 'home' front some very particular thanks must go to Dr Michael Clift, General Secretary of the British Society for the Turin Shroud, for his patience and energy providing me with a near daily link with the UK from my current home in Australia. Also very special thanks are due to editor Carey Smith, formerly of Sidgwick & Jackson, who first commissioned the book, and Judith Flanders, Editorial Director of Weidenfeld & Nicolson, who almost instantly took it over when staff changes at Sidgwick–Macmillan raised concerns on my part that it might not be supported by the requisite editorial care. In the very capable hands of Elsbeth Lindner that care has been most assiduous and I am grateful also to Emma Baxter for her liaison, and to Ilsa Yardley for her copy-editing. Particular gratitude is also due to Anthony Cheetham, chief executive of the Orion Publishing Group, for taking an unusually close interest in the book, including resolving much personal uncertainty over the choice of its title.

Last but not least my thanks as ever must go to my wife Judith, who accompanied almost all my researches, past and present, advised on my every uncertainty, checked every chapter, assembled the bibliography and the basis of the index, and supported me in innumerable other ways.

Ian Wilson,
Bellbowrie, Queensland,
October 1997

Note to the Reader

Many authors sceptical of the Shroud's authenticity write of it as the 'shroud' rather than the 'Shroud', arguing that any author who uses an upper-case 'S' must automatically be a 'True Believer'. To me there is a great deal of woolliness to this particular type of thinking. Although I do not happen to be a 'believer' in either the Bayeux Tapestry or Tower of London, if I use capitals for these they unmistakably establish which tower and tapestry I am speaking of, and my capitalisation of the Turin Shroud, as used throughout this book, has solely this same function. Thus it will be noted that where in this book I speak of Jesus's burial shroud in a context other than as the Turin Shroud, I have happily used a lower-case 's'. Ironically, for me a writer's use of lower-case 's' actually indicates his or her recognition of the Turin Shroud as a true burial shroud, something which many clearly do not intend.

With regard to notes and references, I have provided these at the back of the book, but there are places, particularly with regard to the Shroud's history, where some readers may want more detailed background sources than actually appear. These they will find in my two earlier books on the Shroud. To have repeated all sources in this book would have made the notes and references very top-heavy and unnecessarily repetitive.

THE
BLOOD
AND THE
SHROUD

Cloth of Passion: The 'bloody' controversy that still rages over whether the Shroud is fake or genuine

B y any measure the Turin Shroud is a Cloth of Passion. Literally *and* metaphorically. If it is genuinely the cloth which wrapped Jesus's dead body, then it is spattered with some of the very blood that once flowed through his veins. And even if it is a mediaeval forgery of this same, its first known owner's fate was to die the bloodiest of deaths on the battlefield of Poitiers.

As for metaphorical 'blood', very few of those of modern times who have become drawn into the Shroud mystery have escaped some form of serious wounding, almost in the manner of Tutankhamun's infamous 'curse'. Of this there can be little more recent or poignant example than Turin's archbishop, Cardinal Giovanni Saldarini, whom Pope John Paul II appointed the Shroud's 'Custodian' in September 1990, shortly after the cloth's traditional repository, the seventeenth-century Royal Chapel linking Turin's Royal Palace and cathedral, had to be closed because lumps of stone were falling from its dome.

Saldarini is a most genial, conscientious and capable individual who quickly recognised that the Royal Chapel, with its Guarino Guarini dome and soaring, wedding-cake-tiered altar that has been the Shroud's home for the last three centuries [pl. 2a], could not be allowed to fall into ruin. Accordingly, in concert with the Italian State government (who technically own all the former 'royal' properties), he initiated major structural repairs. To give the Shroud optimum protection while these were in progress, he arranged for its transfer, still rolled up inside its traditional silvered wooden casket, to a state-of-the-art new bullet-proof display case specially built just behind the cathedral's High Altar [pl. 2b]. Aware that May 1998 represented the historic one hundredth anniversary of the discovery of the Shroud's now world-famous negative 'photograph', he ordered public expositions of the Shroud (the first held for twenty years), between that year's 18 April and 14 June. In line with the Pope's call for events com-

memorating the second millennial anniversary of Christ's birth he scheduled a further round of these for the year 2000. And as at the beginning
of April 1997 all seemed to be going almost perfectly according to plan,
with even a lift installed for those wanting closer inspection of Guarino
Guarini's chapel dome, and preparations comfortably in readiness for the
three million or more visitors expected to pour into Turin during the eight
week period that the Shroud would be on view.

Then, shortly after 11 p.m. on the night of 11 April, disaster struck. The
first intimation was a cryptic warning to the local police that a fire 'might'
break out in the cathedral. The next, at 11.35 p.m., was a frantic call from
cathedral parish priest, Fr Francesco Barbero, that the cathedral's fire
alarms were ringing and that the Royal Chapel was already uncontrollably
ablaze. Although Turin's XXI fire brigade was quickly upon the scene,
confronting them as they burst into the cathedral was a mass of smoke
and flame at the High Altar end, with almost directly above this an already
unstoppable conflagration consuming the first floor, glass-fronted Royal
Chapel.

Then, amidst all the smoke and confusion, fireman Mario Trematore
spotted the new display case to which the Shroud had so recently been
moved, its normally gleaming glass already near-unrecognisable from the
debris raining down from above. As he quickly realised, if the chapel's
three-hundred-year-old dome were to crash down it would be bound to
consume the display case and its precious contents in an avalanche of
fiery rubble. Without hesitation (although, as a good Catholic, not without
a silent prayer), he raised his fireman's sledge-hammer and swung it with
all his might against the near two-inch-thick specially toughened glass. It
went a milky colour, but didn't even begin to shatter. As some of his fellow
firemen crowded supportively around, again and again he swung at it, at
last creating a hole big enough to reach into and pull through the Shroud's
bulky, four-and-a-half-foot-long silvered casket. Moments later, as TV
cameramen on the scene zoomed in on a visibly tearful Cardinal Saldarini,
the casket was rushed through the cathedral nave to safety.

Three days later, having made his own residence the Shroud's temporary
place of refuge, Cardinal Saldarini assembled there a small gathering of
specially invited specialists and officials. On his instructions these solemnly opened up the Shroud casket and unrolled the cloth onto a long
table [pl. 1c] to find, to their very considerable relief, that it had survived
unscathed. But as Saldarini was acutely aware, there were a host of indications that the fire had been deliberately lit. Also, almost the entire High

2

Altar environs where the Shroud would have been exhibited was now a blackened ruin, with repairs likely to last into the next century. So what was to become of the scheduled expositions? Should they simply be cancelled until further notice?

Meanwhile I was another individual to have felt more than a little bloodied by this same turn of events. In April 1997 I was at my newly adopted home in Australia, just days from the scheduled completion of this book. The very moment that I heard the news I knew that some serious revision of my manuscript would be needed (ironically, only the day before, in rewriting the first draft of chapter 9, I had spoken of the Shroud's location in the new bullet-proof display case as one of the few definite facts!). But this aside, the news just represented one more trauma on top of the many to which I had become almost inured in the course of my now forty-year association – some might deservedly call it obsession – with the Turin Shroud.

As a very agnostic London schoolboy I had first come across it in a popular magazine article published in 1955. What immediately shook me to the quick, challenging all my previously smug scepticism towards matters religious, was the so obviously lifelike 'photograph' of a crucified body that can be seen on the negative whenever the Shroud is photographed in black and white. So profoundly did this affect me that, albeit ten years later, I began the spare-time historical and other researches that gradually persuaded me, not without continuing self-questioning, that the Shroud must indeed be the cloth which had wrapped Jesus's body in the tomb two thousand years ago. A cloth somehow (and this was the aspect of it which really gripped me) imprinted with his very 'photograph' in death.

In November 1973, while I was living in Bristol, England, a call came through from the United States alerting me that for the first time in forty years the Shroud was to be brought out for public gaze from its then normal repository in the Royal Chapel. It was to be shown on Italian television, and there was also to be an unprecedented opportunity for journalists and interested individuals such as myself to view the cloth at first hand.

It was one of those moments in life that you either seize immediately, or regret ever after. By lunch-time on 22 November I found myself, with some thirty others, being given a brief preliminary introduction by Turin's then archbishop, Cardinal Michele Pellegrino. The group was escorted up a grand marble staircase of Turin's Royal Palace and into a huge, frescoed

3

hall, the Hall of the Swiss. At the far end of this the Shroud hung upright in a simple oak frame, its fourteen-foot length brilliantly illuminated by high-powered television lights.

Then came the second shock. It did not look at all as I had expected. Everything that I knew of the Shroud up to this point – and I thought I knew quite a lot – had been based on black-and-white photographs that, whether they are in positive or negative, make it look a lot darker than it really is [pls 6–7a & b]. To see the original's faintness and subtlety was really quite breath-taking. Framed by the burns and patches from the *other* fire in which the Shroud came perilously close to destruction – a similarly ruinous chapel blaze while it was being kept at Chambéry in 1532 – there was the familiar 'body image' that to me was the Shroud's central mystery. If you stood back you could make it out readily enough: a bearded face, a pronounced chest, crossed hands, legs side by side, together with, as one looked up at the back-of-the-body image, a long rope of hair, taut shoulders and buttocks, and soles of the feet.

But the image colour was the subtlest yellow sepia, and as you moved in closer to anything like touching distance (and I saw to my astonishment that the cloth was unprotected by any glass), it seemed virtually to disappear like mist. Because of the lack of outline and the minimum contrast to the ivory-coloured background, it became wellnigh impossible to 'see' whatever detail you were trying to look at without stepping some distance back again. To me, as a practising life-painter and an enthusiast of art history, it seemed absolutely impossible that any artist-faker could have created an image of this kind, certainly not one of centuries ago. The succeeding day and a half during which I was allowed some eight hours of further direct examination served to reaffirm my conviction, despite all the obvious rational objections, that this cloth simply *had* to be genuine.

The next five years passed in something of a whirl, with world interest in the cloth growing sufficiently that in October 1978, following a six-week public exhibition of the Shroud (the first since 1933), an assemblage of some thirty American scientists, the so-called STURP[1] team, were allowed five days in which to subject the cloth and its image to a battery of high-powered scientific tests. These included visual, photographic and spectroscopic examinations and the taking of over thirty sticky-tape samples representative of 'body image', 'blood-image' and non-image areas. In the wake of these, the STURP team's conclusion, like my own, was that the Shroud is no painting.

While their sticky tapes revealed the presence of all sorts of microscopic

4

debris littering the Shroud's surface, including some particles that might be paint, their interpretation was that whatever had created the image proper was not paint or any other artificial substance. Instead it was some physical force that had in effect 'flashed' itself onto the cloth in a very precisely controlled manner according to the cloth's distance from the theoretical body at any one point. As for the 'bloodstains', they found these indeed to be genuine human blood.

By the end of 1978 the expositions and the STURP testing had given the Shroud a higher public awareness and acceptance than it had ever enjoyed before, and I for my part had been invited by the American publishers Doubleday to write a book on the subject which was published that year.[2] In it I had set out my hypothesis of where the Shroud might have been in its history prior to its emergence in the 1350s in the tiny French village of Lirey, all the way back to the first century AD.

As I was the first to acknowledge, mine was a mere hypothesis, more than a little weak in places and thereby needing further supporting evidence, for which the ideal was one test which the American STURP team had not carried out in 1978 – radiocarbon dating, the method of determining an archaeological artefact's age by calculating the extent to which it has lost its very mildly radioactive carbon-14 content, this being known measurably to 'decay' year by year after an organism's death. This particular test had not been included in STURP's programme mainly because at that time it would have needed a pocket-sized sample of the Shroud's linen, rather more than those responsible for the Shroud were prepared to sacrifice.

However, in May 1977 American nuclear physicist Professor Harry Gove of Rochester University, together with some like-minded colleagues, successfully tested a new accelerator mass spectrometry (AMS) technique of carbon dating, one requiring a sample something of the order of a thousand times smaller than that which had been needed before. And although this method was too new and undeveloped to be used in 1978, it represented the obvious one for the future.

In the event, it took innumerable wranglings before, in October 1987, Turin's Cardinal Anastasio Ballestrero, Archbishop Pellegrino's successor (and Cardinal Saldarini's immediate predecessor), approved a list of three radiocarbon laboratories which were to be allowed sufficient sample from the Shroud for them to be able to carry out this test. These were the Research Laboratory for Archaeology and the History of Art, Oxford, the Swiss Federal Institute of Technology's radiocarbon-dating facility at

Zurich, and the University of Arizona's facility at Tucson, all of these having successfully developed the new Gove AMS method. After some preliminary discussions in the January of 1988 at London's British Museum, representatives of each of these laboratories travelled to Turin in April where, in the early hours of the morning of the 21st, they were escorted into the cathedral.

Shown into the bench-lined sacristy, they found that the Shroud had been laid out before them on a large table, having been brought down during the night from its normal location in the Royal Chapel. As they waited, Turin microanalyst Professor Giovanni Riggi, the man deputed to take their samples, together with his colleague Professor Gonella, first lengthily and noisily conferred concerning the best location on the Shroud from which these should be removed. When this was resolved, Riggi very dextrously and ceremoniously cut an 8-cm-×-1-cm sliver from the left-hand corner at the foot end of the Shroud's frontal image. He then cut this in half and divided one of the halves into three for apportionment between the laboratories, retaining the other half. Each sample was then carefully weighed before being taken to a side room where Dr Michael Tite (later to become Professor), of the British Museum, the project's chosen scientific co-ordinator, packed it into a special coded stainless-steel canister sealed with the Cardinal's own seal. During this same operation Tite also provided each laboratory with a set of similarly coded canisters containing pre-selected samples of cloth of both mediaeval and first-century date intended as 'controls'.

As the laboratory representatives returned home with their canisters, the Turin authorities released the news of their mission to the world and during the succeeding months, first the Arizona laboratory personnel, then Zurich's, then Oxford's ran their particular samples through their equipment. Despite the fact that they had all been sworn not to disclose their findings until these could be collectively released, all sorts of rumours began circulating, almost all of them suggesting that the Shroud had been found to date to the Middle Ages.

During the second week of October 1988 press personnel of the English-speaking world were notified that the results would be announced on Thursday, 13 October in the British Museum's Press Room, with a near-synchronous press conference to be held in Turin that same day.

Accordingly, early that Thursday afternoon I joined this gathering in a dingy, poorly lit and overcrowded basement room of the British Museum. At one end of the room had been set a low platform which three men mounted, reminding me of some of the past Shroud expositions when three bishops on a platform would hold up the Shroud for veneration.

But in this year of 1988 these men were no bishops. They were the already mentioned Dr Michael Tite, with the Oxford radiocarbon-dating laboratory's Professor Edward Hall and Hall's chief technician, Dr Robert Hedges. Nor did they have any Shroud to display. Instead their only 'prop' was a blackboard behind them on which someone had rather crudely scrawled: '1260–1390!' [pl. 3b].

And this was my third, and this time most unpleasant, shock, nothing less than a real body blow. For as Dr Tite explained, these numbers represented radiocarbon dating's calculation, to a ninety-five per cent degree of probability, of the upper and lower dates of when the Shroud's flax had been harvested. Representing an average of the laboratories' findings, which had proved in excellent agreement with each other, they indicated that the Shroud's raw flax had most likely been made into linen on or about the year AD 1325, give or take sixty-five years either way.

This statement rendered worthless all my historical researches on the Shroud, on which I had then been working for more than twenty years. It also negated much of the medical and other evidence which had equally impressed me. The Shroud simply could not possibly be any true shroud of the historical Jesus. For as those on the platform collectively insisted, the odds against this were now 'astronomical'. The radiocarbon dates matched unerringly closely to the time in the 1350s when the Shroud had made its European début in the suspiciously tiny French village of Lirey. They seemingly confirmed a memorandum that the French Bishop Pierre d'Arcis had written to his Pope in the year 1389[3] [pl. 3a] advising him that according to his (d'Arcis's) predecessor of the 1350s, Bishop Henri of Poitiers, the Shroud had been '... cunningly painted, the truth being attested by the artist who had painted it, to wit, that it was a work of human skill and not miraculously wrought or bestowed.'[4]

The radiocarbon dating had therefore confirmed Bishop Henri's insights, all the more believable given the Middle Ages' notorious credulity towards religious relics. As this was expressed by the characteristically forceful Professor Hall: 'There was a multi-million-pound business in making forgeries during the fourteenth century. Someone just got a bit of linen, faked it up and flogged it.'[5]

Thus it was that on the morning of 14 October 1988 most of the world woke up to newspaper headlines – by no means always front-page news – that the Shroud had been 'proven' to be a mediaeval fake. At his Turin press conference Cardinal Ballestrero, true to his earlier expressed insistence that the Church has nothing to fear from the truth, declared that he accepted the laboratories' findings even though, as he carefully added, 'the problems about the origin of the image and its preservation still remain to a large extent unresolved'. England's *Daily Telegraph* newspaper duly translated this into the headline 'Turin shroud is a forgery, says Catholic Church'. On the same day *Independent* newspaper journalists Michael Sheridan and Phil Reeves cheerfully linked the Shroud to other products of 'mediaeval tricksters' such as 'a feather from the Archangel Gabriel ... the last breath of St Joseph, several heads of St John the Baptist',[6] rather as if the Shroud were in the same mould as these and that its fraudulence should all along have been obvious to everyone.

Scientifically the *coup de grâce* came on 16 February 1989 with the scientific journal *Nature*'s publication of the radiocarbon-dating laboratories' formal technical report. Authored by no less than twenty-one of the scientists who had played some part in obtaining the final result, this claimed 'conclusive evidence that the linen of the shroud of Turin is mediaeval'.[7] As the Oxford laboratory's Professor Edward Hall repeatedly stressed in accompanying interviews and talks, no one of any scientific worth could any longer believe in the possibility of the Shroud being genuine. If they did, they might just as well join the Flat Earthers.

Thus it seemed that anyone who had previously upheld any serious case for the Shroud's credibility, among whom I numbered myself, had been dealt a fatal stab to the heart. And sadly, the quality of argument on the part of those who refused to accept that they were 'dead' quickly degenerated into the unworthy. For some Shroud supporters in continental Europe, for instance, the chief defence offered was that it was the radio-carbon dating, not the Shroud, that must be the fraud.

As foremost spokesperson for this particular viewpoint there surfaced the French priest Brother Bruno Bonnet-Eymard, of the very right-wing Catholic group the 'Catholic Counter-Reformation in the Twentieth Century'. As he noted, although the main proceedings of the taking of samples had been videotaped, this was not the case with the putting of the samples into their coded canisters. During this the British Museum's Dr Michael Tite had been accompanied in the side room only by the elderly Cardinal. Bonnet-Eymard therefore outrightly accused Dr Tite of having 'switched' the control samples so that the pieces which the laboratories thought to be the Shroud were in actuality control samples of mediaeval date, while the pieces that they thought to be control samples of first-century date were in fact the genuine Shroud.

Although there was not the slightest serious evidence to support such allegations, even distinguished European Shroud scholars such as the Jesuit Professor Werner Bulst and others became persuaded to follow some variant or other of this party line. Exacerbating this, similar claims were made by the sensationalist German writers Holger Kersten and Elmar Gruber, and with the ingenious extra twist that Dr Tite had allegedly performed his sleight of hand as a result of a clandestine 'deal' with the Vatican. As this duo explained in their book *The Jesus Conspiracy*, certain high officials at the Vatican did not want the Shroud to be found genuine, for the reason that they knew that it and its bloodstains proved that Jesus did not die on the cross. This meant that the 'Resurrection' was not the miracle that Christians believe it to be, which was why the Vatican was so keen to conspire with Dr Tite, because if ever the news got out it would put all the world's clergymen out of business overnight.

But if this was the best that those who still believed the Shroud to be first century could come up with, oddly, little greater light came even from those who fully accepted the radiocarbon dating's findings. All these needed to account for was how someone of the fourteenth century could have 'faked the Shroud up' as Professor Hall would describe it. In other words how someone of an artistically relatively backward period managed to create on the Shroud an image that so convincingly looks to be a positive photograph when it is viewed in negative, despite the fact that no one of the Middle Ages could have seen it in this manner.

And there has been no shortage of theorists in this regard. The Chicago microanalyst Dr Walter McCrone, for instance, had been vigorously maintaining from the early 1980s that a mediaeval artist created the Shroud by simply painting its image onto the cloth using iron-oxide pigments in a gelatin binding medium. According to him, this artist's so successful production of the negative was just a lucky chance deriving from his deliberately painting in reverse of positive tones. In the light of the radiocarbon-dating result McCrone triumphantly declared his argument one hundred per cent vindicated.

Likewise Kentucky teacher, stage magician and die-hard sceptic Joe Nickell has argued for a mediaeval hoaxer having created much this same effect with the aid of a bas-relief of a body laid out in the manner of the man of the Shroud, thereupon splashing on the bloodstains for effect. University of Tennessee forensic pathologist Emily Craig and textile specialist Professor Randall Bresee have put forward the idea that a medi-aeval forger first must have carefully painted the Shroud's image on a sheet of paper, then transferred this to the linen of the Shroud proper using a burnishing technique, the Shroud's image thereby being some-thing between a brass rubbing and a xerox photocopy.

British physician Dr Michael Straiton has explained the so convincing bloodstains by suggesting that the Shroud is simply that of a dead Crusader crucified by the Saracens in mockery of Jesus's crucifixion, although he has some difficulty explaining the negative. Popular writers Christopher Knight and Robert Lomas have gone one further, actually naming the Crusader as Jacques de Molay, the last Grand Master of the Knights Templar, according to them crucified by the Inquisition as a sardonic torture prior to his being burned at the stake in 1314.[8]

South African art professor Nicholas Allen has quite recently argued for the Shroud being a genuine photograph, the world's first, created by a mediaeval artificer using a natural lens and photographic salts known and understood in the Middle Ages. His theory readily accounts for the nega-tive but he has trouble accounting for the bloodstains.

Closely related to Allen's theory has been that of London journalist Lynn Picknett and partner Clive Prince that the Shroud was created, again photographically, by none other than Leonardo da Vinci. According to this duo Leonardo, undoubtedly well known for his pioneering anatomical dissections, used a specially crucified body, but his own face, for a fake that had been ordered by Pope Innocent VIII.

Yet ingenious as so many of these ideas are, the plain fact is that they are extremely varied and from not one of them has come sufficient of a groundswell of support to suggest that it truly convincingly might hold the key to how the Shroud was forged – if indeed it was forged.

For however heretical and unscientific it might sound even mildly to suggest that the radiocarbon dating might have been wrong in the case of the Shroud, what cannot be stressed strongly enough is that all that it has produced, and ever can produce, is an instrument reading that seems to indicate a serious finding, but in itself can explain noth-ing.

By way of analogy we might cite the case of a jumbo-jet pilot who mid-way during a routine flight across the Atlantic suddenly finds that his fuel gauges – scientific instruments upon which he can normally rely – are telling him that his plane is out of fuel. What should he do? Should he blindly accept what his instruments are telling him, and proceed immediately to ditch his plane and its passengers into the ocean? Or should he make a few other checks first?

In effect, this is precisely the situation that has pertained since 1988 with regard to the Shroud and its carbon dating. In which context, just as our airline pilot would need, as a matter of basics, to have trusted those who assured him they had loaded his fuel, so let me rule out straight away any challenge to the integrity of Dr Michael Tite and the radiocarbon-dating scientists of the kind that has been indulged in by Bonnet-Eymard, Kersten and Gruber, and others.

For during both the preliminaries to and the immediate aftermath of the Shroud radiocarbon dating I struck up a moderate acquaintance with the British Museum's Dr Tite, the Oxford laboratory's Professor Hall and the Arizona laboratory's Professor Damon, from which experience I can say with some confidence that any scenario suggesting that one or more of these men may have 'rigged' the radiocarbon dating – let alone con-spired with the Vatican – may be judged as absurd and far-fetched as it is unworthy. Professor Damon's chief technician at Arizona, Professor Douglas Donahue, is a devout Catholic who reportedly paled visibly on becoming the first man to learn the Shroud's dating to the Middle Ages as this was printed out on the Arizona laboratory's computer.[9] He had fully expected the dating to indicate the Shroud's genuineness, but equally, fully accepted the validity of the result when it came. Damon himself is a practising Quaker. As for the bespectacled and very 'English' Dr Tite, the idea of him entering any kind of conspiracy with Roman Catholic cardinals is risible in the extreme. Besides all of which the radiocarbon laboratory scientists photographed the samples they brought back with them from Turin, in each case recognising immediately (despite the coding of the canisters), which specimen was the Shroud, because of its distinctive weave. Any sample switch would have been very easily spotted had there been one, which there was not. The 'skulduggery' scenario may therefore be dismissed out of hand.

Instead what we need to confront is that three reputable international radiocarbon-dating laboratories, using the very best of modern technology, radiocarbon dated the Shroud to some time around the early part of the fourteenth century, a date uncomfortably close to the time when a mediaeval French bishop said it had been forged, and equally uncomfort-ably far from the lifetime of Jesus. If the Shroud really is of the fourteenth century then we need to try to understand very clearly how on earth it was created, mendaciously or otherwise, by someone of that time.

Conversely, if it really is of the time of Jesus, we need to try to understand equally clearly how three state-of-the-art radiocarbon-dating laboratories could have got their datings so seriously wrong.

Now while this is a task that might preferably have waited another generation, and the application of technologies yet to be born, what has made it of sudden urgency is the very same plan we heard announced by Cardinal Saldarini at the beginning of this chapter, that the Shroud is to be publicly exhibited again in Turin April to June 1988, followed by another exposition in the year 2000. For despite the massive setbacks of the fire *and* the seemingly so damning carbon dating, the official word from Cardinal Saldarini, apparently with the full backing of Pope John Paul II, is that the expositions *will* still go ahead, virtually come what may. It is a determination that makes it yet more remarkable that the Church should ever have decided to hold the expositions at all, when this is in such apparent defiance of the Shroud having been so publicly declared a fraud.

For throughout all the centuries of the Shroud's known history, when it was owned not by the Church but by the Savoy family who became kings of Italy, it was the Church's official policy always to avoid giving any too overt endorsement of its genuineness, just as there was similar avoidance in the case of other relics, also of people exhibiting miraculous-seeming phenomena such as stigmata.

Yet less than two decades since the Shroud came into the Church's ownership, and less than a decade since radiocarbon dating declared the Shroud a fake, the Church has begun to behave as if it has the genuine article, against all the odds, including a determined attempt to destroy that article (for all the latest findings suggest that the Chapel fire *was* indeed arson).

So why this sudden volte-face? Does the Church have some very good reason for believing that the radiocarbon dating was wrong and that the Shroud may be genuine after all?

Like our hypothetical jumbo-jet pilot, all we can do, faced with an instrument reading that says that the flax of the Shroud's linen did not 'die' until thirteen centuries after Jesus's lifetime, is to review the whole subject again. We must check anew every aspect, every assumption, every facet of the subject, including the radiocarbon dating, in order to deter-mine just how much that may hitherto have been accepted as fact can or cannot any longer be trusted.

For this is not a time for trying to salvage any egos, mine or anyone else's, however deeply injured they might feel by so publicly being pronounced wrong. Today, in the cold light of the radiocarbon dating the alternatives posed by the Shroud are even starker than they ever have been. It has either to be the most astonishing, most mind-blowingly 'out-of-time' product to come down to us from the Middle Ages. Or, despite all the contradictions, it has to be the genuine article, equally mind-blowingly created by the body of Jesus himself. Huge passions underscore each of these positions. Yet somehow, in the interests of all future understanding of the subject, we need to resolve within which of these two alternatives lies the greater truth.

With these aims firmly in mind it will therefore be the task of this book to rescrutinise every genuinely worthy hypothesis, whether for or against authenticity, with equal *dis*passion. It is my pledge that I will treat those seriously sceptical of the Shroud's authenticity with the same respect as those supportive of it. And from this point of view no aspect of the Shroud presents any greater challenge than its seemingly 'photographic' image – the subject's central mystery and *raison d'être*, without which I for one would never have become involved.

Accordingly it is with this so mysterious image, and with absolutely anything and everything that the eye may reasonably understand and interpret of it, that we will now begin.

Part 1

Cunning Painting – or Genuine Photograph? The Shroud reassessed as an Image

Chapter 1

How can we be sure we are looking at a genuine human body?

O ver the six centuries that the Shroud has been historically known and shown to the European public, observers have always been able to discern with the unaided eye the same ghost-like imprint of a bearded man with crossed hands that I viewed in 1973. As the sceptical Bishop d'Arcis remarked in 1389 (not necessarily from his own first-hand observation), it comprises 'the two-fold image of one man, that is to say, the back and the front ... thus impressed together with the wounds he bore'. Fake or genuine, the long-standing understanding of this imprint has been that the body it represents was laid on one half of the cloth, with the other half then drawn over the head and down to the feet, thereby creating the head-to-head or 'two-fold' effect.

But as is now well known, the Shroud's truly spectacular feature is revealed when its light values are reversed, light to dark, dark to light, by any camera using black-and-white film. The first man to discover this effect was the Italian councillor and keen amateur photographer Secondo Pia [pl. 4b], who was appointed to take the first ever official photograph of the Shroud during the eight-day exposition of 1898. At around 9.30 p.m. on the evening of 28 May, Pia set up his cumbersome box-like camera before the Shroud as it hung above the cathedral altar, made two long exposures using large glass photographic plates, then hurried back to his dark-room to develop these.

As he would subsequently relate, his first thoughts were of relief when he saw pin-sharp negatives of the cathedral altar's ornamentation, which he knew would appear at the edges of his composition, emerge under the developer. But then to his astonishment, as he studied the long oblong that had to be the Shroud itself, there slowly appeared on this not the traces of the ghostly figure that he expected, but instead an unmistakably photographic likeness.

What Bishop d'Arcis had called the 'two-fold image of one man' had undergone a dramatic qualitative change. Now, natural light and dark shading gave the impression of relief and depth. Instead of the man seeming to have a rather grotesque and deformed appearance, he could be seen to be well proportioned and of an impressive physique, the apparent bloodstains from his injuries, because red registers dark in black-and-white photography, showing up in a flat white on his naked body. Most striking of all was his face, quite astonishingly dignified and lifelike against the black background.

As Pia himself immediately recognised, the clear implication was that the Shroud itself was, in effect, a photographic negative that had been waiting dormant, like a pre-programmed time capsule, for the moment that photography's invention would release its hidden true 'positive'. It seemed to him that he had been privileged to become the first man to look upon Jesus's earthly likeness since the days of the apostles.

With the gradual spreading of the news of this discovery, accompanied by the image's publication in newspapers and journals around the world, so there surfaced every form of doubt that anything of this kind could possibly be genuine. In particular, doubts focused on Pia's technically amateur status as a photographer and on his integrity. In an age less conversant with photography than our own, some ignorantly claimed that his photographic plate had simply been 'over-exposed'; others that it had been made by 'transparency'. Particularly wounding for Pia, and a classic instance of our metaphorical 'blood', were malicious insinuations that he had deliberately faked his photograph and that it was all just a hoax.

In the event it took thirty-three years for Pia's competence and honesty to be vindicated, though thankfully he survived to see this day. In May 1931 the Shroud's owner, King Victor-Emmanuel III of Savoy, agreed to fresh photography to accompany a twenty-one-day Shroud exposition being held in that year, the chosen photographer for this occasion being a professional, Commander Giuseppe Enrie. Allowed to work without the Shroud being covered by glass (a facility not accorded to Pia[1]), and taking full advantage of the considerable technical advances in photography since 1898, Enrie photographed the Shroud full length, just as Pia had done, and additionally made a series of life-sized close-ups of the face, the back and shoulders, and a bloodstain to the lower forearm.

In doing so, not only did Enrie confirm Pia's 'photographic negative' effect, he also revealed it with markedly greater clarity and detail [pls 6–7a]. In Enrie's richly atmospheric old studio, still part of a Turin photographic business, I have personally held in my hands the original glass negative of his life-sized close-up of the Shroud face. Its detail and photographic realism are quite stunning [pl. 5a]. To try to interpret it as the product of some unknown mediaeval faker seems rather like trying to argue for the Taj Mahal being a mere geological accident. Nor is this a purely personal view. In 1967 the British photographic professional Leo Vala, inventor of several new photographic techniques and a complete agnostic, commented of this same negative: 'I've been involved in the invention of many complicated visual processes and I can tell you that no one could have faked that image. No one could do it today with all the technology we have. It's a perfect negative. It has a photographic quality that is extremely precise.'[2]

Following Enrie's black-and-white work, in June 1969 Giovanni Battista Judica-Cordiglia took the first ever colour photographs of the Shroud, both full-sized and of selected areas, along with yet more renditions in black and white. In November 1973 numerous further photographs were taken during the showing I attended, followed in 1978 with photography being freely allowed by members of the public during the six-week-long expositions held in that year. At the closure of these expositions it was the turn of the American STURP team, whose photographic work not only included more use of black-and-white film, but also complete X-radiographs, macrophotography of tiny details and colour photography of sufficiently high quality to make life-sized colour transparencies. Jewish-born Barrie Schwortz [pl. 5b], one of the most senior of the STURP photographers, has described how he initially hesitated to join the project on the grounds that he must surely be out of place in a team examining a cloth with such intense Christian associations.[3] In the event he became so fascinated that he has continued his interest over nearly twenty years, even creating a special Internet site for Shroud photographs and information.

From all this photographic work, which today allows even children to check out for themselves the negativity effect on their home computers, what can be said with absolute confidence is that the Shroud's so lifelike photographic negative derives from no modern-day photographic trick. The hidden 'photograph', whatever its origin, is a fact of the Shroud that has to be faced by the Shroud's detractors just as fairly and squarely as its supporters must face the results from the radiocarbon dating. And exactly as in the case of the radiocarbon dating, no assumption should be allowed to pass unchallenged.

As has been pointed out by the British archaeologist Christopher Frayling, it is surely a circular argument to call the Shroud a photograph and thereby to conclude that it cannot be any kind of painted forgery.[4] Yet while this is true, our only recourse for determining within which of these two alternatives lies the greater truth is to try to analyse this image element by element in order to come to at least some reasonable judgement on what exactly it is we are seeing. And given that Dr Walter McCrone contends it to be a painting, and 'cunning painting' was the term used by the sceptical Bishop d'Arcis as long ago as 1389, one of our first priorities has to be to decide whether it might be just that, or whether we really could be seeing a genuine human body.

In order to help us resolve this question there can be few better guides than professional painter and specialist in studies of the naked human figure Isabel Piczek [pl. 11a]. A child prodigy in her native Iron-Curtain Hungary, Piczek held her first professional painting exhibition at the age of eleven and graduated from Budapest's Academy of Fine Arts at only thirteen. Peremptorily summoned to communist Moscow to complete her studies, within a day she fled her home without papers or belongings, crossing four borders, including the Austrian Alps in early winter. Reaching Rome she entered and as quickly won an open public competition to paint a large and very prestigious mural for the city's Pontifical Biblical Institute, horrifying the competition's pre-Vatican II clerical judges when they discovered that they had awarded the commission to a slightly built thirteen-and-a-half-year-old girl.

In the event, Piczek's highly accomplished completed work confirmed the wisdom of their choice. There followed forty-two more highly acclaimed murals in Italy before, in 1956, she emigrated to the United States to specialise in ever vaster murals, up to 3000 square feet in scale, for cathedrals and other major shrines around the states of California, Nevada and elsewhere. Today resident in Los Angeles, she continues with relentless energy to tackle similarly ambitious murals, along with large-scale projects in mosaic, ceramic tile and stained glass. Versatile in painting in oils, tempera, acrylics, even pure iron oxide – the pigment McCrone claims to have been used to paint the Shroud – and with a style neither too traditional nor too modern, Isabel Piczek may be said to know a thing or two about the craft of painting.

So what, then, is her view on the question of whether the Shroud image is some kind of 'photograph' of a genuine human body, or just an artist's 'cunning painting'? Although she first became actively interested in the subject only within the last few years, to see her perched atop her fifteen-foot studio ladder, Shroud 'negative' photograph in hand, carefully checking from this the pose of a totally naked male model laid out Shroud-style directly below her, is to realise that she takes it very seriously indeed – particularly when one learns that she has vetted literally dozens of models for this pose, trying to find one with absolutely the right height and physique.

Immediately needing to be stressed in this context is that for Piczek the use of a nude model, male or female, is neither out of the ordinary nor a matter of the slightest embarrassment. As an advocate of the classical method of making preliminary studies from the nude, she routinely hires professional life models to assume the poses that her compositions demand. For those of her works depicting Jesus's crucifixion she has sometimes required a model to pose roped to a studio cross for several hours at a time, repeating this over several days. As she has commented matter-of-factly of one of the lesser-known physiological effects of this: 'After a lapse of two or three hours, the genitals begin assuming a boyish and even a childish size.'[5] In short, Piczek also knows more than a thing or two about human anatomy, even 'crucified' human anatomy, and we should therefore reasonably anticipate her ability to distinguish between any 'cunning artist's' mere painted depiction of a human body and any 'photograph', created by whatever means, of the real thing.

So what, then, is her professional opinion on the Shroud? As expressed in highly illustrated talks and articles, it is emphatic in the extreme: 'Although there is an argument that no artist of the Middle Ages could have painted a negative image, the fact is that even today, with or without the aid of a camera, no one could paint a negative image with anything like the *perfection* exhibited on the Shroud.'

Since this matter is central to the whole Shroud issue, worth considering in the first instance, by way of demonstration, is the purported Christ face on the negative. If the visible light levels to this are arbitrarily broken into just three, light, medium and dark, it may be observed on the forehead how the bridge of the eyebrows appears light, then this subtly fades into medium for the general broad expanse across the brow, then the tones become dark, denoting the skull's recession towards the hairline. As Isabel Piczek would describe this in artistic terms, we are looking at perfectly realised 'modelling', all the more astonishing since it is without outlines, a device that every artist has used almost without thinking, right up to the present century.

21

And this 'modelling' is equally perfectly realised, totally convincingly conveying the subtleties of genuine facial contours, virtually everywhere that we look on this same face. Thus we can discern serene, refined-looking features that include closed eyes, a raised right eyebrow, a large, distinguished-looking nose, a well-formed mouth, seemingly centre-parted hair falling to near shoulder length either side of the face (the right side seeming longer and bushier than the left) and a full beard trimmed to no more than a couple of inches below the chin line. The only instances of apparently imperfect modelling, such as the right eye's lack of the perfect contours of the left, may very reasonably be interpreted as indicating some disfiguring injury.

Now as Piczek stresses, if any artist, whatever the era, truly had painted such an image we would have to acclaim him as a master of chiaroscuro – that is, painting in light and shade. This artist would be a superior to art history's greatest exponents, Caravaggio and Rembrandt, even though both of these were born centuries later than the latest date attributed to the Shroud by the radiocarbon dating. But even if we could somehow attribute the Shroud to a particular artist, this would be very far from explaining it as a painted work.

For the image that we see on the photographic negative is, of course, not the one that the mediaeval artist theoretically created. Instead, whoever this person might have been, he could only have worked in the vanishingly faint 'positive' stains that so astonished me when I first viewed the Shroud in 1973. In order to create the 'negative' that became revealed in 1898, he would have consistently and unerringly to have selected, in these same tones, the exact opposites to the natural light and shade with which we are all familiar. And he would have had to have done so blind, given that the Middle Ages had no means of enabling him to see the negative, either so that he could check his own cleverness, or show it to anyone else. Quite aside from it simply not making sense that anyone of the Middle Ages should have worked in such a way, it does not seem even remotely possible technically. As Isabel Piczek and any other professional figure painter will confirm, drawing and painting from a life model is quite difficult enough even in normal positive tones of light and shade. To do so in the reverse of these, particularly without any means of checking your work, is all but impossible.

Nor is what Isabel Piczek calls the 'perfection' of the Shroud's modelling solely confined to the face. As she goes on to stress, the rest of the body is every bit as 'perfect' and meaningful. The negative images [pls 10a & 14a] convey so precisely the pose and physical condition of a human body that both can be checked out point by point with some help from studio models.

Thus, although virtually nothing of the man of the Shroud's frontal shoulders can be seen because of the damage from the 1532 fire, below where we would expect these to be the negative's tonal values graduate quite dramatically from dark, to 'mid', to 'light', and then back to dark again. The contours associated with these tonal changes convey quite unmistakably, even to the non-artist, that we are seeing the pectoral muscles of a very prominent and therefore greatly expanded, male chest.

For Isabel Piczek the expansion of the chest muscles presents absolutely no surprise whatsoever. Indeed she says that she would expect nothing less, since she has observed precisely the same phenomenon as an effect of suspending live models on her studio cross. Hardly would she have begun sketching before the models' chests would begin to swell alarmingly, followed within a few minutes by profuse sweating, the physiological strains being so intense that they would sometimes almost faint, although after being allowed a short break, they would recover and go on for perhaps several hours. Medical practitioners independently researching crucifixion have reported very similar effects.[6]

When we look on the Shroud negative to below the chest, we may note a dark area between the ribs, suggesting that what is medically termed the epigastrium, i.e. the above-navel area, was tightly drawn in. This again is one of the effects that Piczek and others have observed of crucifixion-style suspension. Below an indentation reasonably interpretable as a navel there can also be seen an area of highlight convincingly conveying a well-rounded abdomen, then where the lower part of this recedes into shadow the man of the Shroud's forearms may be seen to end in long-fingered hands that cross over each other. And particularly worthwhile at this point is to compare this detail of the negative image with that visible on the Shroud proper.

On the Shroud itself the forearms – aside from the trickling 'blood-stains' – seem to be conveyed by the merest smudges of discoloration, and to be more than a little disarticulated from where we would imagine the upper arms and shoulders to be. Although on each hand we can just make out four distinct fingers, each again seems to be represented by little more than a smudge, so that no one would even begin to anticipate any 'depth' to what is visible.

Yet when we look at the negative we immediately see an arrangement

23

of the hands that if this were by a 'cunning painter' we would again have to acclaim as of the very highest level of artistic skill. Thus although some have pointed out that the man of the Shroud's right hand looks as if this has much longer fingers than the left, such criticisms seem to be based on little-thought-out expectations that his body ought to appear as flat as a pressed plant, or as if run over with a steamroller.

Instead what we are looking at is a most complex yet perfectly realised structure on at least three distinct levels, as any Isabel Piczek-type check against a studio model makes clear. For if we again arbitrarily divide all the tones into lights, mid-tones and darks, we can unerringly see lights for virtually each and every knuckle and joint, mid-tones for the general run of the fingers and backs of the hands, and darks for each and every division of the fingers. We can see darks where the left hand falls over the right, where the left hand's fingertips extend downwards beyond the extent of their clasp, and in the areas at the base of the stomach and inner part of the upper legs where all falls into shadow. We can also see the fingers of the left hand to be quite evidently in *clasp* mode over the wrist area of the right hand (this is why it looks shorter), with the extended fingers of this latter resting on the upper part of the left leg just about at the level of the groin. There is even a feature consistent with the tip of a penis protruding just below these fingers. As anyone who has attended an art life class knows, clasped hands are exceptionally difficult to convey realistically even when one is dealing with natural lights and shadows and can use outlines. For a 'cunning artist' to have done this so successfully in reverse lights and shadows and without outlines simply boggles the mind.

Nor is this all. If now we turn to the legs, still on the frontal view, the thighs change tonally from full dark where they commence at the junction with the torso, to mid-tones at mid-thigh, to light at the region of the knee joint. Below the knee joint the tones commence as light steadily regressing through to near-complete dark where we would expect the ankles. If we refer to the back-of-the-body image, we may also observe that where we would expect to see the backs of the knees there is just dark, though the calf muscles show up light before again darkening towards the ankles. As pointed out by Isabel Piczek, the only reasonable interpretation of all these changes of tone is that the man of the Shroud must have lain with his legs quite significantly flexed at the knees, an effect which, if the Shroud were by the hand of our 'cunning artist', we would describe as foreshortening.

In this regard, because we have become so familiar with foreshortening (that is the representation of an image shortened in relation to its perspective), from the photographs with which we are daily bombarded, we often fail to realise that artistically the technique's modern development only began with the Italians Paolo Uccello (1397–1475) and Piero della Francesca (*c*.1410–92). Obviously, neither artist had even been born when the Shroud was already being condemned by the fourteenth-century French bishops. And talented though Uccello and della Francesca were, they would have been hopeless at chiaroscuro. Once again, therefore, the Shroud seems 'out of time' from the point of view of having been produced by any 'cunning artist'.

An ideal way of demonstrating that the Shroud negative image really does carry some form of 'photograph' of a genuine human body rather than just an artist's representation is of course to reconstruct as closely as possible the appearance and pose of the original body, then check out the 'fit' of this against a cloth of the Shroud's dimensions. And it was partly for this purpose that Isabel Piczek perched so precariously on a high ladder to view her life models posed Shroud-mode immediately below her [pl. 11b], it being only from this vantage point that she could obtain a true sight line, and even then by standing on only one foot.

As she has pointed out, this is yet another reason why no artist painted the Shroud, certainly not from any life model. She found it so difficult to make even small-scale sketches from this uncomfortable position that the very idea of anyone trying to paint on a fourteen-foot cloth in this way has to be absurd. Furthermore, for similar reasons, she became obliged to abandon altogether attempts to reconstruct the back of the body image. For these the model would have been required to lie on his front, his hands crossed beneath his pelvis, balancing himself by just his nose, the top of one hand, and one knee, a pose which though she briefly asked for it, quickly looked so unprofessional and embarrassing for the model that she called it off. The only other way that she could have achieved a true back-of-the-body view would have been to have posed the model Shroud-mode on a sheet of plate glass, then suspended him above her. But since plate glass had not been invented in the Middle Ages, this seemed hardly worth attempting.

Confronted with all these impossibilities for any professional artist, Piczek's firm conclusion is that no painterly forebear of hers painted the Shroud, but that a genuine male human body lay in the cloth and somehow imprinted its image on it. She estimates this man to have been just under six feet tall (approximately 181 cm), and of an impressive physique. The man would not seem to have lain completely flat, rather his head seems to have been partly raised and the whole upper part of his body likewise, a deduction duly requiring Piczek to improvise a resting block on which to lay her models. The man seems to have had a dislocated shoulder (inferred from the right shoulder being lower than the left on the back-of-the-body image) and his hands were crossed across his pelvis in a mode that, according to Piczek, would have completely covered his genitals. His knees seem to have been partly flexed and, as deduced from the back-of-the-body image, his left foot lay partially over his right instep [pl. 10b].

Piczek is not the only individual to have tried to reconstruct the man of the Shroud's body and the conclusions of other researchers have not always been in total accord with hers. For instance, so far as the man's height is concerned, Italy's Monsignor Giulio Ricci calculated this to be as low as five feet three inches, or 160 cm, while the British 'Leonardo da Vinci' exponents Lynn Picknett and Clive Prince, without giving any clear reasons, have claimed an astonishing six feet eight to six feet ten (203 to 209 cm). Fortunately such estimates, both by non-professionals, represent the extremes. Calculations by medical specialists such as the United States' Dr Robert Bucklin, France's Dr Pierre Barbet and Britain's Dr David Willis all support Isabel Piczek. These and similar specialists have also corroborated Piczek's deductions concerning the dislocated shoulder and other features.

Despite Piczek's exhaustive use of studio models, the one serious limitation of her approach has been that it has been rather too exclusively based on visual observation of these *vis-à-vis* the Shroud frontal image. Some most useful supplementary work here has been done using replications of the Shroud to reconstruct the original body it wrapped. A pioneer of this process back in the 1960s was Italian sculptor and anatomy expert Lorenzo Ferri, a professor at the Studio of Sacred Arts in Rome, who photographically transferred the Shroud image life-size onto a sheet of clear plastic and from this proceeded to build up a convincing life-size model of the original Shroud body, very closely matching Isabel Piczek's, corroborating in particular her deductions concerning the raised head, the upwardly hunched upper back and the flexed knees.

A method similar to Ferri's has also been developed and improved upon to this day by the American physicist Dr John Jackson, one of the leaders of the American STURP team which scientifically examined the Shroud in 1978. An enthusiast for the Shroud from a young age, in the early 1970s, while working as an instructor at the US Air Force Academy in

Colorado Springs, Jackson teamed up like-minded colleague Dr Eric Jumper, with the aim of trying to determine the physics of how the Shroud's image might have become projected onto the cloth. Like Ferri before them, Jackson and Jumper made a life-size mock-up of the Shroud, in their case in cloth, cutting this to the Shroud's exact dimensions, projecting the Shroud's image onto it with the aid of a slide projector, then marking this up with every salient body image detail.

Working as they were at an Air Force Academy, Jackson and Jumper appealed for volunteer cadets to come forward to 'fit' this image, rather in the manner of Cinderella and her slipper [pl. 12a]. Unlike Isabel Piczek with her professional life models, they neither expected complete nudity nor long hours of immobility from their volunteers, their aim instead being to calculate exactly how the cloth draped over the body [pl. 12b] and the latter's distance from the cloth at any one point, in order to try to understand how the image came to be formed.

After what has now been more than twenty years of research, Dr Jackson has managed, like Ferri before him, to assemble something at least approximating the real human body that he is fully convinced once lay in the Shroud. Today this can be seen in the special Shroud research centre that Jackson and his Jewish-born wife Rebecca have set up in Colorado Springs. Unlike anything that might have been made by the artist Piczek or a Ferri, this is an essentially utilitarian manikin made from polystyrene cut into the general shape of a human body, as CAT-scanned from an appropriately proportioned volunteer.

Even so, it acts as a useful counterpoint to the Ferri and Piczek versions from the point of view of revealing where researchers approaching the same problem from completely different directions do and do not agree. For instance, Jackson's manikin's height is five feet ten and half inches (approximately 179 cm), only a little shorter than Piczek's, Ferri's and the medical specialists' estimates. On the other hand, while we noted Piczek's and Ferri's reconstructions to indicate the head and upper back having been raised from the horizontal plane, Jackson's manikin lies quite flat. Unlike Isabel Piczek, who posed her models with their spines lying essentially flat against the horizontal plane, Jackson's manikin has his quite significantly arched. Whereas Piczek saw the man of the Shroud's legs as having been bent at something like twenty degrees from the horizontal, Jackson's manikin has these almost completely flat and therefore essentially parallel to the horizontal. Whereas Piczek, from her ladder vantage point, adjudged her model's position correct when his genitals were completely covered by his crossed hands, Jackson's manikin suggests only a partial coverage, consistent with the already mentioned possible penis visible below the fingers.

There is probably little point in trying to reconcile these differences, the likelihood being that both reconstructions have their imperfections due to the different methodologies. Thus while the Jackson method has the virtue of demonstrating how a volunteer of a particular size and pose seemingly exactly 'fits' the replica 'Shroud', this cannot preclude a slightly taller volunteer with his legs slightly more bent also proving an exact match. Conversely, while it could be argued that the Piczek method relies rather too much on the artistic eye, that eye's professional judgement of what the Shroud 'photograph's' light and shade actually convey in terms of the lie of a human body may actually outweigh the otherwise seemingly remorseless logic of pure science.

Whatever the answer, and we will find such ambiguities wellnigh endemic in Shroud studies, the weight of evidence in this particular instance has nevertheless to be overwhelmingly against the Shroud's body image being any kind of painting, however cunningly contrived. As just some indication of the unlikelihood of the Shroud having been created by an artist we may cite the fifty or so surviving life-size direct copies of the Shroud that were made by artists during the sixteenth and seventeenth centuries and are now preserved in churches in Italy, Spain and, in one instance, the United States.[7] Compared with the Shroud, each and every one of these direct copies is simply not in the same league [for three representative examples, see pls 8 & 9, b, c & d]. They shriek their production by a human hand, even though the painters concerned lived at a time artistically far more competent than that in which the Shroud theoretically first surfaced.

Conversely, in favour of the Shroud image being some kind of photograph is not only all the evidence we have seen but also some other odd properties to it, particularly the famous three-dimensionality effect, of which the already mentioned Dr Jackson was one of the co-discoverers. In 1976, while he was visiting the Sandia Laboratories in Albuquerque, New Mexico, Jackson was invited by one of the technicians, Bill Mottern, to try putting the Shroud image into a VP8 Image Analyzer, a spin-off of space-age technology which translates shades of black and white into the impression of vertical relief on a TV monitor. To the astonishment of all present, while ordinary photographs can often give a very distorted result if, say, the shading to a nose is the same as that of a feature twenty feet distant, the Shroud face and body showed up in essentially perfect relief, strongly indicating that whatever created their image was something acting very much in the manner of light.

Another odd property is that the image seems not only to register the surface of the theoretical body, but also, at least in part, its subsurface, in the manner of an X-ray. As several medical specialists have pointed out, among these Michael Blunt, Challis Professor of Anatomy at the University of Sydney, in the case of the hands we seem to be seeing the metacarpal bones and the three phalange bones of each finger.[8] Similarly Professor Alan Whanger of Duke University has argued for features of the skull to be visible.[9] While trying to come to any interpretation of why we should be seeing these simply confounds the mystery of the image, it hardly gives support to the 'cunning painting' hypothesis.

In the case of the Shroud body image, then, in terms of its visual appearance the overwhelming weight of evidence favours it being some form of photograph – from whatever era being yet to be determined – of a genuine body. But if we really are 'seeing' a human body, as seems to be the case, then its physical height, physique and pose are far from the only data about it visible on the Shroud. For additionally, as we have already noted, there are apparent bloodstains and other injury marks, as if from a crucifixion. So can these be construed as what we would expect from a real-life crucifixion, or mere daubings for effect?

Just as in this chapter we have relied principally on a very professional artist to determine that the Shroud is not by one of her kind, so now the appropriate experts to turn to are doctors, pathologists and other professionals. For surely these should be able to detect the hand of some mediaeval trickster faking 'bloodstains' as of crucifixion? Or can they?

Chapter 2

And is it a genuinely crucified human body?

Throughout all our discussion of the so-called body image on the Shroud negative, there was one point which we quite deliberately ignored, rather as if it was to be taken for granted. This was consideration of whether any genuine dead body has ever been known to make a similar imprint to the kind seen on the Shroud.

The blunt answer to this has to be no. If it were quite normal for dead bodies to make imprints of themselves, then the Shroud's image would not retain the mystery it has. Which does not mean to say that dead bodies cannot and do not sometimes leave strange stains. For instance, among the exhibits in the British Museum's 'Byzantium' exhibition held in 1995 there was a pair of sixth-century Byzantine curtains that had subsequently been used for an Egyptian's burial shroud. These unmistakably bear brownish stains from their contact with this Egyptian's body.[1] Likewise, in the wake of a UK television documentary on the Shroud transmitted in October 1988, retired London undertaker Ronald Warrior wrote to the programme's producer remarking on indelible brownish stains that he used 'frequently' to find in the white-painted interiors of the wooden 'shells' in which he and his fellow undertakers routinely transported corpses.[2] Also, in 1981 a West Indian who died of cancer of the pancreas in a Liverpool hospice left remarkable and equally indelible outlines of his arm, hand and buttocks on a mattress cover [pl. 13a].[3] The problem with these is that none has exhibited images even remotely comparable to the Shroud's 'photographic' body imprint. Whatever this latter's derivation, it has essentially to be considered unique.

A similar uniqueness pertains to the Shroud image's clearly closely related set of apparent wound marks and bloodstains. Although bloodstains can be seen on various undoubtedly historical 'relics', such as the shirts in which England's King Charles I, and the United States' President Abraham Lincoln met their bloody deaths, the clarity and completeness of those on the Shroud must again be considered in quite a different league.

Whereas blood transferred to linen normally turns brown and crusty, and often scales off, the Shroud's 'blood' has to this day an unnervingly clean, clear carmine hue. And each stain has a surprisingly complete and even-looking appearance, given that blood from, say, the 'crown of thorns' ought to have dried much earlier than that from, say, the wound in the side. As the Shroud's critics have not been slow to point out, such clarity and completeness actually constitute a strong argument against the Shroud's authenticity, from the point of view that dead bodies simply do not normally leave such complete and perfect traces of the injuries from which they died.

Yet while this must be faced fairly and squarely, it utterly fails to explain, let alone constitute evidence for, how the Shroud could be a mediaeval fake. Accordingly, just as we tried to be very clear and realistic regarding whether the man of the Shroud's body image could readily be dismissed as a 'cunning painting', so now, regarding what we can see of this man's injuries, we need to try to determine the extent to which these may somehow be representative of the crucifixion of a genuine human body (of whatever origin or date), or just some mediaeval hoaxer's daubings to suggest the same.

There are essentially four categories of injuries that anyone, whatever their viewpoint, may reasonably 'see' and identify on the Shroud:

(i) a set of injuries as from a severe whipping
(ii) a set of injuries as from various forms of incidental abuse (including apparent 'crowning with thorns')
(iii) a set of injuries as from piercing at the hands and feet
(iv) a single injury as from the driving of a bladed weapon through the chest

To which may be added as a final category:

(v) evidence of apparent post-mortem blood spillages from (iii) and (iv)

In each of these categories we need to evaluate how these have been interpreted by medical professionals and how they relate to mediaeval artists' depictions of such traumas, in which regard the first category, the marks of a whipping, comprises by far the most numerous and widely distributed of any of the Shroud man's injuries.

Superimposed upon the Shroud body image, in a significantly denser

31

tone of yellow-sepia (registering white on the negative image), are more than a hundred dumb-bell-shaped markings. Each of these, where it has fallen 'true', may be found to measure some one and a half inches (3.7 cm) long [pl. 15a]. On the back-of-the-body image such markings can be seen all over the back and on the cheeks of the buttocks, extending down the legs even as far as the ankles [pl. 14a], and on the frontal image they can be seen on the chest and upper thighs.

It is the distribution of these – grouped generally in threes and with a 'fanning out' appearance – that enables them to be reasonably interpreted as from a whipping, the apparent instrument having been a two- or three-thonged whip that had dumb-bell-shaped metal pellets at the tip of each thong [pl. 15b]. Additionally the STURP ultraviolet fluorescence photography as carried out in 1978 showed up some hitherto unnoticed lines at the top of the shoulders which seem to have been from thongs of the whip cutting into the shoulders as they were lashed from behind, to strike at the chest.

Of the many physicians and pathologists favouring the Shroud's authenticity, those who have studied the dumb-bell-shaped marks have unhesitatingly defined them as contusions, that is, severe swellings or bruises seemingly caused by the percussion of the whip tip with the body's surface. Sceptics, on the other hand, have been rather less impressed, perfectly legitimately pointing out that the sometimes lurid depiction of Jesus's body covered with whip marks was quite a favourite theme of mediaeval art, as for instance, in a late fourteenth-century manuscript in the Bibliothèque Nationale, Paris, in which we find a miniature of the dead Jesus being propped up by angels, the upper part of his body profusely peppered with whip marks not dissimilar to those on the Shroud.[4] Likewise Westminster Abbey's Litlyngton Missal, created at much the same date, depicts Jesus on the cross, his body again bearing distinctively dumb-bell-shaped whip marks, while the British Library's early fourteenth-century Holkham Bible Picture Book similarly features graphic scenes of Jesus being lashed with a knot-tipped whip, his body again peppered with wounds [pl. 15c].

Since the two first examples date from after the Shroud was already reportedly extant in France, there is an argument for the Shroud itself possibly having influenced these. However the overriding issue with regard to all such artists' depictions of Jesus's whipping, from whatever period, is that they simply do not bear the slightest serious comparison with the sheer logic of the markings as on the Shroud. As readers ought to be able to judge for themselves, the subtlety of the Shroud whip marks' distribution pattern is such that if they were made by a forger, this individual would have to have thought out literally everything of how a pellet-tipped whip would fall in relation to the contours of a human body. For instance, it can be seen where the whip wielder's hand was as he repeatedly lashed over the man of the Shroud's shoulders, left and right across his back, laterally (seemingly with some obvious sadism) around his thighs and buttocks, then downwards towards his ankles [pl. 14b]. Since in essence, all the whip-mark evidence suggests genuine injuries to an equally genuine human body, any forger would have to have been a first-class medical researcher as well as an artist.

The second category of injuries, those of incidental abuse suffered by the man of the Shroud, can in some instances only be guessed at from deformities and disharmonies to the body image. For instance, we noted in the last chapter how the right eye[5] looks seriously bruised or disfigured compared with the left. Similarly, both the right and the left cheeks appear to have been badly bruised, also the nose seriously damaged, possibly broken. Some further injuries can be inferred to the backs of his shoulders, which appear chafed as from the carrying of some heavy object. Also the knees seem to have been damaged as from falls. Because such observations are based on the merest subtleties in the Shroud's image, the sceptic may legitimately dismiss them as far too heavily dependent on the rather over-enthusiastic visual judgements of people already favouring the Shroud's authenticity, as a result of which we will omit them from discussion.

Rather less easily dismissable, however, are a set of visible 'bloodflows' that may be included in this same category of injuries. Quite unmistakable on the Shroud's frontal image are several 'blood' trickles visible at the level of the forehead, together with others extending down the hair [pl. 16a]. Most pronounced of these, as visible on the negative, is a full-bodied rivulet that begins at the apex of the forehead, trickles downwards in a '3' shape (as if it has met a couple of diversions along the way), then terminates in a final glob just above the left eyebrow. As has been pointed out by several physicians, including Britain's Dr David Willis and Italy's Dr Sebastiano Rodante, not only is the way that this rivulet has flowed absolutely characteristic of venous blood, but the 3 shape is consistent with where the muscles of the brow would have contracted and formed ridges under intense pain [pls 16b & c].[6]

There are also four or five other trickles above the eyes, one of these seeming to derive from a puncturing of the artery to the right temple (hence apparent arterial blood in this instance), while others seem to run down the hair. If we had any doubts how to interpret these, reference to the back-of-the-head area on the dorsal image quickly provides the answer, for here can be made out at least eight more streams of apparent blood, not counting those which have divided on themselves. Some veer to the left, others to the right, as if from a head that has tilted from one side to the other. All the flows cease along a line convex to the back of the head. The only reasonable interpretation is that these flows came from injuries that were caused by something spiked that was worn on the head, their path checked by the band which kept this in place. And in looking for what that 'something' could have been it is virtually impossible not to envisage an object very like a crown of thorns.

When we look to artists' depictions of Jesus's crowning with thorns, whether from the Middle Ages or from any other time, it is absolutely impossible to find any example with bloodflows even remotely as convincing as those that we see on the Shroud. For instance, there is Mathias Grünewald's brutally realistic *Christ on the Cross* [detail, pl. 17] at the centre of the famous Isenheim Altarpiece in the Unterlinden Museum, Colmar, Germany, in which the crown of thorns is so fearsome-looking that some of its broken-off spines can be seen sticking into the flesh of Jesus's shoulders, his chest and even his lower stomach. Yet although Grünewald painted this crucifixion *c.* 1512–15, in the High Renaissance and more than a century and a half after the purported faking of the Shroud, his portrayal of the bloodflows looks amateurish in the extreme compared with those visible on the Shroud. Equally unconvincing are the 'bloodflows' added to the modern-day replication of the Shroud[7] produced by Lynn Picknett and Clive Prince of 'Leonardo da Vinci faked it' theory.

Which leads us to the third category of injuries visible on the Shroud, the bloodflows as from piercings to the hands and feet. First let us take the trickles that can be seen on each forearm [pl. 18a]. As various medical and other researchers have demonstrated, if these are projected and painted onto a living model's arms and his arms are then moved to the position that their gravitational flow would seem to indicate, it can immediately be seen that at the time the blood flowed each arm must have been stretched out sideways at an approximate angle of sixty-five degrees, i.e. a crucifixion position [pl. 18b].

We cannot see the source of the trickle down the right forearm because its wrist and upper hand are covered by the fingers of the left hand. But this is more than compensated for by the fact that a '/\'-shaped bloodstain is clearly visible on the left wrist, the apex of this, at the centre of the bending fold, being obviously the site of the puncture wound from which the blood flowed. The '/\' shape to the bloodstain also theoretically seems to indicate the two different positions that the man of the Shroud must have adopted while suspended, either denoting his agonising shifting from one position to another or, as some have suggested, the position his arms took at death.

Clearly we are looking at a nailing, but the real surprise is to find the Shroud indicating this to have been through the wrist, rather than through the palms, as so many artists imagined Jesus's crucifixion. Although the sixteenth-century Archbishop Alfonso Paleotto of Bologna was the first to go on record noting this location,[8] it was the French surgeon Dr Pierre Barbet, in the 1930s, who first properly demonstrated how convincing it is anatomically.[9] Using cadavers and freshly amputated limbs that were available to him from his surgical work at St Joseph's Hospital, Paris, Barbet tried suspending these first by the palms, then by the wrist point indicated on the Shroud. He found that whereas in the case of the former the flesh simply tore through, when he drove a nail through the wrist this provided perfect support to a suspended body, however heavy this might be. Furthermore, in conducting this experiment Barbet not only found a hitherto unsuspected passageway through the highly compacted carpal bones at the point the Shroud indicates [pl. 19a], he also discovered an unexpected motor reaction that such nailing provoked in the thumb. Triggered by the nail's touching of the median nerve at the wrist, the thumb would automatically snap itself into the palm, making perfect sense of the fact that although all eight fingers of the man of the Shroud's hands are fully visible, neither of the thumbs is. As Barbet commented: 'Could a forger have imagined this?'

In the manner of anything to do with the Shroud, Barbet's findings have not escaped criticism, even from supporters of the cloth's authenticity. Thus American physician the late Dr Anthony Sava hypothesised that the nailing, although still through the wrist, might have been through the wrist end of the forearm's radius and ulna bones, rather than through the wrist proper,[10] while New York medical examiner Dr Frederick Zugibe has suggested that the nail might first have been hammered through the palm at the base of the thumb, but then driven onwards at such an angle that it emerged at the wrist.[11]

However these are minor quibbles that should not be allowed to detract from the overwhelming medical consensus that the Shroud's wrist and forearm bloodflows convincingly represent how a human body might genuinely have been suspended by nails from a cross. Leading anatomists such as Dr Robert Bucklin, retired Professor of Pathology at the Universities of Texas and California, Professor James Cameron, retired head of the London Hospital's School of Forensic Medicine, and Professor Michael Blunt, retired Challis Professor of Anatomy at the University of Sydney, Australia, are among innumerable members of the medical profession who have all agreed on this.

By contrast, among the literally thousands of artists of history who have painted or sculpted Jesus's crucifixion, the overwhelming majority of these have represented Jesus transfixed by nails through the palms. Of the few exceptions the German Baroque artist Georg Petel, working in the 1630s, certainly created a very naturalistic ivory crucifix featuring wrist-nailing that is now in the Residenz Treasury, Munich Residence.[12] Likewise one of Van Dyck's painted crucifixions features Jesus suspended from the wrists [pl. 19b]. But these artists worked in the Baroque period, a far more advanced era than that in which the Shroud was theoretically forged, and they were in any case more than likely directly influenced by the Shroud, which was then being regularly displayed in Turin. But for a 'cunning painter' back in the 1350s to have single-mindedly thought out the wrist-nailing feature, and to have known of the 'snapping of the thumbs into the palms effect' that this would cause, also to have painted on bloodflows consistent with the principles of gravity (the discovery of which lay three centuries into the future), simply beggars belief.

Nor is this by any means all, even within this category, for obviously closely related to the bloodflows from the man of the Shroud's hands are those visible at his feet. Here, although the Shroud's back-of-the-body image bears the full and very bloody imprint of the sole of the right foot, with even a few centimetres to spare, the frontal image is a little too short, the cloth having apparently extended only part-way down the foot, visible only as a smudge of blood.

Had the Shroud been the creation of an artist, he would almost inevitably have made sure that he represented the frontal half of the body in full, even if he missed part of the back. But if someone laid a genuine human body on one half of the Shroud, and then brought the other half over the head, it would have been a very understandable and natural misjudgement to have allowed too much length for the lower part and not enough for the upper. And in any case, in any other circumstances but deliberate creation of an image such a misjudgement would have been of no consequence, since there was quite sufficient spare cloth to cover the feet using the underside half.

With regard to the foot injuries themselves, as visible on the Shroud, even though we can see only the right sole [pl. 20a] with any clarity (the left foot seemingly having been overlaid over the right) anyone who might find this unconvincing is recommended to step with wet feet onto a tiled surface and then compare the resultant watery impression with that imprinted in apparent blood on the Shroud. A concavity suggests the foot's plantar arch and a dark, rectangularish stain, between where we would anticipate the second and third metatarsal bones, has been widely interpreted as the entry point for a crucifixion nail driven through both feet as these were laid one atop the other. Overall, what would again seem to be evident is a pure, hundred per cent naturalistic impression of a foot light-years removed from what we would expect any artist of the Middle Ages to have created. Indeed, it is impossible even to point to a single mediaeval artistic representation of the soles of Jesus's feet in this manner, essentially every known artist having represented Jesus's feet from the front. If the radiocarbon dating really is correct, how some unknown mediaeval forger managed to be so brilliantly and so accurately innovative even in this feature alone needs more than a little explaining.

The fourth category of obvious-to-all injuries represented on the Shroud is a very dramatic elliptical-shaped wound that is visible in the man of the Shroud's right chest [pl. 21a], immediately below the ridge of his pectoral muscles. This wound measures some one and three quarter inches (4.4 cm) wide, and a copious quantity of 'blood' can be seen to have flowed from it, the angle of flow indicating that this must have occurred while the body hung upright. The elliptical shape suggests it to have been inflicted by a bladed weapon such as a lance or spear and, according to surgeon Barbet's generally agreed anatomical calculations, this would have been driven between the fifth and sixth ribs. As Barbet also noted, because the blow was delivered into the right rather than the left chest, it would have caused bloodflow even after death; had it been from the left side, the left ventricles would already have been empty, resulting in little or no emission. Among this flow's many medically convincing features is that its undulations, just like those on the forehead, do not merely follow the flow of gravity downwards, but indicate even the projection of the middle ribs and other body features.

Depictions of Jesus in mediaeval art reveal plenty of renditions of the lance wound, often repeating the elliptical shape, and sometimes with copious flows of blood. Mid-fourteenth-century sculptured Christ figures in Germany such as a Man of Sorrows in the Frauenkirche, Munich,[13] give this wound particular attention, as does the painted *Grande Pietà Ronde* of *c.* 1390 in the Louvre, Paris [pl. 21c].[14] But again there is all the difference in the world between the medical convincingness of these and the wound visible on the Shroud.

Which brings us to the fifth and final category of readily visible injury marks on the Shroud, apparent post-mortem spillages, that is, bloodflows that do not appear to have come from the body during life or its immediate expiry, but which broke loose from it while it was being laid in the Shroud. Two examples of this may be cited, both readily visible on the back-of-the-body image. First, by the right foot there can be seen a spillage that has broken away at the level of the ankle, extending several centimetres laterally [pl. 20a]. Second, right across the small of the back can be seen a large, similarly lateral splash of blood [pl. 22a]. In the case of this latter, from its position and from the absence of any other obviously related injury, it can only have come from the lance wound in the chest. As interpreted by Dr Joseph Gambescia, a professor of medicine at the Hannemann University Hospital, Philadelphia, this: '. . . makes sense only if the body were tilted on its side with the side-wound oriented momentarily toward the ground and then turned up on the other side so that the flow could make its way transversedly across the back toward the ground.'[15]

A feature of importance here is that people of the Middle Ages and later actually failed to understand this bloodstain properly, the nuns who patched the Shroud after the fire of 1532, for instance, supposing it to have derived from a chain.[16] Is this another indication of the Shroud's forger being 'out of time'? Worth comparison with this bloodflow are those on an extremely graphic fifteenth-century medical illustration of wounds, from a manuscript of Galen's writings, as preserved in the collection of the Wellcome Institute for the History of Medicine, London [pl. 22b]. Despite this illustration having been painted a century and a half after the theoretical forging of the Shroud, the wide variety of injuries depicted on this so-called 'Wounds Man' can only be described, by comparison, as hopelessly crude and childish.

Accordingly, from straight observation of the behaviour of the Shroud's wounds it can be said with considerable confidence that they are medically convincing. Against the innumerable physicians and pathologists who have attested this – not one of whom has retracted his views in the light of the radiocarbon dating – it is only fair to cite one serious dissident in the person of Dr Michael Baden, one-time chief medical examiner for New York City and professor of pathology at the Albert Einstein School of Medicine. However, even in Baden's case his chief objection has been the one point that we acknowledged at the very beginning, that the Shroud's bloodflows are just 'too neat' and that dead bodies simply don't leave on their grave wrappings images of themselves and their wounds of the kind that we see on the Shroud.[17]

Of course, views such as Baden's must be respected and it has been particularly because of this that some of the physicians favouring the Shroud's authenticity have tried to come to a better understanding of how the Shroud's 'blood' might have transferred so neatly onto it, just as we earlier noted how Dr John Jackson tried to do the same in respect of the body image. In this respect a prime researcher on the 'blood' image-making process has been the American physician Dr Gilbert Lavoie, a former consultant to the World Health Organisation. After repeated experiments Lavoie, in partnership with his wife Bonnie, was able to demonstrate that transfer images of blood clots onto cloth very similar to those visible on the Shroud could be successfully made, providing that the contact between the cloth and a moist clot took place no more than two and a half hours after cessation of the bleeding.[18]

Lavoie and his wife also found this transfer process to be quite separate from whatever was responsible for the body image imprinting. To demonstrate this the Lavoies created a John Jackson-type replica of the facial portion of the Shroud [pl. 23a ii], cut out all the 'crown of thorns' bloodflows from it, then draped it over the face of a bearded volunteer model [pl. 23a iii], carefully positioning it so that the facial features matched it point for point. Then, in the exact manner of a stencil, they applied red paint wherever the replica had 'bloodflow' holes. To their astonishment, when they removed the cloth, instead of some of the bloodflows being in the volunteer's hair, as it seemed they ought to be from the Shroud image, they were actually on his forehead, temples and cheeks [pl. 23a iv]. The strong implication was that the Shroud body and 'blood' images were created by two quite separate processes, the former having transferred by normal contact, the latter by something quite different, the two not necessarily being in perfect register.

Although no one can yet be close to a final answer on how the Shroud's 'bloodflow' images came to be 'too good to be true' (as Baden would express it), there is one of these, by no means the most obvious, that deserves a special concluding mention. This is one on the back-of-the-

39

body image, comprising the furthest-but-one main splash from the already mentioned post-mortem spillage at the ankle. For if we take a life-size model of the man of the Shroud, lay this on its imprint on a Shroud replica, then bring the other half of the cloth over the head and down to the feet, this stain can be seen to have a precisely matching 'twin' at its exactly opposite point on the frontal image [pls 6 & 7c, where marked N]. This 'match' was first noticed by the German Jesuit theologian Professor Werner Bulst and is one that Dr John Jackson now takes great delight in demonstrating very convincingly at his Shroud research centre in Colorado Springs. Although ostensibly no more than the tiniest and most insignificant detail, none the less it represents a further powerful addition to the argument that the Shroud really did once wrap a human body that had undergone a real-life crucifixion.

Of course, as must be recognised, this does not necessarily contradict the carbon-dating verdict. It is, after all, perfectly possible to conceive of some cunning and determined mediaeval faker having perhaps procured and deployed a genuinely crucified corpse to achieve his ends. But what if the Shroud also bears hallmarks indicating that this was a crucifixion which took place well before the Middle Ages – indeed, some time around Jesus's own era?

Chapter 3

And is it what we would expect of a genuine first-century crucified body?

E ven if we can accept the weight of evidence reasonably to favour the Shroud having once wrapped a genuine, crucified human body, there is one commonly voiced argument against this body dating from around the time of Jesus. This is that he was far too tall for such an early period. As we have already determined, his likely height was just under six feet (181 cm) and for many laymen, nurturing the widespread belief that people of antiquity were considerably shorter than ourselves, this has been regarded as a serious argument against the Shroud's authenticity, quite aside from the findings of the radiocarbon dating.

In reality there is rather more myth than fact to the idea that there has been any significant increase in the height of *Homo sapiens* during the last few thousand years.[1] English kings such as Edward I and Henry VII were six footers, as were many of the drowned soldiers whose skeletons were found on Henry VIII's *Mary Rose*. As more general archaeological studies of skeletal bones have revealed, while the mean height for Mediterranean peoples of the Roman period was around five feet five and a half inches (167 cm), there was a perfectly reasonable incidence of six footers. For instance, in a Jerusalem cemetery directly contemporary with the time of Jesus, of ten adult male skeletons examined, one was found to be six feet (181 cm), another between five feet seven and five feet ten (170–178 cm).[2] In other words, while six feet would have been an impressive height for Jesus's time, just as it is in our own, it would in no way have been beyond the normal order.

This difficulty duly set aside, we may now turn to those other features that may or may not help us distinguish whether the Shroud's image is of a man who died in the Middle Ages, or in some significantly earlier period. While the body's total nudity hardly helps any such assessment, worth noting at least in passing is the style of the hairdressing. On the frontal image we can see sidelocks, long strands of hair falling either side of the face that have been *de rigueur* among orthodox Jews for umpteen centuries and remain so to this very day. On the back-of-the-body image there also appears to be a long rope of hair running half the length of the spine, rather in the manner of an unbound pigtail. Now while I have yet to come across any mediaeval artist who has imagined such a style of hairdressing for Jesus, highly reputable Biblical scholars such as H. Gressman[3] and H. Daniel-Rops,[4] both writing without any consideration of the Shroud, have reported this as a specific fashion among Jews of Jesus's time. According to Daniel-Rops, for instance, they typically kept the hair 'plaited and rolled up under their headgear' except on public holidays.

From the historical–archaeological point of view, however, the most tell-tale features of the Shroud's image have to be the injuries that the man of the Shroud seemingly sustained, and what these can tell us of the weapons and punishment procedures from which they derived. With regard to the extensive series of whip marks, for instance, we noted earlier how these seem to have been inflicted by a whip with three thongs, tipped with dumb-bell shaped pellets. Consultation of the *Dictionary of Greek and Roman Antiquities* reveals this readily to conform with the *flagrum*, or scourge, a fearsome whip which the Romans used both for their gladiatorial combats and as an instrument of punishment. During the excavations of Herculanaeum, the Roman city that was buried with Pompeii during the Vesuvius volcanic eruption of AD 79, an actual *flagrum* was discovered sufficiently intact to be put on display, its dumb-bell-shaped metal tips readily matching those on the Shroud. While the possibility has to be allowed that such a dumb-bell-tipped whip might also have been used in the Middle Ages, the Shroud's whipping injuries undeniably correspond to the type of implement that the Romans would have used for Jesus's scourging as described in the Christian gospels.[5] Likewise, the elliptical shape of the wound in the man of the Shroud's right chest conforms to just the sort of injury that we would expect from the Roman *lancea*, or lance, the very weapon the John gospel describes as being plunged into Jesus's side,[6] examples of which can be seen in the Landesmuseum, Zurich [pl. 21b], and other major collections of Roman antiquities.

Inevitably, however, the Shroud's most potentially illuminating feature from the historical–archaeological point of view has to be its apparent documentation of a real-life crucifixion, a mode of punishment which, at least so far as the Christian world was concerned, became universally banned from the early fourth century AD. Of course, as has been very pertinently pointed out by the American anthropologist John R. Cole, 'Any fraud worth its salt would try to fulfil Biblical prescriptions,'[7] in which regard, just to see evidence on the Shroud conforming to the Biblical description of Jesus's crucifixion ought theoretically to prove nothing.

However, the interesting feature here is that in actuality the Christian gospels tell us remarkably little about how Jesus was crucified, there being likewise very little information even outside the gospels regarding how crucifixion was carried out. We know that the Romans were not the only peoples of antiquity to have used this method of execution. The Scythians and the Persians certainly did so before them, as did the Jews themselves before their assimilation into the Roman Empire. In the time of Alexander Jannaeus (103–76 BC), for instance, one Simon bar Shetah was recorded as having 'hanged' eighty women near Ashkelon,[8] the word *tlh* used for this now being recognised by reputable scholars as most likely denoting crucifixion. Likewise, the famous Temple Scroll found among the Dead Sea Scrolls is thought to refer to crucifixion in the following passage:

> If a man informs against his people, and delivers his people up to a foreign nation, and does harm to his people, you shall hang him on the tree, and he shall die. On the evidence of two witnesses and on the evidence of three witnesses he shall be put to death ... And their body shall not remain upon the tree all night, but you shall bury them the same day, for those hanged on the tree are accursed by God and men; you shall not defile the land which I gave you for an inheritance.[9]

Following the Roman take-over of Jewish-occupied territories from 63 BC, such 'hangings on a tree' dramatically increased. The late-first-century Jewish historian Josephus described in his *Antiquities* how the Romans crucified some two thousand rebels as part of their suppression of the riots which broke out following the death of Herod the Great in 4 BC.[10] And in his *The Jewish War* Josephus went on to relate how the Romans crucified up to five hundred a day during the revolt of AD 66–70,[11] the horror associated with this mode of execution being such that even their merely going through the preparations for crucifying a popular Jewish captive could bring about the surrender of a whole citadel.[12]

Despite the practice's common usage and high profile, however, almost entirely lacking is any detailed description of exactly how it was carried out. Even in the case of Jesus the only gospel indication that he was specifically nailed to his cross is but glancingly in Doubting Thomas's famous remark: 'Unless I see the holes that the nails made in his hands, and unless I can put my hand into his side, I refuse to believe.'[13] It is noteworthy that even here there is no reference to any nailing of the feet. Among the Roman literary sources, throughout the whole period that crucifixion was a recognised punishment, no writer provides any clear and full description of its physical details, almost certainly because they were regarded too abhorrent and distasteful.

Accordingly, when in June 1968 the first known actual remains of a crucifixion victim were discovered in Jerusalem, these seemed to hold enormous promise for shedding some significant new light on the subject. The discovery happened when builders, bulldozing a rocky hillside at Giv'at ha-Mivtar[14] to Jerusalem's north, uncovered an extensive Jewish burial ground dating to around the time of Jesus. When archaeologists arrived on the scene, they opened up several of the dozens of ossuaries (or bone boxes) littering the tomb chambers and it was in one such ossuary that they found a skeleton, the ankle-bone of which was pierced by a large nail [pl. 20b], enabling even a layman to deduce that this had most likely been a victim of crucifixion.

Israel's powerful ultra-orthodox faction immediately put the archaeologists under great pressure to rebury all the disturbed bones, as a result of which it was with undue haste that these were passed to the Anatomy School at Jerusalem's Hebrew University-Hadassah Medical School for as much expert appraisal as could be managed in a very short time. Here, the crucifixion victim's bones came under the particular scrutiny of Romanian-born anatomist Dr Nicu Haas, who duly reported them to have belonged to a cleft-palated young man in his mid to late twenties who had been some five feet seven inches tall, and whose name, from epigraphists' reading of his ossuary's inscription, had been Jehohanan.

According to Haas, the nail that was the tell-tale indication of Jehohanan's crucifixion measured 17–18 cm (i.e. *c*. seven inches) and had been driven through both his right and left heel bones. It had pinned these to an upright of olivewood, fragments of which still remained on the nail's pointed end, which had been bent into a hook shape from having hit some obstruction such as a knot in the wood. From a scratch at the wrist end of the radius bone Haas inferred that other nails, not found in the ossuary, had been used to fasten Jehohanan by his wrists to a cross-beam, while a fragment of wood found between the head of the nail and the heel bone, seemingly of acacia or pistacia, he thought to have been some placard affixed to Jehohanan's feet that bore details of his crime. From

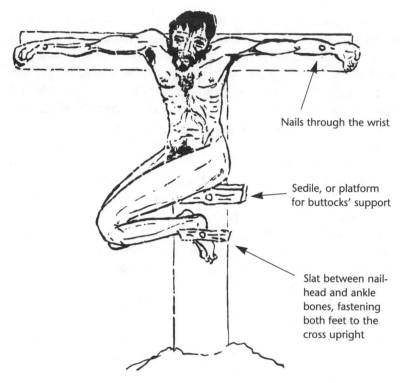

Nails through the wrist

Sedile, or platform for buttocks' support

Slat between nail-head and ankle bones, fastening both feet to the cross upright

Fig 1   The now flawed reconstruction of crucifixion victim Jehohanan
Israeli anatomist the late Dr Nicu Haas's original reconstruction of the crucifixion of Jehohanan, the victim whose remains were found at Giv'at ha-Mivtar, north Jerusalem, still with a nail in the foot bones. Haas's deductions concerning wrist nailing were the first archaeological corroboration, independent of the Shroud, that crucifixion victims were nailed through the wrists, and this aspect of Haas's reconstruction may still be valid. But the awkward side-saddle position is thought very unlikely. (*Courtesy, Israel Exploration Journal*)

visible breakages to one of the lower leg bones, Haas deduced that this must have been deliberately smashed in life in order to hasten Jehohanan's death, exactly as in the case of the two robbers crucified alongside Jesus, as reported in John gospel (ch. 19, vv. 31–33). Because the fastening at the feet did not seem particularly secure, Haas's impression was that Jehohanan may have been provided with some form of *sedicula* or support for his buttocks. After several attempts to deduce how Jehohanan's feet had been arranged, Haas eventually settled for him having been forced into an awkward side-saddle position and commissioned a drawing depicting Jehohanan perched on his buttocks-support in this manner [fig. 1].

When Haas published his findings in a 1970 issue of the prestigious *Israel Exploration Journal*[15] they essentially represented a major scientific advance in the understanding of how crucifixion had been practised in the time of Jesus. They also seemed to be particularly helpful and supportive from the point of view of those interested in the Turin Shroud. Because one of the few things positively known about crucifixion was that methods could vary upon the whim of the executioners, there was no need necessarily to believe that Jehohanan's crucifixion had been absolutely identical either to that supposed of Jesus, or that visible on the Shroud image (assuming a distinction). None the less the scratch to the radius bone represented the first proper independent indication that wrist-nailing was the method used in antiquity, thereby vindicating Dr Barbet's now thirty-year-old researches. And there was absolutely nothing positively to contradict the mode of crucifixion as seen on the Shroud.

However, following Haas's premature death and prompted by the many disputes surrounding his reconstruction (quite independent of the Shroud), in 1985 Haas's findings were re-appraised by the Israeli scholars Joseph Zias and Eliezer Sekeles, using the photographs, casts, radiographs and notes that Haas had made seventeen years before. From these Zias and Sekeles drew some radically altered conclusions. Thus, although they continued to accept that Jehohanan had been a victim of crucifixion, they firmly rejected, supported by the expert opinion of six specialists of the Johns Hopkins University Medical School, that Jehohanan had ever had a palatal-cleft facial deformity. They rejected also Haas's concept that the small scratch on Jehohanan's radius bone necessarily denoted that he had been nailed by the wrists. According to them, this mark was more likely to have been due to rubbing against other bones in the ossuary, there being similar marks on others parts of the skeleton. Quite possibly, therefore, Jehohanan's arms had been fastened by ropes rather than by nails.

Zias and Sekeles also termed 'inconclusive' Haas's finding that Jehohanan had had his legs broken, their interpretation being that this breakage may have been mere incidental damage during later handling of his bones. As for the 'plaque' between the nail-head and Jehohanan's ankle, they found this to be neither acacia nor pistacia, but olive wood [fig. 2]. Most likely it had not been a plaque at all, but instead a simple slip of wood that had had the function of enlarging the nail-head. According to their reconstruction Jehohanan had been made to straddle the cross upright, nails were then driven sideways into this upright through each heelbone, the slip of wood thereby preventing any desperate attempt by

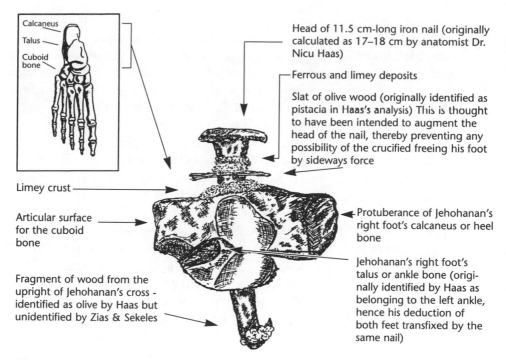

Head of 11.5 cm-long iron nail (originally calculated as 17–18 cm by anatomist Dr. Nicu Haas)

Ferrous and limey deposits

Slat of olive wood (originally identified as pistacia in Haas's analysis) This is thought to have been intended to augment the head of the nail, thereby preventing any possibility of the crucified freeing his foot by sideways force

Calcaneus
Talus
Cuboid bone

Limey crust

Articular surface for the cuboid bone

Fragment of wood from the upright of Jehohanan's cross - identified as olive by Haas but unidentified by Zias & Sekeles

Protuberance of Jehohanan's right foot's calcaneus or heel bone

Jehohanan's right foot's talus or ankle bone (originally identified by Haas as belonging to the left ankle, hence his deduction of both feet transfixed by the same nail)

Fig 2   Nailing through the ankles – the evidence from the crucifixion victim excavated by archaeologists
Crucifixion victim Jehohanan's heel and ankle bones, showing these transfixed by a large iron nail. Based on Dr Nicu Haas's original drawing, but incorporating the modifications to his deductions as made by Zias and Sekeles. (After the original drawing in *Israel Exploration Journal* vol. 20, 1970, p.56)

him to break free by forcing his feet sideways over the nail-head. Particularly tellingly, Zias and Sekeles found that Haas had not even managed to measure the crucifixion nail anything like correctly, their calculation being that this was only 11.5 cm (or four and half inches) long, much too short to have fastened both Jehohanan's feet to the cross. This not only further reinforced their argument for each foot having been nailed separately transversely through the heel, it also obviated the need for anything of the buttocks-rests and foot-platforms that scholars had endlessly argued over, following Haas's reconstruction.

Given Zias's and Sekeles' radically different conclusions from those of Haas (who was no longer alive to defend himself), our first decision has to be how much we should accept even their findings as necessarily the last word on how Jehohanan, or any other similar victim of antiquity, was crucified. For instance, as has been remarked by the archaeologist Dr Eugenia Nitowski, Zias's and Sekeles' rejection of the clear indentation on Jehohanan's radius bone as evidence of wrist-nailing is very far from conclusive. In her words: 'If we argue merely from photographic evidence, in plates 22A, B and C of Haas's *Israel Exploration Journal* article a dent can be seen exactly where a nail would be driven, and at no other place can dents or scratches be found on the radius. Coincidence?'[16]

None the less several of Zias's and Sekeles' new insights deserve to be taken seriously as is some quite independent, though equally ambiguous, data concerning how crucifixion may have been carried out in Jesus's time deriving from two Roman graffiti, one found more than a hundred years ago in a palace on Rome's Palatine Hill [fig. 3, left] the other more recently on a wall at Pozzuoli, near Naples [fig. 3, right]. No more than the very crudest depictions of crucifixion, both are difficult by any standards to interpret, the Palatine Hill example, for instance, as part of its mockery, depicting the crucified individual as having an ass's head.

Nevertheless in the former, while whatever holds the crucified's out-stretched arms to the cross-beam (represented by just a line) is by no means clear, there can be no mistaking that his legs are apart, with his feet either standing on some transverse foot-support, or else transversely pierced through with very long nails in the manner deduced by Zias and Sekeles.

As for the Pozzuoli version, in which the crucified's arms are similarly conventionally shown outstretched on a transverse beam, again his legs are the surprise, being shown most curiously bent outwards, in a manner quite different from the conventional crucifixion as traditionally depicted by Christian artists. Here the feet would again seem to be either pinned by a single nail to the front of the cross upright (which is represented as a very slim pole), or, in full conformity with the Zias and Sekeles recon-struction, fastened to either side of it, the bent mode of the legs favouring this latter posture.

What we also seem to be seeing in the Pozzuoli graffito (though it may also be true of the Palatine Hill one) is the crucified represented *facing* his cross, rather than with his back to it, since his body is clearly represented as occluded by the upright. This has the effect of making fresh sense of the bent-legs mode, since if the crucified were positioned facing the upright, with his heels nailed either side of it, he would necessarily have had to straddle it in a most undignified manner, his legs no doubt

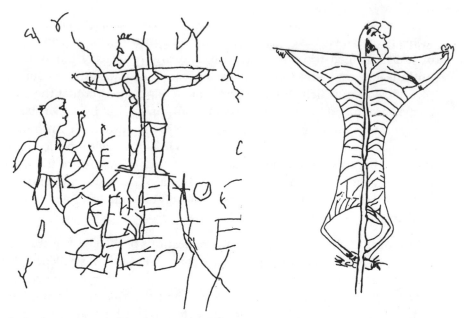

Fig 3 Roman era graffiti depicting crucifixion:
(*Left*) As found in 1856 on the wall of the Domus Gelotiana, a palace of the Emperor Nero's time (AD 54–68) on the Palatine Hill, Rome. This shows a figure with an ass's head as if standing on a lower crossbar or *suppedaneum* of a T-shaped cross, while another figure at left stands and gestures as if in adoration. The Greek inscription reads: 'Alexamenos worships his god'. The palace was used as a training school for boy slaves, and Alexamenos was probably a Christian among these. It is unclear whether the ass/man is facing, or has his back to, the cross. (*Right*) As found on a wall at Pozzuoli, near Naples. Note the crucified's feet fastened quite differently to the Palatine Hill example, and the apparent clear indication of his being suspended facing his cross. In both instances the cross is represented surprisingly slim, possibly suggesting the use of a defoliated, but unfelled tree-trunk for the upright.

contorting violently as he vainly tried to break free. It also makes sense of the undoubted custom (despite Zias and Sekeles) of the breaking of the legs to hasten death. Experiments have shown that if volunteers are suspended crucifixion-style solely by their arms they have great difficulty breathing. So once the already weakened crucified was unable to push himself up on the nails through his heels, he would have expired relatively quickly of asphyxia, exactly as appears to have happened in the case of the two thieves crucified with Jesus.

The crucial aspect of all these latest insights derived from the Jehohanan bones and the graffiti is that they are very far from detracting from the case for the Shroud's fidelity to such a Roman-era crucifixion.

49

For instance, let us take the idea of the crucified having been fastened facing his cross. We have been so conditioned by artists' endless depictions of Jesus crucified with his back to it that any other way might seem unthinkable until we actually reconsider that very same $\wedge$-shaped double bloodflow from which Dr Pierre Barbet made his deduction that the man of the Shroud had been suspended not by his palms, but by his wrists. As was pointed out to me as long ago as 1978 by the South Australian physician Dr Victor Webster, it is so obvious to anyone with medico-legal training that this stain derives from a blood clot to the back of the wrist that everyone utterly overlooks that this stain has most mysteriously gone 'completely undistorted and completely undamaged'. As Webster explained:

> Just meditate for a moment on the implications of this [i.e. the absence of any distortion or damage]. If the man of the Shroud[17] was nailed by the wrists to the wood of the cross, taking into consideration the inevitable pressing of the hand against the wood, and the 15-degree movement [i.e. the shifting of position denoted by the $\wedge$], which presumably lasted a considerable time, then the complex blood clot and therefore its present-day image must have been rubbed, smudged or abraded and could not possibly persist as the clear 'blood clot' which we see today.
>
> Only two possibilities exist. First, a long nail may have been used, one long enough to hold the wrist out away from the wood. This seems most unlikely. Second, the man must have been crucified with his ventral surface against the cross. In other words, *facing the cross*! There seems to me no alternative.[18]

Long before Zias and Sekeles had made their revisions to Haas's findings, Webster even came to similar conclusions with regard to the nailing of the feet. Firmly rejecting Haas's feet together, side-saddle reconstruction pose as quite 'ludicrous', Webster opined instead that the man of the Shroud had '. . . stood on a small platform or *suppedaneum* and the nailing of the feet took place by driving the nail obliquely through the heel bone firmly into the wood of the *suppedaneum*. There would of course be two nailings, the feet being placed side by side.'

Back in 1978, Webster very understandably inferred a *suppedaneum* or platform, as did many others who read and argued over Haas's report, simply because Haas had reported the crucifixion nail to have been driven obliquely through Jehohanan's heel bone. However in view of Zias's and Sekeles' correction of Haas, i.e. that the direction of the nail was in fact laterally, or sideways through the heel bone, Webster would almost certainly now agree that no platform would have been necessary. Harrowing though it is even to contemplate, the crucified would seemingly have had to stand on the nails through his heelbones in order to give himself some relief from his suspension from his wrist bones. For those carrying out a crucifixion, such a method, demanding neither buttocks-support nor foot-rest, would have had the great virtue of simplicity, always a strong argument for this being the way it actually happened.

For many Shroud researchers who, under the influence of their traditional crucifixes, have 'seen' the nail wound in the man of the Shroud's right foot as a slightly darker patch between his tarsal or toe bones, this may seem highly damaging to what they may hitherto have taken as near 'holy writ' regarding the Shroud. Yet if they carefully reconsider the Shroud's foot area 'bloodstains' they might realise that this is far from the case. As we have already noted, the whole sole of the man of the Shroud's right foot can be seen imprinted in blood, together with a post-mortem blood spillage that has broken away from his *heel* or ankle area [pl. 20a]. Likewise, on the frontal image the flow of blood at his feet looks to have its origin at his ankles–heels rather than at instep height. Since we would not expect blood to flow upwards, arguably, the Shroud points to an ankle–heel-bone nailing very compatible indeed with the latest insights from Zias and Sekeles. And is not the ankle–heel an exact counterpart to the wrists? And may we not perhaps also anticipate that something of the same nerve-jangling horror associated with the wrist-nailing also happened at the ankles?

What cannot be emphasised enough is that all the above interpretations are based on evidence that is far too fluid and ambiguous for anyone, whether Zias and Sekeles, Dr Victor Webster, or myself, to claim that they represent the last word on the subject. Shroud or no Shroud, to 'see' Jesus not only nailed by the wrists, but facing his cross and writhing with his heel bones pinned to what, given the fairly diminutive size of olive trees, is likely to have been a fairly low upright of olive wood [for reconstruction, see fig. 4, overleaf], demands a fundamental change in perceptions that may be impossible for many even to contemplate. Although as is quite evident from Josephus, a real crucifixion was a great deal more horrifying than the typically rather static affair portrayed by Hollywood's filmmakers, no one can yet claim to know what it was *really* like.

But from the historical–archaeological point of view, far from simply conforming to the traditional conceptions of mediaeval artists, among

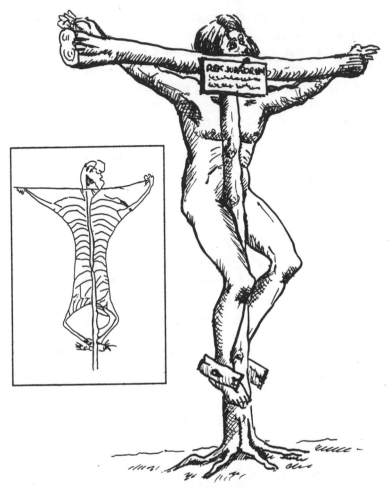

Fig 4   How the man of the Shroud was crucified?
Reconstruction based on Dr Victor Webster's argument for the man of the Shroud having
been nailed through the back of the wrists, and the evidence from the Jerusalem crucifixion
Jehohanan for nailing through the heels, obviating the need for any *sedile* or *suppedaneum*.
Note the close compatibility of this reconstruction to the Pozzuoli graffito (see inset). Since
the upright of Jehohanan's 'cross' was of olive wood, this suggests the use of the trunk of
an olive tree *in situ*, corresponding to Simon Peter's description of Jesus having been hung
on 'a tree' in Acts 10.3. Note the slats of wood designed to prevent the crucified pulling his
feet free of the nails with any strong sideways movement.

52

whom wrist-nailing was almost unknown and heel–ankle-nailing completely unknown, the Shroud can be seen to be fully compatible with, and
a complement to our understanding of, the very latest insights concerning
how crucifixion may have been practised in Jesus's time.

Yet even if it is historically convincing as a portrayal of a crucifixion of
someone genuinely from Jesus's era, can we be equally sure it is convincing
with regard to how such a person would have been buried?

Chapter 4

And is it what we would expect of a genuine first-century crucified body's burial?

Anyone who has ever witnessed a Jewish wedding will know what long-drawn-out and exuberant occasions these can be, the Christian gospel story of the wedding at Cana being but one indication of how far their roots go back into historical tradition. Jewish funerals, by contrast, are mostly hastily arranged and very simple, yet all the indications are that the traditional rites for these too stretch back a very long way indeed.

So does the Shroud and the image of a body that we see on it conform to what we would expect of a typical Jew's burial back in the time of Jesus? Ostensibly no. Whereas the man of the Shroud's body was apparently laid out in death still covered with blood from his wounds (and as we shall see later, even with dirt still adhering to his feet), traditional Jewish funerary preparations required the corpse to be washed scrupulously from head to foot according to the practice of *taharah*. Whereas it is quite evident that the man of the Shroud's body was buried stark naked, apart from his envelopment in the Shroud itself, according to the traditional Jewish Laws enshrined in the *Mishnah* the corpse needed to be dressed in *tachrichim*, that is, a complete set of burial garments typically including a head covering, shirt, breeches, surplice and girdle. And whereas on the Shroud we see a body apparently intact and devoid of any signs of decomposition, the norm for Jewish burials of Jesus's time was for the corpse to be taken within twenty-four hours to its appointed resting place, left for many months for it and its wrappings to rot to a skeleton and rags, and then for its bones to be gathered up into an ossuary or bone box of the kind in which the crucified Jehohanan's remains were found.

So does this mean that the Shroud and its image are quite incompatible with the burial of a Jew as crucified back in the first century AD? Absolutely not. As any true expert in Jewish burial tradition will point out, the particular deceased person whom we see on the Shroud would have needed some very different funerary arrangements, because he self-evidently died a violent death – i.e. of crucifixion – during which his body became extensively stained with his life-blood.

As has been explained by Jewish-born Victor Tunkel of the Faculty of Laws, Queen Mary College, University of London,[1] in these circumstances, and only in these circumstances, traditional Jewish burial rites positively and unequivocally insisted upon absolutely no *taharah*, or washing of the body. The belief among the Pharisees of Jesus's time, shared by Jesus's own followers, was that the body would be *physically* resurrected at the end of time, thereby requiring that anything and everything that formed an essential part of it, such as an amputated limb, or its life-blood, should be buried together with it in anticipation. This has been expressed in an abridged version of the *Shulhan Aruch*, the great sixteenth-century *Code of Jewish Law* which modern-day Jewish scholars recognise as codifying laws and practices that go back to ancient times: 'One who fell [i.e. in battle] and died instantly, if his body was bruised and blood flowed from the wound, and there is apprehension that the blood of the soul was absorbed in his clothes, *he should not be cleansed.*'[2]

Likewise, as both the *Shulhan Aruch* and the great Jewish authority Nahmanides (1194–1270), go on to prescribe, over any clothes, however bloodstained, that the deceased may have been wearing when he died, those preparing him for burial were expected to wrap a white shroud – in the words of the *Shulhan Aruch*: 'a sheet which is called *sovev*'. A further requirement from the *Shulhan* was that whatever garments the deceased may have worn when he died were all that he should be buried in, clearly implying that if he had died naked, then he should be left that way, except for the *sovev*.

Of particular importance here is the exact form that this *sovev* took. As explained by Victor Tunkel, in the case of a heavily bloodstained corpse the ritual required as much avoidance as possible of any disturbing of the blood (and as we have seen, one of the Shroud's marvels is the lack of disturbance to its bloodstains). The *sovev* therefore had to be an all-enveloping cloth, that is, a 'single sheet ... used to go right round' the entire body.[3] The Hebrew verb from which *sovev* derives specifically means 'to surround' or 'to go around', thus perfectly corresponding to the 'over the head' type of cloth that we see in the case of the Shroud, and also, incidentally, to the *soudarion* which the John gospel describes as having been 'over his [Jesus's] head' and 'rolled up in a place by itself'[4] as observed by Peter and John during their discovery of Jesus's empty tomb.

Now if these elements so far may seem quite remarkably supportive of the Shroud being convincingly the burial cloth of a Jew crucified back around the first century AD, it is important also that we take account of an element that some have considered rather less convincing, the burial pose, and specifically the crossing of the hands over the genitals. While the laying out of a body flat on its back incontrovertibly conforms to the Jewish rite, the crossing of the hands over the genitals has been regarded by the Revd David Sox[5] and other detractors as suspiciously indicative of pious 'artistic modesty' denoting the hand of an artist rather than any true historical burial practice.

In fact such an objection may be easily disposed of. Despite the ancient Egyptians, for example, being far less prudish than the Jews, the Cairo Museum has (or certainly had), literally rows of mummies of ancient Egyptian priests buried with their hands 'modestly' across their genitals, exactly as in the case of the Shroud.[6] Likewise, an ancient Egyptian black basalt sarcophagus in London's British Museum, dating to *c.* 340 BC, features a carving of its original occupant with his hands crossed again in what is virtually an exact Shroud attitude [pl. 23b i]. Crossed-hands burials are also commonplace among other nationalities, including the ancient British,[7] while in the case of the Jews themselves, although the custom of gathering up deceased's bones into bone boxes has generally deprived us of knowing how they were originally laid out, none the less examples have again been found of Shroud mode burial. In particular, near contemporary with Jesus, a woman's skeleton with crossed hands came to light in 1951 when the French archaeologist Père Roland de Vaux excavated the cemetery at Qumran, the community responsible for the Dead Sea Scrolls [pl. 23b ii].[8] Although the pose proves nothing, since one can also point to innumerable mediaeval manuscript illuminations depicting the dead with their hands crossed in the same mode [pl. 24a],[9] Sox's objection essentially has no validity and may be dismissed.

But the question nevertheless arises: does the Shroud, although it accurately conforms to the rites by which Jesus may have been buried, perhaps also conform to how someone of the Middle Ages might have expected Jesus to be buried, this hypothetical forger producing his fake to these specifications?

The answer this time has to be a firm no. For a start, both before and during the Middle Ages there was a virtually universal Christian belief that Jesus's body was washed before burial, this being the recognised interpretation of the John gospel reference to Jesus having been buried 'following the Jewish burial custom'.[10] Supporting this, Constantinople came to possess what purported to be the very stone upon which this washing had been carried out, the 'Red Stone of Ephesus'. It is also a fact that throughout most of Christianity's first thousand years Christian artists had absolutely no concept of Jesus having been buried in a 'shroud' of the kind preserved in Turin, instead depicting him being buried wrapped in mummy-style swathing bands, and with his face exposed.[11] Later, as we will be showing, this view came to be changed, with an over-the-head type of shroud gradually emerging in art. But this latter was directly as a result of awareness of the existence of the Shroud as we know it today and not because this was what people understood from the gospels concerning how Jesus had been buried.

The other major question that arises concerns whether the Shroud, albeit compatible with burial procedures in the time of Jesus, perhaps also conforms to the type of shroud-burial that would have been being practised in mediaeval France and its environs around the time that it was theoretically forged, i.e. the fourteenth century.

The answer to this has again to be a firm no. Although in mediaeval French manuscripts such as the *Rohan Book of Hours* there are plenty of graphic depictions of burial in shrouds,[12] these exhibit some fundamental differences to the enshrouding procedure that we see in the case of the Turin Shroud. The typical mediaeval example features the body laid in the cloth bag-style, the feet being fully enclosed and the bottom ends of the cloth bunched up over the head, with any excess material left to sprout like the end of a Christmas cracker. This is the very reverse of the Turin arrangement in which the head was fully enclosed and the cloth's ends (unbunched) were left loose at the feet. Indicative of the long-term and widespread popularity of the mediaeval 'Christmas cracker' arrangement, a seventeenth-century sculpted tomb in St John's Church, Bristol, England, is but one example featuring its Civil War period owner in much the same type of shroud. Conversely, I have yet to come across a single example, mediaeval or later, of the Turin 'over-the-head' mode.

Furthermore, if we want to get some real 'feel' for how a true mediaeval shroud was used, there can be nothing finer than two shrouds removed by Leicester University archaeologists from the corpse of an English mediaeval knight in 1981. During summertime excavations at St Bee's Priory in Cumbria, Dr Deirdre O'Sullivan and her archaeological team came upon a lead coffin that from the Priory's known history they gauged must date to around 1300, i.e. within a generation or so of the Shroud's purported forgery. When they opened it up, to their astonishment, inside was not the rubble of skeletal remains that they expected, but instead the fully intact and enshrouded body of a partially bearded, bald-headed man who, from his injuries, had seemingly died either in battle, or during jousting [pl. 24b]. Although he was so well preserved that his flesh was even still pink and supple, O'Sullivan and her helpers sadly failed to maintain this preservation. After a rushed and ruinous autopsy, their only recourse was to rebury him and to draw as little attention to their find as possible.

Thankfully, a much better preservation job was done on the knight's two shrouds, despite their initial slimy and highly odoriferous state. Through the efforts of conservation specialist Jean Glover of the North West Museum and Art Gallery Service,[13] these can be studied at leisure by visitors to Cumbria's Whitehaven Museum. The inner of the pair [pl. 24c], an eight-foot-square rectangle, would seem originally to have been first folded to a quarter of its width and the knight's naked body then laid on this doubled-up portion, the rest of the material being wrapped over and that at the top of the head gathered up in the already mentioned 'Christmas cracker' mode. As for the outer shroud, measuring some nine feet long by four and half feet wide, this was folded upwards from under the wrapped body to envelop the feet, probably because these had been somewhat inadequately wrapped by the inner shroud, and the head end then brought over the covered face, bunched up over this and bound up with cord. A portion of the inner shroud was also found to have been cut off and used as a kind of apron between this and the outer shroud, though the exact function this served has not been determined.

Clearly the St Bee's knight's shrouds, although they correspond very well with the mediaeval-manuscript depictions of shroud-wrapped bodies, are completely different from the Turin Shroud [fig. 5] in terms of their dimensions (half the length, twice the width), their mode of wrapping (sideways, rather than over-the-head), and their mode of fastening (with a lot of string, evidence of which is absent in the case of the Shroud). They also consisted of bits of cloth rather crudely joined to each other, quite unlike the Shroud's spectacular fourteen-foot length.

Yet none of this, of course, means that the Shroud cannot be the work of a 'cunning' mediaeval forger. Perhaps, whoever he was, this individual enjoyed such power that he could arrange for a six-foot man, possibly some prisoner, to be crucified in the exact manner of Jesus Christ? Perhaps he was able to obtain authentic ancient weaponry for the carrying out of details such as the scourging? Perhaps, given that Jews were well estab-

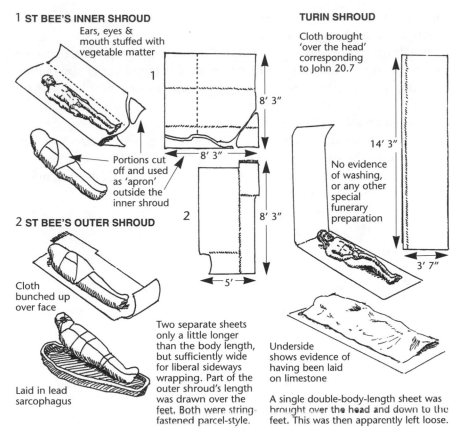

1 ST BEE'S INNER SHROUD

Ears, eyes & mouth stuffed with vegetable matter

1

8' 3"

8' 3"

Portions cut off and used as 'apron' outside the inner shroud

2 ST BEE'S OUTER SHROUD

Cloth bunched up over face

Laid in lead sarcophagus

2

8' 3"

5'

Two separate sheets only a little longer than the body length, but sufficiently wide for liberal sideways wrapping. Part of the outer shroud's length was drawn over the feet. Both were string-fastened parcel-style.

TURIN SHROUD

Cloth brought 'over the head' corresponding to John 20.7

14' 3"

No evidence of washing, or any other special funerary preparation

3' 7"

Underside shows evidence of having been laid on limestone

A single double-body-length sheet was brought over the head and down to the feet. This was then apparently left loose.

Fig 5 Mediaeval and Turin Shroud burial arrangements compared
Plan of a mediaeval shroud burial (*left*) as based on the well-preserved wrappings of the knight found at St Bee's, Cumbria, compared to the arrangement evident from the Turin Shroud (*right*)

lished throughout Europe during the Middle Ages, he knew the special burial requirements that pertained to those of this religion who had died a bloody death and arranged for an all-enveloping cloth accordingly?

Of course, even if he had managed all this, how he managed to get the image onto the cloth still remains unexplained. Also is it not rather incredible that this unknown individual should have gone to so much trouble and effort to deceive in an age in which, as twentieth-century journalists have reminded us, a large proportion of the populace would

59

have been very easily duped by a feather of the Archangel Gabriel or a phial of the last breath of St Joseph?

Whatever the answer, it is important to stress that everything that we have discussed so far has been based on mere external visual observation and appraisal of the Shroud's 'photographic' image of an apparently crucified human body and its burial.

So what about the Shroud as a physical object, as something that can be examined 'hands on' for the composition of its body image, its blood image, and other mysterious features? Just how much, when these are studied and analysed by modern technology's every available tool, might it continue to stand serious scrutiny?

Part 2

'Cunning Painting' – or Genuine Gravecloth?
The Shroud reassessed as a physical object

Chapter 5

What can the Shroud's fabric tell us?

Everything that we have so far discussed concerning the Shroud has been based on what anyone can deduce about it from good photographs, whether these be in positive or negative, black and white or colour. Information derived from direct physical access to the cloth has not been necessary.

For this section of the book, however, almost everything is based on what has been learned by those specialists who have been allowed some form of direct access either to the Shroud itself, or to some sample of it. And while some religious relics remain even now perpetually locked away, a prime example being Rome's so-called 'Veronica', the Shroud has been made quite surprisingly accessible, there having been some six occasions[1] during the last three decades in which it has been opened up for some form of specialist appraisal. The most spectacular of these, inevitably, was the five-day, round-the-clock, ultra-high-tech examination conducted by the American STURP team in 1978.

However, for all the qualifications of some of the persons who have been allowed direct access on such occasions, they have not necessarily always been the right people to tackle the questions crying out for straight answers. Typical in this regard has been the Shroud's appraisal as a historic textile, from the point of view of whether, the radiocarbon dating aside, it might be mediaeval or more ancient. Despite the American STURP team having comprised some thirty highly qualified personnel, all of whom crossed the Atlantic in 1978 for the specific purpose of making a thoroughly definitive scientific examination of the Shroud, not one of these had had proper professional experience either of mediaeval textiles, or of ancient textiles, nor did anyone possess professional expertise regarding the technology of textiles – despite the Shroud being first and foremost a piece of historic fabric.

So given that we may expect some limitations to the data deriving from at least some of those who have been privileged to have had such hands-on access to the Shroud, just what can we glean concerning this cloth, specifically from the point of view of its characteristics as a piece of fabric?

In fact, what has been preserved in Turin throughout the past four centuries as the Shroud is rather more than just a single item of fabric. Whenever its custodians of recent times have opened up its four foot four inch (133 cm) long, gilded wooden casket they have found inside a parcel beautifully wrapped in a modern red cloth, bound with red tape and sealed four times with the seal of whoever was Turin's cardinal archbishop the last time that such an opening-up was authorised. Only after their removing this protective covering and another three inside this have they reached the Shroud bundle proper.

On unrolling this bundle they have found it to consist of three main cloths and a variety of minor ones, one below the other and all sewn to each other. The topmost of these, yet another protective cover made of red taffeta, was personally sewn the length of one side of the Shroud by the then twenty-five-year-old Princess Clotilde of Savoy in 1868, to replace a black cover cloth that had been formerly provided in 1694. Below this there is the Shroud itself, patched in places with pieces of sixteenth-century altar cloth to cover where it was scorched and holed in the fire of 1532. And immediately beneath this there is a backing cloth of sixteenth-century holland cloth, onto which the Shroud was sewn in 1534 in order to strengthen it, following the fire of two years earlier, the whole ensemble surrounded by a blue fabric frame to protect everything at the edges. Year by year these three cloths and their attachments have lived in the most intimate contact with each other, rolled up so tightly together around a 4-cm-diameter velvet-covered staff that invariably each opening-up produces additions to the innumerable crease and tension marks that have long been scattered across the Shroud's surface.

As a piece of fabric, then, the Shroud is something of a monument to the wisdoms and failings of its conservators both ancient and modern, and it is important that we comprehend something of the history of these as part of our understanding of the cloth as a whole.

The conservators' biggest failure was undoubtedly the major historical predecessor to the recent fire of 1997, that back in 1532. In that year the Shroud, which by then had been owned by the Savoy family for nearly a century, was being kept in a grille-guarded niche in the back wall of the beautiful Sainte Chapelle that the Savoys had built as their personal place of worship adjoining their castle at Chambéry, high in the French Alps.

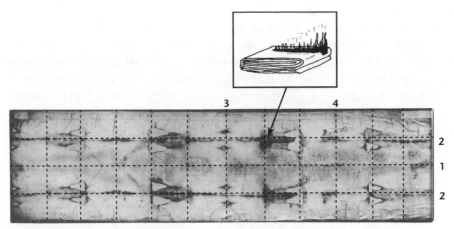

Fig 6   Plan of the damage caused by the fire of 4 December 1532
Plan of the damage caused by the 1532 fire, showing how the Shroud was folded into 48
folds at the time of this incident. Remarkably, the image was almost entirely untouched by
the damage

As a protection from theft they had arranged four different locks for the
grille, the keys for these held by different individuals, a not uncommon
security ploy for sacred objects and one that might have seemed ideal.

However, the one circumstance in which such security is not ideal is
when quick and unexpected access is needed, like in a serious fire, as broke
out in the chapel the night of 4 December. With the whole edifice quickly
ablaze, and there being no time to summon the four key-holders, the
caretaking clergy's only recourse was to a blacksmith, Guillaume Pussod,
who managed to prise open the protective grille. However, the beautifully
crafted silver casket housing the Shroud had already become irreparably
molten. By the time that the Shroud, which lay inside neatly folded into
forty eight, could be lifted out, a drop of superheated silver had already
set one corner ablaze. And although this was immediately doused with
water, when the cloth was opened out full length the effect was like a
paper-tearing act, the cloth being extensively branded with scorch-marks,
gaping burn holes, and water-damage marks. But uncannily and of no
little wonderment to those of the time, the all-important central image
remained almost completely unscathed.

Today those damage marks, albeit mostly covered over with triangular-
shaped patches sewn on by Poor Clare nuns [fig. 6], represent part of the
known history of the Shroud's fabric, the Poor Clares' Mother Superior,
Louise de Vargin, even having left a graphic memoir of the two weeks

during which she and her fellow nuns performed this delicate task.[2]

Other blemishes, however, have gone altogether less well documented, most notable of these being four sets of burn holes which similarly adjoin but do not harm the body image [fig. 7]. Two of these can be seen either side of the buttocks on the Shroud's back-of-the-body view, and two either side of the crossed hands on the frontal one. Each group of these sets can be seen to comprise three black-edged holes with varying amounts of ancillary damage [pl. 35b] and, from the way that they back each other up when the Shroud is folded in four, in a clear descending order of penetration, it is a reasonable inference that something like a red-hot poker was run through the cloth three times on some occasion when the Shroud was folded in this manner. Yet there is absolutely no documentation of when, how or why this might have occurred,[3] the only certainty being that it must have been before 1516. This is because the holes can clearly be seen in a Shroud copy reliably dated to this year (and

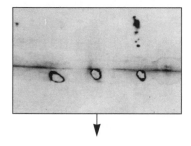

4	. ' '	Bottom	1	0	Topmost
	'			0 0 0	
3	0 0 0	3rd	2	0 0 0	2nd
	\			0	

Fig 7 Plan of the so-called 'poker hole' damage
The distribution of the four groups of so-called poker-holes on the Shroud. The four groups of these can be seen to have a descending order of penetration, showing that the cloth must have been folded in four at the time the damage occurred, and that the four sets of holes derive from a single damage incident. The blackened appearance of their edges suggests that something like a red-hot poker was thrust three times through the centre of the folding arrangement. One possibility is some form of 'trial by fire' – a Dark Ages equivalent of the carbon dating test, but all that is certain is that the damage pre-dates 1516.

thereby sixteen years before the 1532 fire), preserved in the Church of St Gommaire, Lierre, Belgium [pls 8–9b].

Similarly unknown are the circumstances surrounding the cutting off of certain portions from the Shroud. Although some have been snipped away on well-publicised occasions in recent years (as in the case of the radiocarbon dating of 1988), the fate of others is completely unknown. Thus on the frontal image half of the Shroud a 14 × 8 cm (five and a half by three and a half inch) portion can be seen to be missing at the spectator's left from the foot end; likewise a 36 × 8 cm (fourteen inch by three and a half inch) portion on the equivalent back-of-the-body half of the cloth [pls 6–7c, where marked K]. Historically the only reliably documented removal of anything of this kind was Dowager Duchess of Savoy Margaret of Austria's stipulation in her will of 1508 that a portion of the Shroud be given to her beloved church of Brou at Bourg-en-Bresse. Yet even in this case, whether such a bequest was actually executed, how much of the Shroud was taken and if so how much, if anything, might survive today at Brou, remain unknown. Such instances of serious damage aside, there are also many minor surface blemishes that show signs of having been darned at different times and by different hands, though the early history of these similarly fades into obscurity.

Which leaves us with the original Shroud fabric itself, and its uncertain origins. At least from the structural point of view there is complete agreement, among Shroud enthusiasts and detractors alike, that it has been woven from linen, that is, from fibres of the *linum usitatissimum* or domesticated flax plant. Since despite the complications of its manufacture, linen-making has been known throughout at least the last nine thousand years,[4] with Jesus's Galilee having been an important manufacturing centre, this presents no obstacle to the possibility of the Shroud being 2000 years old.

Likewise, although non-specialists often express disbelief that anything as frail as linen could survive 2000 years, certainly in as complete a form as that exhibited by the Shroud, this objection is again easily dealt with. For providing that linen is kept dry it is one of the most enduring of fabrics. Moth grubs ignore it because it lacks the keratin that their diet needs and many other insects find it too hard to masticate. As proof of this durability the world's museums abound in ancient Egyptian linen mummy-wrappings, many of these 4000 years old, yet still strong and intact. Turin's Egyptian Museum, for one, has some ancient Egyptian linen shirts that are as perfect as if they came off the loom but yesterday.[5]

Accordingly, while there is no real difficulty to the Shroud possibly being 2000 years old, the far more crucial question is whether, from what can be gauged of its fabric, it really is that old, particularly in the light of the adverse carbon-dating result. Does its weave, for instance, offer any clues to its age? This weave was reliably identified in the 1930s as a three-to-one herringbone chevron twill, a complex variety for which the weaver would have had to pass each weft (or transverse) thread alternately under three warp (or vertical) threads, then over one, creating diagonal lines, the direction of which he or she would then have reversed at regular intervals [pl. 25b].

But is such a weave more typical of the Middle Ages, or of the first century, or of both? The straight answer to this has to be that it is typical of neither period, examples in fact being so rare that the British Museum's Dr Michael Tite, when trying to obtain specimens to use as controls for the Shroud radiocarbon dating, completely failed in this endeavour, thereby being obliged to abandon the original intention for the radio-carbon-dating test to have been done blind, that is, with the laboratories ignorant of exactly which sample came from the Shroud.

For the fact is that in the case of ancient Egyptian linens, which are overwhelmingly the most common variety of linen to survive from antiquity, all are of plain weave, that is, they have been created in a simple 'one over, one under' style [fig. 8]. So does this mean that the herringbone weave had not even been invented at the time of Jesus, a point which, if it were true, would necessarily destroy at a stroke any argument for the Shroud dating back to that period? Happily this is not the case.

For instance there is a cloth from Palmyra in Syria, known definitely

Three-to-one twill weave

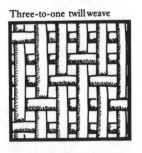
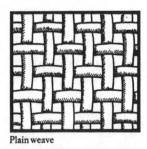

Plain weave

Fig 8   Plan of the Shroud weave
(Left) Plan of the Shroud's three-to-one weave, showing its greater complexity compared to the simple plain weave at right

Fig 9   Very rare mediaeval example of the Shroud's herringbone twill weave
A block-painted fragment of linen of 3.1 chevron twill (or 'herringbone') weave, in the
collection of the Victoria and Albert Museum. From the painted design, known from silks
of the second half of the 14th century, a similar date is attributed to this fragment, making
it a near unique example of herringbone weave from the mediaeval period. The shaded
portions are a reconstruction. (Victoria and Albert Museum ref. no. 8615–1863)

to date from before AD 276, which is in herringbone weave. Another
herringbone example, definitely dating from the Roman era, was found
in a child's coffin at Holborough, Kent, England. Yet other examples have
been found at Trier, Conthey, Riveauville, and Cologne.[6]

The complication to all these, however, is that they were woven not in
linen, but in silk. And although there are other examples of essentially
the same weave, some dating back to the late Bronze Age, these were
created in wool. It has to be acknowledged that no actual examples of
linen directly matching the herringbone twill of the Shroud survive from
antiquity, but this is far from saying that examples did not and could not
have existed in this fabric. As any of the world's community of specialists
in the history of textiles will readily confirm, the number of surviving
specimens of ancient textiles represents but the tiniest proportion of the
amount long lost to us, so that what we do not know about them vastly
outweighs what we do know.[7]

Herringbone woven linen was certainly not commonplace in the mediaeval European world in which the Shroud was purportedly forged. Dr

69

Donald King, the Keeper of Textiles at London's Victoria and Albert Museum, was only able to find one possible example in his collection [fig. 9], in the form of two seven inch by four inch (18 × 10.5 cm) cuttings from a stole or maniple.[8] Because this bears a printed design of foliage and birds inspired by patterns from late-fourteenth-century woven silks, it is thought to have been made around this same date. But it represents a lone example and as has been pointed out by Manchester textile specialist the late John Tyrer[9] its texture is very much coarser than the Shroud. So the Shroud is the only known example of plain herringbone twill linen dating from before the second half of the sixteenth century.[10]

The other data deriving from specialist study of the Shroud's fabric shed little greater light. When in November 1973 Belgian Professor Gilbert Raes of the Ghent Institute of Textile Technology was invited to Turin to take part in a one-day specialist examination of the Shroud, he was provided with a 13-mm warp thread, a 12-mm weft thread and two postage-stamp-sized portions (taken from the left-hand corner of the Shroud's frontal half), to take back to his home laboratory for study.

From these samples Raes was able to identify the twist of the yarn used for the Shroud as 'Z' twist, meaning that whoever had held the original spindle must have rotated this clockwise. All ancient Egyptians, seemingly to a man (or woman), spun their linen yarn 'S' twist, that is, by rotating it anti-clockwise. However, this distinction is in fact no more of a deter-minant of age or provenance than the weave. In the post-pharaonic era Z twist began to appear in Egypt and other parts of the Middle East, and almost all European linen from around 300 BC through to mediaeval times was Z spun.[11] And although most Syrian and Palestinian linen was S spun, there are Z-spun examples from around the time of Jesus that are known from Palmyra (whence we noted one of the herringbone twill silks), and from the desert of Judaea.[12]

Another deduction that Raes was able to make from his samples was that the linen is undoubtedly fine, thereby confirming my own rather surreptitiously gleaned observation of the same year. By counting the number of threads to the centimetre on his samples, Raes found these to average of 38.6 warpways and 25.7 weftways, a sure indicator of the use of a very fine thread. This again provides no threat to authenticity, it being well recognised that antiquity's weavers could produce fabrics readily rivalling those of the present day for fineness. One cloth from 3600 BC, for instance, is half again as fine as the Shroud.[13]

Yet another of Raes's findings was of minute but unmistakable traces of cotton adhering to the linen threads, suggesting to him that wherever the Shroud had been woven, it had been done on equipment that had also been used for cotton. Since the particular variety of cotton that Raes found was *Gossypium herbaceum*, a characteristic Middle-Eastern variety, this initially led him, and as a result myself and others, to regard this as rather good evidence for the Shroud having originated in the Middle East.

In the event, such an interpretation was seriously misplaced. The British archaeologist and textile specialist Elisabeth Crowfoot,[14] and American Donald M. Smith,[15] have both pointed out that cotton manufacture was introduced into Europe by Arab Moslems when they invaded Spain in AD 711, thus bringing into being a Spanish cotton industry that was quite a flourishing one by the thirteenth century, at which time it was controlled by several Jews.[16] Furthermore, as the French textile specialist Gabriel Vial pointed out in the wake of the Shroud examination that he was allowed to make in 1988 (at the time of the taking of the carbon-dating samples), the presence of traces of cotton may in any case be altogether incidental. Despite Raes's perfectly feasible idea that whatever loom was used for the Shroud could have been used for weaving cotton as well as linen, the Shroud's surface is so littered with microscopic debris, including innumerable particles and fibres from the garments of those who have brushed up against it, that the presence of cotton might simply have derived from the wearing of cotton gloves by people handling it – as in fact the members of the STURP team did in 1978, even though this was five years after his finding.

One particularly informative element of the Shroud's fabric ought to have been its edges, given that these must bear at least some data concerning how the original weaver finished them in the form of a selvedge and how people from times past may have made modifications to this edge in order to display it. Sadly, however, the Shroud's now centuries-old attachment to its backing cloth and the blue fabric surround has mostly prevented any examining and/or photographing of the edges, the only exception having been during the STURP examination in 1978 when the Turin microanalyst Giovanni Riggi (the same man who cut off the samples for carbon dating in 1988), unpicked a section of the Shroud from its backing cloth in order to try to view the image from the Shroud's underside [pl. 25a].

Although Riggi was no textile expert, he found himself surprised and intrigued by some of the stitching that he encountered at the edges. In his own words:

During the separation of the two cloths ... it was discovered, much to our surprise, that rows of invisible stitches approximately 2 cms apart run parallel to the main longitudinal axis. At least, that was the case in the areas that I separated. Obviously I cannot say for certain that the same kind of stitching is to be found elsewhere. But what is certain is that the colour of the thread used for this stitching blends in perfectly with the threads of the Shroud itself, and being no thicker than warp or weft, it cannot be detected by the naked eye. Today ... I very much regret not having kept any of these little strips of stitching which I spent eight hours removing, one by one. It would have been interesting to know more about these.[17]

What Riggi seems to be describing here are threads set two centimetres apart at the Shroud's edges that, given their indistinguishability from the Shroud's threads, were very possibly part of the Shroud's original manufacture, but which in 1534 became utilised by the Poor Clare nuns to help fasten the Shroud to its backing cloth. It is therefore a matter of considerable regret that being no textile expert, Riggi actually destroyed what by his own admission may well have been some rather crucial historical evidence.

One final mystery element of the fabric is what appears to be a seam line three and a half inches from the Shroud's edge (as seen to the left of the frontal image when viewed face on), that runs the cloth's full length. It is from inside this seam line that the Shroud's two missing portions have been removed at its two ends, but what is as yet still far from clear is the exact function of the seam itself, if that is indeed what it is.

Before the STURP examination of 1978 I had hypothesised that the three-and-a-half-inch-wide strip of cloth which the seam appears to join to the main body of the Shroud was a 'side-strip' added close to the time of its original manufacture, perhaps in order to balance the appearance of the image on the cloth, since only by its addition does the body image appear central.

But then in 1978 X-radiographs made by the STURP team showed that the same weft-run could be traced through from the original Shroud into the side-strip, suggesting that the cloth had been made as a single piece, with the seam being just that, a seam. However, if that was the case, why on earth had anyone gone to all the trouble of very carefully cutting off a three-and-a-half-inch strip, only then equally carefully to sew it back on again?

Fortunately, French textile specialist Gabriel Vial threw some fresh light on this mystery. After carefully examining the make-up of the Shroud's individual warpways rows of threads, he concluded that the Shroud must originally have been woven wider than its present width, but then someone cut it lengthways, removed either one or three warpways rows and carefully sewed it up again. Vial has favoured three rows having been removed, since just one would (a) have been hardly worth the effort; and (b) extremely difficult to cut and sew up again as accurately as would appear to be the case.

However, as has been suggested both by my wife (a practised needlewoman), and by the STURP X-radiograph technician Bill Mottern (and his wife),[18] rather than any cutting of the fabric, what could have been responsible for the very same effect is just a simple tuck or flat-fell seam run the length of the Shroud, which any proper textile specialist ought one day to be able to confirm, if given the same access to the Shroud's underside accorded to Giovanni Riggi and the STURP team.

If the seam is some kind of tuck, the mystery, of course, is why it was made? Might it have been to centralise the image on the cloth? Or was it a purely decorative device? Whatever the answer, and whether the Shroud be a cunning fake or a genuine gravecloth, we can only acknowledge that our understanding of some of its most basic details as a textile is still far from complete, despite five ostensibly intensive scientific and technical examinations, three of these involving textile specialists.

Overall, our only conclusion concerning the Shroud's physical fabric has to be that it is essentially neutral with regard to the case for the Shroud's antiquity, or otherwise. In truth, such evidence as we can rely on neither overly supports nor undermines the radiocarbon-dating findings.

Chapter 6

What of the Shroud's so-called body image?

Ve have already studied the apparent 'photograph' of a human body that the Shroud reveals when seen in negative. But what is the substance that gives rise to this image on the Shroud proper? Surely this must be scientifically analysable? And if so, surely it must be possible to determine whether it is merely a 'cunning painting', as the fourteenth-century Bishop d'Arcis claimed, and as the radiocarbon dating seemingly confirmed, or something else? As we are about to see, the answers are far from straightforward.

What we have chosen to call the body image may be broadly defined as all the visible body features – i.e. hair, body parts and body disfigurements – that are not actual 'bloodstains'. And although what comprises this image can be seen readily enough on colour photographs of the Shroud's natural appearance, there is really no substitute for seeing it on the cloth itself.

Even its colour is extraordinarily difficult to define. Dr Pierre Barbet, who viewed the Shroud at close quarters when it was briefly displayed in daylight on Turin Cathedral's steps on 15 October 1933, described it as 'brownish'.[1] From my personal impressions when I saw it illuminated under strong television lighting in 1973 I spoke of it as 'pure sepia monochrome' and 'pale sepia akin to yellow',[2] while American journalist Robert Wilcox, who stood shoulder-to-shoulder with me at that time, quite independently chose exactly the same word 'sepia' for his colour description.[3] However, the American STURP scientific team of 1978, who took their own very high-powered artificial lighting with them to Turin to conduct their scientific work, chose to reject all such earlier descriptions and instead to define the image as yellow or straw-yellow. In essence what we all ought to be able to agree on is that the image's hue is very subtle, and appears differently in different types of lighting at different times of the day.[4] The best available analogy is that it resembles both the colour and character of faint scorchmarks on a well-used ironing-board cover.

Whatever colour description you give to it, the image looks far paler than it appears in photographs, particularly in black-and-white photographs. The best explanation for this is the seemingly magical transformation that can happen with a very old sepia-coloured family photograph if you happen to have it copied in black and white. Almost invariably the picture will turn out to have far more detail than you had ever previously suspected, a phenomenon due to your eyes' greater difficulty distinguishing gradations in shades of pale sepia-yellow than if you were distinguishing the same gradations reproduced in shades of black. However, even on colour photographs the image consistently appears rather sharper than it does on the original Shroud, this seeming to be a property of the reduction in scale (in the case of non life-sized photographs), serving to sharpen the focus.

Also deserving of a reminder is the image's almost vanishing subtlety as you view it on the original, seemingly melting into the cloth the closer you get to it. For me, having, as earlier mentioned, some art-school experience of drawing and painting the human figure, this effect seemed demonstration in itself that no artist could possibly have created the image in any conventionally understood way. Not only would there have been extreme difficulty working in tones optically so indistinguishable from each other, but any artist would have needed at least a six-foot paintbrush to see what he was doing and make adjustments to it at the same time.

Making such a task that much more difficult still would have been the theoretical artist's additional handicap of choosing to work without the slightest semblance of any outline. Essentially, every artist throughout history, at least up to the time of the Impressionists, has used outlines as the base point of reference from which to build up images, because outlines enable you to see what you're doing, and where, particularly when your 'canvas' is fourteen feet long. Yet if the Shroud's image is truly a work of human artifice, then whoever was responsible for it created the world's first outline-less painting, a quite remarkable achievement in itself.

All this, of course, only makes more crucial our coming to the right judgement concerning whatever science can determine of the chemistry of the Shroud's body image. However, this is a particularly bloody battle-field of scientist fighting scientist, on which the non-scientific layman is likely to find himself ever more confused with every blow.

What no one can deny is that the most exhaustive, though not necessarily the most conclusive, approach to determining the nature of the Shroud's body image was that of the American STURP team. Although they took with them to Turin a huge armoury of what was in 1978 state-of-the-art image-analysing equipment, in fact one of their more meaningful approaches involved simply mounting the Shroud on their purpose-built vertical-or-horizontal-mode test frame, then flooding it with so-called 'transmitted' light from behind, enabling a viewing of the Shroud much as though it were a very large colour transparency.[5] The effect of this on the body image was fascinating. Although the 'bloodstains' showed up well against the light, clearly having some substance sufficiently solid to 'block' it, the body-image stains did not seem to show up at all, suggesting that they had very little, if any, solidity or substantiality to them.

Life-size X-radiographs that the team took of the Shroud section by section also turned out very similar. Although these were sufficiently sensitive to register very clearly even the ring-stains from the water that had been used to douse the Shroud during the 1532 fire, of the body image and of even a single bloodstain they showed not a trace. When, as mentioned in the last chapter, the microanalyst Giovanni Riggi, as an associate of STURP, did his unstitching of one edge of the Shroud from its backing cloth in order to see whether the body image might show up on the cloth's underside, the unequivocal finding was that nothing of it did. Likewise, when STURP's optical physicists tried exciting or irradiating the body image with ultraviolet radiation they found that it did not fluoresce or reflect the excitation back, as might have been expected of any reflective substance such as an artist's pigment.

So what, then, might the Shroud's body image be composed of, that it can be readily visible to the naked eye as a browning or yellowing effect on the linen, yet be so subtle that it appears on one side of the cloth only, with neither transmitted light nor X-rays registering it? Part of the equipment that the STURP team took with them to Turin in 1978 was a Wild M400 Photomakroscope specifically for viewing the tiniest details on site, and it was via this, and with the Shroud hanging vertically before him on its test frame, that optical physicist Sam Pellicori of the Santa Barbara Research Center, California, set about studying all he could of its body image [pl. 26a].

Selecting for this purpose what was logically one of the most intense of 'body image' areas, the tip of the nose, Pellicori routinely tried viewing this at various magnifications [pl. 24b], only to find himself baffled by it. Even when he homed in on the merest fibrils of threads, he could not discern anything like an overlying pigment that might be responsible for what the unaided eye readily enough 'saw' as a nose-tip. All that the eye registered as body image seemed to derive merely from a slightly increased yellowing of the fibrils of thread in an 'image' area, compared with those in an area where there was no image. This change of colour affected only the very topmost fibrils and was so vanishingly subtle that, for instance, where one fibril crossed another, the lower fibril could be seen to be unyellowed at this point, having apparently been protected by the topmost one from whatever was responsible for the image-making process. As for the idea of any sort of liquid, such as a paint medium, having been applied to the cloth to create such a yellowing, in Pellicori's judgement there seemed absolutely no sign of this. Whereas in the case of any conventional water-colour or oil-painting process it might have been expected that the fibres would appear stuck or matted together by whatever had been used in the paint medium, the Shroud fibres appeared unaffected by anything of this kind.

The magnifications that Pellicori had available to him on-site in Turin were not high by microscopy standards, and he and his colleagues were further hampered by the less than ideal conditions of the test-room with which they had been provided. This was a large, draughty, wooden-floored chamber in the fifteenth-century Royal Palace, where uncontrollable breezes repeatedly wafted the free-hanging cloth and where the slightest footfall could ruin any microscopy photograph unless all present were ordered to stop in their tracks at the critical moment. Much therefore depended on what could be learned of the Shroud's image-bearing fibres if these were viewed elsewhere under higher magnifications. So with the approval of the Turin authorities the STURP team applied more than thirty specially formulated five-centimetre-long sticky tapes to carefully selected sectors of the Shroud's surface, both image-bearing and non-image-bearing, then transferred these sticky side down to glass microscope slides for shipment with them back to the USA.

There the choice of the best analyst for these fell to Dr Walter McCrone, a Chicago-based microscopist who had created world headlines in 1973 with the claim that he had found Yale University's famous Vinland Map – a map showing America purportedly drawn a century before Columbus had discovered it – to be a modern fake. Studying minute samples of the Map's ink via his favourite instrument, the light microscope, McCrone had discovered one of the substances this contained to be anatase, a crystalline form of titanium oxide that had only been developed in 1920. Such virtuosity with the microscope seemed excellent credentials for an impartial study of the Shroud, which indeed was what prompted me to be the first to contact McCrone on the subject in January 1974, finding him encouragingly enthusiastic and apparently devoid of any pre-conceived ideas concerning its authenticity or otherwise.[6]

Accordingly, McCrone was introduced to the American STURP project, even signing their agreement to maintain secrecy on any findings about the Shroud until they were able collectively to reveal their results. Regret-tably, he then made a most ill-advised[7] approach to the exiled ex-King Umberto of Savoy, whose approval he sought for a unilateral radiocarbon-dating initiative. This resulted in his peremptory dropping from the 'hands-on' STURP team of 1978 and consequent failure to gain close access to the Shroud that he would otherwise have had. None the less, when senior STURP member Ray Rogers of the Los Alamos Laboratory, New Mexico, was *en route* back from the Turin examination, he stopped over in Chicago specially to hand-deliver to McCrone's laboratory thirty-two (almost the sum total) of the sticky-tape slides, twenty-two of these having been taken directly from image areas.

McCrone immediately found himself distinctly unimpressed by the specially formulated sticky tape that STURP had used. Whereas it is usually possible to view whatever samples have been taken directly through normal sticky tape, some anisotropic property of the STURP tape pre-vented this, demanding the samples' remounting. None the less, on Christ-mas Day 1978 the workaholic McCrone was able to enter in his notebook for the commencement of his work on the Shroud samples:

> This seems to be an appropriate date to start ... My objective is to find out what the image is. It is visible, therefore it has atoms, and we should be able to analyse those atoms. This will tell us what makes up those atoms and perhaps how it got there. Most likely it will turn out to be body fluids yellowed with age. It is well known that almost any organic fluids darken with time (varnish on paintings for example). Underarm perspiration also obviously yellows cloth...[8]

However, if these were genuinely McCrone's expectations, within just a few days he started to reach some conclusions fundamentally at variance with them. In the teeth of what Sam Pellicori had observed via the Photomakroscope, McCrone began finding what to him was clear and unequivocal evidence for the Shroud's body image not only being by the hand of an artist, but its having been painted by that artist in an essentially conventional artistic manner. Scrutinising the fibres specifically taken from body-image areas, he observed these to be coated with what he interpreted as particles of a very finely powdered iron oxide.

As he was well aware, iron oxide, which can take the form of rust, jeweller's rouge, yellow ochre, red ochre, burnt sienna and weathered coal fly ash, is a natural artist's pigment that has been used since the very earliest cave paintings. As he was also aware, any artist would have needed some form of binding medium to apply this to the surface he had chosen (particularly in the case of such a resistant one as untreated linen). Evidence of this he duly found in what he called 'definite indications of a very thin dried paint medium with occasional tiny thickened residue layers with well-dispersed pigment particles embedded within'.[9] To determine the chemical nature of this binding medium he then applied a series of tests which enabled him to rule out the theoretical artist having used any drying oil or gum, as might have been expected in the case of an oil painting. Instead, however, they registered positive for the presence of some form of proteinaceous, or protein-containing medium, which by a further process of elimination he concluded to have been a collagen tempera, such as an artist or his assistant might have made from boiling up scraps of parchment. Aside from the iron oxide, McCrone also found among the Shroud's general surface debris various incidental particles of artists' pigments such as mercuric sulphide (artists' vermilion), ultramarine, orpiment and madder, all of which served to confirm in his mind that the Shroud must have been 'cunningly painted', just as Bishop Pierre d'Arcis had claimed back in 1389.

When, on the weekend of 24–5 March 1979, the STURP team held its first post-Turin debriefing in Santa Barbara, California, McCrone specially travelled from Chicago to discuss these adverse findings with them, only to receive a less than effusive welcome in view of their having independently reached quite diametrically opposed conclusions. In the summer of 1980 he severed all connection with them, but remained fettered by the secrecy agreement he had signed, until that same September when a Shroud-watching English journalist, Peter Jennings, unauthorisedly reported the gist of a lecture that McCrone had given to a theoretically 'closed' meeting in London.[10] This effectively obviated the need for him to keep a lid on his findings any longer, as a result of which he quickly published a series of articles in his own 'house' journal, *The Microscope*. Following this, the news gradually spread around the world, accompanied by a prediction by him that whenever the Shroud came to be radiocarbon dated the result would be a date around 1350, one that to his considerable satisfaction he

79

lived to see fulfilled. He has also continued steadfastly to uphold the conclusions that he first reached in 1980, right up to the present time.

Now McCrone is a microanalyst of international repute. His six-volume *Particle Atlas* is a standard reference work in the field of microanalysis. In a personal acquaintance going back now more than twenty years, he has never given me cause for anything but admiration for his lucidity, integrity and professionalism. As I have told him, I respect him rather more highly than I do many of the pro-Shroud scientists and researchers theoretically on my 'side', and of his own stance he himself has written with typical robustness: 'I am no Don Quixote and I do not knowingly tilt at windmills. When I "tilt" I have good reasons for doing so, and in this case I can assure you I have compelling, rational and straightforward reasons for saying the "shroud" of Turin was painted with a thin water-color paint by an artist.'[11]

But the key question is, is he right in such findings, even with the carbon-dating result having come out so firmly in his favour? After he had had his samples for several months he was asked to return them to the STURP team, a request with which he duly complied, but even before he had done so the STURP reaction was stoutly to challenge him. Although they did not deny the presence of iron oxide on the Shroud – indeed they could hardly do so since even those who had worked on the X-ray fluorescence analysis had found signals for iron, along with calcium and strontium, all over it – they were adamant that in the body-image areas this was present only in trace amounts and was not responsible for what the eye sees as image. Indeed, they demonstrated how if you daubed iron oxide onto a piece of cloth in sufficient intensity for it to show up as some semblance of the body image, this registered clearly under X-radiography, while that on the Shroud did not. The only locations on the Shroud that they acknowledged to have significant iron signals were the bloodstain areas, where it would be expected, since blood contains iron. They also acknowledged strong iron at the foot, where another factor was in play, to be discussed in chapter 8.

Accordingly, for a second opinion the thirty-two sticky-tape samples were passed to the now late Dr John Heller of Connecticut, a professor of internal medicine and medical physics at Yale University, and to Heller's long-time colleague, research chemist Jewish-born Dr Alan Adler of Western Connecticut State University. Analysing under the microscope the very same sticky tapes that McCrone had studied, Heller and Adler specifically tried to find the iron oxide that both sides, from their different perspectives, were already agreed was present. They quickly found it, but the immediate surprise to them was that it was quite exceptionally pure. As they were already aware, most artists' pigments tend to be contaminated by impurities. Accordingly, they began badgering museums to be allowed to study their ancient textiles, immediately finding that these, too, often exhibited the same chemically pure iron. As they gradually determined, the answer to where this iron came from probably lay in the fact that when flax is retted, that is, soaked in water, during the linen manufacturing process, it draws up into itself iron, along with calcium and strontium, as trace elements from the water. As Heller and Adler reasoned, at the time of the 1532 fire this very fine iron probably migrated from where it had been taken up within the fibres and became washed to the edges of where the fire-dousing water had been splashed on the cloth. This was why it showed up at these edges under the X-rays and from there, with the Shroud's repeated handling, became lightly distributed all over the cloth. But they felt adamant that wherever this iron came from, it was not responsible for what the eye sees as the Shroud's body image.

What, then, in Heller's and Adler's judgement could have created this image? After studying the body image under any and every variety of magnification, they came to the firm conclusion that it derived from nothing at all that had been added to the Shroud, in the manner that any conventional artist would have used. For instance, when they applied the tests for proteins by which McCrone claimed he had been able to identify an artist's use of a tempera binding medium, they found no evidence for such proteins.

Instead, the impression they gained was that the image derives from something taken away. Thus, if high magnification photographs of body-image fibres are studied, some of these actually appear to show an eating away of the fibres, as if they have been aged, or degraded significantly more than their non-image-bearing counterparts [pl. 26c]. STURP's Ray Rogers described the image just resting on the tops of the fibrils, and as there are fibrils in the off-image areas that look exactly like those that make up the image itself, this: '... suggests that what we are dealing with is some change in the chemistry of the cloth itself. It has been aged. For some reason, the fibrils that make up the image got older faster than the rest of the fabric.'[12]

A homespun equivalent of this might be the yellowing, or accelerated ageing, that can be observed to happen very rapidly to a newspaper (like flax, made principally of cellulose), that has been left out in strong sunlight. If we could imagine some process in which this worked selectively, with the Shroud body acting as the source of the sunlight, then we might have an appropriate model for what *could* have happened to create the Shroud body image, though both Heller (in his lifetime) and Adler have consistently declined to become drawn into such speculation. All they have been insistent upon is that McCrone, despite his microanalytical eminence, is wrong. Even his findings of the various incidental artists' pigments on the Shroud are judged as having nothing to do with the body image, but instead have a completely different explanation, as will be addressed in a later chapter.

So what, for his part, does McCrone think of Heller's and Adler's objections to his arguments? 'Asinine', 'drivel' and 'Adler is an *ass* and you *may* quote me' are among some of the comments that he has made about them in the course of our correspondence. Of the photographs that Adler interprets as Shroud body-image fibres that have seemingly been eaten away by the image-forming process, his explanation is that these are actually non-image fibres, the 'corroded' appearance being simply due to air bubbles in the adhesive of the sticky tape.[13] When asked how the hypothetical mediaeval artist managed to create the effect of a real photograph, working in negative, he has remarked:

> He [the artist] ... tried to imagine just how a shroud might look. It should not be a typical portrait based on light and shadow. He must have considered a dark tomb with a cloth in contact with a body. If he then formed the image based on contact points between shroud and body he would have darkened the brow, bridge of nose, moustache, beard, cheekbones, hair, etc. Then as an artist he would shade the image intensities aesthetically into non-contact areas. In doing so he in effect assigns image density values equivalent to cloth–body distance. This would explain the appearance of the Shroud image and, as well, STURP's 3-D image construction. Even more importantly, a photographic negative of such a painted image would automatically appear to be a true positive image. In ordinary light the nose, brows, cheekbones, etc., would appear darker and the recesses lighter, just the opposite of an artist's Shroud rendition but fulfilling the photographic positive-negative relationship.[14]

As might be expected, the professional artist Isabel Piczek has been more than a little underwhelmed by this explanation by McCrone, pointing out that besides it being unbelievable that any real-life artist could have achieved so spectacularly successful a result working in negative, getting everything anatomically right, and so on, it would have been absolutely automatic for a mediaeval artist to have prepared a ground for his paint to stick to, something for which there is no evidence whatsoever on the Shroud.

At least part of the blame for why there continues to be such heated controversy between otherwise respected scientists concerning the Shroud's body image must be laid at the door of the STURP team. Even in 1978 it ought to have been obvious that the Shroud's image was either by the hand of a mediaeval artist, as Bishop d'Arcis had directly claimed, or that it was the imprint that a genuine crucified body left on its grave-cloth. As a basic minimum the STURP team ought therefore to have included, in order to deal with the first possibility, at least one specialist in mediaeval art; in order to deal with the second possibility, either a medical specialist with archaeological knowledge or an archaeologist with medical knowledge. In the event their team included none of these, just as it did not include a textile specialist.

Furthermore, as has been pointed out to me by Joyce Plesters of London's National Gallery scientific department[15] (levelling her criticisms evenly at McCrone as well as STURP), had any properly professional art specialist been invited to try to determine whether the Shroud was a painting, he or she would not have used anything as crudely indiscriminate as sticky tape for obtaining samples. Instead a needle and/or scalpel would have been used invisibly to remove minute and very specific samples. Also the person would have ensured that whoever did this was the same one who would also carry out the microscopy. As an investigation of an object that was either a gravecloth or a mediaeval painting the STURP operation was ill conceived from the very outset. The issue, however, may not be one of a straight choice between the Heller and Adler and the McCrone interpretations. Given that the very sampling procedure was flawed, both may be wrong.

Another seriously thought-out argument for how the body image may have been formed has been put forward within only the last two years by British physicist Dr Allan Mills of the University of Leicester. Noting that pressed plants often leave very Shroud-like sepia-coloured images of themselves on the sheets of paper between which they have been laid, Mills has postulated that these images may have been generated by the release of a gas molecule, singlet oxygen, triggered by the trauma that the plant suffers through being cut and thereby killed for such a purpose. Mills has long been fascinated by the Shroud and suggests that conceivably some similar singlet oxygen release might lie behind its image formation.[16]

Across the Atlantic, yet another not altogether unrelated possibility has been advanced by Mexican-born paediatrician and microbiology specialist Dr Leoncio Garza-Valdès of the Santa Rosa Hospital, San Antonio, Texas. According to Garza-Valdès, what McCrone interpreted as the protein-aceous medium used by the hypothetical mediaeval artist may in fact be a bioplastic coating that bacteria and fungi have formed on the Shroud's surface, rather in the manner of the build-up of a coral reef. For Garza-Valdès, that which the eye sees as body image might have been formed by greater and more variegated concentrations of these bacteria and fungi, the images created by pressed plants again arguably providing a very close parallel. He also notes that since bacteria of this kind produce their own natural iron it may have been this, rather than the retting process, which is responsible for the very fine iron that is to be found not only on the Shroud, but also on other ancient textiles affected by the same kind of coating.

As yet, this new way of looking at McCrone's findings must be accounted a mere possibility, since most of Dr Garza-Valdès's researches in this field have still to be fully explored and published. Already clear, however, is that instead of the riddle of the Shroud's body image having been explained by the present generation of scientists researching the Shroud, a proper understanding of it may so far hardly have begun. All we can say with certainty is that any claim of proof of the hand of a mediaeval artist would at the very least be premature.

Chapter 7

What of the Shroud's wound marks: are they actual blood?

As we have remarked earlier, the very colour of the 'bloodflows' as they appear on the Shroud proper (as distinct from on the negative, where they appear white), raises some very justifiable suspicions. We all know that if we cut a finger and tie a handkerchief around it, the initially vivid red of the fresh blood will rapidly change to a dull brown, usually within a few hours. Yet as long ago as the early sixteenth century one Antoine de Lalaing described the Shroud bloodstains as 'clear as if they had been made today'.[1] Vignon, viewing the Shroud in the 1930s, described the colour as 'mauve carmine'.

Whatever interpretation one makes of them, I would readily endorse both of these descriptions. In the course of my own viewing of the Shroud in November 1973, I was present on occasions when the television lights were both on and off. When the lights were switched off and the room where the Shroud was displayed remained in what may be best described as subdued interior daylight conditions, colour-wise the 'blood' marks appeared not much different from the body image. When they were switched on the bloodstains took on a very distinctive 'clean' mauve-carmine colour that strongly reminded me, from occasions when I have checked proofs of colour printing, of the magenta that printers use for their primary red. Again reminiscent of colour printing, the bloodflows had a very thin and flat appearance, more like portraits of bloodflows than blood proper.

Again, from our experience with cut fingers we know that blood upon clotting quickly becomes crusty and flakes off, both from the skin and from any covering bandage, regardless of what injury it may have derived from. Yet one of the extraordinary features of the Shroud's bloodflows is that they appear suspiciously complete – effectively, whole images of stains, without any indications of anything having flaked away.

So how is any of this possible, without the Shroud being an obvious forgery? Back in the early 1930s the French surgeon Dr Barbet recognised these anomalies but set them aside on the grounds that they were not incompatible with certain chemical and other conditions. But today, in the light of the radiocarbon dating, we cannot fudge the issue in this way. Given that these stains so convincingly appear to have behaved as bloodstains, as attested by pathologists, they must either be genuine blood, of whatever origin, that has somehow left a complete, non-flaky carmine-mauve image of itself, or they must be extremely clever paintings of bloodstains, complementing the extremely clever painting of the body image as attested by Walter McCrone.

Now as we have already noted, in 1978 the STURP experiment of shining a strong light behind the Shroud, as if it were a colour transparency, revealed the 'bloodstains' as showing up solid against the light, in a manner that the body image did not. This seemed clearly to indicate that whatever may be responsible for these stains has some definite substance. When the bottom edge of the Shroud was unpicked and the image areas viewed from underneath, the 'bloodstains', again unlike the body image, could be seen to penetrate right through to the underside of the cloth. Yet the X-rays registered neither the body nor the blood images, suggesting that whatever the image-producing substance was, it was either genuine blood, which would produce little or no signal, or some pigment of too low an atomic weight to register on an X-ray. (A really cunning mediaeval painter this, to have anticipated X-rays!)

As for Sam Pellicori and his work with the Wild M400 Makroscope, whereas we earlier noted that he could see no significant particulate matter in any of the body image areas, in the case of the 'bloodstain' areas he found a definite substance, just as the transmitted light experiment suggested there should be [pl. 27b]. Optically this certainly looked like what one might expect of blood at high magnification – although, consistent with their other omissions, the STURP team had also not brought with them to Turin anyone professionally experienced at looking at blood under the microscope.

Again, all therefore depended on the opinion of non-participant specialists looking at sticky-tape samples of this 'blood' back in the USA and once more the task of first examining these 'blood' samples fell to Dr Walter McCrone. It was on Boxing Day 1978 that McCrone set under his microscope a sticky-tape sample labelled as having come from the area of the wound in the side. As he recorded in his notebook: 'Starting with 3–CB a heavy image area blood from the lance wound. Using low magnification 10× & 10× ...) I could see heavy encrustations (of blood?) – too red! I've never seen dried blood look like this. The sample we used for the *Particle Atlas* is spray-dried but is yellow to black depending on thickness of the particles. Why is this blood different?'[2]

Exploring further with his polarised light microscope, trying a variety of magnifications, McCrone came to the view that this 'blood' was iron oxide, just like the body image, simply in greater concentrations. Later, using the scanning electron microscope, he also found that it was mixed with mercuric sulphide or cinnabar, better known as the artist's pigment vermilion. And this cinnabar–vermilion was present not simply as stray particles, but in significant amounts.

Then, exactly as in the case of the body-image samples, it fell to John Heller and Alan Adler [pl. 27c] to give the second opinion on these 'blood' tapes. Isolating from them one fibril that was clearly encrusted with the red particles that McCrone had identified as iron oxide and vermilion, Adler applied a so-called birefringence test by which, if the specimen is placed between two polaroids set at right angles to each other, the particles should show up as bright-red speckles if they really were iron oxide. They did not do this. Neither did they behave like iron oxide for another test, for pleochroism, by which, if they really were iron oxide, they should have sent light scattering out in all directions. Adler also expressed serious doubts that the 'blood' could contain significant amounts of vermilion from the fact that nothing of it had shown up in the X-radiographs. As he pointed out: 'If you've ever seen an X-ray of tooth fillings, the mercury stands out. You can't "see" the blood in the X-rays. If the blood were one third cinnabar [i.e. vermilion] like McCrone claims, the mercury would show up on the X-ray studies, and it doesn't.'[3]

To which Isabel Piczek, user of vermilion in her everyday work, has added:

Vermilion is ... the heaviest pigment known ... opaque, a brilliant red, and very poisonous. It is erratically permanent. [Cennino] Cennini [a mediaeval painter who wrote a book on the painting techniques of his time] warns that when exposed to air and light, vermilion turns black. Its light fastness is very poor ... Vermilion *repels* water. It is very difficult to mix with aqueous mediums ... Painted on an untreated canvas, exposed to air, sun, fire (as the 1532 fire in the Chambéry chapel), the chances are almost nil that vermilion would have retained its red colour.[4]

Next Heller and Adler tried microspectrophotometry, a now well-developed method of identifying particles of unknown composition by analysing their wavelength spectra, every different substance exhibiting on the computer screen a pattern of peaks and valleys as distinct from other substances as if it were a fingerprint. As Adler was aware, if a Shroud particle was blood, its heme-porphyrin components should exhibit a pronounced peak, the so-called Soret band, at approximately 410 nanometers, thereafter falling off sharply. At Yale University, where he had been a professor of medicine and medical physics, Heller managed to beg the use of a microspectrophotometer and help from a well-known biologist, Dr Joseph Gall. When a Shroud 'blood' particle was fed into this, it showed an extremely large peak at 410 nanometers, then falling off very sharply, which Adler interpreted as unequivocal evidence that it must be haemoglobin, denatured as would be expected of a very old blood sample.

In the teeth of McCrone's 'iron oxide and vermilion' verdict, a variety of well-recognised chemical tests similarly produced positive results for the various individual constituents that make up what we call blood. Thus they registered positive for the presence of bile pigments. They registered positive for the presence of proteins. As had already been visually observed via ultraviolet photography, the bloodstains seemed to have a halo around them, as if they had oozed some form of serum, and when samples from these areas were tested by the standard Bromcresol Green test, one routinely used by physicians to check for albumen in the urine, they registered positive for serum albumen.

But if, despite McCrone's opinion, the bloodstains really are blood, why should they be so clear and complete? Gilbert Lavoie threw some significant light on this question by dripping fresh blood onto various surfaces, then applying a linen cloth at various intervals during the clotting process, finding that the impression had to be transferred onto the cloth within two hours in order to produce imprints like those on the Shroud.[5] From such experiments both he and others have formed the opinion that what is seen on the Shroud is not so much whole blood as an exudate from clotted wounds. This contains very few actual cells of blood and would give us more in the way of images of blood rather than whole bloodstains, just as we suggested back in chapter 2.

Furthermore, Alan Adler tumbled upon one very important explanation for why, as has been agreed by everyone, the 'blood' looks too red. A particular oddity that he discovered of the Shroud 'blood's' bile pigments was that these seemed to contain what he called 'an extraordinarily high' level of the pigment bilirubin, giving rise to the question why this should be so. As he explained:

> One possibility is that the person had a severe malaria, but this does not seem very likely. But a torture, scourging and crucifixion leading to shock – that would produce a tremendous hemolysis [break-up of red blood corpuscles-IW]. In less than 30 seconds the haemolyzed hae-moglobin will run through the liver, building up a very high bilirubin. If that blood then clots the exudate forms, and all the intact cells with haemoglobin stay behind, only the haemolyzed goes out along with the serum albumin which bind the bilirubin. So what one ends up with on the cloth is an exudate which has an enhanced bilirubin index with respect to the haemolyzed haemoglobin. You now mix bilirubin which is yellow-orange with methaemoglobin in its para-hemic form, which is an orangey-brown, and you get blood which has a red colour.[6]

From tests for protein on the Shroud 'blood', Adler further found that when the tiny 'blood' sample was dissolved away by these, as it should be by the particular protease method used, the fibril beneath appeared clean and untouched by any body image. This suggested that the blood had become transferred to the cloth first, the formation of the 'body' image then occurring later, the very reverse of the way that any artist might have been expected to work.

However plausible and convincing all this may sound, coming as it does from a world-acknowledged specialist on the porphyrins to be found in blood (and one who, as a Jew, can hardly be accused of pro-Christian leanings). McCrone has written dismissively of Adler's findings, 'All this is fiction – there is *no* blood in the Shroud image.'[7]

This means that we are once again confronted with the unedifying spectacle of two well-qualified and well-respected sets of American scientists disagreeing, with the lay reader left thoroughly confused in the middle. McCrone also seems to have been distinctly underwhelmed by the fact that Italian forensic medicine Professor Pierluigi Baima-Bollone, after analysing full threads that he extracted from the Shroud's 'small of the back' bloodstains during the STURP examination of 1978, claimed to have positively identified these as human blood of the group AB.[8] Similarly ignored went the highly respected French geneticist Professor Jérôme Lejeune's confident identification of human haemoglobin on a Shroud 'blood' sample that he had obtained. Lejeune, a discoverer of the gene responsible for Down's Syndrome, had been intending further genetic-type research but died in April 1994.

While all might seem a total impasse there is, in fact, thanks to the recent advances of science, one further approach to the problem that ought to help act as some kind of arbiter. This is based on the fact that if the Shroud's 'bloodstains' truly are composed of just iron oxide and vermilion, as McCrone claims, then they could not possibly provide meaningful results for the presence of DNA, the code of life. Conversely, if they are truly 'blood', as claimed by Alder and his colleagues, then at least some vestiges of DNA should be present and lend themselves to meaningful interpretation.

In the event, vestiges of DNA do seem to be present. The first indication of this came from Italy, based upon two 1.5-cm-long threads that Italian scientists had taken from the bloodstained foot region of the Shroud when they worked alongside the STURP team in 1978. When in 1995 these threads were examined specifically for DNA at Genoa's Institute of Legal Medicine, the Institute's Professor, Marcello Canale, duly reported: 'We have extracted the DNA present on these tiny threads and have amplified this with a chain reaction that allows us, via a particular enzyme, to keep on replicating the DNA an infinite number of times. It is a method that can be used even in the case of a single cell ... The DNA chain is very long, and we are able to identify very small sectors representing individual characteristics which can ultimately enable us to identify the individual from whom they derive.'[9]

However, if the sceptic distrusts any claim of such a kind coming from 'pro-Catholic' Italy, a second analysis, using quite different samples and carried out in the United States, may be more acceptable. As the Turin archbishopric's official minutes show, although the taking of the radio-carbon-dating samples from the Shroud was completed by 1 p.m. on 21 April 1988, the Shroud was not returned to its casket until 8.30 that evening. By way of explanation of what happened to the Shroud during those seven and a half hours it has recently been revealed that Giovanni Riggi, the Turin microanalyst who performed the cutting-off of the samples for the radiocarbon dating, used them to remove some small samples from the Shroud's crown-of-thorns 'bloodstains', apparently with Cardinal Ballestrero's consent. Having no immediate plans to research them, he seems then to have deposited them in a bank vault to await future circumstances in which he might be able to use them to advantage.

Those circumstances emerged four and a half years later when Dr

Leoncio Garza-Valdès, as part of his researches into the bioplastic material which he believes coats the Shroud's fibres, visited Turin in the hope of being allowed some kind of first-hand access to it. On his meeting Professor Gonella, he was introduced to Giovanni Riggi, thereby learning of the latter's private collection of the 'bloodstain' samples. A few months after his return to San Antonio he managed to enlist the help of the University of Texas's special Center for Advanced DNA Technologies to make a study of these, whereupon, on his informing Riggi of this opportunity, Riggi crossed the Atlantic with the samples, destination San Antonio.

Upon Riggi's arrival at the Texas University Health Science Center his 'blood' samples were swiftly brought to two highly qualified individuals who had no previous connection with the Shroud, Dr Victor Tryon, Director of the Center for Advanced DNA Technologies, and his wife and chief technician, Nancy Mitchell Tryon. In fact, on his receiving the first item of Shroud material, a 1.5-mm 'blood' fragment on sticky tape, Victor Tryon merely handed it to his wife as if it were another item for routine processing. Nancy, although she noticed that the sample seemed unusually tiny and old, had no idea that it was from the Shroud. None the less she had no difficulty obtaining a positive reading that it was human blood, and in the subsequent work she and her husband quickly established the presence of both X and Y chromosomes confirming (if it were not already obvious visually), that the individual of the Shroud was of the male sex. They further corroborated these findings by a rerun of the same tests using a sample that Riggi had taken from a different area of the Shroud.

But would the Tryons be able to identify DNA? Indeed, yes. According to Victor Tryon, by employing routine polymerase chain reactions which can detect pieces of double-stranded DNA they have found three quite unmistakable gene segments:

Beta globin gene segment from chromosome 11
Amelogenin X gene segment from chromosome X
Amelogenin Y gene segment from chromosome Y

Such is the importance and interest value of this claim that I decided to check its credibility independently with American-born specialist in ancient DNA, Dr Thomas Loy, who happens to be conveniently near to me at Queensland University's Centre for Molecular and Cellular Biology and is sufficiently famous in his field that he is mentioned in its connection in the book *Jurassic Park*. He confirmed to me that he finds absolutely no cause to doubt the Tryons' findings.

Thus, as I learned, the DNA in blood and tissue from archaeological finds even several thousands of years old is now quite routinely being analysed and evaluated. One current study is examining what can be gauged of the inbreeding indulged in by the Egyptian pharaohs. Unlike in the case of McCrone-type microscopic analysis, in which so much depends upon the microscopist's eye, DNA analysis is instrument based and a far more exact science. The amelogenin X and Y genes, as found by the Tryons, are absent from bacteria and fungi, and genuinely suggestive of a human source. Loy was also supportive of the credibility of Alan Adler's explanation for the 'too red' blood. He himself had come across 300,000-year-old blood of a similarly vivid colour, it always being the circumstances of the deceased's death, rather than anything to do with the sample's age, that is responsible for this.

As Loy stressed, the one major factor that everyone has to be on guard for when dealing with DNA, both ancient and modern, is that of contamination. However, when I put this point directly to Nancy Tryon she assured me that because the Center's work often has to be presented in courts of law, they have the most stringent controls to guard against it. Only if someone secondary to the original individual whose blood appears on the Shroud had happened to bleed again onto the very same spot could serious contamination have been introduced – and (nuns pricking their fingers while carrying out repairs excepted), that scenario has to be considered reasonably unlikely.

For those supportive of the Shroud's authenticity the good news of the DNA findings is that they provide a powerful, though as yet far from conclusive, riposte to the McCrone 'iron oxide and vermilion' verdict on the Shroud 'blood'. The bad news is that they represent a huge source of worry that someone may draw from them some conclusion undermining central tenets of the Catholic faith, such as the Virgin Birth. There is even the science-fiction nightmare of someone of the future perhaps producing from the Shroud a cloned Jesus of Nazareth, a theme that has indeed already spawned one highly imaginative novel to this effect.[10]

With regard to the latter scenario, any such fears on the Church's part may be accounted essentially groundless. As Nancy Tryon pointed out to me, cloning from the Shroud is not only not on the San Antonio agenda, it would actually be impossible from the material available, given that they have isolated only seven hundred base pairs (the basic units of DNA), as against the three billion that make up the entire human genome.

Even so, when in the spring of 1996 Garza-Valdès informed Cardinal

Saldarini of these and related researches by sending him a copy of an article about them that had appeared in the Health Science Center's house journal *The Mission*, the Cardinal's response was far from warm or congratulatory. He bluntly pointed out that when he took over from Cardinal Ballestrero as the Shroud's custodian he did not reappoint Giovanni Riggi, who thereby had no authority to make samples available for use in DNA or any other research. Any proper authority for this could only have come from the Shroud's owner, Pope John Paul II, and had certainly not been granted.[11] Independently Saldarini issued a public statement calling for any Shroud samples taken since the 1978 examination and still in private hands to be returned to him, at one and the same time specifically forbidding and disowning any scientific research that might be carried out on materials not so returned.

Not only did this salvo effectively stop the Tryons' work dead, it also represents a huge stumbling block for us, since whatever may be the validity of their findings as a refutation of McCrone, technically they cannot be recognised as such because of the Church's disclaimer.

In like manner to the body image, therefore, identification of the Shroud's 'bloodstains' as true blood cannot be considered proven, adding yet further to the uncertainties surrounding what theoretically ought to be the easiest evidence of the Shroud to deal with, its physical composition.

However, we are still not finished with that physical composition. For even though we have dealt with the body image, the blood image and the physical fabric, we have yet to consider what further clues may lie among the microscopic debris that is known to litter every inch of that physical fabric's surface.

Chapter 8
What of the Shroud's surface debris?

As we all know, leave any surface exposed to the air even for just a few days and it will gather dust. If we were to look at that dust under a microscope we would find it to have quite a variety of constituents depending on the particular environment to which it had been exposed. If this were a modern-day urban industrial area, for instance, we might expect fly ash from power stations and lead from the exhausts of vehicles still running on leaded fuel. If it was a country area there might be pollen and plant spores.

Now whether the Shroud is six hundred or two thousand years old, it is historically known to have been exhibited in some quite different locations. This inevitably impinges on the varieties of incidental debris that may be found on its surface and what clues these may carry regarding phases of the Shroud's past, unknown as well as known.

On the occasion of my own examination of the Shroud in 1973, one homespun experiment I tried was viewing the Shroud's surface from the extreme vantage point of one edge, running my eye across its width at various points along its length. Although this had been chiefly intended to determine whether there was any raised matter visible in the image area (which there was not), it also revealed a scattering of irregularities which turned out to be tiny droplets of wax. Of course it was hardly surprising to find these, given the many recorded occasions on which candles were known to have been used when the Shroud was exhibited. Also, in relative terms such droplets were rather large to count as microscopic detritus. Even so, the method at least produced a satisfyingly immediate result.

On my scrutinising the Shroud more conventionally from the front, particularly looking for any unusual discolorations additional to those that had already been documented, it also struck me that the apparent rope of hair at the back of the head had a distinctly more greyish hue than the rest, a possible indication that the man of the Shroud had had his hair dressed with oil. Although, on my returning to Turin for the 1978 exposition, I suggested to members of the STURP team that they might try taking samples from this during their examination (which they were conducting at that time), they proved far too preoccupied with just keeping to their pre-arranged programme – a pity, since it seemed to me that conclusive identification of hair oil in such a location could have constituted quite a significant addition to the evidence for the Shroud genuinely having contained a human body.

Even so, a near equivalent indicator of this kind actually did come to light quite unexpectedly during the reflectance spectroscopy work that STURP married couple Roger and Marty Gilbert carried out as part of the project. While the Gilberts were working on the Shroud's back-of-the-body image, they happened to come upon some unusual reflectance spectra, with very definite high iron traces, specifically and exclusively in the area of the soles of the feet, particularly the heel. Accordingly, in order to determine what, if anything, might be special about this area, they called over optical physicist Sam Pellicori to try training his Wild M400 Makroscope on it. After spending some time studying the foot area at full magnification, Pellicori solemnly pronounced: 'It's dirt!' And, as the others present were able to observe through the viewfinder, there were indeed significant quantities of dirt particles deep into and between the threads very specifically in this area, as in no other on the Shroud. As Dr John Heller subsequently commented, 'What could be more logical than to find dirt on the foot of a man who has walked without shoes? Obviously no one was crucified wearing shoes or sandals, so he was barefoot before they nailed him to the cross. There is not enough dirt to be seen visually, so it follows that no forger would have put it there, because artists aren't likely to add things that cannot be seen ... It was a single data point, but ... not a trivial one.'[1]

These are, however, but incidentals to some of the more deliberate gatherings and analyses of Shroud dust debris that have been performed during the scientific examinations of the last quarter century. They began in 1973, when the Swiss criminologist Dr Max Frei first applied pieces of sticky tape to the Shroud's surface in order to sample it for pollen, of which more later. But they then escalated dramatically in 1978 with the STURP team's already noted use of sticky tape for the purpose of analysing the image, also with further sticky-tape applications by Dr Frei and again, during this same occasion, an actual mini-vacuuming of the Shroud's underside by the Turin microanalyst Giovanni Riggi as part of his programme of procedures following his unpicking of the Shroud at one edge.

From the concerted efforts of these different researchers quite a considerable variety of detritus has been gathered from the Shroud, the interpretation of which, as usual, has been the area of greatest difficulty.

For some materials, such as power-station fly ash, the reasons why this should be found on the Shroud ought to be obvious enough to anyone. As the main manufacturing centre of the Fiat motor car, Turin is a large industrial city and the ash from power plants and so on is in the very air that everyone breathes. It is therefore bound to find its way eventually onto everything, even if it is as closeted as the Shroud.

Almost equally explicable is the presence of specks of various metals. In the dust vacuumed from the Shroud's underside, a part of the cloth which had been effectively sealed in since 1534, Giovanni Riggi found not only iron, but also particles of bronze, silver and even gold. Since the Shroud is known to have been kept in a variety of containers in the course of its history, of which probably the most elaborate was the ill-fated silver casket which melted during the fire of 1532, the reportedly blackened appearance of some of the silver particles makes it obvious enough that these derived from that incident. Other precious-metal particles are likely to have come from gold and silver ecclesiastical vessels placed in close proximity to the Shroud during exhibitions and special ceremonies held in its honour. Also, we should not forget that many mediaeval ecclesiastical vestments were embellished with precious metals. And it is a matter of record that the Shroud was temporarily kept in an iron box following the 1532 fire, almost certainly not the first such container.

While still on the subject of metals, the STURP X-rays showed up several wire-like objects, some slightly broader, looking like metal shavings, embedded into the fabric at seemingly indiscriminate points. Although the sampling and metallurgical analysis of even just one of these might conceivably have furnished an important clue to their and the Shroud's historical origins, frustratingly, this was yet another of the American team's omissions.

Minute particles of fabric also proved abundant among both the sticky tape and the vacuumed debris, those listed by Heller and Adler alone including red silk, blue linen, plain cotton, plain wool and even pink nylon.

The red silk appears easy enough to identify since, as we have already noted, the Shroud is stored day by day in immediate contact with a red taffeta covering that was provided by Princess Clotilde in 1868. However, we also know that the Shroud had a red silk drape as early as 1453, which appears to have been a predecessor to the black cover that Princess Clotilde replaced. So any properly exhaustive analysis would need to distinguish which fibres came from the modern and which from the mediaeval red silks.

The origin of the blue linen is also easy enough to pin down, almost certainly deriving from the blue frame surround that, like the red coverlet, was provided by Princess Clotilde in 1868. When in July 1988 I visited Professor Hall at the Oxford radiocarbon-dating laboratory, where the Shroud sample was at that time awaiting processing, Hall mentioned his and his assistant Dr Hedges's puzzlement at the number of tiny red and blue fibres that they had observed on it. These I was easily able to blame on Princess Clotilde's red and blue additions to the Shroud.

As for the cotton, the wool and the nylon, these and other particles like them are most likely to have fallen from the vestments and ordinary clothing of people who directly handled the Shroud, or have been in its close proximity, over the centuries. But in these instances, determining any exact provenance is all but impossible. In the case of the cotton, for instance, we know that even in 1978 alone at least four different varieties of cotton gloves were worn by those who handled the Shroud, without counting all the other occasions in history when cotton might have been worn by those displaying it, or when it was perhaps overlaid or underlaid with some cotton sheet. Wool is also such a common fabric that it could have come from anywhere at any time.

The biggest puzzle of all is the pink nylon, very much a twentieth-century product (therefore hardly attributable to Princess Clotilde) and surprisingly well distributed. Heller and Adler found it on their tapes and it has also been noted on those taken by Dr Max Frei. It is said to be of the same variety as that used for ladies' girdles and pantihose, giving rise to all sorts of dark speculations concerning the underwear of the comparatively few women who have had access to the Shroud during the age of nylon.[2] According to one American cleric, the simple explanation may be that it derives from the nylon that is used in some modern-day ecclesiastical vestments, though this has yet to be substantiated.

And if there can be this kind of mystery concerning materials that can only have been dropped on the Shroud in recent, well-documented years, small wonder that other less easily dateable materials remain matters of intense debate. Thus, as we have already noted, McCrone found undoubted artists' pigments among the detritus on the STURP tapes, these comprising, besides the already mentioned iron oxide and vermilion, madder (a duller red, made from the root of the plant rubia tinctorum), ultramarine (a very costly artist's blue, made from oriental lapis-lazuli) and orpiment (artist's yellow, made from arsenic trisulphide).

Although no one has challenged McCrone's finding of these, and very understandably he himself has interpreted them as buttressing his claim for the Shroud being the work of an artist, in fact the discovery of a particle of pigment as expensive as ultramarine on a work that needs no blue in its composition itself indicates that this particular fragment, at least, can never have been intended for the Shroud, but instead must have derived from something more adventitious.

One obvious reason why all manner of stray paint particles must almost inevitably have found their way onto the Shroud is the common practice in the sixteenth and seventeenth centuries for artists who painted copies of the Shroud to lay their finished product upon the original with the pious intention of imbuing their work with something of its holiness. For example, the life-size[3] Shroud copy preserved in the Royal Monastery at Guadalupe, near Toledo, Spain, bears the inscription: 'At the request of Signor Francesco Ibarra this picture was made as closely as possible to the precious relic which rests in the Sainte Chapelle of the Castle at Chambéry [i.e. what is now our Turin Shroud] and *was laid upon it* [my italics: the original Spanish is '*estata distesa dissopra*'] in June 1568.'[4]

Across France and Spain there are some fifty copies of this kind, several of which have similar inscriptions describing their having been placed 'in contact' with the Turin original.

The STURP team also noted from their work on site in Turin one other easy way for the Shroud to have acquired quite a sprinkling of paint particles, without these having anything to do with it being by the hand of an artist. In virtually every one of the seven rooms of Turin's Royal Palace that the team were allocated for their testing work the ceiling was a magnificent Renaissance creation, richly decorated with frescos from which tiny paint fragments would fall like confetti as the team members worked below. Accordingly, there need be no argument concerning the presence of paint pigments on the Shroud's surface. It is the distinction between those that are definitely strays and those that may have been deliberately applied that forms the basis of the continuing dispute.

If this facet is hotly debated, so is the presence of yet another item of surface debris, the pollen, as collected by Dr Frei. It was in 1973, on his being invited to Turin to notarise the genuineness of colour photographs of the Shroud taken in 1969, that Frei happened to notice the amount of dust on the cloth's surface, and asked if he could take some sticky-tape samples of this. His request was granted and Frei took twelve tapes of this kind, which he studied under the microscope in his Zurich laboratory.

As Frei expected, the tapes bore microscopic debris from the very same cross-section of materials we have just discussed – e.g. ash, metal fragments, fabric fragments. But what he was particularly looking for, because as a botanist by training it was the area of his greatest expertise, were grains of pollen. For as he knew, every pollen grain, although so minute, has a very hard outer shell, the exine, which can survive literally tens of thousands of years. And as he also knew, each grain differs quite markedly from the next according to the type of plant it has come from. This means that if you can identify the type of plant from which a pollen has originated you can tell at least something of the terrain in which it grew, be it temperate, desert or tropical.

In his criminological work Frei routinely used analysis of pollen on a suspect's clothing to assess whether he might or might not have been at a particular scene of crime. But with the Shroud, if he could make a really thorough analysis of its pollens, then he might be able to throw some light on the different terrain to which it had been exposed in the course of its history. Thus, if its pollens were only of flora typical of France and Italy, the only two countries within which it has moved during its known history from the fourteenth century to our own time, then of course this would suggest that it had never been outside those countries, strongly reinforcing the argument for it having been forged. Conversely, if pollens from more Eastern climes were found, while this would not prove the Shroud genuine, it would at least show that the forger, in addition to all his other 'cunning', went to the lengths of obtaining a non-European piece of cloth for his purpose.

As Frei painstakingly manipulated the tiny pollens to facilitate studying them under the microscope, he evolved certain important rules for himself. For instance, he needed to be careful not to impart any significance to the finding of something like cedar of Lebanon pollen. This tree has been planted in far too many European parks and gardens for it and others like it to be regarded as having any significance. But as he steadily identified one pollen after another, many of these either of native European varieties, or popular imports, so there began emerging certain specimens that had to be of import [pl. 29]. In particular, he found himself identifying pollens from halophytes, that is, from plants typical of the desert regions around the Jordan valley and specifically adapted to live in soils with the high salt content found almost exclusively around the Dead Sea. In his own words: 'These plants are of great diagnostic value for our geographical studies as identical desert plants are missing in all the other countries where the Shroud is believed to have been exposed to the open air. Consequently a forgery, produced somewhere in France during the Middle Ages in a country lacking these typical halophytes, could not contain such characteristic pollen grains from the desert regions of Palestine.'[5]

Frei also found pollens from plants that he identified as indicating that the Shroud had spent some time in a terrain with steppe-plan vegetation. This seemed to suggest to him Turkey, and particularly the more easterly parts of the Anatolian region.

However, in order to assemble a really conclusive argument to pin-point the Shroud to these places Frei needed more data, as a result of which he made a second sticky-tape sampling during the 1978 examination, followed by five more years of researches, including field trips to Turkey and Israel, all with the aim of publishing a fully definitive book on his findings. Then, in January 1983 he died, before being able to complete any of this. And although five years later both his written papers and his Shroud pollen collection were acquired by an American pro-Shroud group, faction-fighting and other eventualities within this group have largely denied us his researches right up to the present time.

Equally deleterious to Frei's researches (and further symptomatic of the 'blood' of our title), have been doubts concerning his professional competence that began to be expressed, even during his lifetime, by none other than the STURP group. Working alongside Frei in 1978, they observed with no little horror his seemingly amateurish method of obtaining sticky-tape samples. Unlike the pressure-sensitive 'torque applicator' and specially formulated Mylar tape that they had brought with them from the USA [pl. 28b] Frei, Colombo-style, took out of his pocket the sort of Scotch tape dispenser that can be purchased in any supermarket and proceeded to press pieces from this into the Shroud with what seemed quite inordinate vigour [pl. 28a]. When it came to the examination of their sticky tapes, the STURP team found that on all the thirty-four they had taken there was but one pollen, from a ragweed which grows in considerable profusion around Turin.[6] So how had Frei managed to collect so many specimens on his mere twelve tapes? It began to be put about that Frei was at best a bad scientist, at worst, a charlatan.

The unfortunate effect of this was to give the Shroud's detractors encouragement to denigrate further Frei's competence, particularly with the man himself dead and unable to defend himself. As Frei has been painted by the American sceptic Joe Nickell, he 'once taught an evening course in microscopical techniques in the Zurich University extension system' and was 'subsequently ... asked to create a crime laboratory for the local police'.[7]

The truth is that Frei founded the city of Zurich police's central scientific department in 1948 and was its director for twenty-five years. From 1952 he began lecturing in criminology at the University of Zurich's Faculty of Law, at the Swiss Police Institute at Neuchâtel and at the German Police Institute at Hiltrup. He was scientific editor of the German review *Kriminalistik*, was regularly consulted by police forces in Germany and Italy, as well as his native Switzerland, and in 1961 was appointed by the United Nations to become one of the senior investigators into the death of their Secretary-General Dag Hammarskjöld.

Which leaves the original STURP charges of Frei's amateurism, on which the plain facts are that whereas STURP's specially formulated Mylar sticky tape proved unsuitable for microscopic use because of its anisotropic characteristics, this was not the case with Frei's 'dime-store' variety. Also, whereas the STURP torque applicator extracted so little pollen precisely because of its scientifically controlled light pressure, Frei, the professional criminologist, quite deliberately pressed his thumb hard into the linen in order to obtain the most deep-seated, and thereby arguably most original, materials.

That Frei genuinely obtained hundreds of pollens with this 'amateurish' method is beyond doubt. When in July 1988, thanks to the generous co-operation of his widow Gertrud, his collection was acquired by the US-based pro-Shroud group ASSIST,[8] Dr Walter McCrone was invited to attend a special workshop of study of the pollen at the Philadelphia Academy of Natural Sciences, chaired by the Academy's head of botany, Dr Benjamin Stone. All present at this meeting were able to view what was on each slide via a microscope specially linked to two video monitors, and not only did there emerge on these much of the same detritus as on the STURP tapes, but also hundreds of pollens. ASSIST's Paul Maloney, who subsequently attempted to inventorise these, observed:

For example on the tape which Frei took from the bloodflow from the

101

PLANT POLLENS CORRESPONDING TO THE SHROUD'S HISTORICALLY DEFINITE TRAVELS AROUND WESTERN EUROPE AND THE WESTERN MEDITERRANEAN

1. **Varieties best known under their everyday names**
   Anemone (Anemone coronaria L.)
   Beech (Fagus silvatica)
   Castor-oil plant (Ricinus communis L.)
   Cedar of Lebanon (Cedrus libanotica Lk.)
   Cypress (Cupressus sempervirens L.)
   Hazel (Corylus avellana L.)
   Juniper (Juniperus oxycedrus L.)
   Laurel (Laurus nobilis L.)
   Love-lies-bleeding (Amaranthus lividus L.)
   Oriental plane tree (Platanus orientalis L.)
   Pine (Pinus halepensis L.)
   Pistacia (Pistacia halepensis L. & Pistacia lentiscus L.)
   Rice (Oryza sativa L.)
   Rock rose (Cistus credicus L.)
   Rush (Scirpus triquetrus L.)
   Rye (Secale spec.)
   Spina Christi (Paliurus Spina-Christi Mill.)
   Thistle (Carduus personata Jacq)
   Yew (Taxus baccata L.)

2. **Other varieties**
   Alnus glutinosa Vill
   Capparis spec.
   Carpinus betulus L.
   Lythrum salicaria L.
   Phyllirea angustifolia L.
   Poterium spinosum L.
   Ridolfia segetum moris

PLANT POLLENS INDICATIVE OF THE SHROUD AT SOME TIME IN ITS HISTORY HAVING BEEN IN NEAR EASTERN ENVIRONS, PARTICULARLY ANATOLIA AND ISRAEL

1. **Varieties found in desert and semi-desert terrain**
   Acacia (Acacia albida Del)
   Artemisia Herba-Alba A
   Atraphaxis spinosa L.
   Haplophyllum tuberculatum J.
   Helianthemum versicarium B.
   Oligomejus subulata Boiss.
   Peganum Harmala L.
   Pteranthus dichotomus Forsk.
   Scabiosa prolifera L.

2. **Varieties found in steppe type terrain, as in eastern Turkey and southern Israel**
   Glaucium grandiflorum
   Hyoscyamus reticulatus L.
   Ixiolirion montanum Herb.
   Linum mucronatum Bert.
   Roemeria hybrida (L) DC
   Silene conoida L.

3. **Varieties particularly typical of Anatolian (Turkish) environs**
   Epimedium pubigerum DC
   Prunus spartiodes Spach

4. **Varieties found in salty environs, particularly the Dead Sea**
   Althea officinalis L.
   Anabasis aphylla L.
   Gundeli a Tournefortii L.
   Haloxylon persicum Bg.
   Prosopis farcta Macbr.
   Reaumuria hirtella J. & Sp.
   Suaeda aegyptiaca Zoh.
   Tamarix nilotica Bunge

5. **Varieties particularly typical of the environs of Jerusalem**
   Bassia muricata Asch
   Echinops glaberrimus DC
   Fagonia Mollis Del.
   Hyoscymus aureus L.
   Onosma syriacum Labil.
   Zygophyllum dumosum B.

Note: All regionalisations are approximations

Fig 10   The pollen varieties found on the Shroud, as identified by Dr Max Frei.
Chart of the plants represented by the pollens Dr Max Frei claimed to have found amongst the Shroud dust, with the regions from which these plant varieties mostly derive. Dr Frei did not live to complete his research, and this list has been adapted from one published posthumously on his behalf by Prof. Heinrich Pfeiffer

heel I have made a quick count of at least seven pollen. And seven were found in a quick count of the tape from the bloodflow across the back. But such quick counts do not really tell the story. My nearly completed photo inventory of a tape from the dorsal 'side-strip', and the one from the bloodflow down the anatomical left arm, holds more than 160, and one from near the forehead of the man of the Shroud shows more than 275 pollen.[9]

As Walter McCrone, for one, was bound to concede, Max Frei had quite genuinely obtained the pollen he claimed. The one serious question raised by professional pollen analysts was whether he really could make the identification of the individual grains down to species level that he appeared to have done in a list of fifty-eight different plant species, all apparently identified by him, as published by an associate after his death [fig. 10]. Dr Oliver Rackham of Corpus Christi College, Cambridge, although not a pollen analyst himself, works with them and knows their methods. He has commented to me of this list:

> Conventional pollen analysts can make most identifications only to genus (e.g. *Pistacia*), or even to family (Chenopodiaccae). They use terms like '*Ranunculus*-type' or '*Quercus-cerris*-type' for a group of species, all with the same type of pollen, for which no closer identification is possible. Of Dr Frei's fifty-eight identifications, fifty-six are to species; only twice does he identify no more closely than to a genus, and he never uses the '-type' expression. I am suspicious of such great precision of identification. If it is true, then Frei made a very considerable advance at the frontier of what palynology is capable of doing. Maybe he did, but he never explained how he did it. Species, rather than genus or family, identifications are crucial to his argument.[10]

What is known of Max Frei is that his as yet unpublished manuscript (a document, along with everything else, stalled by the ASSIST infighting), includes description by him of a special procedure that he had developed for removing pollen grains from sticky tapes, apparently enabling him to study individual specimens in much greater detail, and with much greater ease, than had hitherto been possible.[11] This may provide the answer to Dr Rackham's concerns. Also worth noting is that the leading Israeli pollen analyst Dr Aharon Horowitz, having studied Frei's list of Israel plant pollens, has expressed his view that the list convincingly established that the Shroud must have been in Israel some time in its history.[12] Dr Avinoam

Danin of the Hebrew University's Department of Botany has even pointed to the Shroud pollen demonstrating an itinerary from Israel's Negev desert northwards to the Lebanon highlands.[13]

And there is one further supportive finding which has come to light, which still concerns the pollen, but which also takes us into yet another variety of extraneous material on the Shroud's surface: mineral deposits. The now familiar Turin microanalyst Giovanni Riggi, during his analysis of the materials that he had vacuumed from the Shroud's underside, reported coming across pollens among these, which he did not have the expertise to identify, but among which he noticed an approximately fifty per cent proportion that would not have been identifiable by Frei, since they bore a thick, calcium-rich mineral covering, coating all their otherwise distinctive features.

Accordingly, it was a matter of some surprise to Riggi when, on his being shown slides of some 160 pollens that ASSIST's Maloney had photographed from Frei's tapes, all but one of these appeared free of any such coating. Since Frei had taken his samples from the Shroud's image side and Riggi had vacuumed his pollens from its underside, i.e. the side which had theoretically lain in contact with the tomb, then the strong implication had to be that the Shroud's underside had been affected by once having lain on some calcium-coated surface in a way that the body-image side had not, raising the question, could this mineral coating have been from the rock of a tomb in Jerusalem?

In this regard it so happens that back in 1982 STURP's Ray Rogers took some of the Shroud sticky-tape samples to his old friend optical crystallographer Dr Joseph Kohlbeck, Resident Scientist at Hercules Aerospace in Utah. All that Rogers wanted from Kohlbeck was for him to make photomicrographs of the sticky tapes taken in 1978, since he knew Kohlbeck to have optical equipment that was superior to anything available at his own Los Alamos laboratory.

However, Kohlbeck began to take a lively interest in some of the particles of calcium carbonate (or limestone) that he immediately spotted among all the other debris on the tapes. Quite independent of the Maloney–Riggi observations (which in any case lay in the future), these raised in his mind the interesting question of whether the chemical 'signature' of these might in any way match that of the stone of the tomb in which Jesus was laid in Jerusalem.

As he was aware, one of present-day Jerusalem's most popular sites for Christian pilgrims is the Church of the Holy Sepulchre, the central shrine of which has a surprisingly good claim to being where Jesus was once buried. Sadly, this has been so badly hacked about in the course of its history, and is at present so well protected against any further hacking about, that Kohlbeck rightly adjudged the chances of obtaining any samples very slim. But he reasoned that limestone rock inside other tombs in the Jerusalem vicinity ought to have roughly the same characteristics. He found a most useful and knowledgeable local research colleague in the person of archaeologist Dr Eugenia Nitowski who, for her doctorate, had made a specialist study of ancient Jewish tombs in Israel. She had excavated the first rolling-stone-type tomb east of the Jordan and, as a result of the contacts she had made, was able to obtain for Kohlbeck the Jerusalem tomb limestone samples that he needed.

He subjected them to microscopic analysis, quickly finding them to have precisely the sort of distinctive characteristics that he had hoped for. As he has explained:

> This particular limestone was primarily travertine aragonite deposited from springs, rather than the more common calcite. Calcite and aragonite differ in their crystalline structure – calcite being rhombohedral [i.e. triangular] and aragonite orthorhombic [i.e. with three unequal axes at right angles to each other]. Aragonite is less common than calcite. Aragonite is formed under a much narrower range of conditions than calcite. In addition to the aragonite, our Jerusalem samples also contained small quantities of iron and strontium, but no lead.[14]

With Nitowski now highly intrigued at what he might find next, Kohlbeck proceeded to examine a sample of calcium taken from the Shroud in the very same foot area in which Roger and Mary Gilbert had come across the now famous 'dirt'. This was chosen because it showed a larger and therefore potentially more significant concentration of calcium carbonate than other areas. To Kohlbeck's considerable satisfaction, the sample turned out to be of the rarer aragonite variety, exactly as in the case of the samples taken from the Jerusalem tombs. Not only this, but it also exhibited small amounts of strontium and iron, again suggesting a close match.

But even these parallels were not enough to 'prove' the needed signature, as a result of which Kohlbeck took both the Shroud samples and the Jerusalem tomb samples to Dr Ricardo Levi-Setti of the famous Enrico Fermi Institute at the University of Chicago. Here, Levi-Setti put both sets of samples through his high-resolution scanning ion microprobe, and as

Positive Secondary Ions   Positive Secondary Ions

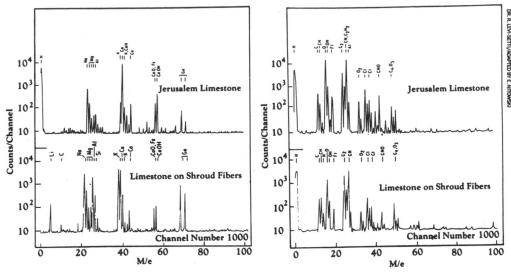

Fig 11   Comparison of the chemical 'signature' of limestone dust from the underside of the Shroud with dust from a Jerusalem tomb

The two graphs show the relative amounts of the chemical compounds found in thin sections of aragonite, the particular crystalline form of calcium carbonate present both on the Shroud fibres and in Jerusalem tombs dating from the first century. The peaks, which indicate the ions from a particular chemical compound, reveal such strikingly similar patterns that the crystallographer Kohlbeck has argued for a strong possibility of the Shroud limestone being of Jerusalem provenance. (As reproduced in *Biblical Archaeology Review* Jul/Aug 1986, p. 23)

he and Kohlbeck studied the pattern of spectra produced by each [fig. 11] it became quite obvious that they were indeed an unusually close match, the only disparity being a slight organic variation readily explicable as due to minute pieces of flax that could not be separated from the Shroud's calcium. As Kohlbeck readily acknowledged, this cannot of course be taken as proof that the Shroud aragonite can only have come from a Jerusalem limestone tomb. It may well be possible to find another area of the world in which the aragonite might prove similar to that on the Shroud and only future research more refined than anything so far conducted might one day be able to make a match that could be considered absolutely conclusive.

None the less from all that we have seen so far, one thing has to be glaringly clear. Not only has the Shroud visually satisfied the criteria for everything that might be expected of the burial of a first-century Jew crucified in the manner recorded of Jesus of Nazareth, but its own intrinsic physical evidence, although by no means lacking in contra-indicators, is also tantalisingly indicative of the same. So should we really dismiss all the Piczeks and Bucklins, the Hellers and Adlers, the Freis and the Kohlbecks as merely fooled by some mediaeval forger, as the radiocarbon-dating verdict would urge us to do? Or is there at least a reasonable case for looking into the possibility that the radiocarbon dating just might conceivably be wrong?

Before we do so, however, it seems high time to review the whole question of the Shroud's history, though with an important new twist: looking not forwards, in the normal manner of history, but backwards. For what we need to find out is whether the fourteenth century really is the earliest that a 'shroud' answering the description of that of Turin can be traced. And if it is not, just how far back *can* we go?

Part 3

Tracking the Shroud
Back through History

Chapter 9

Can we be sure that the Shroud dates back even to the 1350s?

oth before and after the radiocarbon dating it has been commonplace of press reports to say that historically the Shroud can
only be traced back reliably to the 1350s. This derives from Bishop
of Troyes Pierre d'Arcis's memorandum of 1389, which speaks of Bishop
Henri investigating the authenticity of a purported shroud of Jesus at Lirey
in France, 'thirty-four years or thereabouts' previously, meaning around
1355. However, not a single surviving document actually from the 1350s
even mentions a shroud at Lirey, let alone reports any diocesan investigation into its authenticity. Nor is there any guarantee that this Lirey
shroud was the Shroud now preserved in Turin. Yet the 'reliable' fact of
the Shroud being 'only traceable back to the 1350s' is all too often quoted
among the 'hard' evidence corroborating its fraudulence.

This is why, in our reappraisal of everything to do with the Turin Shroud,
we will continue to take absolutely nothing for granted, including all such
so-called 'hard facts' about its historical origins or lack of them. As if
following a thread in a maze, our approach will be to track the Shroud
epoch by epoch back through history, double-checking each change of
ownership and location, and at every stage re-examining why individual
historical references to a purported shroud of Jesus might or might not
pertain to our Turin Shroud. As we will discover, although there are places
where the thread wears decidedly thin, it does seem to extend significantly
further back than the 1350s. But it will be for you the reader to judge at
what point it becomes too fragile for further reliance.

There can be no better example of taking nothing for granted than what
happened the very day that I was working on what I supposed to be the
final draft of this particular chapter. On 11 April 1997, within hours of my
having confidently typed that we can at least be sure that 'ever since 24
February 1993 the Shroud has been reposing, rolled up as usual inside its
casket, in a special bullet-proof display case erected behind the High Altar

of Turin Cathedral', those words themselves became history. For 11 April was the day of the catastrophic fire in Turin's Royal Chapel and cathedral, from which the Shroud had to be so dramatically rescued by fireman Mario Trematore. At that moment every book previously written on the Shroud instantly became out of date.

Not only did the Shroud's new and expensively produced showcase disintegrate among the flames and destruction, but so did almost everything else of seeming 'permanence' and durability that had formed its surroundings during the previous four hundred years. As we will see in the course of our tracing backwards, this has tended to happen so often during the Shroud's history, both certain and reconstructed, that it begins to look almost like a message in itself.

Often unrealised is that the Shroud has only been actually owned by the Roman Catholic Church, in the person of the current Pope, John Paul II, for the last fifteen years. It was as recently as March 1983 that the Pope and his successors were bequeathed the Shroud, following the death of former king of Italy Umberto II of Savoy, among whose forebears [see family tree, fig. 12] the cloth can be traced with as much reliability as can be mustered for anything historical, for a full four hundred and fifty years, all the way back to 1453.

For almost three hundred of those years – that is, back to 1694 – we know the Shroud to have reposed in the same silvered wooden casket that survived the 1997 fire. This was kept inside the multi-locked high-security cage high up in the Baroque altar that formed the centrepiece of the now fire-ravaged private Chapel that the Savoys had had the architect Guarino Guarini build for them at first-floor level between the cathedral and their apartments in the Royal Palace. Traditionally, every time that there was an occasion on which it had been decided that the Shroud should be exhibited to the populace, two of the cathedral clergy would clamber up a ladder set upon this altar, unlock the cage and various inner compartments, and bring down the Shroud casket. The Shroud would then be opened out and displayed, sometimes in the cathedral, as in 1978, 1933, 1931 and 1898, but before then more commonly either from a palace balcony, or on a covered dais specially set up in the palace courtyard. Until Umberto II of Savoy's fall from power in 1946 the most common reason for such 'expositions' was to celebrate Savoy family marriages, as in 1931, 1868, 1842, 1789, 1775, 1750, 1737, 1665, 1663, 1646 and 1620, though in the earlier period showings were also often held annually to mark the Shroud's papally approved feast day of 4 May.

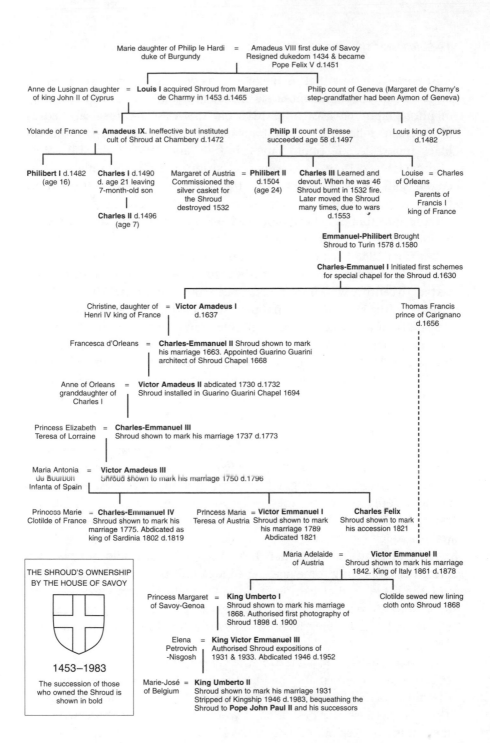

Marie daughter of Philip le Hardi = Amadeus VIII first duke of Savoy
duke of Burgundy   Resigned dukedom 1434 & became
                                    Pope Felix V d.1451

Anne de Lusignan daughter = **Louis I** acquired Shroud from Margaret   Philip count of Geneva (Margaret de Charny's
of king John II of Cyprus   de Charmy in 1453 d.1465   step-grandfather had been Aymon of Geneva)

Yolande of France = **Amadeus IX**. Ineffective but instituted   **Philip II** count of Bresse   Louis king of Cyprus
                     cult of Shroud at Chambery d.1472   succeeded age 58 d.1497   d.1482

Philibert I d.1482   **Charles I** d.1490   Margaret of Austria = **Philibert II**   **Charles III** Learned and   Louise = Charles
(age 16)   d. age 21 leaving   Commissioned the   d.1504   devout. When he was 46   of Orleans
                          7-month-old son   silver casket for   (age 24)   Shroud burnt in 1532 fire.
                                                  the Shroud   Later moved the Shroud   Parents of
                          Charles II d.1496   destroyed 1532   many times, due to wars   Francis I
                          (age 7)   d.1553   king of France

                                                                        Emmanuel-Philibert Brought
                                                                        Shroud to Turin 1578 d.1580

                                                                        Charles-Emmanuel I Initiated first schemes
                                                                        for special chapel for the Shroud d.1630

Christine, daughter of = **Victor Amadeus I**   Thomas Francis
Henri IV king of France   d.1637   prince of Carignano
                                                                                           d.1656

Francesca d'Orleans = **Charles-Emmanuel II** Shroud shown to mark
                        his marriage 1663. Appointed Guarino Guarini
                        architect of Shroud Chapel 1668

Anne of Orleans = **Victor Amadeus II** abdicated 1730 d.1732
granddaughter of   Shroud installed in Guarino Guarini Chapel 1694
Charles I

Princess Elizabeth = **Charles-Emmanuel III**
Teresa of Lorraine   Shroud shown to mark his marriage 1737 d.1773

Maria Antonia = **Victor Amadeus III**
de Bourbon   Shroud shown to mark his marriage 1750 d.1796
Infanta of Spain

Princess Marie = **Charles-Emmanuel IV**   Princess Maria = **Victor Emmanuel I**   **Charles Felix**
Clotilde of France Shroud shown to mark his   Teresa of Austria Shroud shown to mark   Shroud shown to mark
                    marriage 1775. Abdicated as   his marriage 1789   his accession 1821
                    king of Sardinia 1802 d.1819   Abdicated 1821

                                            Maria Adelaide = **Victor Emmanuel II**
                                            of Austria   Shroud shown to mark his marriage
                                                              1842. King of Italy 1861 d.1878

THE SHROUD'S OWNERSHIP   Princess Margaret = **King Umberto I**   Clotilde sewed new lining
BY THE HOUSE OF SAVOY   of Savoy-Genoa   Shroud shown to mark his marriage   cloth onto Shroud 1868
                                               1868. Authorised first photography of
                                               Shroud 1898 d. 1900

                          Elena = **King Victor Emmanuel III**
                          Petrovich Authorised Shroud expositions of
                          -Nisgosh   1931 & 1933. Abdicated 1946 d.1952

1453–1983

Marie-José = **King Umberto II**
of Belgium   Shroud shown to mark his marriage 1931
The succession of those   Stripped of Kingship 1946 d.1983, bequeathing the
who owned the Shroud is   Shroud to **Pope John Paul II** and his successors
shown in bold

Fig 12   The Shroud's ownership by the House of Savoy, 1453–1983

Almost every time that such expositions occurred there was a demand for some form of commemorative picture of the occasion. During the age of photography, at least from 1898 on, this was of course satisfied by photographs reflecting the latest advances in this recording method: first black-and-white still photographs in 1898 and 1931, then still colour photography in 1969, then colour television in 1973, then high-quality colour stills in 1978. As evidence that the Shroud exhibited on those occasions was one and the same as that still extant today, the varieties of photographs that have been produced in the more recent exposition years all have to be the most reliable form of documentation.

But from 1868 backwards the pictures produced had of necessity to be the work of artists, whose chief forte Shroudwise right back to the late sixteenth century was churning out cheap souvenir prints. When we study a print of this kind, such as that published of the 1842 exposition of the Shroud from the palace balcony [pl. 30a][1] (an event for which the taking of an early daguerreotype photograph was actually considered), we are in for quite a shock. Although the artist demonstrated his skill in his accurate rendition of the palace architecture and of the various worthies holding up the Shroud, so far as his depiction of the Shroud is concerned, his fidelity to the original was poor to say the least.

The man of the Shroud's body is rendered extremely crudely. His legs are shown apart, whereas on the original these appear close together. There is at least a foot of cloth depicted below his feet on the frontal image, whereas on the original the cloth terminates at least a couple of inches before reaching the toes. Not least, whereas the man of the Shroud can quite unmistakably be seen to be stark naked, on the 1842 print he wears a baggy loincloth.

It is important to stress that these discrepancies should not be interpreted as supporting some far-fetched idea that the cloth we see today is not the same as that exhibited in 1842. In fact, almost every artistic depiction before the age of photography exhibits similar deficiencies, part of the explanation lying in how souvenir prints in particular came into being.

As somewhat the paparazzi of their day, lithograph artists and print engravers almost invariably had far too little time to make anything but the most fleeting sketch of whatever event they were commemorating. This was because the best money would be made by those who had their finished work out on the streets almost the moment the event had occurred, if not before. It was their common practice, therefore, to make much of the image in advance, copying, for instance, any available portraits of VIPs expected to be present. And in the case of the Shroud, because this was almost never on view except at exposition time, they would necessarily look to whatever engraving had been made for the last exposition, the problem being that that artist might well have drawn upon the work of his predecessor, and that predecessor his predecessor, and so on. As for the loincloth, this can be seen in one artist's 'copy' after another [pl. 30b], right back to 1560, originating in a decree of the prudish Pope Paul IV who, incensed by the nudities of Michelangelo's 'Last Judgement', ordered a general cover-up of these and all similar depictions of 'private parts'. Accordingly, even though the copyists were ones who worked closest to our own time, were competent individuals and were without doubt recording one and the same Shroud that we know today, for a variety of understandable reasons the actual accuracy of their depictions leaves much to be desired.

Indeed the one truly tell-tale feature of their work confirming that they were depicting our Turin Shroud, quite aside from the obvious Turin–Savoy family context, is, ironically, their repeated rendition of the burns and patches of the 1532 fire. The depictions of these patches and also of the back-of-the-body imprint enable us to distinguish the Turin Shroud from representations of a rival 'Besançon Shroud', destroyed in the French Revolution, which lacked these features. And as we will discover, this will not be the only instance of scars and blemishes providing us with an important 'fingerprint' for our 'Turin' Shroud as we try to track it further back through time.

As we move from 1694 back to 1578, the year the Shroud was first 'permanently' in Turin, we find the cloth historically still well recorded. A detailed, year-by-year account is given in the Chronology at the back of this book. We know that from 1587 it lived in a *tempietto* or shrine atop four tall columns in the Turin Cathedral presbytery while awaiting the building of the special chapel as designed by Guarino Guarini. Of its transfer to Turin in 1578 there is similarly abundant record. The real purpose of this was to cement Savoy Duke Emmanuel-Philibert's decision to switch his capital away from Chambéry to the more centrally located Turin – although to soften the loss to Chambéry's faithful, the adroit Duke pretended this was a temporary move to save the saintly Archbishop Charles Borromeo, at that time making an arduous pilgrimage 'on foot' from Milan to venerate the Shroud, the rigours of having to cross the Alps. The very first known print commemorating a Shroud exposition was that published in 1578 as a souvenir of the showing in honour of Borromeo's arrival in Turin, and even the reputed casket in which the Shroud made its journey across the Alps to meet him has survived and can be examined in Turin's Shroud Museum.

During the century and a quarter of the Savoys' ownership of the Shroud, from 1578 back to 1453, the cloth was by no means continuously in Chambéry, although it was of course in the fire in Chambéry's Sainte Chapelle that it received its scars and subsequent patches. This chapel, like its Turin counterpart in 1997, fared much worse than the Shroud itself, all its stained glass and fine fittings being totally destroyed. In the earlier part of this period Savoy's dukes, mostly youngsters who died before reaching maturity, constantly carried the Shroud around with them as they toured their domains with their entourages. Then when from 1502 they made the Sainte Chapelle its theoretically permanent home, first came the disastrous fire, then in 1535 followed a French invasion, which necessitated them sending the Shroud, for its own safety, on a series of refugee journeys to towns and cities as far afield as Turin, Milan, Vercelli, Aosta and Nice. It took until 1561 and the Treaty of Câteau-Cambrésis before Duke Emmanuel-Philibert's diplomatic and military skills enabled its temporary return to Chambéry.

But despite this itinerancy, the Shroud's adventures are consistently well attested throughout this whole period, automatically reducing to fiction the recent theory that Leonardo da Vinci 'invented' it in 1492. An account of June 1485, two months before England's battle of Bosworth Field, clearly records the payment of 2 écus to ducal chaplain Jean Renguis 'in recompense for two journeys which he made from Turin to Savigliano carrying the Shroud'. Two years earlier an inventory drawn up by the same Jean Renguis in partnership with sacristan Georges Carrelet, equally clearly describes the Shroud as 'enveloped in a red silk drape and kept in a case covered with crimson velours, decorated with silver-gilt nails, and locked with a golden key'. Throughout the years 1478 back to 1471 archive sources enable the tracking of repeated movements of the Shroud, to Pinerolo in 1478, from Ivrea to Chambéry in 1475, from Ivrea to Moncalieri and back again in 1474, from Turin to Ivrea in 1473, from Vercelli to Turin in 1473, from Chambéry to Vercelli in 1471, and so on. Leonardo, it should be noted, was a mere nineteen-year-old in 1471.

With regard to artists' 'documenting' depictions of the Shroud at this time, of course as we track back earlier than 1532 these are bound no longer to feature the useful 'fingerprint' of that year's fire-damage marks –

although it is worth observing that of the five known copies of the Shroud painted between 1532 and its transfer to Turin in 1578, all actually omit these already inflicted marks, suggesting that there was some embarrassment on the part of the Savoys of this generation at their failure to keep the Shroud totally safe.

Looking back to 1516, however, any deficiency of this kind is compensated for by an excellent one-third-life-size Shroud copy clearly dated to that year and preserved in the Church of St Gommaire at Lierre in Belgium [detail, pls 8–9b]. This quite unmistakably shows the already mentioned set of four so-called 'poker holes' (see p. 66), and also, because it predates the era of the prudish Pope Paul IV, it faithfully records the man of the Shroud's total nudity. We therefore have some reason to keep a watch out for these two replacement 'fingerprints', albeit for what they are worth, as we continue relentlessly to move ever backwards in time.

The year 1453 marks one of those major changes of ownership episodes that requires special scrutiny in order to guard against any skulduggery or confusion, especially since there survives no actual deed of transfer as such. Instead, what we do have is a set of alternative documents which serve the same function. These comprise, from the year 1443, a petition from the dean and canons of the tiny French church of Lirey, urging the elderly French widow Margaret de Charny to return the Shroud to them; for the year 1453 the conveyance by Duke Louis I of Savoy of a small castle and some estate revenues to this same Margaret in return for some unspecified 'valuable services' (this seems to have been what sufficed as the transfer); for the year 1457 an excommunication of Margaret for her failing to return the alleged Shroud to the Lirey clergy; for the year 1459 a lifting of the excommunication, apparently as a result of a deal having been struck; and finally for the year 1464, four years after Margaret de Charny's death, an agreement on Duke Louis's part to compensate the Lirey canons for their loss of the Shroud.

Despite the lack of a formal transfer document, it is crystal-clear from all this data that a Christ shroud had been in Margaret de Charny's possession and passed into Duke Louis's. And from the fact that Duke Louis's Christ shroud passed all the way down through his descendants to become the Turin Shroud that we know today it follows, despite Margaret's and Louis's rather 'under-the-counter' way of conducting their transaction, that Margaret's Christ shroud must have been our Turin Shroud. Nor does it take too much to guess why Margaret might have wanted to pass it on to a family who were not her immediate relatives. Despite her two marriages she had no surviving children and in her old age she would have seen her distant relative Duke Louis and his wife Anne of Cyprus as a pious and up-and-coming couple eminently suited to take charge of such an important property as the Shroud – unlike her nephew, a wayward character with a false nose made of silver, or the Lirey canons, whose tiny wooden church was very run down and had become hopelessly vulnerable during the Hundred Years War that had raged throughout her lifetime and before.

The really difficult question concerns just how Margaret and her pre-decessors had come to own the Shroud, in which regard we suddenly find our thread-following backwards into time beginning to encounter some serious mist. Looking to 1418, when we know that northern France was full of marauding English troops following the battle of Agincourt three years earlier (in which Margaret de Charny's first husband, Jean, was one of the 10,000 Frenchmen killed), we find Margaret and her second husband, Humbert de Villersexel, obviously amicably taking charge of the Shroud from the Lirey canons in order to keep it and other of the church's treasures safe in their well-fortified southerly castle of Montfort. According to the still extant receipt that Humbert gave the canons:

> During this period of war, and mindful of ill-disposed persons, we have received from our kind chaplains, the dean and chapter of Our Lady of Lirey, the jewels and relics of the aforesaid church, namely the things which follow: first, a cloth, on which is a figure or representation of the Shroud of our Lord Jesus Christ, which is in a chest decorated with the arms of Charny ... The aforesaid ... we have taken and received into our care ... to be well and securely guarded in our castle of Mont-fort.[2]

Despite the description 'figure or representation' we have, in fact, every reason to believe that this was our Shroud, as will become clearer shortly. And because we know that, unlike in the case of the jewels and other precious items, Margaret did not subsequently return the Shroud to the Lirey canons, we may construe it to have been an object of great import-ance to her over and above any considerations of financial gain. Indeed, she was prepared to risk even excommunication in order to secure its future with someone other than herself. Likewise we may construe that financial gain was very much what the Lirey canons had in mind, con-cerning the Shroud since, as their subsequent dealings with Duke Louis of Savoy revealed, they were quite prepared to accept its loss in return for

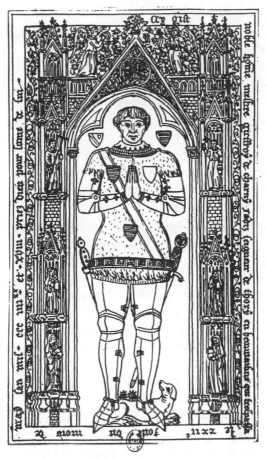

Fig 13 Geoffrey II de Charny (d. 1398)
Effigy of Geoffrey II de Charny, who personally displayed the Shroud in the church of Lirey,
as this appeared on his tombstone in the Cistercian abbey of Froidmont, near Hermes,
northern France. The original tombstone, along with most of the rest of the abbey, was
destroyed in the First World War. (From an ink drawing in the Roger de Gaignières collection,
Bibliothèque Nationale, Paris)

some appropriate compensatory income. This may well have been another
reason why Margaret did not want them to have it back.

But how had the Shroud come to be in this clearly contentious ownership situation between Margaret and the canons? And how had it come
to be in tiny, obscure Lirey? Margaret de Charny we know to have been
the daughter of a French knight Geoffrey II[3] de Charny [fig. 13], whose
inherited fief Lirey was, and of Geoffrey II's close association with this

same Shroud there is absolutely no shred of historical doubt. He figures prominently and very actively in the well-documented goings-on of 1389 in which Lirey's canons conducted the expositions of the Shroud which so incensed local bishop Pierre d'Arcis. Although prior to 1389 the Shroud had been 'hidden' away throughout the previous 'thirty-four years or thereabouts', seemingly under de Charny care, it was in this year of 1389, as d'Arcis's memorandum makes clear, that Lirey's dean, whom from independent sources we know to have been one Nicole Martin: '... suggested to the Lord Geoffrey [II] de Charny, Knight ... to have the said cloth replaced in the said church [i.e. Lirey] that by a renewal of pilgrimage the church might be enriched with the offerings made by the faithful.'[4]

To this, Geoffrey II de Charny apparently readily agreed, prompting what was clearly such an impressive stream of pilgrims to Lirey that Bishop d'Arcis, suspecting some fraud, made his enquiries, learned that Bishop Henri of a little over a generation before had discovered the Shroud to be an artistically created forgery and thereupon very commendably tried to get the expositions stopped. To which end, as d'Arcis imparted in his memorandum to Pope Clement, he outrightly ordered Dean Nicole Martin to cease exhibiting the Shroud, threatening him and his canons with excommunication if they disobeyed.

As is quite clear from both d'Arcis's memorandum and from local government reports of the time, Geoffrey II de Charny's response was not to let the expositions cease, but instead personally to involve himself to the extent even of holding up the Shroud in his own hands before the assembled throng of those who had come in pilgrimage to Lirey. In d'Arcis's words: 'The knight [i.e. Geoffrey] ... by holding the said cloth with his own hands on a certain solemn feast, and showing it to the people ... caused himself ... to be put in formal possession ... of the said cloth and of the right of exhibiting it.'

There can be no doubt, then, that the father and daughter de Charnys, both as individuals and as feudal lords of the church of Lirey, were highly committed to the Shroud, in which regard the most intriguing factor surrounding the expositions of 1389 is how Geoffrey II and his canons officially and unofficially represented it both to outside authority and to the populace. For as d'Arcis makes clear, in order to gain his official authorisation for the expositions Geoffrey II had most suspiciously bypassed d'Arcis, his local bishop and the obvious person to approach, petitioning instead the Papal Nuncio, Cardinal de Thury. To de Thury he represented the Shroud not as the original authentic shroud of Jesus (which might immediately have roused some disbelief and suspicions), but instead merely as a 'picture or figure' of this 'which many people came to visit out of devotion and which had previously been much venerated and resorted to in that church [i.e. Lirey]'. By presenting the cloth as nothing special, he thereby easily obtained his authorisation.

But as d'Arcis also makes clear, by both unofficial word of mouth and by the elaborateness of the ceremonial that they used in conducting their expositions, Geoffrey II and his canons behaved quite unmistakably as though they had the genuine article. In d'Arcis's own words: 'Although it [the Shroud] is not publicly stated to be the true shroud of Christ, nevertheless this is given out and noised abroad in private, and so it is believed by many, the more so because, as stated above, it was on the previous occasion declared to be the true shroud of Christ.'

Likewise, d'Arcis wrote of the ceremonial that Geoffrey and the canons adopted: 'The cloth was openly exhibited and shown to the people in the church aforesaid on great holidays, and frequently on feasts and at other times, with the utmost solemnity, even more than when the Body of Christ our Lord is exposed, to wit, by two priests dressed in albs with stoles and maniples and using the greatest possible reverence, with lighted torches and upon a lofty platform constructed for this special purpose.'

Many pro-Shroud writers have tried to undermine Bishop d'Arcis's and his memorandum's credibility. They have criticised his bad temper and his 'barbarous' Latin, and they have also pointed out that although there are two copies of the memorandum, neither of these is the original, both being just unsigned, undated drafts.

However, although the latter facts are perfectly genuine, the truth is that whatever d'Arcis's command of Latin, he had held the major see of Troyes for some twelve years and before then had had a respectable career as a lawyer. Also, whatever his temper at the time, in his memorandum he set out the facts as he knew them with complete lucidity. And there are just too many ancillary supporting documents for these to be in serious dispute.

For example, there survives a letter of 4 August 1389 from King Charles VI of France, ordering his local magistrate to have the Shroud seized and placed 'under honest custody', clearly reflecting the part of d'Arcis's memorandum in which he describes taking measures to 'have the cloth placed in the custody of the King's officers'. There survives a report by this same magistrate of his officers' visit to Lirey, describing how Dean Martin protested to them that he didn't have all the necessary keys to the church treasury, and that even if the deputation tried to break their way in they would not find the Shroud there. There survives also a letter of 6 January 1390 from Pope Clement VII ordering d'Arcis not to raise any further complaints about the Shroud under threat of excommunication, another by Clement the same day to Geoffrey de Charny, setting out the conditions under which he was prepared to allow the expositions to continue (he was expected to make clear that the cloth in question was not the true shroud of Christ) and yet another by Clement to some independent clerics requesting them to check on his behalf that his instructions had been obeyed.

In sum, the factuality of d'Arcis's information has to be faced fairly and squarely, just like the factuality of the radiocarbon-dating verdict. And on the face of it there are grounds for the utmost suspicion concerning Geoffrey II de Charny, his dean and canons, and the Shroud itself. For it would seem to be absolutely self-evident that while they gained their official permission to exhibit the Shroud just as a 'picture or figure' of whatever the true shroud might have looked like (and this is what Pope Clement upheld), they behaved as if they had the real thing and put it about privately likewise.

Now what is also clear from Bishop d'Arcis's memorandum is that if the Shroud really is a mediaeval forgery – and d'Arcis himself was in absolutely no doubt about this – then its creation could not be laid at the door of Geoffrey II de Charny. If, as d'Arcis insisted, Bishop Henri's original discovery of the Shroud's artistic creation had taken place 'thirty-four years or thereabouts' before 1389, i.e. around 1355, then at least Geoffrey II could have had no direct part in it. We do not know exactly when he was born, but a document of 1356[5] concerning the death of his father, Geoffrey I, makes clear that he was but a child at this time.

Accordingly, whatever we may make of Geoffrey II and his canons' undeniably suspicious-looking behaviour, it is necessarily to the 1350s, the generation before their time, that we must now look for the circumstances of how this extraordinary piece of 'forgery' could have come into being, obviously with the radiocarbon-dating verdict of '1260–1390!' cheering us along all the way.

Except that, as we should, of course, not fail to keep in mind, if Margaret de Charny went to such elaborate lengths to ensure the Shroud's long-term future with the Savoys, also if Geoffrey II, for his part, was privately so insistent that it was the genuine article, then possibly, just possibly, both may have had some very good reasons for believing this genuineness to be right.

Chapter 10

Could the Shroud date back to 1204?

Now if there genuinely were no historical or visual record of the existence of anything resembling our Shroud earlier than the 1350s, as is so often alleged, then given the d'Arcis memorandum and the radiocarbon dating '1260–1390!' verdict, there really would be little point in looking too deeply into the circumstances in which it came to light in Lirey at around this time. Something along the lines of the 'cunning artist' allegation would simply have to be accepted, despite its incredibility, and that would be that.

But the alleged absence of any historical record earlier than the 1350s is simply not true. All there is an absence of (and it is undeniably a serious one), is a properly *continuous* record. For if we seek a beacon that the Shroud genuinely could date significantly earlier than the 1350s, then we need look no further than a manuscript of the early 1200s that reposes in the Royal Library in Copenhagen, Denmark.[1] Unquestionably genuine, it is essentially the campaign memoirs of a French soldier, Robert de Clari, who took part in the infamous sack of Constantinople by the Fourth Crusade in 1204. A few months before this sack Robert and the other crusaders had been allowed to walk round Constantinople as sightseers, and in the course of his wanderings he came across the city's already historic Church of St Mary of Blachernae. According to his characteristically factual description, this was: '... where there was the shroud[2] in which Our Lord had been wrapped, which every Friday raised itself upright, so that one could see the figure of Our Lord on it.'

Now here, quite unmistakably, is a reference to a shroud that certainly sounds like our Turin one (for the original text, see fig. 14). For instance, modern literary scholars[3] confirm that Robert's use of the Old French word 'figure' meant to him just what it would to us today, that he saw what he took to be Jesus's whole body somehow imprinted on the cloth.

Obviously we will need to know more about this 'shroud' in Con-

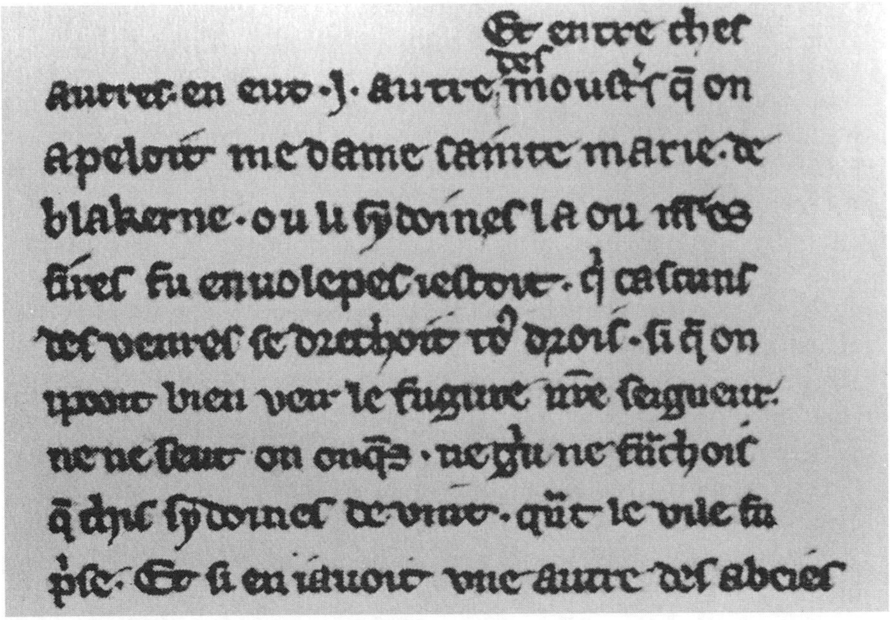

Fig 14 A reference to the Shroud from 1203–4?
The key passage in Crusader Robert de Clari's account of the wonders he saw in Constantinople just prior to the Crusader sack of 1204. In this he speaks of a 'figure'-bearing *sindon* or shroud of Jesus at the Church of St Mary at Blachernae which was made to stand upright every Friday. (Copenhagen Royal Library, MS 487, fo. 123b.)

stantinople, but that will come later. For the present, it can be taken as a matter of fact that something certainly sounding like our Shroud was being displayed in Constantinople (which also sported other alleged relics of Christ), over fifty years earlier than the earliest date of 1260 given to this by radiocarbon dating. And equally important is Robert's immediately following information that: '. . . no one, either Greek or French, ever knew what became of this shroud when the city was taken.' Effectively this is telling us that this shroud with Jesus's imprint disappeared just as mysteriously from a Constantinople full of Frenchmen in 1204, as the one that we know today turned up in the obscure little French village of Lirey in the 1350s. And lest there be any misunderstanding, Lirey was, and continues to be, very obscure – a tiny rustic hamlet of some fifty houses, in which the original wooden church and de Charny mansion, all too typically of the Shroud, have long gone. All of which needs to be kept in mind as we first grapple, as best we might, with just how, whether it is genuine or forged, so spectacular

125

a relic as the Shroud could have come to appear in so unlikely a place some time in the 1350s.

For this our prime guide has, of necessity, to be Bishop d'Arcis, writing from the year 1389. According to him 'thirty-four years or thereabouts' earlier, i.e. *c*.1355, the then dean of the Lirey church, whose name we independently know to have been Robert de Caillac, procured the Shroud, 'cunningly painted' with 'the twofold image of one man, that is to say the back and the front'. Then 'consumed with the passion of avarice' de Caillac falsely declared and pretended the Shroud to be 'the actual shroud in which our Saviour Jesus Christ was enfolded in the tomb and upon which the whole likeness of the Saviour had remained thus impressed, together with the wounds which he bore'. According to d'Arcis: 'This story was put about not only in the kingdom of France, but, so to speak, throughout the world, so that from all parts people came together to view it [i.e. the Shroud].' As d'Arcis went on, Bishop Henri of Poitiers, who was Troyes's bishop from 1353 to 1370, there-upon:

> ... set himself earnestly to work to fathom the truth of this matter ... Eventually, after diligent inquiry and examination, he discovered the fraud and how the said cloth had been cunningly painted, the truth being attested by the artist who had painted it, to wit, that it was a work of human skill and not miraculously wrought or bestowed. Accordingly ... seeing that he [Henri] neither could nor ought allow the matter to pass, he began to institute formal proceedings against the said dean [i.e. de Caillac] and his accomplices ... They, seeing their wickedness discovered, hid away the said cloth so that the Ordinary [i.e. Bishop Henri] could not find it, and they kept it hidden afterwards for thirty-four years or thereabouts down to the present year.

Now we earlier promised ourselves that throughout our tracking back in time we would regularly try to find some check, particularly a visual one, that any shroud being referred to was one and the same as our Turin Shroud. So can we do this in respect of d'Arcis's purportedly 'cunningly painted' Lirey cloth? In fact, there has survived one item, from six and a half centuries ago, which is as good a piece of visual evidence for this as anything anyone could wish for.

It consists of an ostensibly insignificant-looking lead medallion [pl. 31a], little bigger than a large postage stamp, that was fished out of the mud of the Seine in 1855 and is today preserved in Paris's Musée de Cluny. Although parts of it have clearly been broken off and it has no inscription of any kind, the part that survives includes a quite unmistakable depiction of our Shroud. We can clearly see a double body imprint; crossed hands; full nakedness; truncated feet on the frontal image; a turned-in-sole on the back-of-the-body image and a crude but convincing representation of the spillage of blood across the small of the back. Not least, if you look very carefully, you can see a quite brilliant rendition of the Shroud's distinctive herringbone weave.

From broken remnants of clerical albs and broad-trimmed capes just above the depiction of the Shroud, it is clear that the medallion originally included two churchmen, presumably Lirey's 'wicked' Dean de Caillac and one of his canons, holding up the Shroud, though their heads and shoulders have long disappeared. Far more revelatory, however, are two heraldic shields that can be seen immediately below. The one on the left, with three smaller inner shields or inescutcheons, bears the arms of Geoffrey I de Charny, lord of Lirey and father of Geoffrey II. The one on the right, with three floral devices, bears the arms of Geoffrey II's mother (or possibly stepmother), Jeanne de Vergy. Either side of Geoffrey's shield can be seen a lance and pincers, either side of Jeanne's a multi-thonged whip and a column, with in between these a roundel depicting an empty tomb from which rises a cross hung with a crown of thorns.

Quite unmistakably this medallion was a stamped souvenir of the kind that people of the Middle Ages delighted in bringing back with them from visits to holy shrines such as St Thomas à Becket's tomb at Canterbury or St James's at Compostela. They often wore these as badges on their caps, much as people of today sport car stickers declaring 'I ♡ New York' or 'I've seen the lions of Longleat'. Equally unmistakable is the medallion's provenance and date. The de Charny–de Vergy arms, in combination with Bishop d'Arcis's information, pin-point Lirey as the place where this particular souvenir originated, presumably having been dropped by some pilgrim on his return to Paris. The fact that the medallion depicts the Shroud atop other instruments of Jesus's Passion shows that unlike in 1389 when it was officially described only as a 'picture or figure', in this instance it was quite outrightly being displayed as the true shroud of Jesus. This thereby checks out with Bishop d'Arcis's statement that this was what was being openly claimed of the Lirey Shroud in Bishop Henri's time. And since Geoffrey I de Charny died in 1356 and, as I have been assured by heraldic specialists, the heraldry strongly conveys that he was still alive at the time the medallion was created,[4] the medallion is unlikely to date later than 1356.

Much of Bishop d'Arcis's information from thirty-four years later does, then, appear correct. But what of the rest, that Bishop Henri discovered the cloth to be a forgery and instituted legal proceedings? Why should we not believe this even though, as we noted earlier, there survives no immediately contemporary evidence?

One immediate problem is that such contemporary documents as do exist seem directly to contradict d'Arcis by showing no evidence of any controversy. For example, there survives a document of Bishop Henri of 28 May 1356, one year later than the 1355 suggested by d'Arcis, warmly approving the foundation of the church at Lirey, explicitly stating that he 'praises', 'ratifies' and 'approves' this venture. He also speaks glowingly of church patron–founder Geoffrey I de Charny's 'sentiments of devotion ... which he manifests ever more daily'. Although it has been pointed out that the phrases are somewhat stock, nevertheless we can hardly suppose that Henri would have said anything of this kind while in the midst of legal proceedings against the Lirey church. Yet if the controversy broke out after May 1356 there was scant time for it to have done so in Geoffrey I de Charny's lifetime, since he was dead by that September, very publicly and decisively killed by the English on the battlefield of Poitiers. And from even a year later, specifically June 1357, there exists a document issued by the papal court at Avignon, cheerfully granting indulgences to all visiting the Lirey church and its relics, as if oblivious to any scandal that might have surrounded either.

In the face of this sort of puzzle the historian looks to the original source, i.e. Bishop d'Arcis, for clues to how he might have gained his information. Was this perhaps just hearsay? Or was d'Arcis looking at documents of Bishop Henri's that might have been lost to us? D'Arcis's own words put a date to these events, 'thirty-four years *or thereabouts*' before the year of 1389 in which he was writing. Given that it was as automatic then as it is now for official documents to carry a date, if d'Arcis had had those documents before him he would surely have *known* the date. So was his information even then rather less well documented than he might have cared to admit?

Furthermore, there is another point which d'Arcis let slip. He told Pope Clement that it had been put about among the populace '... that I [i.e. d'Arcis] am acting through jealousy and cupidity and to obtain possession of the cloth for myself, just as similar reports were circulated before against my predecessor'.

Although, as we have seen, d'Arcis's information deriving from the 1350s could have been at least partly hearsay, even so he seems to be telling us, possibly accurately, that Bishop Henri of Poitiers had been accused of wanting the Shroud for himself. This casts quite a new complexion on a hitherto almost unnoticed remark of Bishop Henri's in his ratification of the Lirey church in May 1356, that 'we ... ourselves [are] wishing to develop as much as possible a cult of this nature'. The question is raised, could Henri have actually had in mind an attempt to get his hands on the Shroud whenever he could come up with a suitable pretext?

Of course, we have no means of being sure that in his speaking of 'a cult of this nature', Bishop Henri was even referring specifically to the Lirey church's possession of the Shroud. But let us try to put ourselves in his position, albeit from the little that we so far know of him, upon his learning of the Shroud's first exposition at Lirey. When he became Troyes's bishop in 1353 he had taken on responsibility for a diocese which, like many others in France at that time, was beset by huge financial problems because of the continuing depredations of the war with the English and also the major depopulations as a result of the Black Death only four years before. He had also taken on responsibility for a cathedral which had been begun as far back 1208, but which was still far from complete, needing much money for the work still required. As a man of the Middle ages he would have known that the best way to bring in such money was for your cathedral to possess some major relic or relics which might attract pilgrimage trade and offerings. Troyes's chief asset was the body of St Helen of Athyra,[5] hardly what one might call a major draw.

Then Henri learns that only twelve miles from his cathedral, in the little wooden church of the tiny village of Lirey, there is being exhibited what is being claimed as the true Shroud of Christ, imprinted with an image of his body and wounds. As his informants tell him, this is attracting a 'multitude' of people 'from all parts' to view it, many of these bringing offerings. In such circumstances, might not even the most saintly of bishops feel just a little 'jealousy and cupidity'? If Henri of Poitiers were indeed that saintly, which the historical record tells us to have been far from the case.

For even in an age when many bishops were very worldly princes, Henri of Poitiers has to count as one of the worldliest. It is a matter of genealogical fact that at the Abbey du Paraclet, near Nogent-sur-Seine – the very abbey associated with Abelard and Héloïse – Henri kept a concubine, Jeanne de Chenery, by whom he had several children, subsequently referred to in France's official genealogies as the *'bâtards de Poitiers'*. When in 1358 Troyes was threatened by English soldiers marauding after their victory at Poitiers, it was Henri, as Troyes's chief magistrate, who intelligently and resourcefully mustered the city's defences and with the Count de Vaudémont scored a notable military victory at Chaude-foüace, scarcely a stone's throw from where he kept his mistress. Clearly this was a forceful individual unlikely to have been shy of acquiring a money-making relic by any means he could. Although exactly how and when Henri may have made his bid for the Shroud is impossible to determine, the d'Arcis memorandum's excessive insistence on the Lirey dean and canons' 'passion of avarice' just might have been a case of the pot calling the kettle black.

All of this leads us to turn now to Geoffrey I de Charny, Henri's opposite number in this controversy. As was evident from his own and his wife's arms on the Lirey medallion, this Geoffrey, as lord of Lirey, was the Shroud's prime owner. Despite Bishop d'Arcis in 1389 telling Pope Clement that it was the wicked dean of Lirey who had procured the Shroud, in Clement's very response to this the pope remarks, from some apparent inside knowledge (Geoffrey I's widow Jeanne had married his uncle Aymon), that it was 'the father of this Geoffrey [by this latter meaning Geoffrey II] burning with the zeal of devotion' who had obtained the Shroud for the church, rather than the church having obtained the Shroud for him.

Similarly, when on 8 May 1443 Lirey's dean and canons were suing Margaret de Charny for the Shroud's return, Margaret stated on oath that the Shroud had been *'conquis par feu'* by her grandfather, Geoffrey I. Although the exact meaning of her phrase *'conquis par feu'* has been of some bafflement even for the French, all seem to agree that the buck for obtaining the Shroud seems to stop with this Geoffrey I.

So who was he? Was he a man who we can really believe lay behind the whole Shroud hoax? If McCrone and the radiocarbon-dating scientists are right that the Shroud was created fraudulently some time around the mid 1350s, either Geoffrey I was very gullible or a party to the deception. Yet everything that we can determine of Geoffrey I's character – and on this the historical record is surprisingly good – tells us that he was upright, astute and far from avaricious. When he died on the battle field of Poitiers he was holding in his hands France's most sacred battle-standard, the *oriflamme*, the hoisting of which signified 'no surrender'. Because the *oriflamme* was believed sacred, only the very worthiest individuals were accorded the honour of carrying it, the chronicler Froissart specifically remarking of the battle line up before Poitiers, 'the King's sovereign banner was carried by Sir Geoffrey de Charny, as the wisest and bravest knight of them all.'[6]

Everything else that we know about Geoffrey's life bespeaks the same worthiness. From as early as 1337, the very start of the so-called Hundred Years War between England and France, on battlefield after battlefield he fought for his country with conspicuous gallantry. In 1340 he helped defend Tournai against the English. In 1342 he led the first corps at the battle of Morlaix. In 1347 under Humbert, Dauphin of Vienne he took part in a crusade to the Near East that stopped at Smyrna. In 1349 he led a daring attempt at recapturing Calais, during which he was betrayed and slipped over to England for a term of imprisonment, before returning to die a hero's death at Poitiers.

But far more than these and related expressions of his valour, Geoffrey had earned a very special reputation for chivalry, one that has endured even to this day. Open any authoritative book on this and there will almost certainly be discussion of him as one of the ethic's pioneers. His own *Book of Chivalry* has recently been translated into English[7] and the picture of him that emerges from it is of a very devout but thoroughly down-to-earth individual of the utmost integrity. Freely admitting that he was seasick during the crusade, he stresses that 'you must never be cast down by the inevitable setbacks you will receive in life. Although to be a successful knight, physical fitness is important, if a good wine is offered, accept it gladly in moderation. Never believe in achieving everything by your own strength alone. The truly wise man gives thanks to God and to the Virgin Mary for any successes he may achieve'.

Geoffrey's role model was the Old Testament Jewish hero Judas Maccabeus, whom he saw as a man 'handsome without pride, ever honourable, a great fighter who died armed in God's causes'.[8] He had his stern side, for when he was released from his captivity after Calais he sought out the man who betrayed him, arrested him and cut off his head. Quite obvious from his life is that he was never rich, in the manner of most of the great French nobles alongside whom he fought so valiantly. After his capture at Calais it was to the king that his family had to look to pay his ransom money. It was also his king who funded the building of the modest little Lirey church, with its 'college' of six priests.

But if the buck for the Shroud's ownership truly stops with Geoffrey, and if the cloth's image was not concocted by some cunning artist in league with him and Lirey's canons – and all our earlier findings argue against this – where on earth did it come from? Did Geoffrey perhaps obtain it when, as already mentioned, he accompanied the crusade to Smyrna? Even if, despite his seasickness, he actually travelled as far as this 'finest of the Turkish ports' (and he definitely returned to France considerably ahead of the rest of this expedition), the idea of some Turkish hawker standing on the quayside with something as spectacular as the Shroud, fake or genuine, seems highly doubtful, quite aside from which there would then have been no reason for Geoffrey and his successors to be so reticent about where it had come from.

Equally doubtful is the information on a historical notice posted in the second Lirey church some time in the mid sixteenth century, that the Shroud had been a gift to Geoffrey from France's King Philip VI 'as recompense for his valour'. Not only would it have been unthinkable for a king to give such a gift to a man of Geoffrey's comparatively humble status, even if this had been the case the de Charnys would again have had a ready counter to their local bishops' allegations and would hardly have had to resort to expedients like pretending they did not believe it to be the genuine article.

As for Margaret de Charny's already quoted '*conquis par feu*' remark, this seems to have been almost deliberately enigmatic, as if she was either ignorant, or unprepared to divulge what she knew, of the real truth.

And not least of the difficulties surrounding this same question is that despite Geoffrey's writing of his 'Chivalry' book, also the survival of numerous documents relating to his founding of the Lirey church and much else, nowhere do we find mention of his actual ownership of the Shroud. The pilgrim's medallion is the only pre-1389 'document' that attests to this. So was it some secret family heirloom that he brought out only at the very end of his life? Or was it perhaps acquired via Geoffrey's second marriage, to Jeanne de Vergy, the date of which is unknown, but which may likewise have been very late in his life? Or did Jeanne de Vergy bring it out shortly after his death and conduct expositions partly in his name? We simply do not know. All we can say is that until the very first Lirey expositions of the 1350s – whenever *exactly* these may have occurred – no one was prepared to shout their ownership of the Shroud to the rooftops. And when they did, they seem to have burnt their fingers so badly that they quickly shut it away again for that now famous 'thirty-four years or thereabouts'.

At this point, then, we can only track backwards in the dark for a full hundred and fifty years, with that distant beacon of Robert de Clari's Constantinople shroud our sole glimmer of light. Should we look for clues in Geoffrey's family roots? When I wrote my first book on the Shroud, in 1978, I had noted French genealogist Père Anselme's remark that Geoffrey was only '*probablement*' the son of a Jean de Charny (of the Mont St Jean line of de Charnys) and his wife Margaret de Joinville, as a result of which I left open the issue of whether this was indeed Geoffrey's lineage.

In fact, thanks to the amount of French and English genealogical research that has since become available, there seems now no longer any doubt that Geoffrey was indeed Jean de Charny's and Margaret de Join-ville's son. As I had not previously realised, the inheritance of tiny Lirey can clearly be seen to have passed from Margaret de Joinville's chronicler father, Jean de Joinville (described as lord of Lirey around 1290), to Margaret, apparently as part of her dowry and then on to Geoffrey, Lirey being the first and principal lordship with which Geoffrey is associated. Not only has this genealogy been accepted by Professor Richard Kaeuper in his scholarly Introduction to the first English translation of Geoffrey's 'Book of Chivalry',[9] but the family alliances that we know pertained to Geoffrey and his descendants can be seen to be part of a long-standing tradition between the Joinville, de Vergy and de Charny families [see family tree, fig. 15, overleaf], all of whom lived in relatively close proximity to each other.

Once we accept that this really was Geoffrey I's family tree, then it becomes at least a little more interesting. For instance, it would now seem that Geoffrey was probably the youngest of three brothers, the other two being Dreux and Jean; and he had at least one sister, Isabeau. Dreux would seem to have been the eldest, thereby inheriting the main Mont-Saint-Jean title, and in 1313 he can be traced to Greece, where as a result of his creditable part in an expedition led by Louis of Burgundy he won the hand in marriage of heiress Agnes de Charpigny. Back in 1209, after taking part in the sack of Constantinople, Agnes's grandfather, Hugh de Lille Charpigny, had been awarded the barony of Vostitza, a territory today centring on the port of Egion on the north-western shore of Greece's

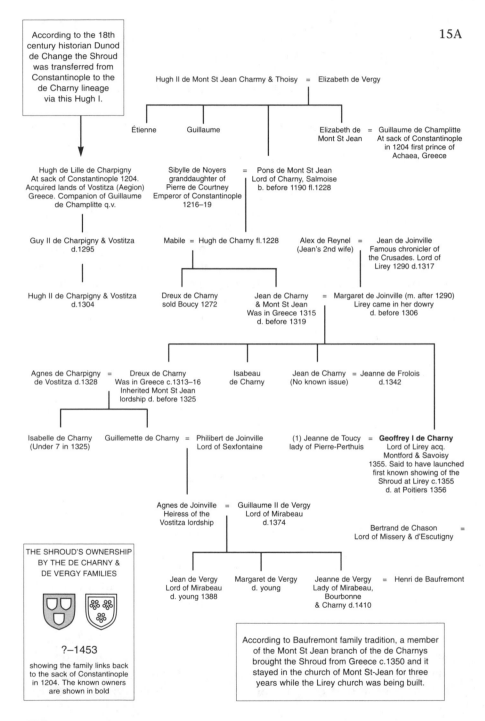

According to the 18th century historian Dunod de Change the Shroud was transferred from Constantinople to the de Charny lineage via this Hugh I.

Hugh II de Mont St Jean Charmy & Thoisy = Elizabeth de Vergy

Étienne   Guillaume

Elizabeth de = Guillaume de Champlitte
Mont St Jean   At sack of Constantinople
in 1204 first prince of
Achaea, Greece

Hugh de Lille de Charpigny
At sack of Constantinople 1204.
Acquired lands of Vostitza (Aegion)
Greece. Companion of Guillaume
de Champlitte q.v.

Sibylle de Noyers = Pons de Mont St Jean
granddaughter of   Lord of Charny, Salmoise
Pierre de Courtney   b. before 1190 fl.1228
Emperor of Constantinople
1216–19

Guy II de Charpigny & Vostitza
d.1295

Mabile = Hugh de Charny fl.1228

Alex de Reynel = Jean de Joinville
(Jean's 2nd wife)   Famous chronicler of
the Crusades. Lord of
Lirey 1290 d.1317

Hugh II de Charpigny & Vostitza
d.1304

Dreux de Charny
sold Boucy 1272

Jean de Charny = Margaret de Joinville (m. after 1290)
& Mont St Jean   Lirey came in her dowry
Was in Greece 1315   d. before 1306
d. before 1319

Agnes de Charpigny = Dreux de Charny
de Vostitza d.1328   Was in Greece c.1313–16
Inherited Mont St Jean
lordship d. before 1325

Isabeau
de Charny

Jean de Charny = Jeanne de Frolois
(No known issue)   d.1342

Isabelle de Charny
(Under 7 in 1325)

Guillemette de Charny = Philibert de Joinville
Lord of Sexfontaine

(1) Jeanne de Toucy = Geoffrey I de Charny
lady of Pierre-Perthuis   Lord of Lirey acq.
Montford & Savoisy
1355. Said to have launched
first known showing of the
Shroud at Lirey c.1355
d. at Poitiers 1356

Agnes de Joinville = Guillaume II de Vergy
Heiress of the   Lord of Mirabeau
Vostitza lordship   d.1374

Bertrand de Chason   =
Lord of Missery & d'Escutigny

THE SHROUD'S OWNERSHIP
BY THE DE CHARNY &
DE VERGY FAMILIES

?–1453

showing the family links back
to the sack of Constantinople
in 1204. The known owners
are shown in bold

Jean de Vergy
Lord of Mirabeau
d. young 1388

Margaret de Vergy
d. young

Jeanne de Vergy = Henri de Baufremont
Lady of Mirabeau,
Bourbonne
& Charny d.1410

According to Baufremont family tradition, a member
of the Mont St Jean branch of the de Charnys
brought the Shroud from Greece c.1350 and it
stayed in the church of Mont St-Jean for three
years while the Lirey church was being built.

15B

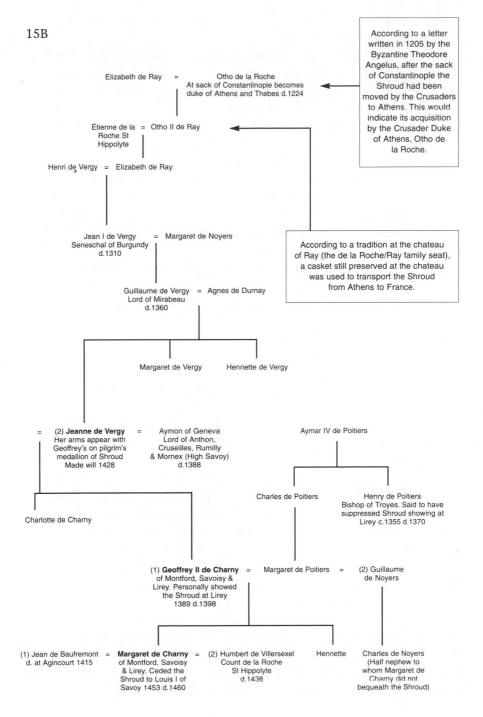

Elizabeth de Ray = Otho de la Roche
At sack of Constantinople becomes
duke of Athens and Thebes d.1224

According to a letter written in 1205 by the Byzantine Theodore Angelus, after the sack of Constantinople the Shroud had been moved by the Crusaders to Athens. This would indicate its acquisition by the Crusader Duke of Athens, Otho de la Roche.

Étienne de la = Otho II de Ray
Roche St
Hippolyte

Henri de Vergy = Elizabeth de Ray

Jean I de Vergy = Margaret de Noyers
Seneschal of Burgundy
d.1310

According to a tradition at the chateau of Ray (the de la Roche/Ray family seat), a casket still preserved at the chateau was used to transport the Shroud from Athens to France.

Guillaume de Vergy = Agnes de Durnay
Lord of Mirabeau
d.1360

Margaret de Vergy   Henriette de Vergy

= (2) **Jeanne de Vergy** =   Aymon of Geneva   Aymar IV de Poitiers
Her arms appear with   Lord of Anthon,
Geoffrey's on pilgrim's Cruseilles, Rumilly
medallion of Shroud   & Mornex (High Savoy)
Made will 1428   d.1388

Charles de Poitiers   Henry de Poitiers
                         Bishop of Troyes. Said to have
                         suppressed Shroud showing at
                         Lirey c.1355 d.1370

Charlotte de Charny

(1) **Geoffrey II de Charny** = Margaret de Poitiers = (2) Guillaume
of Montford, Savoisy &   de Noyers
Lirey. Personally showed
the Shroud at Lirey
1389 d.1398

(1) Jean de Baufremont = **Margaret de Charny** = (2) Humbert de Villersexel   Henriette   Charles de Noyers
d. at Agincourt 1415   of Montford, Savoisy   Count de la Roche   (Half nephew to
                        & Lirey. Ceded the   St Hippolyte   whom Margaret de
                        Shroud to Louis I of   d.1438   Charny did not
                        Savoy 1453 d.1460   bequeath the Shroud)

135

Peloponnese peninsula. So when Dreux married Agnes in 1316 he acquired her Fourth Crusade inheritance.

We can then see Joinville, de Vergy and de Charny marriages, this last being Geoffrey's to Jeanne de Vergy, during which a shroud acquired in the sack of Constantinople could conceivably have been part of Jeanne's dowry. But we also have to acknowledge that historically there's not a shred of hard evidence for this. The de Charnys, the de Vergys, the de Joinvilles and other closely related French families all had antecedents who participated in the sack of Constantinople in 1204, any one of whom *might* have brought back a fake or genuine shroud of Christ and quietly kept it in the family from one generation to the next. But relics acquired in such a way were normally declared quite openly and given to the local cathedral, and there would have been no real reason for the guilty secretiveness that the de Charnys exhibited.

A little more satisfactory is the theory advanced in my 1978 book that it was possibly the Crusader Order of Knights Templars who owned the Shroud during the missing hundred and fifty years. This has just that little bit extra going for it, because the Templars had a very special interest in the tomb of Jesus and everything associated with it, and when they returned from the Holy Land to France in the late twelfth century they were widely rumoured to be secretly worshipping some form of image featuring a bearded man's face. During World War II a Mrs Molly Drew, then living in Templecombe in Somerset, on the site of a Templar preceptory, had the shock of her life when a fall of plaster in the ceiling revealed an old panel painting [pl. 32b], seemingly once having belonged to the Templars, with precisely such a face, strangely disembodied, and bearing a close resemblance to the facial area on the Shroud. Was this the Templars' copy of the Shroud for their members in England? Radiocarbon dating confirmed the panel painting to date back to possibly as early as 1280,[10] certainly the right period, and adding further substance to the theory was that a Templar called Geoffrey de Charny[11] was one of the two leaders of the Order burnt at the stake, following its suppression by King Philip IV of France in 1307. Since whatever the Templars had been secretly worshipping was never found, there must therefore be the possibility that the Shroud secretly passed via the Templar de Charny's family to Geoffrey I, this theory having the additional merit that it would explain the de Charnys' reticence over how they acquired it. But it is all only a theory, which has its critics[12] as well as its supporters, and despite the intriguing Templecombe panel painting – for which no more satisfactory explanation has yet been advanced – substance-wise it gets us little further than delving into family trees.

What about works of art indicative of the Shroud's possible existence prior to the 1350s? Whether we like it or not, we have to face that from now on, in our tracking backwards through time, there is nothing featuring the outstretched Shroud, showing both its frontal and back-of-the-body images, in the manner of the Lirey pilgrim's medallion. Yet this is not to say that during this period back to 1204 there are no works of art strongly indicative of the Shroud's earlier existence *somewhere*.

Take, for instance, a magnificent *epitaphios* liturgical cloth today displayed in the Museum of the Serbian Orthodox Church in Belgrade [pl. 32a]. Originally from the monastery of Krušedol, in the Fruška Gora mountains north-west of Belgrade, its inscription[13] firmly dates it to the reign of Milutin II Uroš, ruler of Serbia from 1282 to 1321, predating the 1350s when, according to Bishop d'Arcis, the Shroud was 'cunningly painted' seven hundred miles and several daunting mountains away in France. Despite its being uncompromisingly linear, we see on it an image so strikingly reminiscent of the Shroud's front-of-body image that, whether directly or indirectly, it can hardly be other than that image's progeny or precursor.

We see the same long-haired, long-nosed, bearded face. We see the same crossed hands. Exactly as in the case of the seventeenth-century G. B. della Rovere aquatint depicting how the Shroud's image was formed,[14] we can see how the Byzantine artist-embroiderer had depicted the lance-wound correctly on the mirror-reverse side to that in which it appears on the Shroud proper, but has forgotten that the same rule must also apply to the crossing of the hands. And in the case of these same hands, although the thumbs are depicted, the way that the long fingers of the lower hand parallel those on the Shroud is particularly striking.

Between 1301 and 1310 the Italian sculptor Giovanni Pisano created for the pulpit of the cathedral at Pisa a sculpture [pl. 33a][15] showing two angels almost running forward to present a linen cloth on which a half-figure of Jesus is imprinted, his hands again crossed across his body in the exact pose of the Shroud.[16] No one knows exactly what inspired Pisano to launch this particular image in western Europe at this time, but even his is not the earliest image of Jesus in this Shroud-like crossed-hands manner. Similar images from the thirteenth century are to be found deriving from the Byzantine world, where they are known variously as the Extreme Humility and King of Glory [pl. 33b]. And these had their antecedents before 1204, as we shall shortly discover.

There is also another oddity to be seen in the Byzantine world. In the Eastern Orthodox Church's rigidly formulated decoration of church walls with religious scenes, depictions of Jesus as a naked child sacrificially laid upon the altar, the so-called *Melismos*, can be seen shortly before and during the thirteenth century to interchange with Shroud-like images of Jesus's crucified body laid out on the same altar. One such can be seen in the prothesis of the Markov monastery, Serbia,[17] and although this dates from 1375, art historians such as Germany's Hans Belting are confident that the type dates back at least as early as 1192.[18]

This also seems to be uncannily paralleled by key elements in the famous Grail stories, which had their widest circulation around this time in the very same Troyes region of France in which the Shroud surfaced in the 1350s. And despite the popular idea that the mysterious Grail was simply the chalice of the Last Supper, what the stories themselves reveal is that any such chalice was only one of several changing aspects of the Grail proper, others taking the form of a container for a Templecombe-type disembodied head, and yet others (and these obviously closest to the *Melismos*) a vessel for a series of changing visions of Christ, varying from a child, often accompanied by his mother Mary, to a mature man covered in the wounds of crucifixion. In some of the Grail stories these changes occur as part of a very special and exclusive High Mass, sometimes described as a 'Mass of the glorious Mother of God' and with Jesus himself present in a very real way, at which the celebrant is often Joseph of Arimathea, the very man who bought the shroud as a container of Jesus's body and blood.[19]

We should not be surprised to find such Byzantine influences upon the Grail stories, for it can hardly be coincidence that they began to circulate in French knightly circles at the very time that, directly as a result of the sack of Constantinople and its preliminaries, those very same knights had witnessed the wonders of the Byzantine world, had envied too much what they saw, had raped, looted and pillaged, and had then brought back home with them to France whatever of value that they may personally have been able to lay their hands on. So was there some particularly privileged person or group who thus brought back the Shroud and decided to keep it for themselves, secret society-wise, at least until the 1350s? Curiously, in one of the Grail stories the

Templars are identified as its guardians, but in essence we have to accept the mist surrounding this period to be far too thick for us to be sure of anything.

Instead, what we can say is that rather than the idea of the Shroud, in the form of a crossed-hands figure on a cloth which went over the head and down to the feet, having *originated* as the brain-child of some brilliantly cunning forger of the 1350s, all the signs are that somewhere, somehow, it actually already *existed* during these 150 'missing' years.

As but one further indication of this, some time around the year 1225 someone decided to repaint the frescos in the chapel of the Holy Sepulchre in Winchester Cathedral, England, and in particular its scene of Jesus being taken down from the cross by Nicodemus and Joseph of Arimathea, with St John and Jesus's mother also in attendance. Whoever the artist was, he painted behind St John and Nicodemus a third man carrying what can only be construed as a double-length shroud [pl. 34a] clearly designed to go over Jesus's head and down to his feet, exactly as we see in the case of our Turin Shroud.

As a further pointer, we find the idea of Jesus imprinting his full-length figure on a piece of cloth in a document dating from as early as 1211. Around this year the Rome-educated English lawyer-chronicler Gervase of Tilbury wrote his monumental *Otia Imperialia* and remarked in one passage: 'The story is passed down from archives of ancient authority that the Lord prostrated himself with his entire body on whitest linen, and so by divine power there was impressed on the linen a most beautiful imprint of not only the face, but the entire body of the Lord.'[20]

So although from the time of the de Charnys back to 1204, tracing the thread of the Shroud's history backwards is quite difficult, equally undeniably during the same period there *are* tantalising hints that *somewhere* there existed something very like the Shroud. We have seen the idea of the bearded crucified figure on cloth with hands crossed over his genitals, as in the Belgrade *epitaphios*. We have seen the concept of the Shroud going over the head and down to the feet, as in the Winchester fresco. We have also seen, from Gervase of Tilbury, that 'archives of ancient authority' were supposed to attest to Jesus having left the imprint of his entire body on a cloth. All we lack, during the 1350 to 1204 period, is the ability to establish with any degree of conviction where a real historical object corresponding to all these characteristics may have been kept.

This brings us back to the shroud with Jesus's figure on it that Robert de Clari saw at Constantinople's Church of St Mary at Blachernae some time around the autumn of 1203. Here we have a definite historical object. The question is, could it have been *our* Shroud?

Chapter 11

Could the Shroud date back
to the sixth century?

L ooking back in time from 1204, we are in a period in which, if the radiocarbon dating is to be believed, there should be no evidence of our Shroud. The year 1260 was the earliest possible date for the Shroud's existence by radiocarbon dating's calculations.

Yet artistic likenesses of Jesus originating well before 1260 can be seen to have an often striking affinity with the face on the Shroud, insofar as anyone would have been able to make this out on the cloth itself, as distinct from the hidden photographic negative. Purely by way of example we may cite from the twelfth century the huge Christ Pantocrator mosaic that dominates the apse of the Norman Byzantine church at Cefalù, Sicily [pl. 36b i]; from the tenth century, the Christ Enthroned from the Church of San Angelo in Formis, Italy [pl. 36b ii]; from the sixth century, a Byzantine-style medallion portrait of Christ on a silver vase discovered at Homs, the ancient Emesa, in Syria [pl. 36b iii]. The common features of all these are a very distinctive rigidly front-facing Jesus with long sidelocks, an individualistic long nose and a slightly forked beard, all strikingly similar to the face on the Shroud [pl. 36a]. And curiously, this type of likeness does not stretch all the way back to the first century, but seems to stop at the sixth, as if there was something which emerged at this time which sparked off this particular way of representing Jesus.

One easy explanation is, of course, that the Shroud's fourteenth-century forger simply copied this likeness as one cunning element of his forgery. But what if there were a firm historical record, specifically between the sixth century and 1204, of an actual piece of cloth, imprinted with Jesus's likeness, that Byzantine artists looked to for inspiring portraits of Jesus of the kind listed above? And what if the Christ portraits produced during these centuries bore certain tiny but tell-tale features suggesting that their artists had been copying, even if at second or third hand, from our Shroud?

Would we feel quite so confident that our Shroud simply *could not* date so far back in time?

So what, according to firm historical record, was this particular cloth? Let us first remind ourselves of what Robert de Clari, sightseeing in Constantinople in the autumn of 1203, told us of the 'shroud' that he viewed in the Church of St Mary at Blachernae, just months before this disappeared amidst all the mayhem of Constantinople's sack by him and his fellow Crusaders: '... about the other marvels that are there [in Constantinople] ... there was another church which was called My Lady St Mary at Blachernae, where there was the shroud in which Our Lord had been wrapped, which every Friday raised itself upright, so that one could see the figure of Our Lord on it.'

As pointed out earlier, this is an unquestionably genuine eyewitness account by a down-to-earth French soldier, one who said of himself that 'he may not have recounted in as fair a fashion as many a good author would have done, yet he always told the strict truth'. And we can be in no doubt that by his using the word 'figure' Robert meant the image of Jesus's full-length body, as additionally conveyed by his puzzlingly describing this as raising itself upright.

But the more immediate puzzle about this passage is that at first (and indeed at second) sight the actual identity of this Christ-image-bearing shroud is by no means clear and indeed has baffled some modern-day editors of Robert's text. Up to Constantinople's sack in 1204 the city's Byzantine rulers certainly possessed the world's most definitive collection of purported relics of Jesus, including pieces of the wood of the cross, the nails, the lance, the crown of thorns and (though it appears in lists very late) the shroud. But these were all kept in a special chapel in the old Sacred Palace adjoining Hagia Sophia and the Hippodrome [see map, fig. 16]. Nor were any of these relics normally shown to the ordinary public, being regarded – in line with traditional Eastern Orthodox thinking – as far too sacred for this. Detailed information about them, accordingly, is as scarce as hens' teeth. And while the twelfth-century Byzantine emperors had recently created a thriving 'country' palace for themselves at Blachernae, which was in Constantinople's north-western corner, the only major relic that the Church of St Mary there was known to possess was the purported Virgin's robe, brought from Capernaum in Palestine in the fifth century.

But this is far from necessitating that Robert de Clari could not have seen at Blachernae the Christ 'shroud' that he says he saw here. For the

1a. Fireman Mario Trematore carrying the Shroud casket from Turin's blazing Cathedral on the night of 11 April 1997.

1b. Cardinal Giovanni Saldarini of Turin.

1c. The Shroud's condition being examined at the Cardinal's residence 14 April 1997, less than three days after the fire. The cloth was found to have been undamaged by this incident.

2a. Photographed before the Cathedral fire, the magnificent Bertola-designed altar in the Cathedral's elevated Royal Chapel, in which the Shroud was housed from 1694 to 1993. The Chapel was badly damaged in the fire, and although scaffolding partly protected the altar, restoration will take several years.

2b. The ultra-modern display case in which the Shroud was housed the night of April 11, 1997. Fireman Trematore had to smash through its bullet-proof crystal in order to reach the Shroud casket and carry it to safety.

3a. The memorandum of Bishop d'Arcis of Troyes, written *c*.1389. Prior to the carbon-dating this provided the prime evidence for the Shroud's alleged mediaeval date.

3b. British scientists Professor Edward Hall, Dr. Michael Tite and Dr. Robert Hedges announcing the results of the carbon-dating at a press conference held at the British Museum 13 October 1988.

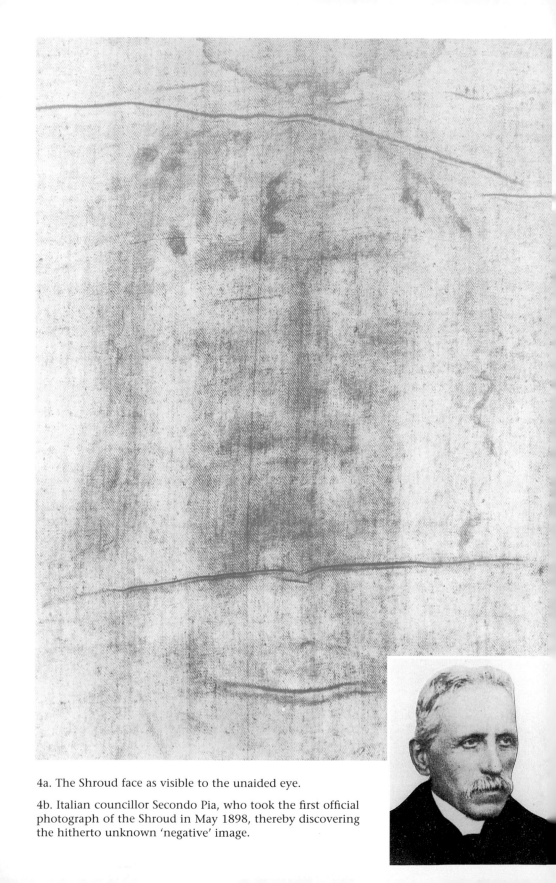

4a. The Shroud face as visible to the unaided eye.

4b. Italian councillor Secondo Pia, who took the first official photograph of the Shroud in May 1898, thereby discovering the hitherto unknown 'negative' image.

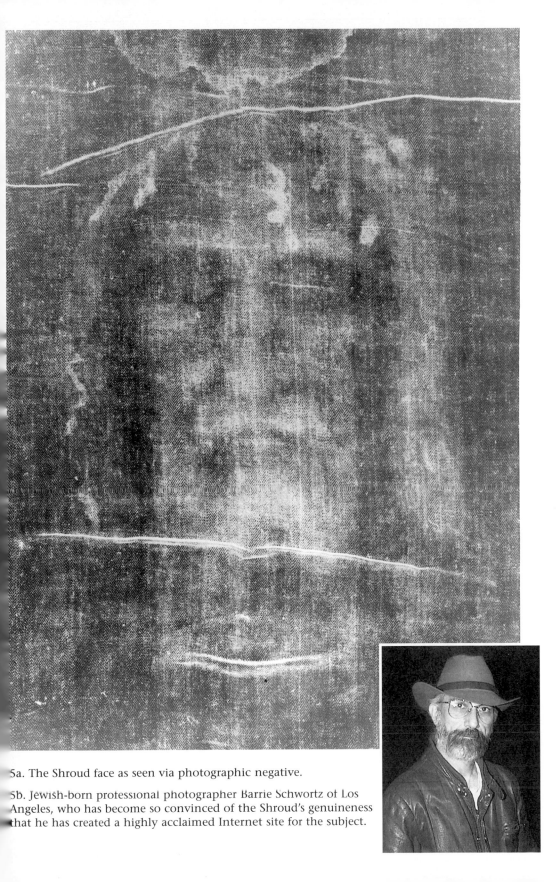

5a. The Shroud face as seen via photographic negative.

5b. Jewish-born professional photographer Barrie Schwortz of Los Angeles, who has become so convinced of the Shroud's genuineness that he has created a highly acclaimed Internet site for the subject.

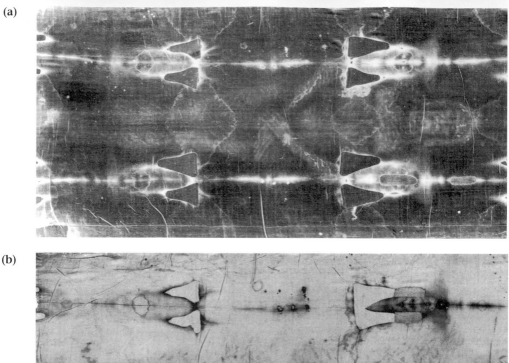

(a)

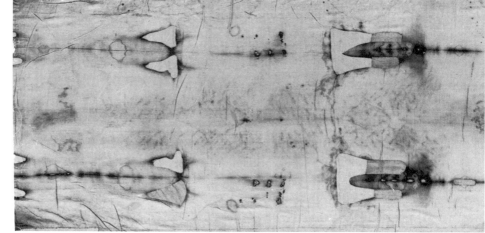

(b)

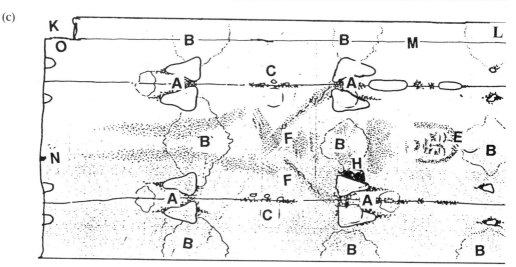

(c)

6&7. The Shroud seen full-length, (a) in negative and (b) in positive, and (c) with explanatory diagram of the salient features: (A) Patched-over burnmarks from the 1532 fire (B) Stains from water used to douse the 1532 fire (C) 'Poker-hole' burns from an unknown damage incident before the 1532 fire (D) Wounds from whipping (E) Bloodflows from a 'crown of thorns' (F) Bloodflows from apparent nailing of the

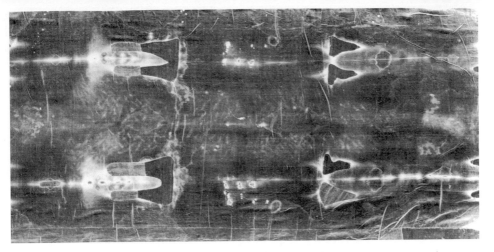

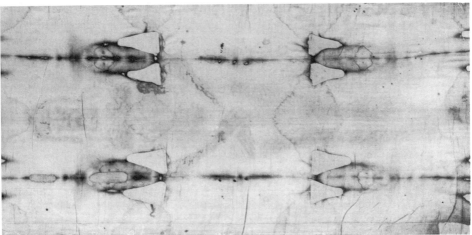

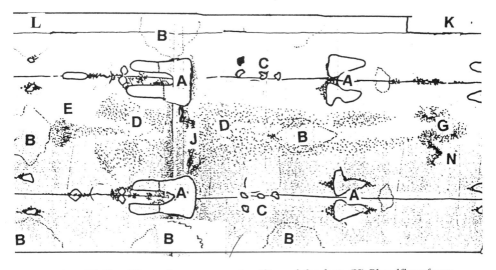

wrists (G) Bloodflows from apparent nailing of the feet (H) Bloodflow from lance-thrust into chest (J) Spillage from (H) across small of the back (K) Cloth portions seemingly removed at some unknown period (L) So-called 'side-strip' (M) Seam-line joining side-strip to main cloth (N) Matching stains (O) Site of removal of the sample for carbon-dating, 1988.

The Shroud frontal image (a) alongside typical artists' copies from the 16th and 17th centuries (b-d), showing the marked qualitative difference between these and the original, and underlining the difficulty attributing the Shroud to the hand of an artist:

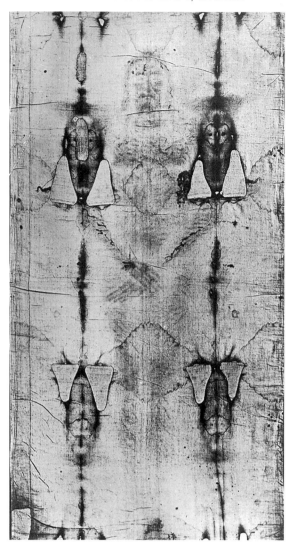

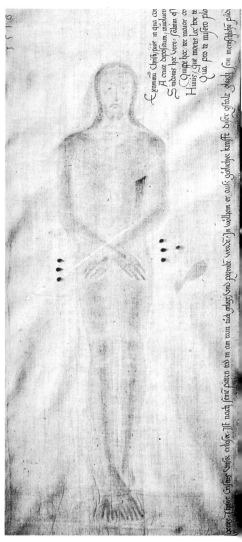

8&9a. The Shroud.

8&9b. Copy of 1516, Church of St.Gommaire, Lierre, Belgium.

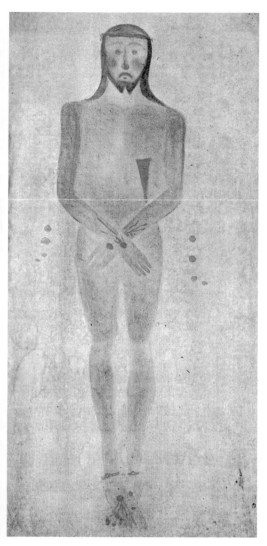 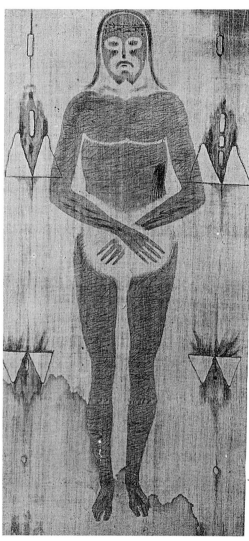

8&9c. Copy of c.1550, Xenobregas,
near Lisbon, Portugal.

8&9d. Copy of 17th century, Church of
Notre Dame, Chambéry, France.

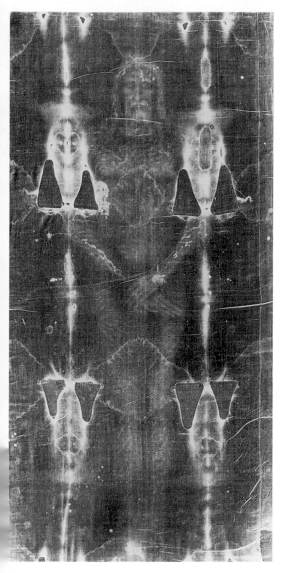

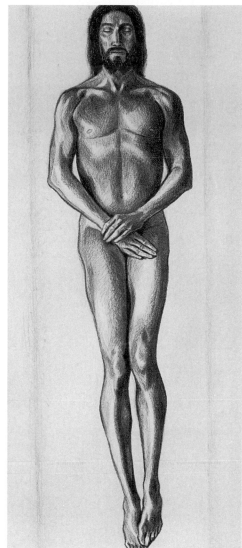

10a. The frontal appearance of the man of the Shroud, as seen on the photographic negative.

10b. Reconstruction of the same by artist Isabel Piczek of Los Angeles, as based on a life model.

11a. (inset right) Hungarian-born Isabel Piczek. A traditionally-trained artist who is convinced the Shroud cannot be the work of an artist.

11b. (right) Isabel Piczek on a ladder in her studio, checking the positioning of a life model posed Shroud-style below her.

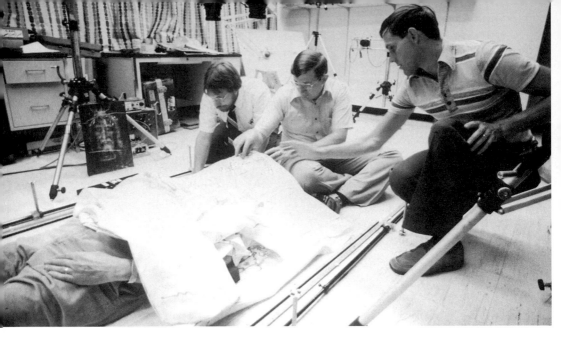

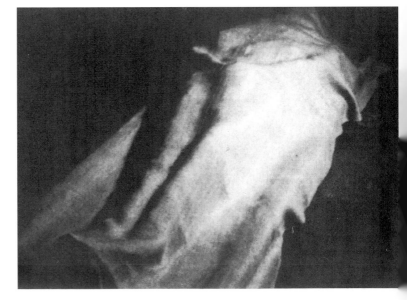

12a. Dr. John Jackson and colleagues reconstructing the Shroud pose shortly prior to their 1978 testing of the Shroud.

12b. The Jackson reconstruction of the cloth drape:
(left) Mathematical representation.
(below) Linen cloth model.

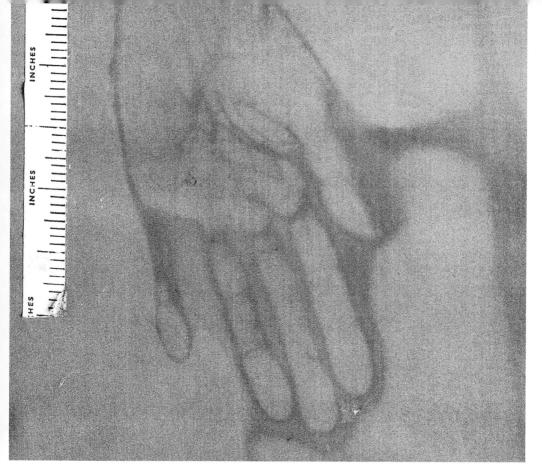

13a. Closest 'natural' parallel to the Shroud image? An outlined hand and buttocks as imprinted on a mattress cover by a patient who died of cancer of the pancreas at a Liverpool hospice, 1981.

13b. Some of the medical specialists who have upheld the Shroud's medical convincingness:

r. Robert Bucklin, tired Professor of hology, universities exas and California.

Professor J.M. 'Taffy' Cameron, retired head of the London Hospital Medical School's Dept. of Forensic Medicine.

Professor Jérôme Lejeune of the French Academy of Medicine, Paris.

Dr. Gilbert Lavoie, consultant, World Health Organization

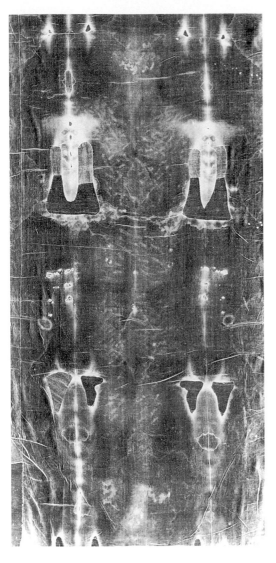

14a. The Shroud back of the body image, seen in negative.

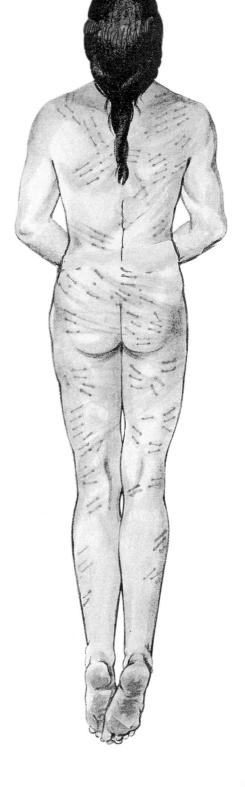

14b. Plan of the distribution of the apparent wounds from whipping.

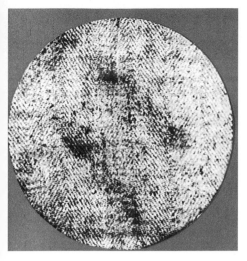

15a. Close-up of the apparent wounds of whipping, reproduced positive.

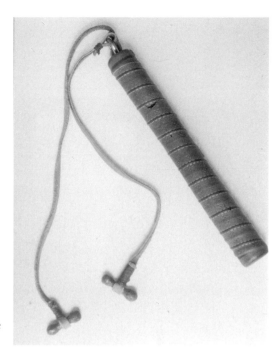

15b. Reconstruction of the apparent whip used.

15c. Typical example of a mediaeval artist's unconvincing depiction of wounds of scourging, from the *Holkham Bible Picture Book*, created *c.* 1326, almost exactly the date radiocarbon-dating attributes to the Shroud.

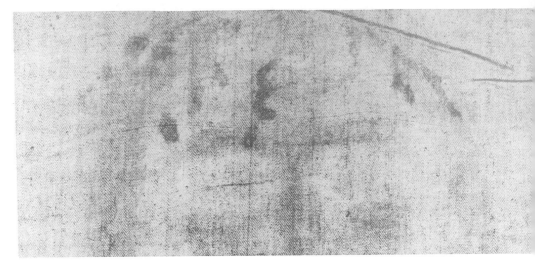

16a. The 'crown of thorns' bloodflows as seen on the forehead of the man of the Shroud.

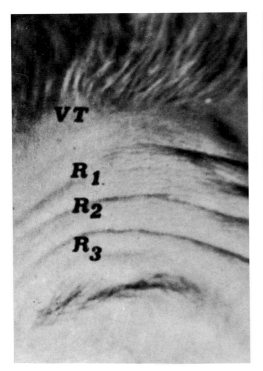

16b. Musculature of the forehead in 'furrowed' mode.

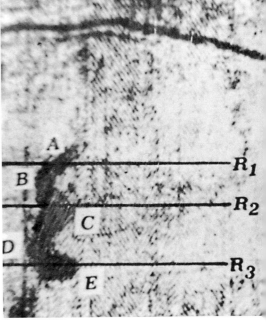

16c. How the interruptions of the flow of the reverse '3' shaped bloodflow exactly matches that musculature.

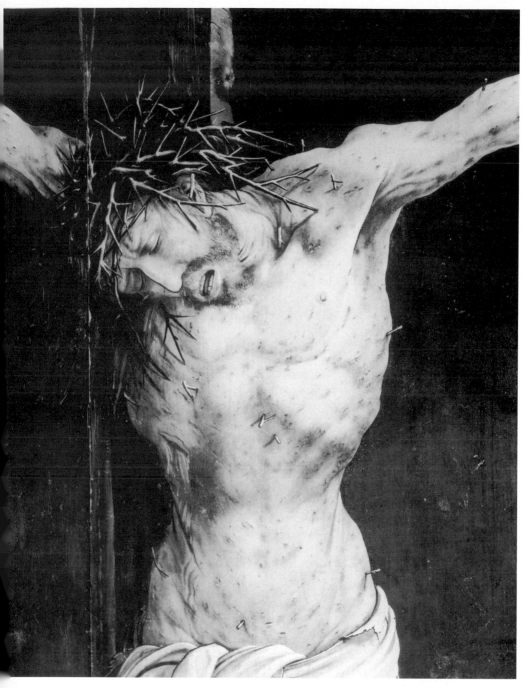

17. Christ crowned with thorns, detail from Grünewald's Isenheim altarpiece, showing unconvincingly depicted bloodflows.

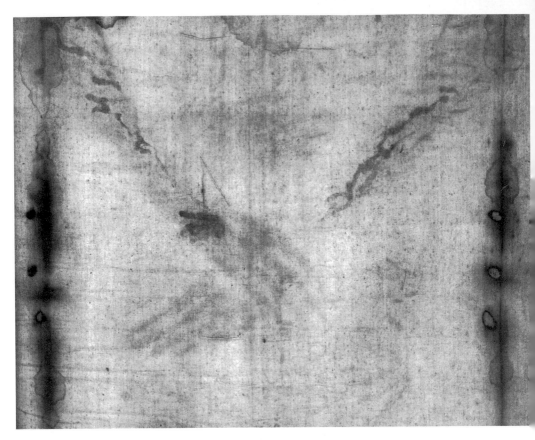

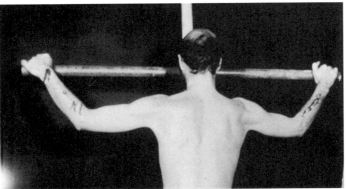

18a. Close-up of the 'crossed hands' area on the Shroud bloodflows.

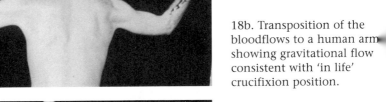

18b. Transposition of the bloodflows to a human arm showing gravitational flow consistent with 'in life' crucifixion position.

18c. The same transposition showing, from one branch the ∧-shaped flow, the body apparent position at death.

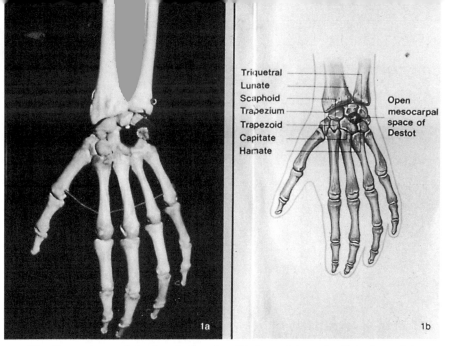

Triquetral		
Lunate		
Scaphoid		Open
Trapezium		mesocarpal
Trapezoid		space of
Capitate		Destot
Hamate		

| 1a | 1b |

19a. X-ray views of the hand, showing likely position of nail in the wrist.

19b. Rare artistic depiction of crucifixion with wrist-nailing, by the 17th-century Flemish artist Anthony Van Dyck. But note how even Van Dyck's rendition of bloodflows has little of the Shroud's medical convincingness.

20a. Close-up of the 'bloody foot' area on the Shroud, showing bloodflow from ankle.

20b. Ankle-bones of the only archaeologically-known victim of crucifixion, showing these fastened by nail.

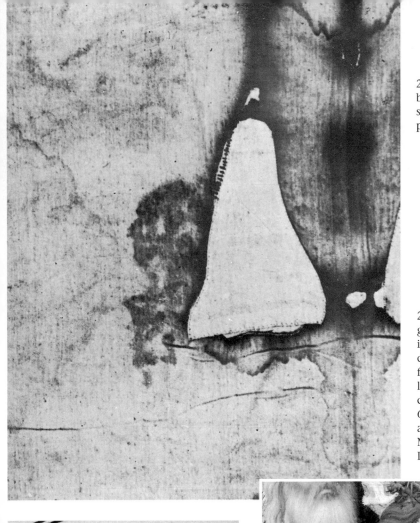

21a. Close-up of the bloodflow in the chest, seemingly as from piercing with a lance.

21c. Mediaeval artist's graphic but still medically unconvincing depiction of blood flowing from the lance-thrust in Jesus's chest, detail from the *Grande Pietà Ronde*, attributed to Jean Malouel, *c.*1390, Louvre Museum, Paris.

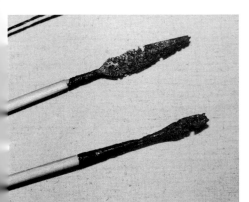

21b. Examples of the Roman lancea, from the Landesmuseum, Zurich.

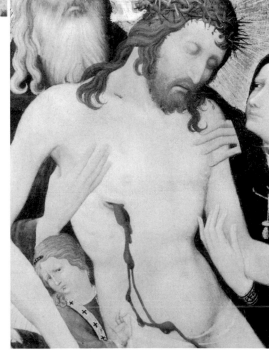

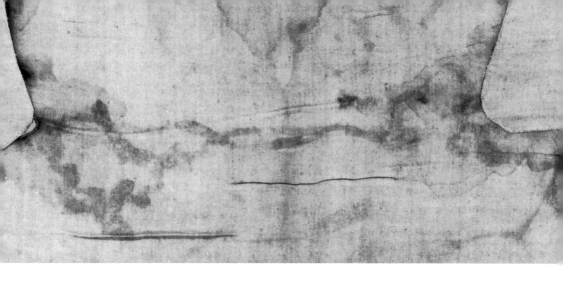

22a. Close-up of bloodflow across the small of the back.

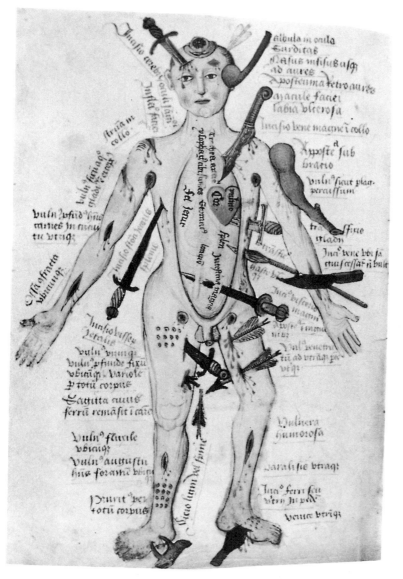

22b. 'Man of Wounds' medical illustration of c.1500, showing poor artistic understanding of bloodflows, even over a century after the Shroud was purportedly painted by an artist.

(i)

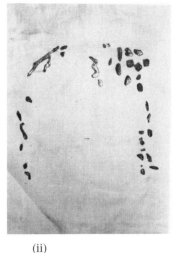

(ii)

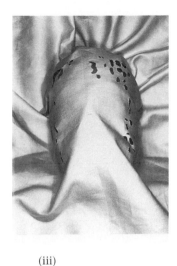

(iii)

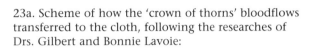

23a. Scheme of how the 'crown of thorns' bloodflows transferred to the cloth, following the researches of Drs. Gilbert and Bonnie Lavoie:

   (i) the Shroud face.

 (ii) the bloodflows marked out on an equivalent piece of cloth.

(iii) this same cloth draped over a human face, with the bloodflow areas cut out stencil style.

(iv) paint applied through the cut-outs, showing with the aid of a present-day model how the bloodflows may actually have fallen on the original face the Shroud wrapped.

(iv)

23b. Examples of burial in antiquity with hands crossed over the genitals:

(right) Egyptian priest laid out in death, from sarcophagus of c.340 BC, British Museum.

(far right) Jewish woman's skeleton from a first century cemetery belonging to the site where the Dead Sea Scrolls were found.

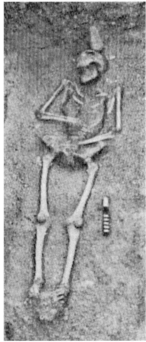

24a. Example of a mediaeval burial with hands crossed over the genitals, from a Book of Hours painted *c*.1410.

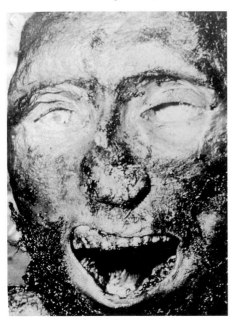

24b. The remarkably preserved face of the mediaeval knight found at St.Bee's, Cumbria, photographed shortly after the removal of the two shrouds which wrapped his body.

24c. The inner shroud of the mediaeval knight found at St.Bee's, Cumbria, photographed still in position before its unwrapping, showing a typical mediaeval mode of enshrouding.

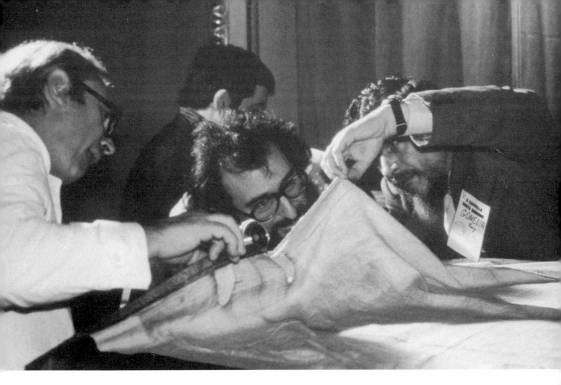

25a. Giovanni Riggi (left) and others examining the Shroud's underside, 1978. Although to reach the underside Riggi had to unstitch the Shroud at the edges, he failed to document the edges' appearance.

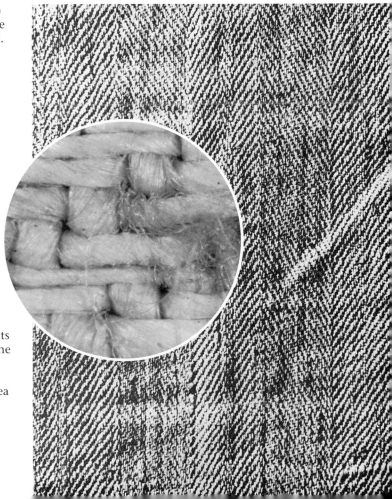

25b. Close-up of the Shroud weave, showing its characteristic herring-bone pattern.

25c. (inset) Magnified area of the Shroud's weave.

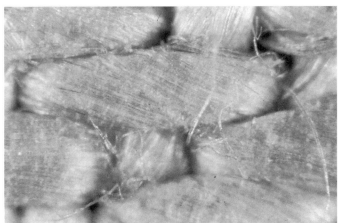

26a. American optical physicist Sam Pellicori viewing the Shroud in 1978 on-site through the microscope.

26b. Shroud 'body' image area seen at low magnification.

26c. Shroud 'body' image area seen at high magnification.

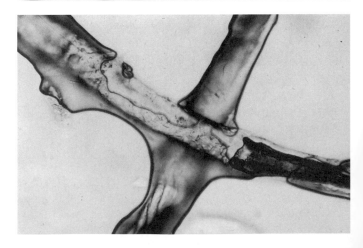

27a. Shroud 'blood' seen at low magnification.

27b. Microbiologist Professor Stephen Mattingly of the University of Texas, seen viewing Shroud 'blood' samples through the microscope. He and his colleague Dr. Tryon confirm these as blood, and claim to have identified DNA gene segments in it.

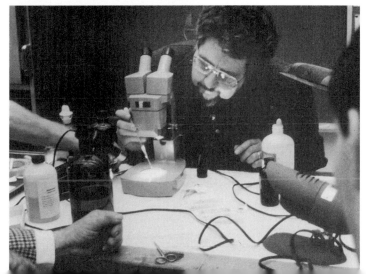

27c. Chemist Dr. Alan Adler examining Shroud 'blood' under the microscope.

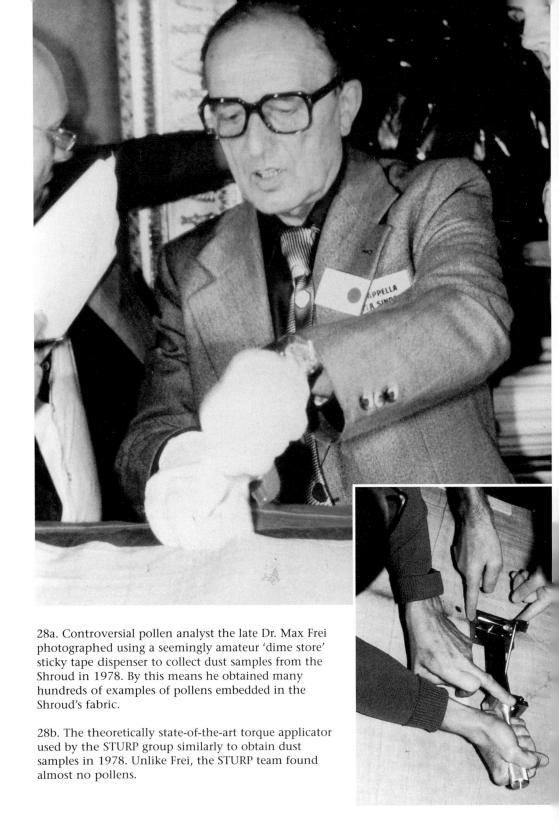

28a. Controversial pollen analyst the late Dr. Max Frei photographed using a seemingly amateur 'dime store' sticky tape dispenser to collect dust samples from the Shroud in 1978. By this means he obtained many hundreds of examples of pollens embedded in the Shroud's fabric.

28b. The theoretically state-of-the-art torque applicator used by the STURP group similarly to obtain dust samples in 1978. Unlike Frei, the STURP team found almost no pollens.

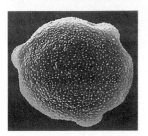

1. Coryllus Avellana L
(Hazel)

To be found throughout
France, Italy, and elsewhere.

2. Althea Officinalis Marsh

Halophyte plant widespread
around Mediterranean area.

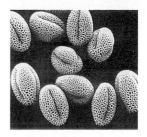

3. Philyrea Angus Tifolia

Plant of the general
Mediterranean region.

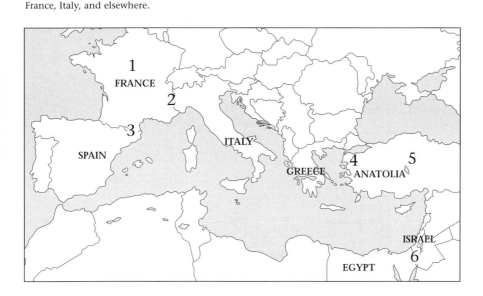

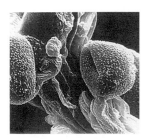

**4. Pteranthus Dichotomus
Forsk**

Plant of the sandy and
limey desert, particulary
Anatolian steppe and
Jerusalem environs.

**5. Haplophyllum
Tuberculatum Juss**

Plant of deserts, particularly
Anatolia and Jerusalem environs.

6. Prosopis Farcta Macbr

Plant to be found in
Anatolia but particularly
common around Dead Sea.

29. Some examples of the 58 different varieties of pollens
that Dr. Max Frei found among the Shroud's surface dust, as
identified by him up to the time of his death in 1983, with
(inset map) the more potentially significant distribution areas
for each parent plant around the Mediterranean and Near East.

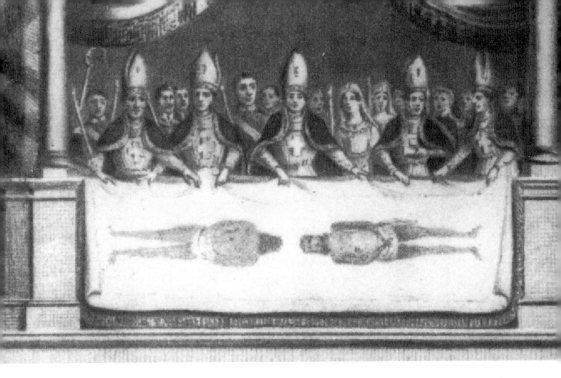

30a. 1842 souvenir print commemorating public exposition of the Shroud from a palace balcony in Turin in that year.

Ritratto del Santiss: Sudario, dedicato alle Altezze Sereniss: di Maria Adelaide, Maria Anna, e Mar
della Real Casa di Sauoia, in questa prima Impressione. *dall'vmiliss.^e* e ossequiosiss. Seruitore. Pietro Ant

30b. *c*.1690 engraving on silk, commemorating exposition of the Shroud from a dais in the palace courtyard.

31a. *c.*1355 Pilgrim's medallion bearing the arms of Geoffrey de Charny and his wife Jeanne de Vergy, the earliest-known depiction of the Shroud in its full-length, double-imprint form.

31b. Attesting to Geoffrey de Charny's renown on both sides of the English Channel for his chivalry, the opening page of the manuscript of one of his books of chivalry, as preserved in the Bodleian Library, Oxford. The coat of arms indicates that it was most likely his personal copy, which was acquired in the 18th-century by the English collector Thomas Coke (1697-1759) of Holkham Hall, Norfolk.

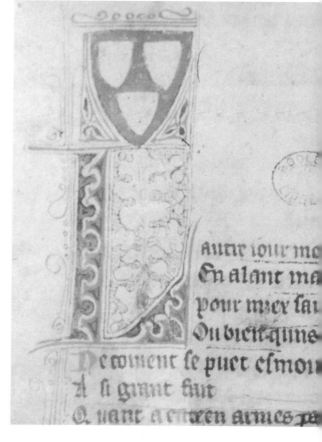

32a. *c.*1300 Embroidered liturgical *epitaphios* from the reign of the Serbian king Stephen Uroš II Milutin (1282 – 1321). Cloths of this kind, directly symbolising the shroud of Jesus, are known to have been used in the Byzantine liturgy well over a century earlier than the 'Turin' Shroud's emergence in Lirey in the 1350s.

32b. *c.*1280 Evidence of Templar ownership of the Shroud? Panel-painting with Shroud-like face, radiocarbon-dated to the Templar period, as discovered during World War II hidden in the ceiling of a cottage in Templecombe, Somerset.

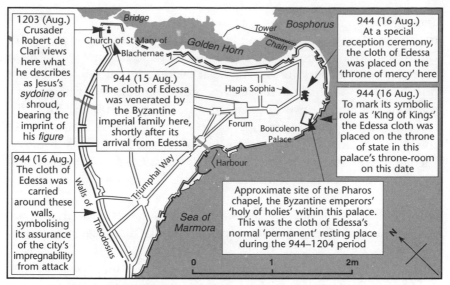

Fig 16 Constantinople c. 1204
Byzantine Constantinople, based on a map of modern-day Istanbul, showing the relative positions of the Blachernae Church, where Robert de Clari saw the 'shroud' he described, and the Boucoleon or Sacred Palace, where the Byzantine emperors' relic collection was normally stored

circumstances were very unusual when he strolled the city some time in the closing months of 1203. The Byzantine people were extremely nervous about their having tall, heavily armed foreigners like himself in their midst, men whom they had seen very forcibly depose their former usurper emperor in favour of a more legitimate but not necessarily more popular candidate. The tensions from this, combined with Crusader anger at not being paid for their mercenary services, would soon lead to the Byzantines firmly shutting their gates against further Crusader 'visits', thereby bringing upon themselves the sack proper of 1204.

Meanwhile, it was always in tense circumstances such as these that the Byzantines, a very devout and superstitious people, traditionally looked to their purportedly 'palladian' religious objects for protection. The Blachernae church was their recognised rallying place for this, as it had been in 626 when they had been threatened by the Avars, and again in 860 by the Russians. On both occasions Blachernae's Virgin's robe had helped send these foes packing.

Why, then, was the robe not deployed again in 1203? The simple answer is that a little more recently than 860 Constantinople had acquired a new

143

and arguably yet more powerful palladian in the form of a piece of cloth imprinted with the image of Jesus himself. Everyone knew the cloth with this imprint to have protected most powerfully the eastern city of Edessa from the Persians back in 544 BC. What everybody did not know – not least because there had never been any previous public exposition of it – was that the imprint was of his whole body, the cloth being his burial shroud. Instead, the popular supposition (and one largely maintained to this day), was that the cloth bore the image only of his disembodied face, the same face that had inspired the already mentioned Christ portraits in Byzantine art and which, it was thought, had been created while Jesus was alive.

So how can we be sure this Edessa cloth, which was certainly in Constantinople in 1203, and which equally certainly disappeared following the Crusader sack, was the same 'shroud' which Robert de Clari viewed, and one and the same as our Shroud? If only our knowledge of it had been confined to Constantinople's later years then the answer might have been more straightforward than it is. For when we quoted, in the last chapter, Gervase of Tilbury's reference of *c.* 1211 to the linen cloth on which Jesus had 'impressed ... a most beautiful imprint of ... [his] entire body', we omitted to make clear that Gervase had been referring to this very same cloth of Edessa. He told how its history could be traced right back to the time of Jesus when a King Abgar of Edessa, a quite definite historical individual, had written a letter asking Jesus to come to see him, to which Jesus had responded: 'If indeed you desire to see my physical appearance, I send you a cloth on which the image not only of my face *but of my entire body* has been preserved.'

Nor was Gervase of Tilbury the only western author to write of this Edessa cloth as bearing the full imprint of Jesus's body. In about 1141 the chronicler Ordericus Vitalis (1075–1143?), a monk who was born in England but spent the major part of his life at St Evroult in Normandy, recorded in his *Ecclesiastical History*: 'Abgar reigned as toparch of Edessa. To him the Lord Jesus sent ... a most precious cloth, with which he wiped the sweat from his face, and on which shone the Saviour's features, miraculously reproduced. This displayed to those who gazed upon it the likeness and proportions of the body of the Lord.'[1]

However, the one major problem with these accounts is that being by western writers, two thousand miles distant from the original in Constantinople, they can scarcely be considered the best of witnesses. Added to which, neither writer described this cloth as a shroud as such. Although they explicitly stated that Jesus had imprinted his full body on the linen, they both rather incongruously conveyed that he did so while he was alive and well, thereby falling back into line with those who believed the image to be of a face only.

And we look in vain among eastern writers for any clear physical description of the shroud latterly referred to as preserved with the other major Passion relics in Constantinople's Sacred Palace. The closest we get to this, and the authority at least is a good one, is a mention by Nicholas Mesarites, the relic collection's actual overseer in 1201, that included in his charge were: '... the burial shrouds[2] of Christ: these are of linen. They are of cheap and easy to find materials, still smelling of myrrh and defying decay since they wrapped the outlineless, fragrant-with-myrrh, naked body after the Passion.'

'Outlineless' (and this is indeed the meaning of the Greek word *aperilepton* that Mesarites uses), is inevitably fascinating from the point of view that such outlinelessness is indeed a major characteristic of the Shroud image that we know today. Likewise, that Jesus's body was 'naked' is something that Mesarites could hardly have known unless he were looking at some form of imprint of this on the cloth. But because in his cryptic manner Mesarites does not actually directly say that there was such an imprint on the cloth, no real weight can be accorded to his information. And the issues are further complicated by some lists of the imperial relic collection that refer both to Jesus's shroud and to what might be construed to be the Edessa cloth as two separate objects, although no one should seriously regard such lists as properly reliable inventories.

Now in line with our promise to ourselves that at every stage of our tracking back we would try to check whether there were any directly contemporary *pictorial* indications of the Shroud's existence, this seems quite an appropriate point to do so. As we have already indicated, we cannot at this period expect explicit depictions of expositions in the manner of the Lirey medallion and the Turin souvenir prints, because quite regardless of whether or not Constantinople's shroud and cloth of Edessa were one and the same, neither was normally ever publicly exhibited in such a manner. The 1203 showings seem to have been quite unique in this regard.

However, if we look to images from this time of Jesus laid out Shroud-like in death with crossed hands – the Shroud pose that has so unjustifiably been criticised as indicative of artistic 'modesty' – we are far from disappointed. In Budapest's National Széchenyi Library is a book called the

Pray Manuscript,[3] greatly prized by Hungarians as the first surviving text in their language, and reliably thought to have been created at their Boldva Benedictine monastery between 1192 and 1195. But from the Shroud point of view by far its greatest interest is its four pages of coloured drawings, and in particular the third of these [pl. 35a], which shows in its upper register Joseph of Arimathea and Nicodemus preparing Jesus's dead body for burial, with in the lower register the three Marys visiting the angel-guarded empty tomb.

When I first came across this back in the 1970s, I was particularly struck by the way, in the upper register, Jesus's dead body is depicted in a quite unmistakably Shroud-like pose and totally nude, this latter feature alone certainly atypical of most Byzantine art. This seemed sufficient reason in itself for including it in my first book published in 1978. However, what I had failed to spot were other features linking it and its associated drawings even more closely to our Shroud, features which subsequently came to be noticed by French scholars, most notably by the earlier mentioned Professor Jérôme Lejeune, who specially visited Budapest to view the manuscript in the original.

For instance, first, and specifically in the case of the manuscript's Shroud-like depiction of Jesus's dead body, the drawing shows all four fingers of each of Jesus's hands, but no thumbs, exactly as on the Shroud. Whereas in the manuscript's other drawings Jesus's thumbs are depicted perfectly normally. Second, in this same drawing of Jesus's dead body, just over Jesus's right eye there is a single forehead bloodstain, delineated in red, located in exactly the same position as the very distinctive '3'-shaped stain on the man of the Shroud's forehead. Third, in one of the manuscript's other drawings, of Christ Enthroned, while Jesus's left hand is depicted with the nail wound through his palm, the wound in his right hand appears unmistakably, and most unusually, to be through his wrist.

Possibly the most tell-tale feature of all, however, is one that was first reported in 1986 by the Dominican monk Père A. M. Dubarle of St Joseph's Convent, Paris. In the lower register of the manuscript's page with the Shroud body there can be seen a shroud, obviously Jesus's, partly rolled up on the lid of the sarcophagus representing Jesus's tomb. If this piece of cloth is studied very closely, it can be seen that it bears a set of tiny 'poker holes', three in a line and then one offset [see close-up, fig. 17a], precisely corresponding to the four groups of these still visible on the Shroud [pl. 35b] and known to predate the 1532 fire. Another, larger, set of this same arrangement of holes can be seen on the sarcophagus lid itself

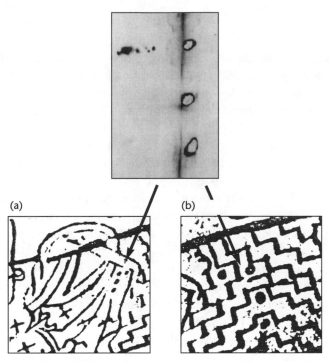

(a)   (b)

Fig 17   Seemingly Turin-Shroud inspired 'poker-holes' on the shroud of Jesus depicted in the Hungarian 'Pray' manuscript of 1192
(a) a group of holes (slightly enhanced for clarity) on the rolled-up shroud depicted lying on the casket; (b) a group of similar holes depicted on the sarcophagus which, as has been noted, has a herring-bone pattern

[fig. 17b]. Is it mere coincidence, also, that the lid bears a distinctively herringbone type of pattern?

As Professor Lejeune felt bound to conclude from his study of all these different features: 'Such precise details are not to be found together on any other known [Christ] image – except the Shroud which is in Turin. One is therefore forced to conclude that the artist of the Pray manuscript had before his eyes ... some model which possessed all the characteristics of the Shroud which is in Turin.'[4]

And while the Pray manuscript is the best surviving example of a Shroud-like body from this period, similar depictions of Jesus exist from as early as the eleventh century, among these a Byzantine ivory, in this instance depicting Jesus clad in a loincloth, preserved in the Victoria and Albert Museum, London [pl. 34b]. Also, in a twelfth-century Byzantine enamel preserved in the Hermitage, St Petersburg, immediately below a scene of the crucifixion is a similar depiction of Jesus laid out in death on his shroud, the inscription to which specifically reads 'Christ lies in death, manifesting [or 'making visible'] God'.[5] There are also Shroud-like half-length images of Jesus with crossed hands appearing to rise out of his casket jack-in-the-box style – the already-mentioned 'King of Glory' images [pl. 33b] – perhaps reminiscent of Robert de Clari's shroud 'raising itself upright' each Friday.

Intriguing though such possible artistic reflections of our Shroud are, however, they are essentially mute. Of themselves they cannot prove that our Shroud was the same as either the Constantinople 'shroud' or the Edessa cloth, whether or not these in their turn were one and the same.

However, historically at least we are comparatively well informed about the Edessa cloth before 1204. And having so far referred to this only somewhat tantalisingly, it is now only right that we should address it directly. As earlier mentioned, its origins, so far as these are known, were in Edessa, today the provincial city of Urfa in south-eastern Turkey, not far from the border with Syria. After having been Byzantine in the sixth century, Edessa and its Christ-imprinted cloth fell into Moslem hands in the seventh century, as a result of which it was only in 943 that the Moslems became sufficiently weak, and the Byzantines proportionately strong, for the latter to make a determined attempt to win the cloth rightfully back for Christendom.

Accordingly, Constantinople's Emperor Romanus sent a whole army eastwards for it, headed by his best general, John Curcuas who, on camping before Edessa's gates, astonished the Moslem emir by promising the town immunity from attack, the release of two hundred Moslem prisoners and the payment of twelve thousand silver pieces, all for just one thing – the cloth with Jesus's imprint.[6] Despite such an offer seeming too good to refuse (particularly for a Moslem), the perplexed emir actually sent to his superiors in Baghdad for advice, with Curcuas and his army cooling their heels in the meantime. But then at last word came back that the Byzantine terms should be accepted, as a result of which the high-ranking Orthodox clergy whom Curcuas had brought with him, after making checks that they had been handed over the true cloth (there was apparently at least one attempt to deceive them[7]), duly transported this the breadth of Antolia, the troops of Curcuas escorting them all the way.

On 15 August 944, clearly chosen because it was the Feast of the Assumption (symbolically, Mary Mother of Jesus was regarded as a 'vessel' of Jesus and the Edessa cloth repeatedly associated with her), the cloth was carried by boat across the Bosphorus to St Mary at Blachernae, where it was viewed and venerated by Byzantine's royals. The next day, which would become the cloth's own special feast day (still celebrated in the Eastern Orthodox Church) it was carried around Constantinople's walls, thereby specifically establishing it as the city's new palladian, theoretically yet more powerful than Blachernae's Virgin's robe. Then both at Hagia Sophia and in the throne-room of the Sacred Palace it was accorded a special coronation and enthroning, symbolically establishing (or reaffirming) it as Constantinople's very special 'King of Kings'. Finally after all this and other ceremonial it was laid to rest in its own special place in the Sacred Palace's Chapel of the Pharos, there joining the emperor's matchless collection of relics of the Passion.

What, then, *was* this cloth, that it held such enormous importance to the Byzantine people? If one talks to some modern-day scholars, such as the now-venerable Crusades historian Sir Steven Runciman, or the classicist Professor Averil Cameron[8] of King's College, London, they will summarily dismiss it as merely 'some old icon whose origins we cannot possibly hope to trace.'[9] They will also insist that it could not possibly have been our Shroud because the word 'Mandylion', the name often later given to the Edessa cloth in Byzantine art, could not have denoted anything of such a size. In Sir Steven's words: 'The Image of Edessa was always described by the Byzantines as a *'mandelion'*, a kerchief, which is quite different from a *'sindon'* [or shroud]'.[10]

But were the Byzantines, the successors of the ancient Greeks, really so gullible that they would have gone to such elaborate lengths, and indulged in such excessive ceremonial, just for some old *painting*, particularly given that the Empire had only just got over a great deal of antipathy towards painted images, a controversy that had raged only little over a century before, during the era of Iconoclasm? Also, can we really be sure that the Edessa cloth was the handkerchief size that Sir Steven and Professor Cameron contend? Distant though Gervase of Tilbury and Ordericus Vitalis were from Byzantium, how could they have come to believe that the Edessa cloth bore the full imprint of Jesus's body, if it was really that small? And what did the Byzantines themselves say about this cloth that they had acquired at such expense in 943–4?

It so happens that one year after the Edessa cloth had been brought to Constantinople a special Official History of it was written for its feast day, copies of which survive in manuscript form.[11] In this the author unmistakably speaks of Shroud-like characteristics in the cloth's key

149

feature, its imprint. He was clearly perplexed about this, because he went to the lengths of providing two quite different versions of how it may have been formed, freely admitting that 'it would not be at all surprising if the facts had often been distorted in view of the time that has elapsed'.

Thus according to the first version of the story that he gave – and it is one that can be found from as early as the sixth century – the image became formed when Jesus asked to wash himself and left it on the towel he used to dry his face. According to the second version, for which no surviving antecedent is known, it purportedly came about following Jesus's agony in the Garden of Gethsemane, when according to Luke's gospel 'his sweat fell to the ground like great drops of blood'.[12] Reputedly Jesus again took a piece of cloth, wiped his face on it and produced an imprint, this time obviously a bloodier one.

Now clearly neither of these versions tells us that the Byzantines knew as at AD 945 that this cloth was Jesus's burial shroud. For if they had, we would have none of our present difficulties. In the face of such initially conflicting information we can only provisionally suggest that perhaps at that time the Shroud was folded so that only the face was visible and knowledge of its full figure only came later, when the cloth had been more fully examined. This would account for Ordericus Vitalis's and Gervase of Tilbury's quite different ideas about the size of the cloth, even though they otherwise followed the original story. Also we can at least say that the water/sweat details in the Official History's author's accounts of the Edessa cloth image's creation sound uncannily like the characteristics of the Shroud's image. At the very beginning of the Official History the author also speaks of the image as 'a moist secretion without colouring or painter's art ... made in the linen cloth'. It is his speaking only of a face on the cloth, as if unaware of any other feature, that represents the biggest stumbling-clock.

But crucially, can we establish exactly what this face looked like? There are only a few surviving direct copies of the cloth of Edessa dating from its two and a half centuries in Constantinople, all varying one from the other, Byzantine art being notoriously non-naturalistic. Some of these, such as the 'Holy Face of Laon', the 'Holy Face of Genoa' also, arguably, Rome's famous 'Veronica', reached the West, where they achieved their own cult status and became prey to overpainting and adaptations of their size.[13] However, even these convey at least one essential characteristic, that the Edessa cloth's face was a brownish monochrome, rigidly front-facing and disembodied-looking on its cloth, certainly rather more than a little reminiscent of the Shroud.

Arguably more reliable, because they would have been less prey to alteration, are copies that can (or in some cases could) be found among murals in Serbian, Russian and Cypriot churches, such as at Gradac, Studenica, Kato Lefkara [pl. 37b], Spas Nereditsa [pl. 37c], and elsewhere.[14] These convey other recurring possible clues to the original's appearance, such as (on some) a lattice-type decoration, possibly from some kind of grille that once covered the cloth, also the face being set on a landscape-aspect cloth – i.e. something much wider and emptier at the sides than any artist would normally have chosen if he were setting out to paint a face on just any piece of canvas.

One particularly interesting Edessa cloth copy [pl. 37a] was discovered only a few years ago by the acknowledged expert in Cappadocian frescos Lennox Manton (a retired dentist), who very kindly brought it to my attention. This is painted above an arch in the Sakli or 'Hidden' church in the Goreme region of central Turkey, roughly halfway between Urfa/Edessa and Istanbul/Constantinople. It dates to the tenth or early eleventh century and, despite some damage to the face, its general resemblance to the facial portion on the Shroud is really quite remarkable. There is the same sepia-coloured, disembodied, rigidly frontal face on the same landscape cloth. (If we isolate the Shroud's facial area, then its sides are indeed wide in relation to the face [pl. 36a]). And when we know, as we do from the Official History, that this same Edessa cloth's imprint had the appearance of 'a moist secretion without colouring or painter's art', then can we really believe that this could *not* have been our Shroud?

Obviously much depends on whether there really was more to the Edessa cloth than ostensibly met the eye, or whether Sir Steven Runciman and Professor Cameron are right that this can solely have been a face only on a handkerchief-sized piece of linen. Deserving mention is that the term 'Mandylion', which Sir Steven Runciman seems to have regarded as so crucial to his argument, is used nowhere in the lengthy Official History of the cloth, its earliest known incidence being in *c.*990, and then only in the biography of an ascetic, Paul of Mount Latros, who merely receives a vision of this cloth. Out of several dozen references to the cloth of Edessa collected by the German scholar Ernst von Dobschütz, only three use the term. Even if it does specifically denote something tiny, this may have no more significance than Robin Hood's dubbing his burliest 'merry man' 'Little John'.

Furthermore, when we look to other indications of the cloth of Edessa's size we find that the eighth-century Greek theologian John of Damascus described it as a *himation*, evoking the two-yards-wide by three-yards-long outer garment worn by the ancient Greeks. Although these latter were not known for their prudishness, even they might have found a pocket-handkerchief-sized *himation* a little skimpy. Likewise, in the late tenth century Leo the Deacon spoke of the image as on a *peplos*, unequivocally denoting a full-size robe.

For myself, however, by far the most illuminating of all the words used for the Edessa cloth has to have been *tetradiplon*, even though it only occurs twice, once in a sixth-century manuscript and once in the Official History. As a word in Greek, this is extremely rare and completely unknown outside the two above-mentioned texts. Yet it is perfectly understandable, since it is a compound of the two ordinary words *tetra* meaning 'four' and *diplon* meaning 'doubled' – thus 'doubled in four'.

Why should the cloth of Edessa have been described as 'doubled in four'? Inevitably this can only have had something to do with the way the cloth was once folded. It provided my cue, more than a quarter of a century ago, to experiment with what might happen if one tried folding the Shroud in four-by-two folds, as the word seemed to suggest [fig. 18]. When I tried this with the aid of a photograph, the revelation was something akin to Secondo Pia's discovery of the hidden negative. To my utter astonishment, the Shroud face appeared strangely disembodied, on a landscape-aspect cloth, exactly as it appears on the pre-1204 Edessa cloth copies, such as at Sakli, Gradac and Studenica, some of which I did not even know of at that time.

Now if one imagined the cloth folded in this way, mounted on a board and decorated with some kind of gold covering, preventing easy access to the inner folds (and all this is precisely what the Official History describes of the Edessa cloth's early mode of conservation), then it is very easy to see how anyone viewing it might well suppose there was no more to the image than this face. It is also easy to understand how anyone, not knowing of the Shroud's hidden negative, would 'see' Jesus's eyes as open and staring, for that is exactly how they look on the cloth itself and it is indeed how later copyists of what was undoubtedly the Turin Shroud often depicted them.

It would therefore be very understandable for people at any time when the cloth was displayed in this manner to suppose that its image had been made while Jesus was still alive (particularly if this was what earlier

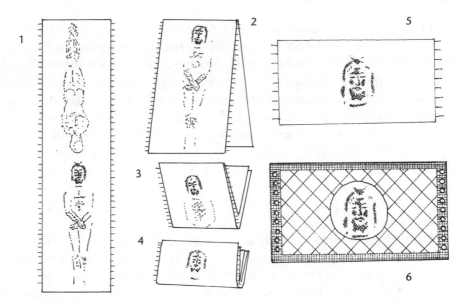

Fig 18   How if 'doubled in four' the Shroud takes on the appearance of artists' copies of the cloth of Edessa

1. The Shroud full length
2. The Shroud 'doubled'
3 & 4. The Shroud doubled again, making 4 × 2 folds
5. How when 'doubled in four' in this way, the Shroud face appears disembodied on a landscape aspect cloth, closely corresponding to the earliest known artists' direct depictions of the cloth of Edessa
6. How the Shroud may have appeared if mounted on a board and covered with gold decoration, as described of the cloth of Edessa. A lattice-shaped decorative covering would explain the lattice work seeming to cover the cloth on some artists' copies of the cloth of Edessa. Some copies also show the fringe at the side fastened to nails either side of the board. Frustratingly, the edges of the Shroud have never been properly documented photographically, due to Princess Clotilde's blue surround

tradition dictated), the only jarring feature being the bloodflows on the forehead and hair. And this seems to have been precisely what disturbed the author of the Official History, hence his second version of the story of the image's creation that it derived from the 'bloody sweat' that flowed down Jesus's face during the agony in Gethsemane.

There is even an indication that only shortly after the Edessa cloth's arrival in Constantinople some people, in a more privileged position than the rest, were actually able to see more on it than just the face. In 1987 Professor Gino Zaninotto,[15] a classics scholar living in Rome, browsing in the Vatican Library, happened to come across a Byzantine manuscript that

I was completely unaware of when I did my original research in the 1960s and '70s, and which had largely escaped even the encyclopaedic German von Dobschütz. This was a sermon written by one Gregory, archdeacon of Constantinople's Hagia Sophia Cathedral at the very time of the Edessa cloth's arrival in Constantinople in 944, in which, as a man who had obviously seen at least something of its image for himself, Gregory made clear that he could not agree with the idea of it having been formed by Jesus washing himself. Instead, obviously following the same thoughts as expressed by the author of the Official History, he remarked that the cloth must have become: '. . . imprinted with the drops of sweat from the agony [in Gethsemane], which flowed from the face of the Prince of Life [i.e. Jesus] like drops of blood.'

But then he went on with a statement that hardly makes any sense unless he was referring to something so very like the Shroud as to make little difference. In his words: 'And the image, since those flows, has been embellished by [blood] drops *from his very side*, the two [things] are full of symbolism, blood and water here, and there the sweat of the face.'

In other words, according to Gregory, who had seen it for himself, the Edessa cloth's imprint included, in addition to watery blood on the face, a stain from the lance-wound in Jesus's side. In all logic, such a stain could only have become transferred onto the cloth after Jesus had been brought down dead from the cross. Hence, and even though Gregory, back in the tenth century, declined to pursue this further, since to do so he would have had to deny tradition, this cloth had to be Jesus's burial shroud.

Nor does the evidence stop here. For if the Edessa cloth was indeed one and the same as our Shroud, then we ought to find some evidence on the latter, in the form of old crease-marks, that it was 'doubled in four' for some lengthy period. In fact, when the American STURP team did their exhaustive examination and photography of the Shroud in 1978, one of the lesser-known parts of their programme was raking light photography specifically to show up such creases. The photographs revealed the cloth's surface to be criss-crossed with literally hundreds of old marks of this kind, but a truly significant set of ridge and valley fold marks showed up almost

Fig 19 Ancient foldmarks on the Shroud
With raking light photographs taken in 1978 Dr Jackson has identified ancient foldmarks, individually distinguishable as of ridge and valley type, consistent with a one-time 'doubled-in-four' folding arrangement. The multiplicity of these foldmarks at points D and F also offers additional clues to the one-time folding arrangement (see fig. 20). (Based on original plan by Dr Jackson, though his lines are more uneven than they appear here.)

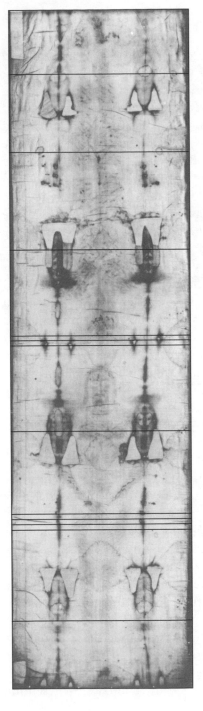

A – Ridge foldmark

B – Ridge foldmark

C – Valley foldmark

D – Band of many foldlines, plus
7cm-wide discolouration band

E – Ridge foldmark

F – Three valley foldmarks
One ridge foldmark

G – Valley foldmark

155

exactly where the 'doubled in four' reconstruction dictated that it should [fig. 19].[16]

Furthermore, from the slightly uneven way that these creases fall and the fact that there is an evenly spaced bunch of four at one particular location, STURP's Dr John Jackson has even very convincingly reconstructed how the doubling in four followed a particular order that included part of the Shroud being folded around a square-shaped block of wood that would have run its full width.[17] As Jackson further deduced, if the Shroud were kept in a casket slightly wider than its full width and there were a mechanical device for pulling it upwards from the fold line level with the front shoulders, then the Shroud body would appear to raise itself jack-in-the-box style from its casket in exactly the manner Robert de Clari reported of what he saw at the church of St Mary at Blachernae [fig 20].

It is perhaps difficult for us modern-day sceptics to imagine the awe that such a 'rising from the tomb' would have had for those few deemed worthy to view it while the cloth was in Constantinople. Not only could such a scenario readily account for some of the Grail stories of the crucified Christ appearing in all his wounds at exclusive Masses, but the gadgetry involved is typical of Byzantine ingenuity. Foreign ambassadors attending the Constantinople court are known to have reported with astonishment how one moment the emperor would be enthroned before them at only a moderately elevated level, then the next magically whirled aloft to the ceiling, with even a change of garments. Mechanical lions would roar. At Robert de Clari's Blachernae the veil on a particularly precious icon of the Virgin Mary was made 'magically' to part every Friday. Without doubt the Byzantines had the necessary skill to create a dramatic 'rising from the tomb' of our Shroud, if they possessed it. And all the signs are that they did.

So if we accept, at least provisionally, that the cloth of Edessa and our Shroud could have been one and the same, is there any more evidence of this identity as we track back yet further in time, to the years before the cloth's transfer to Constantinople in 944? Indeed there is. During the three immediately prior centuries the cloth's historical existence was essentially as well recorded in Edessa as we found it to have been in Constantinople. In this regard it is important to visualise Edessa not as the totally Islamic place that (as Turkish Urfa), it is today [pl. 40a], but instead as bristling with already historic Christian churches, despite its Moslem occupation from the seventh century. The many churches, representing

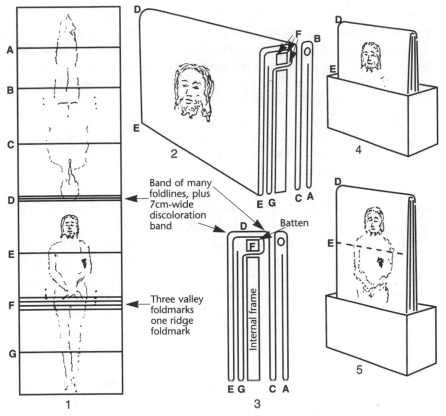

Fig 20 'The Shroud ... every Friday raised itself upright'
From the fall of its foldmarks, a suggested reconstruction of how the Shroud could have been made to rise upright from its casket in the manner that the Crusader Robert de Clari described of the 'shroud' he saw in Constantinople in 1203: (1) The Shroud foldmarks, as deduced by Dr John Jackson; (2) Reconstruction by Dr Jackson, based on the foldmarks, of how the Shroud may have been wound around a batten at point F; (3) Dr Jackson's plan of the Shroud's folding arrangement inside its casket; (4) First stage of the Shroud appearing to raise itself upright; (5) Second stage of the Shroud appearing to raise itself upright. Although exactly how the cloth was made to rise is necessarily conjectural, the Byzantines delighted in gadgetry of this kind, and Dr Jackson has produced a yet-to-be-released full-scale reconstruction of how this was technically possible

though they did some bitterly divided denominations, were a reflection of Edessa's fame throughout the Christian world both for its cloth imprinted with Jesus's likeness and for the story of its very early conversion to Christianity.

The biggest and most beautiful of the churches was the cathedral, completely rebuilt and redesigned after an earlier one was destroyed in a disastrous flood in 525. And it was in this cathedral that our cloth of Edessa came to be stored in its own special chapel with its own caretaker, brought out once a year or so for a special ceremony, but too holy ever to be shown publicly in the manner of the Lirey and Turin Shroud. A hymn datable to 569[18] likens the colour of the cathedral's marble to that of 'the image not made by human hands', a common way of describing the imprint on our Edessa cloth, and this is the earliest positive reference to its historical existence during this period.

Frustratingly, however, for the first time in our tracking back, and whether or not the cloth of Edessa was one and the same as our Shroud, there have survived from this period no *direct* artistic copies of it, even freehand, of the kind that we noted at Sakli, Spas Nereditsa, Gradac, etc. There can be little doubt that this was because of the great debate reverberating at this time, the Iconoclastic controversy, concerning the permissibility of representing Jesus at all. What seems to have happened is that the cloth likeness was translated into an acceptable *indirect* image of Jesus as Pantocrator, or Ruler of All.

Certainly it seems no coincidence that it was precisely from the time of the cloth of Edessa's emergence as a historical object – tradition had it that it was found above a gate when the Persians were besieging Edessa in 544 – that there appeared in art the distinctive front-facing Christ likeness remarked on at the beginning of this chapter. And the affinities of this likeness, even back in the sixth century, to the face on our Shroud (alias the cloth of Edessa), are very striking indeed.

As but one demonstration, though worth citing, because they inevitably carry a date far firmer than any radiocarbon dating, are the gold coins of the Byzantine Emperor Justinian II, who had two reigns, the first between 685 and 695, the second between 705 and 711.[19] Justinian was the first Christian ruler ever to mint coins with Jesus's facial likeness on them and in doing so, in what is thought to have been AD 692, he had his coin engraver display the Jesus face on the coins' obverse or 'heads' side, with Justinian's own standing image, in palpable inferiority, on the 'tails' or reverse. A splendid specimen of one of these gold *solidi* is in the museum at St Gallen, Switzerland [pl. 38a], and the general resemblance to the face on the Shroud, particularly given the tiny size of the coin, is quite astonishing. Numbers of these superbly crafted coins are to be found in numismatic collections all over the world.

A clearly painted variant of the same likeness, and dating even earlier, can be seen on a Christ Pantocrator icon in St Catherine's Monastery, Sinai [pl. 38b]. Among the several indications that this dates to the sixth century, accepted by specialists such as Princeton University's Professor Kurt Weitzmann, are that it was painted using a special encaustic wax technique, the methodology of which subsequently died out. Again, the most striking parallels to the Shroud face can be pointed out. An American researcher, Dr Alan Whanger, has developed a special polaroid projection technique that has shown up some one hundred and seventy points of 'congruence' between this and the Sinai icon.[20]

But is there some way, perhaps akin to fingerprinting, to demonstrate the absolutely specific influence of the Shroud, and no other, on such early Christ likenesses? Indeed there is. Even before World War II the French scholar Paul Vignon most exhaustively traced numerous recurring oddities on such early portraits, features such as a raised eyebrow, a 'V' shape between the eyebrows, an enlarged left nostril, a heavy line under the lower lip, a transverse line across the throat and much else [pl. 39b], all of which seemed to indicate some common source of inspiration and all of which, as Vignon showed, corresponded to identical features to be seen on the Shroud [pl. 39a].[21]

To recount these again here would be wearisome, particularly as I addressed them at length in my first book. However, one example may serve for the rest. Behind an insignificant-looking locked door in the via Alessandro Poerio in Rome's Trastevere district is one of Rome's lesser-know catacombs, that of S. Ponziano, and deep within this, just above a steeply descending walkway lined by bone-filled burial niches, can be seen a fresco of a Christ Pantocrator [pl. 39c] of the essentially identical kind to that on Justinian II's *solidi* and reliably datable to the same period. At Christ's eyebrows (though lamentable neglect has caused recent fading), the artist painted a distinctive topless square, starkly geometrical and quite at variance with the naturalism of the rest of the portrait.

Why should the artist have chosen such an odd way to represent the eyebrows? On the Shroud, readily visible in exactly the equivalent place, is precisely the same topless square. But might this be just another feature which the Shroud's mediaeval forger incorporated to give his image extra authenticity? Hardly, since the Ponziano catacomb was closed down in AD 820 and not reopened until well after the Middle Ages. In a very real sense, therefore, the Ponziano catacomb Pantocrator represents the exact equivalent of Robinson Crusoe's finding the footprint of someone other than himself on his supposedly uninhabited island. It tells us that instead of there being no evidence for the Shroud before the 1350s, it really was in existence as early as the sixth and seventh centuries. And if it indeed was, then it can hardly have been other than the cloth of that time that we have called the cloth of Edessa.

Giving rise to what is automatically the next question: what do we know about the even *earlier* origins of the cloth of Edessa? Is it remotely possible that this might even be traceable all the way back to the very time of Jesus?

Chapter 12

Could the Shroud even date back to the time of Jesus?

I f our Shroud really were one and the same as the Byzantines' cloth of Edessa, then of one thing we can be sure: no Byzantine would have been in any doubt about it dating back to the time of Jesus. For them the cloth's origins were obviously and incontrovertibly linked with the world-famous story of Edessa's evangelisation back in the time of King Abgar. And although Edessa had had several kings of this name, for them the Abgar in question was the one who was Jesus's direct contemporary.

Yet even for the Byzantines, tracking the cloth of Edessa back in time was not without its difficulties. Just as we 'lost' (and have yet properly to find), the Shroud during the period from the 1350s back to 1204, so they 'lost' the Edessa cloth before the sixth century. Except that in their case it was obvious where it had been. According to the story of its finding, as enshrined both in the Official History and some fine icons [pl. 40b], it was discovered 'above the city gates' of Edessa, having apparently been deliberately hidden there at some earlier period. Reportedly two other objects were with it, the first a piece of tile bearing the same facial likeness as on the cloth (this would become a revered relic in its own right, called the Keramion); and the second an old oil lamp.

According to the Official History it was a bishop of Edessa who made this discovery during the historically known siege of Edessa by Persian forces under the Kusraw (or Chosroes) I in 544. Purportedly the bishop was guided to find the cloth via a dream, then when he did so, it helped miraculously to rout the Persians. But although a similar story was told by the ecclesiastical chronicler Evagrius in c. 593, the more secular Procopius, writing almost contemporaneously with the siege, made no mention of a miraculously imprinted cloth playing any part. The date of 544 cannot therefore be considered certain. All we can be sure of is that at least as early as c. 569 the Edessa cloth was being referred to as already extant, as if it had been so for some while, whereas in 521 the very prolific Edessan

161

scribe, Jacob of Serug, died without having accorded it a mention. Furthermore, when we look back to earlier writers who might have been expected to refer to it, such as the peripatetic Spanish abbess, Egeria, who wrote a detailed account of her sightseeing visit to Edessa *c.* 383, we hear of her having been shown statues of Abgar and his son, but nothing about any cloth bearing Jesus's imprint.

So how far back in time are we expected to believe that our Shroud, alias the cloth of Edessa, might have lain in some niche above one of Edessa's gates? Edessa was in fact hardly the safest place for it to be hidden during the centuries immediately preceding, and including, the sixth. Edessa's local river, the Daisan or 'Leaper' had unpredictable tendencies to live up to its name, as a result of which the town was flooded, with 30,000 fatalities, in 525.[1] From Edessa's highly-respected 'Chronicle' we also learn of similar major floods in 413, 303 and 201, this earliest occasion, when 2000 died, apparently also having damaged the nave of the 'church of the Christians', information notable in itself as possibly the first record of the existence of a purpose-built and obviously tolerated Christian church anywhere in the world.

Now clearly our Shroud, if it was one and the same as the cloth of Edessa, would actually have to have been in some high, and dry, location, such as above a city gate, to have survived all these disasters. If it was kept above Edessa's west gate, as tradition indicates, then it would indeed have been safe. The original location of this is known: it stood on higher ground than other areas of the city [see map, fig. 21]. But why should a piece of cloth that, as we have seen, became so highly prized by Byzantium's emperors, have been hidden away like this in the first place? And why in such a curious hiding-place? This necessarily presupposes some time before the sixth century, when Christians in Edessa found themselves in such extreme danger that they were unable even to flee the town, leading them to some very desperate measures to ensure the cloth's long-term safety. It also implies that prior to this danger there had been at least some establishment of Christianity in Edessa. In fact, the traditional story of Edessa's evangelisation, one that became most widely disseminated from Iran in the east to Britain in the west, not only involved such a scenario, it is also as tangled and riven with controversy as anything that we have so far had to deal with concerning the Shroud proper.

For it is the story's undoubted garbling directly as a result of its widespread early popularity that has understandably more than a little undermined its credibility among scholars of the present day. Thus the most

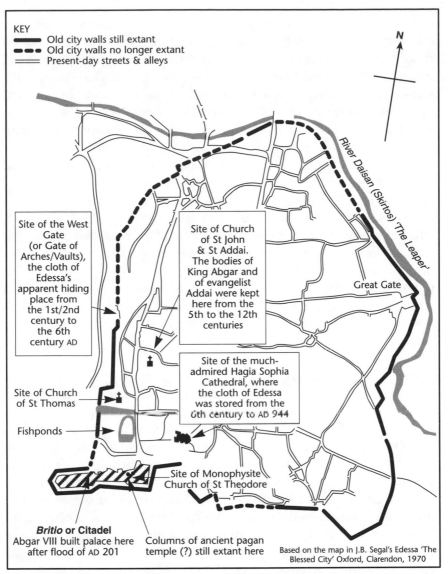

N

River Daisan (Skirtos) 'The Leaper'

Site of the West Gate (or Gate of Arches/Vaults), the cloth of Edessa's apparent hiding place from the 1st/2nd century to the 6th century AD

Site of Church of St John & St Addai. The bodies of King Abgar and of evangelist Addai were kept here from the 5th to the 12th centuries

Great Gate

Site of Church of St Thomas

Fishponds

Site of the much-admired Hagia Sophia Cathedral, where the cloth of Edessa was stored from the 6th century to AD 944

Site of Monophysite Church of St Theodore

Britio or Citadel
Abgar VIII built palace here after flood of AD 201

Columns of ancient pagan temple (?) still extant here

Based on the map in J.B. Segal's Edessa 'The Blessed City' Oxford, Clarendon, 1970

Fig 21   Edessa – Home of the Shroud for nearly a thousand years?
The topography of Edessa, based on a map of Urfa as it is known today, showing the sites of some of the city's major Christian and other landmarks as these existed at the time that it was home to the cloth of Edessa (arguably) alias the present-day Turin Shroud. Once a major place of Christian pilgrimage, today the city is 100% Moslem, with all historical traces of Christianity deliberately obliterated (Based on the map in J. B. Segal's *Edessa: 'The Blessed City'*, Oxford, Clarendon Press, 1970).

complete of the surviving original Syriac manuscript versions, a late fourth century *Doctrine of Addai* text preserved in St Petersburg,[2] is very demonstrably badly corrupted. This has Edessa's King Abgar, sick with an incurable disease and hearing of Jesus's healing 'miracles', send, via a messenger called Hanan, a letter to Jesus entreating him to cure him of his disease. On Hanan's reaching Jerusalem he reads Abgar's letter to Jesus, to which Jesus responds that although he cannot come in person 'because that for which I was sent here is now finished and I am going up to my Father', he will send a disciple who will cure Abgar and convert him and his entourage to 'everlasting life'. By virtue of being Abgar's court painter as well as his messenger, Hanan then paints Jesus's likeness 'with choice paints', which portrait he brings, with Jesus's message, back to Edessa, where it is 'placed with great honour' in one of the royal palaces.

As the text goes on, after Jesus's ascension St Thomas fulfils Jesus's promise by sending Addai, one of the seventy-two 'outer circle' of disciples[3] to Edessa. On Addai's arrival he is taken by a fellow Jew, Tobias, to Abgar's court whereupon, at the very moment of Addai's entry, Abgar alone sees a 'wonderful vision' upon Addai's face. Amazed, he prostrates himself at Addai's feet, declaring his belief in Jesus, and is cured of his disease the moment Addai lays hands on him.

Abgar and his courtiers are then given some lengthy Christian instruction, in the course of which they are told an equally lengthy story of how 'Protonice', apparently a widow of the Roman Emperor Claudius, went to Jerusalem, where she found both the site of Jesus's crucifixion and his tomb, this latter still containing three crosses. Addai then preaches to all the citizens of Edessa at an open space called Bethtabara, urging them to abandon their former pagan, idolatrous ways. After this, Abgar approvingly urges Addai to build a Christian church, even some of the city's chief priests becoming moved to pull down their traditional sacrificial altars, with the notable exception of 'the great altar which was in the midst of the city'. Likewise, large numbers of inhabitants of the surrounding countryside are converted. At gatherings of these new Christians the 'Old and the New Testament' are read, together with a book called the 'Diatessaron'. One 'Narsai', a neighbouring 'king of the Assyrians' is described as becoming sympathetically interested, likewise the Roman Emperor Tiberius, who duly punishes 'some of the chiefs of the Jews' for their part in Jesus's crucifixion.

After several years Addai dies a natural death, to widespread sorrow, with Abgar honouring him as if he were one of his own dynasty by burying him in a large, ornamentally sculptured sepulchre. As leader of Edessa's Christians, Addai is succeeded by Aggai, maker of the royal tiaras and one of the many 'converts', and for a while all continues to go well for Christianity, until King Abgar's death. Despite his eldest son and immediate successor continuing his father's pro-Christian policy, a more 'rebellious' son succeeds, who quickly reverts to the old religion and insists on Aggai making him a traditional pagan-type tiara. When Aggai refuses, this son orders his legs to be broken, so swiftly bringing about Aggai's death that he has no time to appoint his obvious successor, Palut, in his stead. This necessitates Palut going to Antioch for its bishop, Serapion, to lay his hands on him; Serapion, we learn, having received his bishopric from Rome's Pope Zephyrinus.

Now what has immediately to be recognised is that the story as given in this fourth-century *Doctrine* manuscript is, at best, shot through with anachronisms and interpolations pertaining to a time significantly later than that of Jesus. For instance, the term 'New Testament' only properly came into being with the African Church Father Tertullian, who lived between *c.* 160 and *c.* 220. The work called the Diatessaron, a conflation of the four gospels into a continuous narrative, was compiled by the Syriac writer Tatian, quite possibly actually in Edessa, no earlier than 160. The story of the finding of the True Cross by Protonice, widow of Claudius, seems to derive from the western legend of this having been discovered by the Emperor Constantine the Great's mother, Helena (*c.* 255 to *c.* 330).[4] The Serapion mentioned as bishop of Antioch held that see only from AD 199, while Pope Zephyrinus had his pontificate between 198 and 217. As for 'Narsai, king of the Assyrians', by which the *Doctrine*'s author would have meant Narseh, head of Edessa's neighbour-state Adiabene, he lived at the same time not as Abgar V, Jesus's contemporary, but as Abgar VIII, whose reign was between 177 and 212.

It is equally apparent, however, that many elements of the story have an authentic period ring. There is good knowledge, for instance, of Edessa's geography and traditional pagan religion. With regard to the fatal dispute over the royal tiara, this item of headgear was indeed extremely important to Edessa's kings, repeatedly being featured on their coins.[5]

So it is perfectly feasible that all these anachronisms and interpolations may simply represent accretions to an original story of Edessa's that may not necessarily go back quite as far as the time of Jesus, yet which cannot be far short of it either. Around AD 325, for instance, Bishop Eusebius of Caesarea, who is often referred to as the father of Church History, wrote in his *History of the Church* an abbreviated account of the same events. This lacks the anachronistic references to the Diatessaron, Pope Zephyrinus and so on. and also any mention of the portrait of Jesus purportedly painted by Ananias. Yet it again talks cryptically of a 'wonderful vision' that appeared to Abgar alone when Addai[6] had his first meeting with him. And before quoting verbatim from the letters between Abgar and Jesus, Eusebius matter-of-factly assures us that: 'Written evidence of these things is available, taken from the Record Office at Edessa, at that time the royal capital. In the public documents there, embracing early history and also the events of Abgar's time, this record is found preserved from then till now.'[7]

According to Eusebius, then, there were in Edessa's Record Office documents supportive of at least the essentials of the Abgar story that dated from substantially before the Romans annexed Edessa to their empire in AD 214, and therefore presumably free from the interpolated elements.

Whatever we may make of Eusebius's testimony (and historians generally express their admiration for his shrewdness and dependability), one indisputable fact is that there was indeed an Abgar who was king of Edessa in AD 30. He was Abgar *Ukkama* (the Black), a Syriac name which Eusebius specifically reproduces. He is usually numbered as Abgar V and historically his reign is known to have been from 4 BC to AD 7, then from AD 13 to AD 50. He was therefore Jesus's exact contemporary and whatever date we may put upon Jesus's crucifixion, which cannot have been later than the end of Pontius Pilate's governorship in AD 36, he outlived this by at least fourteen years. Yet of his religious affiliations absolutely nothing is known outside the Abgar legends themselves to suggest that he may have been even mildly receptive to Christianity. He issued no coins with his own likeness, only that of whichever Parthian overlord to whom he owed suzerainty. And his only appearance in the *Annals* of the Roman historian Tacitus is as a 'deceitful ruler' whose main claim to fame was having sufficiently diverted a young prince whom the Romans wanted as their puppet-king of Parthia for Parthia's rightful king, Gotarzes, to be able to capture him and send him away minus his ears.

While none of this necessarily negates Edessa's conversion having happened in Abgar V's reign, it certainly fails to offer much confirmation either. However, an altogether different situation pertains to the long reign of Abgar the Great, who is generally numbered VIII of the Abgars, from 177 to 212. As we have already seen, Edessa must have had a properly tolerated Christian church in this Abgar's reign, since this is specifically recorded as being damaged in the flood of AD 201. As we have also seen, many of the 'interpolated' names mentioned in the fourth-century *Doctrine* manuscript – Serapion, Pope Zephyrinus, etc. – were people who flourished in this particular Abgar's reign. Also, Abgar VIII is known to have abandoned the cultic castration that formed one of the more barbaric elements of his people's traditional rites.

Perhaps the most fascinating feature, however, is what we find happening to his coinage.[8] For in the time of his father Ma'nu VIII, who had gained his throne by pursuing a pro-Roman, anti-Parthian policy, Edessa's copper coins typically featured the reigning Roman emperor on the obverse or 'heads' side, and Ma'nu wearing an unornamented tiara on the reverse. When Ma'nu died and Abgar VIII succeeded him, the pro-Roman policy continued and Abgar adopted for his official forenames the names Lucius Aelius, in honour of the reigning Roman Emperor Lucius Aelius Commodus, a broadly tolerant individual greatly influenced by his pro-Christian wife Marcia.

Far more spectacular, however, is what he ordered for his tiara, the tiara that, as we learned from the *Doctrine* story, was so important to an Abgar as a statement about himself. On his earliest coins we see Commodus's head on the obverse, with Abgar on the reverse, wearing a plain tiara. But then, quite fascinatingly, there occurred a dramatic change. He suddenly had himself represented wearing a tiara quite unmistakably ornamented with a distinctive solid-armed cross [pl. 41a].

Was this a declaration of his Christianity, and a very bold one too, given that executions by crucifixion were still widely practised by the Romans? When Commodus was assassinated, to be followed, after a period of confusion, by Septimius Severus, who had no known Christian sympathies, Abgar reverted to a significantly more cautious approach, sometimes having his tiara represented plain, sometimes decorated with pellets forming a cross-like shape, and sometimes with an ostensibly pagan-style crescent ornament, except that mixed up with stars, the setting often featured one, two or three crosses [fig. 22]. It was as if he were deliberately blurring the issue of whether he was or was not a full Christian.

Historical caution, just like Abgar's own, prevents us from claiming totally conclusively the cross on Abgar VIII's tiara to be a Christian cross, even though it would be of no small interest if this were the case, since it would be easily the first example in all history of a monarch displaying the Christian cross as part of the very headgear of his or her monarchy.

But if we cannot claim full proof, the cumulative evidence at least for Christianity's toleration in Edessa during Abgar VIII's long reign is

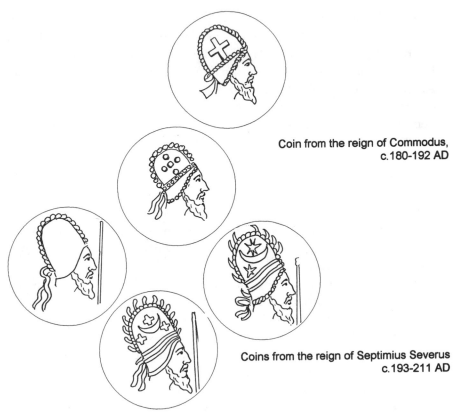

Coin from the reign of Commodus,
c.180-192 AD

Coins from the reign of Septimius Severus
c.193-211 AD

Fig 22 Edessa's king Lucius Abgar VIII's mysteriously changing tiaras
The changing tiaras of Edessa's king Lucius Abgar VIII, as displayed on examples of his
copper coinage issued under Roman suzerainty. While he overtly displays the Christian cross
on his tiara during the reign of the tolerant Roman emperor Commodus, during the reign
of the harsher Severus, Lucius Abgar's religious affiliations become much more blurred.

overwhelming. Noteworthy in the Edessa chronicle account of the flood
damage to the 'church of the Christians' is that this very phrase suggests
that Christianity was not the official religion of state, but was none the
less fully tolerated. By the same token the fourth-century *Doctrine* carefully
acknowledged that although many pagan altars were torn down, the city's
great central one was not. Abgar VIII was therefore quite definitely the
sort of monarch who might have created a sufficiently favourable climate
for Christians to convince someone that his city was the safest place to
bring the Shroud. And given that the art of Edessa, under heavy Parthian
influence,[9] was characterised by rigidly frontal-facing likenesses, the rigidly

front-facing Shroud face could have been considered almost made for the city.

But does this mean to say that it was Abgar VIII, not Abgar V, who was the true Edessan monarch behind Edessa's conversion, and was the entire saga of Hanan, Addai, Aggai, etc. all therefore an invention? Not necessarily. It was, after all, the Romans who took over Edessa almost immediately following Abgar VIII's death; there then ensued some quite definite persecution of Edessan Christians, particularly under Diocletian, in a period of suppression that had its own documentation and its own martyrs. And this appears to have been quite distinct from the persecutions of Addai, Aggai, etc., whose fate would seem definitely to have been at the hands of one of the Abgar dynasty [see fig. 23], and in the context of traditional Edessan rather than Roman paganism. Furthermore, whoever Addai was, he was certainly sufficiently real for his tomb continuously to be described as an Edessan landmark from as early as *c.* 190 to when a particularly destructive breed of Turkish invaders effectively obliterated all such Christian monuments in the mid eleventh century.[10] And what were believed to be his bones were also kept with ones supposed to be those of Abgar V. Accordingly, given that the language of Edessan Syriac was very close to that of Jesus's Aramaic, and that Edessa had a flourishing Jewish community in Jesus's time, there is nothing inherently impossible in Edessa having been evangelised very shortly after Jesus's crucifixion along something of the lines that the story suggests.

There is one further, and highly relevant, insight on Edessa's earliest Christian origins that has only recently come to light, thanks to some brilliant pioneering on the part of American Dan Scavone [pl. 41b], Professor of History at the University of Southern Indiana at Evansville.[11] Moreover, it intriguingly links the origins of the Grail story with the evangelisation of Edessa.

We may remember observing earlier that the Grail seems to have been a holy receptacle for the body and blood of Jesus that was very firmly linked with Joseph of Arimathea. We may also recall how this was closely associated with a very special vision, reserved for a select few, which sometimes took the form of a disembodied head of Christ, sometimes a full body covered with wounds of crucifixion. Although this suggested something to do with the Shroud, hopelessly complicating it were major elements in the mainstream twelfth- and thirteenth-century versions that Joseph of Arimathea had brought the Grail to Britain, and that Britain's King Arthur and his knights (who, if they were historical at all, were five

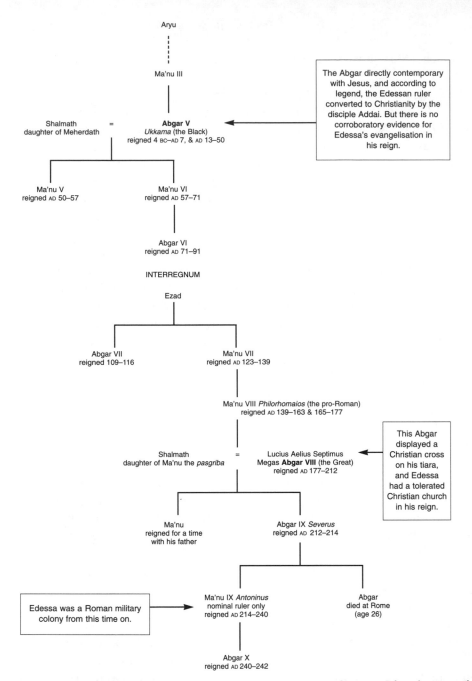

Aryu

Ma'nu III

Shalmath
daughter of Meherdath = **Abgar V**
Ukkama (the Black)
reigned 4 BC–AD 7, & AD 13–50

The Abgar directly contemporary
with Jesus, and according to
legend, the Edessan ruler
converted to Christianity by the
disciple Addai. But there is no
corroboratory evidence for
Edessa's evangelisation in
his reign.

Ma'nu V
reigned AD 50–57

Ma'nu VI
reigned AD 57–71

Abgar VI
reigned AD 71–91

INTERREGNUM

Ezad

Abgar VII
reigned 109–116

Ma'nu VII
reigned AD 123–139

Ma'nu VIII *Philorhomaios* (the pro-Roman)
reigned AD 139–163 & 165–177

Shalmath
daughter of Ma'nu the *pasgriba* = Lucius Aelius Septimus
Megas **Abgar VIII** (the Great)
reigned AD 177–212

This Abgar
displayed a
Christian cross
on his tiara,
and Edessa
had a tolerated
Christian church
in his reign.

Ma'nu
reigned for a time
with his father

Abgar IX *Severus*
reigned AD 212–214

Edessa was a Roman military
colony from this time on.

Ma'nu IX *Antoninus*
nominal ruler only
reigned AD 214–240

Abgar
died at Rome
(age 26)

Abgar X
reigned AD 240–242

**Fig 23   The kings (or toparchs) of Edessa, from the time of Jesus to Edessa's annexation
by the Roman Empire**
It can be seen how from the historical perspective the story of an Edessan king's conversion
to Christianity followed by a second son reverting to paganism better suits the reign of
Abgar V than of Abgar VIII, even though there is much more direct evidence for the latter's
Christian leanings.

centuries removed from Joseph of Arimathea), were somehow an integral part of the story.

It was this problem that led to Dan Scavone probing the earliest roots of the Grail stories, with some quite astonishing results. First he began enquiring into why Joseph of Arimathea, a figure consistently most closely identified with Jesus's burial shroud in the gospels and early apocryphal writings, came also to be associated with the Grail in mainstream Grail writings in the twelfth and thirteenth centuries. In the course of these researches he came across a little-known Georgian manuscript of the sixth century[12] that quite specifically and unmistakably described Joseph as collecting Jesus's blood, not in any chalice or dish, as in the later stories, but in a shroud. In the words of this manuscript, in which Joseph speaks in the first person: 'But I [Joseph] climbed Holy Golgotha, where the Lord's cross stood, and collected in a headband *and a large sheet* [my italics] the precious blood that had flowed from his holy side.'[13]

To Scavone this seemed to be a 'missing link' in the Grail story, indicating that the Grail's true origin might be Jesus's shroud. This would certainly accord with Joseph of Arimathea's close association with it. But if this were the case, how on earth did King Arthur and Britain ever get themselves into the story?

First Scavone found that because St Philip had been thought to have evangelised France, this could easily have led to the supposition that Joseph of Arimathea, with whom he was first linked in the same Georgian manuscript, continued on to Britain to evangelise that country. Except, as Scavone discovered, the idea of Philip's evangelising France was actually a mistake due to a ninth-century French bishop's having misread a reference to Galatia in Turkey, where St Philip is far more reliably known to have evangelised and been buried, as *Gallis* or Gauls, the old name for the people of France.

But how might any misreading for Britain have come about? The clue lies in Bede's eighth-century *History of the English Church and People* which reported Britain's evangelisation as deriving from a British king called Lucius sending a letter to Pope Eleutherus (AD 175–89) asking to be made a Christian, a request which Eleutherus duly followed up.[14]

So where did Bede get his information? And who was King Lucius? First Scavone traced Bede's source to an almost identical passage concerning Pope Eleutherus compiled for the official *Liber Pontificalis*, or Book of the Popes, and dating *c.* 530. This then led him to some findings by the great German Biblical scholar Adolf Harnack,[15] who had no clue of any possible

171

relevance to the Turin Shroud. As determined by Harnack, the *Liber Pontificalis* copyist, in transcribing from whatever earlier document had lain before him, had misread one vital word, 'Britio'. Although both in the early centuries, and now, it would have been very easy to assume that this meant 'Britain', in fact, as Harnack knew from a surviving fragment of the otherwise lost *Outlines* of the early Christian theologian Clement of Alexandria (*c.* AD 150–216), the tombs both of St Thomas and of Edessa's reputed evangelist Addai were reportedly in '*Britio Edessenorum*'. And this had nothing to do with Britain. Instead it meant the *Britio*, or to give its Syriac equivalent *birtha*, that is, the castle or citadel of the Edessans, a cliff-like landmark of present-day Urfa immediately to the city's south [pl. 41c].

But if Bede's Britio was not Britain, but Edessa, who was King Lucius? As determined by Harnack, there never was any British king called Lucius. Instead, this had to be Lucius Aelius Abgar, our Abgar VIII, the first monarch in all history known to have had sufficient interest in Christianity that he could indeed have written to Pope Eleutherus, one of his direct contemporaries, asking for Christian evangelists to come to his city. Arguably, it may have been upon these two simple mistakes, made back in the sixth century, that there evolved the whole idea of Britain's evangelisation by Joseph of Arimathea, upon which became superimposed King Arthur's involvement and ultimately the whole tangle of Grail legends as these are known today.

But does this mean that the whole story of Edessa's evangelisation, in its turn, hailed from Abgar VIII writing to Pope Eleutherus rather than Abgar V writing to Jesus? Again, not necessarily. The very strong evidence for Edessa's Christian evangelisation in Abgar VIII's reign at the end of the second century does not mean that something very similar could not have happened earlier in the reign of Abgar V. All it does mean is that while the evidence of Christianity in Edessa in the reign of Abgar VIII may be considered nearly good enough for history, whatever of this kind that may have happened in the reign of Abgar V must still remain legend.

But what about the cloth of Edessa/Shroud? Arguably, it is no coincidence that during the particular period of some three or more centuries in which it would have lain, whereabouts unknown, in its niche above Edessa's gate (whoever put it there presumably having been killed during the time of persecution, hence its non-recovery), Christian art was at its vaguest concerning what Jesus looked like, and this despite this same period's comparative proximity to Jesus's own lifetime. Thus by far the greater majority of portraits of Jesus from this time show him as a beardless youth, as in many catacomb frescos, also in the fourth-century mosaic discovered on the floor of a Roman villa at Hinton St Mary, Dorset. And although there are a few bearded examples, such as in the catacombs of Commodilla and Ss Peter and Marcellinus, these are vague and markedly lacking in the Shroud-like frontality of the later, 'authoritative' Christ portraits. It is seemingly as if they derived just from some vague oral tradition of Jesus's human appearance, there being not a jot of guidance to this in the gospels.

This same disappearance of our Christ-imprinted Edessa cloth, at whatever early date, may also well account for why the one single literary reference to it during this time, that in the already acknowledgedly garbled fourth-century *Doctrine of Addai* text, unequivocally describes it as painted 'with choice paints', in the teeth of the unanimous opinions from the sixth century on (when at least some privileged individuals were definitely able to see the original for themselves), that this was an 'impression', an image 'made without hands', a cloth seemingly miraculously imprinted with a 'moist secretion without colouring or painter's art'. In this instance, therefore, we need take no account of the fourth-century 'painted with choice paints' description, despite the fact that it is actually the earliest of all to survive, since we have good reason to believe that the author could never have seen what he was talking about. Instead, what is important is that he mentioned any kind of portrait at all, since it means that there must have lingered even into the fourth century a memory that some special portrait of Jesus *had* earlier been brought to Edessa during the time of the Abgars. Certainly this was what the Byzantines recognised in the sixth century when, high above one of Edessa's gates, they found the cloth that we have labelled the Edessa cloth (and which we believe to have been the Shroud), and hailed it immediately as having been made in some totally mysterious way by the very body of Jesus himself.

Many details, of course, have to remain speculative. What was the 'wonderful' vision seen by Abgar, mentioned even in Eusebius's more interpolation-free version of the story? Given the Grail stories' cryptic vision of a Christ covered in wounds, could Abgar privately have been shown the Shroud (he is described as having 'alone' seen the vision), this being instrumental in his conversion?

If our Shroud was the cloth of Edessa, why was it folded and mounted on a board in the 'doubled in four' arrangement we reconstructed? Could this have been specifically to disguise its nature as a gravecloth? If Addai, or whoever, had wanted to show Abgar what Jesus looked like, wouldn't it have been natural for him to present it as a kind of portrait, thereby making it more manageable size-wise, the face in any case being the Shroud's most readily meaningful feature? And if this were the case, it would of course explain all the subsequent misleading misconceptions that the imprint was created while Jesus was alive.

As for the time of persecution, why did someone decide to hide the cloth above one of Edessa's city gates and why was a 'twin' image of Jesus on a tile found with it when it was rediscovered? These two questions may actually have a single answer. Because it was typical of Parthian rulers to display images of their 'gods' above their cities' gates,[16] Abgar may well have ordered a ceramic, or 'tile', version of Jesus's likeness, obviously based on the Shroud likeness (something along these lines is actually confirmed in the Official History). Then, when at the time of the persecution the 'rebellious' successor ordered this removed, what more practical ruse than for some life-threatened early Christian to prise the tile out, slip the Edessa cloth/Shroud behind it, then replace it face inwards, thereby making good the gateway's outward appearance once more?

Whatever the answer, here we have at least a plausible explanation for how our Shroud, whether brought to Edessa in the reign of Abgar V or Abgar VIII, might have been rediscovered in the sixth century in the manner described in the last chapter. As a result of which, instead of there being absolutely no record of our Shroud before the 1350s, as is so often contended, we have been able historically to trace an object that sounds and looks most uncannily like it, almost all the way back to the very time of Jesus himself. The idea of the Shroud having been located in Edessa and Constantinople for its first 1200 years checks out perfectly with a significant number of Dr Max Frei's pollens indicating that it spent some time in an Anatolian environment [fig. 10, p. 102]. And this is in addition to our having found, earlier in this book, so much compelling evidence for the Shroud being an actual gravecloth of a Jew crucified in the manner of Jesus, including many suggestions that it originated in Jesus's time.

All this inevitably gives rise to the question, can anyone any longer be quite so sure of radiocarbon dating's claim 'conclusively' to have proved the Shroud a mediaeval fake? Can we really still believe in a mediaeval forger?

Of course, it may still be difficult to conceive that the radiocarbon dating of 1988, as conducted by three internationally respected scientific laboratories, could have erred by as much as 1300 years. But is it not time, now, to look just a little more critically at the technique's own credibility when its scientists so confidently claim 'accuracies' to within a hundred years or so?

Part 4
Carbon Dating:
Right or Wrong?

Chapter 13

'Odds of one in a Thousand Trillion'?

J ust in case all that hot and dusty tracking back through nearly 2000 years of history got your blood racing with optimism for the Shroud's authenticity, how about a quick cold shower? According to Professor Harry Gove [pl. 42a], prime inventor of the state-of-the-art accelerator mass spectrometry method that was used to carbon date the Shroud, the very same scientific criteria that provide a ninety-five per cent degree of probability in favour of the Shroud's manufacture between 1260 and 1390 also provide odds of 'about one in a thousand trillion'[1] *against* it dating back to the time of Jesus. Feeling refreshed?

Now Professor Gove is an amiable and intelligent man whom I know and greatly respect. Numbers, even ones in trillions, hold real meaning for him and he doesn't claim such daunting odds lightly. Yet the Shroud aside, can we really believe that *any* scientific test can carry *that* degree of confidence in its accuracy? And particularly carbon dating, despite the air of supra-papal infallibility that those who understand it (and even those who don't), confidently impart to it.

Highly important, if we are even to begin to question radiocarbon dating's trustworthiness, is that we understand at least something of the principles upon which it is based. This is that all living things, in their taking-in of carbon dioxide, also take in, as a tiny proportion of this, the radioactive isotope carbon 14, which is continually being formed in the upper atmosphere. After carbon 14's filtering down into the air we breathe it becomes, via photosynthesis and the food chain, an integral part of all plant and animal life. Whatever living organism we may be, while we are alive its proportion to our stable, non-radioactive carbon will be maintained at about one part in a trillion. Then, when we die, our carbon 14, being radioactive, begins to decay, reducing its proportion to the stable carbon (carbon 12) in whatever may be left of us. And since the halfway stage of this process, better known as the half-life, is known to be around

5730 years, if centuries after we die someone measures the proportion of carbon 14 to carbon 12 in whatever remains of us (whether this be bone, wool, leather, wood, linen or grains of rice), it is theoretically possible for them to work out the year we died, rather like reading off the time from a conventional clock.

The first man to realise the usefulness of this for archaeology, the University of Chicago's Willard F. Libby, hit upon the idea during four years' development work on the first atomic bomb. After adapting the Geiger counter into an apparatus to 'count' the rate of decay, he began running archaeological samples through it in the late 1940s, among the first of these linen wrappings from the then recently discovered Dead Sea Scrolls. As so-called 'carbon dating' developed from these early beginnings it was gradually realised that Libby's original calculation of 5568 years for radiocarbon's half-life was wrong and that it should be 5730 years. From comparative work with wood samples of known age (because of their tree-rings), it also became clear that, instead of the radioactive decay being a steady fall-off, as Libby had assumed, in practice variations in cosmic-ray activity had caused some fluctuations at different periods. Although this necessitated a recalibration that is now routine for every radiocarbon-dating test, in no way did such adjustments undermine Libby's fine achievement and in 1961 he was very deservedly awarded a Nobel Prize for the whole new branch of science that he had founded. Intriguingly (and this has only recently been learned from Italian sources), it was almost immediately following the award of this prize to Libby that he asked permission to radiocarbon date the Shroud.[2] In the event, despite his impeccable credentials, his request was turned down, on the not unreasonable grounds that far too large a piece of the cloth – no less than 870 square centimetres – would have needed to be destroyed for this purpose.

The die was, however, cast, and as succeeding generations of scientists refined the original dating methods so that smaller samples became needed, it was inevitable that calls for the Shroud to be radiocarbon dated would increase. By far the most dramatic of such refinements occurred in May 1977, when Professor Harry Gove and two colleagues successfully experimented with a process whereby, instead of the months'-long counting of beta particles' emissions that the Libby method required, they used the University of Rochester's massive accelerator mass spectrometer to separate and count the actual number of radiocarbon atoms. Although Gove and his colleagues' initial 'samples' were merely some barbecue charcoal and some graphite, from their very first results they knew that the process worked. Not only could it be done in just a few minutes, but the size of sample needed was a thousand times smaller than anything previously required, without the slightest loss of accuracy. Hardly had an article breaking the news of this method appeared in *Time* magazine before the Revd David Sox, then General Secretary of the British Society for the Turin Shroud, sent a confidential letter to Professor Gove to test out his interest in the process being used for the Shroud.

Gove's initial response to Sox was that his method was really still too much at the developmental stage for him to be able to accept samples for dating. However, when in October 1978 the Turin authorities staged an international conference alongside the expositions and examination held in that year, Gove attended to argue for his method being used as soon as the time was right. On his way to Turin he called in at Oxford University's Research Laboratory for Art and Archaeology, which he knew to be developing a new radiocarbon-dating unit based on his method, and on his merely mentioning the Shroud project to the laboratory's director, Professor Edward Hall, Hall unhesitatingly declared his enthusiasm to 'get in on the act'.[3]

With the American STURP team's positive scientific work coming under increasing challenge from Walter McCrone during the ensuing years, the need for the new method's use on the Shroud became more and more pressing. Additional to the Oxford and Rochester laboratories, the accelerator mass spectrometer laboratory at Tucson, Arizona, together with the proportional counter laboratory at Brookhaven, New York (which had been developing a stretched version of the Libby method), now declared themselves enthusiastic to participate. Even when the Shroud's former owner, ex-King Umberto of Italy, died in March 1983, bequeathing the Shroud's ownership to the Pope, this seemed but a minor setback to the growing optimism that the Shroud's submission to carbon dating would only be a matter of time.

Thus when on 1 June 1985 at Trondheim Norway Drs Tite and Burleigh, both then of the British Museum, presented the results of an inter-comparison experiment conducted on textiles apportioned between four accelerator mass spectrometer laboratories (Oxford, Tucson, Rochester and Zurich) and two proportional counter ones (Brookhaven and Harwell), this was confidently regarded as opening the way for a radiocarbon dating of the Shroud. With this very aim Gove then took charge of organising a special exploratory meeting between these laboratories, with the British

Museum as co-ordinator. By way of acknowledgement of the Shroud's new ownership, Gove invited the President of the Pontifical Academy of Sciences, Professor Carlos Chagas, to be the meeting's chairman.

As anyone might, Gove felt such a move to be the very model of diplomacy, but he failed to appreciate that almost any Shroud dealings favouring Rome provoked deep resentment from those in Turin, particularly the Cardinal's chief scientific adviser, Professor Luigi Gonella, who had co-ordinated much of the 1978 testing. Thus when British journalist Peter Jennings made public that he knew the June date of the confidential exploratory meeting that Gove had arranged, Turin had its excuse for demanding a calling-off of the whole plan. In the immediate aftermath some extremely heated telegrams flew between the US, Britain, Turin and Rome, with even myself becoming called upon to act as an intermediary to soften some of the more ill-considered remarks that the English-speaking laboratories' heads had hurled in the Italians' direction. After allowing the dust to settle Professor Chagas re-scheduled the meeting and under his chairmanship, generally recognised to have been exemplary, a set of recommendations for the Shroud radiocarbon dating were drawn up, to become known as the 1986 Protocol.

This Protocol recommended that the time was now right for the carbon dating, and that the seven radiocarbon-dating laboratories interested in being 'in on the act' (to the former six had been added France's Gif-sur-Yvette), should all be allowed Shroud samples of the size sufficient for their purposes. The target date for the taking of samples was set for 10 May 1987 and for logistical reasons it was recommended that this be done 'immediately before' further experiments that had already long been planned by several interested groups as a follow-up to the STURP work in 1978.

As set out in the Protocol, the person chosen to perform the sample removal was the well-respected Swiss textile specialist Mme Mechthild Flury-Lemberg of the Abegg Foundation in Bern. She was given clearly to understand that she should select sites away from charred areas, also away from the image and from any other area of obvious information value. It was agreed that the British Museum, as represented by the head of its Research Laboratory, Dr Michael Tite, would act in a supervisory capacity. To make the test properly scientifically 'blind', Dr Tite was to use his Museum connections to provide at least two suitably ancient 'control' samples per laboratory, additional to the Shroud and of very similar weave, so that the laboratories should not know which of their samples came from the Shroud.

This Protocol also stipulated that the laboratories would not charge for their work, and would submit their results for analysis by the Pontifical Academy, the Turin Institute of Metrology and the British Museum, who would only inform the media after the analysis had been carried out. This set of proposals having been agreed by all at the meeting, including Turin's Cardinal Anastasio Ballestrero, it was then formally submitted to the Pope.

Five days after the meeting the Turin newspaper *La Stampa* announced, obviously with full authority, that the 'Protocol' meeting had been held and that the Pope had given his approval to its recommendations that all seven laboratories date the Shroud. But what became evident during the succeeding weeks, as the May 1987 target date began to look less and less achievable, was that there was some intense politicking going on behind the scenes. Some of the radiocarbon-dating laboratories, now within a whisker of getting the go-ahead they had been waiting for, began to voice their disapproval of the idea of other scientific experiments being carried out on the Shroud at the same time as theirs, concerned that these might steal some of the thunder from their work.

Another person also highly concerned about his thunder being stolen was Professor Gonella, who in interminable telephone calls to me and others spoke of Professor Chagas as if he were public enemy number one, rather than the Pope's most senior scientific adviser. As early as April 1987 there were indications of the direction his mind was taking when, in an interview with *La Stampa*, he imparted that only two or three laboratories would be involved in the testing.

Then on 10 October the real bombshell struck with a letter from Cardinal Ballestrero to the seven 'appointed' institutions, informing them that only the Oxford, Arizona and Zurich laboratories would take part in the testing. This decision he had apparently taken on Gonella's advice that these laboratories had greater 'experience in the field of archaeological radio-carbon dating'. He had also decided that the Pontifical Academy of Sciences (and thereby Professor Chagas), should have no further part in the project. Likewise thrown out was any participation by the textile expert Mme Flury-Lemberg. The British Museum's Dr Michael Tite was now to be the man to have sole overall responsibility for the project's international scientific credibility.

As a demonstration that real hands-on power over the Shroud rested not with Rome but with Turin, the Cardinal's letter and its scrapping of the 1986 Protocol stunned even the three chosen laboratories and in an initial joint response drawn up by Arizona's Professor Douglas Donahue they declared themselves 'hesitant to proceed' and urged 'further consideration' of the decision.

But this hesitancy was as nothing compared with the outright ire of the rejected Professor Harry Gove, who had spent nearly ten years bringing the project into being and was now not even to have a look-in. Suspecting that part of Gonella's motivation had been a deliberate slight to him for bringing in Chagas, Gove first fired off a letter to the Pope (useless, as he anticipated), then on 15 January of 1988, in partnership with Garman Harbottle of the Brookhaven laboratory, issued a press release detailing the decision's many irrationalities.

Contradicting, for instance, Gonella's argument that the three chosen laboratories had greater experience dealing with archaeological samples, Gove and Harbottle pointed out that 'the Harwell laboratory, left out, has had more experience than the three chosen laboratories put together'. They also confided that during the preparatory inter-comparison exercise of 1985 it had been the chosen Zurich laboratory which had committed a serious error, causing a misdating of 1000 years. As they concluded: 'The Archbishop's plan, disregarding the Protocol, does not seem capable of producing a result that will meet the test of scientific rigour' and 'it is probably better to do nothing than to proceed with a scaled-down experiment'.

Had the three chosen laboratories held their nerve and insisted that the original Protocol be maintained, history might have been very different. But as Gonella rightly anticipated 'the prize was too great', particularly for the Oxford laboratory's Professor Hall, who was in a fight-to-the-death struggle with the Harwell laboratory (still using the old Libby method), for the controlling share of the UK's radiocarbon-dating work. When Gonella merely hinted that if the three chosen laboratories declined to co-operate he might bring in Italy's Pisa and Udine laboratories, they duly capitulated.

As early as 22 January – little more than one week after Gove's press conference – Arizona's Damon and Donahue, Oxford's Hall and Hedges, and Zurich's Wölfli all met up with Gonella in the British Museum's Board Room to work out the final details of how and when they would take the samples.

Up to the day of this meeting STURP and other Shroud groups had been encouraged by Gonella to formulate what had become very elaborate

plans for ancillary testing work on the Shroud, utilising the rare opportunity of it being out of its casket. For instance, the British Society for the
Turin Shroud's intended programme included hands-on involvement by
Scotland Yard forensic scientists and world-class experts in ancient textiles,
and it had been envisaged that this work would be carried out immediately
after the removal of the samples for the carbon-dating laboratories. Following the British Museum meeting, however, Gonella let it be understood
that these plans all had to be scrapped. The radiocarbon-dating laboratories
thereby had total exclusivity, ensuring that whatever result might be
arrived at, the publicity would be theirs and theirs alone, with no other
possibly conflicting findings to interfere with it.

The rest, as they say, is history. As we learned in the very beginning of
the book, the samples were taken on 21 April 1988 and during the ensuing
months were processed by the three laboratories, all very closely in touch
with each other because they used the same radiocarbon-dating method,
amidst ever more insistent 'leaks' that the result would date the Shroud
to the Middle Ages. Then on 13 October 1988 came the official announce-
ments that they had found the Shroud to date, with a ninety-five per cent
degree of confidence, to some time between 1260 and 1390.

Gove, who had known the result in advance (having been present as an
invited guest the day Arizona processed their sample), somewhat forgot all
his earlier warnings that the test as conducted by just the three laboratories
would not meet 'the test of scientific rigour'. In a private bet on the
outcome he had won himself a pair of cowboy boots, and consoling
himself that it was his accelerator mass spectrometer method that had
been used by all three laboratories, he declared the result to be a 'triumph'[4]
for this technique. From his enthusiasm, one might be forgiven for thinking that it had been his method that was being tried and tested, not the
Shroud.

On the other side of the Atlantic, Professor Hall was similarly upbeat.
In a lecture provocatively entitled 'The Turin Shroud: A Lesson in Self-
Persuasion' he told a packed audience of the British Museum Society in
London that radiocarbon dating had so conclusively proved the Shroud
to be a fake that anyone who continued to believe it genuine had to be a
'Flat Earther'. And in the March of 1989 his efforts to drum up the
maximum publicity reaped their rewards when he was able to announce
(for publication on, of all days, Good Friday) that his laboratory's future
was secure. Following his retirement from the Oxford laboratory, this was
now to be awarded a permanent professorship, financed with a million

185

pounds donated by forty-five rich businessmen. Who was the person chosen for this post? Dr Michael Tite.

It is only fair to say that the seeming unchallengeability of the radio-carbon-dating verdict, so forcefully put over by Tite, Gove, Hall, and via them by the world's media, stunned almost everyone who had favoured the Shroud's authenticity, including myself. There was simply no immedi-ately available explanation for how such a verdict could be wrong, if indeed it was wrong. The best response seemed to be quietly to bide time while someone worked out either, if the carbon dating was right, exactly how the Shroud was forged, or, if it was wrong, how three internationally respected laboratories could have committed such a huge error.

Unfortunately some of the more hot-headed enthusiasts for the Shroud's authenticity in continental Europe did not have such patience, particularly in the light of their interpretations of Dr Michael Tite's elevation to the Oxford professorship. They launched into a succession of unedifying conspiracy theories, mostly emanating from the French priest, Brother Bruno Bonnet-Eymard who, as I noted at the very beginning of this book, outrightly accused Dr Tite of having switched fourteenth-century cloth for the Shroud samples at the time that he packed these in their coded canisters out of sight of any videocameras. And as I stressed back then, and will continue to do now, this totally unworthy and unfounded type of allegation will form no part of my argument.

Even so, it is important for us to understand at least some of the background 'facts' that the conspiracy theorists have twisted, not least in order to eliminate them from the argument. For instance, it is an unde-niable fact that on the very day of the taking of the samples Frenchman Gabriel Vial of the Textile Museum, Lyon, whom Gonella had invited as token textile specialist in place of Mme Flury-Lemberg, unexpectedly brought with him an extra 'control' sample, in the form of a piece of a late-thirteenth-century cope that had once belonged to St Louis d'Anjou. Although some of the conspiracy theorists looked to this as being what Dr Tite 'switched' for the true Shroud samples, the fact is that this was of plain-weave linen, quite different from the Shroud's herringbone. It also happened to have been supplied in the form of threads, not the whole fragments we know the laboratories to have received.

Providing further fuel for the conspiracy theorists was the fact that the Turin microanalyst Giovanni Riggi, Gonella's friend and personal choice to perform the actual cutting of the Shroud samples in place of Mme Flury-Lemberg, seems to have had something of a hidden agenda. Instead of cutting off just the sample that was needed by the laboratories, he would cut off twice the amount, halve it, and divide only one of the halves into three for the laboratories, retaining the other. On his discovering that he had made the Arizona portion too small to meet the agreed weight, he snipped off a small portion from the retained piece. Arizona thus received its sample in two parts (for a complete scheme of this apportionment, see fig. 24). It is also little known that he kept the trimmed edges, trimmings that are no longer extant. There is some dispute in Turin concerning whether he did this with official approval, though photographs of the trimmings that I have seen certainly show Cardinal Ballestrero's seal. As for the rest of the retained portion, probably enough to do another carbon dating, whoever may have this and where it is is by no means clear, though it is said to be personally held by Cardinal Saldarini.

None of this was initially declared. It only emerged when *Nature's* report that the Shroud sample cut off measured 70 × 10 mm – a seemingly exact figure in a report dealing in seemingly exact measurements – was found to be irreconcilable with the amounts that the laboratories had actually received. Complicating matters further, although the scientists at each of the radiocarbon-dating laboratories photographed their Shroud samples when they opened them up on bringing them back – necessary, as the samples would be destroyed by the carbon-dating process – some photographed one side, some the other, and without including any scale.

Such discrepancies were therefore all that were needed for two German conspiracy theorists, Holger Kersten and Elmar Gruber, to concoct a new and yet more elaborate scenario whereby, although the Shroud is genuinely of Jesus and dating from the first century, Dr Michael Tite and certain high officials at the Vatican plotted together to make sure it would be found to be otherwise. Purportedly, what the Vatican officials had wanted to keep hidden at all costs was the shock secret, known of course only to them, that the Shroud proves that Jesus did not die on the cross and that therefore the whole Resurrection story is a hoax, a secret that, if it ever got out, would lose clergy their jobs and destroy all Christianity. Hence it was apparently in the Church's interest for the Shroud to be proved a fake.

Such is the age we live in that the Kersten–Gruber book achieved a wide distribution. Its central argument does not, however, merit even the slightest serious consideration, as ought to be obvious, not least from the Church's recently demonstrated absolute determination, against all the odds, to hold the two intendedly full-blooded Shroud exhibitions of 1998 and 2000 very much as if the Shroud is still the genuine article. Kersten's and Gruber's claim that the samples the laboratories received did not fit together and were therefore not from the Shroud is readily disproved by the plan showing how all the samples do fit, reproduced here as fig. 24.

Let it be a hundred per cent clear, therefore, that I am in not the slightest doubt that the Shroud radiocarbon dating was conducted honestly, by scientists of the highest competence, on the Shroud itself and in accord with the best available scientific methods. Nor am I in much doubt that if the Shroud were radiocarbon dated again tomorrow, the same result would be arrived at. It is perhaps worth noting that Professor Douglas Donahue of the Arizona laboratory, the first man to know the result, is a practising Catholic and genuinely had high expectations that the Shroud would be found to be of the first century. Likewise, his close colleague Professor Damon is a practising Quaker. These men had every reason to uphold a first-century result, if that was the way their technology pointed.

However, I most seriously question the near-infallibility that almost everyone, including scientists, journalists and lay people, has imparted to this same result. It is as if, because it had been produced by a nice, clean, high-tech method, and by highly professional, hard-nosed scientists claiming margins of error of little more than a hundred years, everyone must blind themselves to everything else that had been deduced regarding the Shroud and accept this single scientific test as the ultimate arbiter, overriding all else.

But should we? Had the laboratories unanimously produced a first-century result in the way that they produced the fourteenth-century one, surely one thing that would have come under the most intense scrutiny would have been the abandonment of the 1986 Protocol. As we may recall, one of the stipulations of this, in line with any well-conducted scientific experiment, was that suitable 'control' samples should be provided so that the receiving laboratories, of whatever number, should not know which of their samples was the true Shroud.

As we have already learned, the Shroud's three-to-one twill weave is so unusual that despite strenuous efforts on Dr Tite's part – and he even approached me for help at one point – it proved impossible to obtain anything of identical weave to the Shroud, either of first- or fourteenth-century date, for use as controls. As a result, controls of different weave had to be used instead, meaning that the laboratory staff had no difficulty recognising which sample was the Shroud, the original idea of a proper 'blind' test necessarily, therefore, having to be abandoned.

This is accepted, just as it is also accepted that it was perfectly legitimate

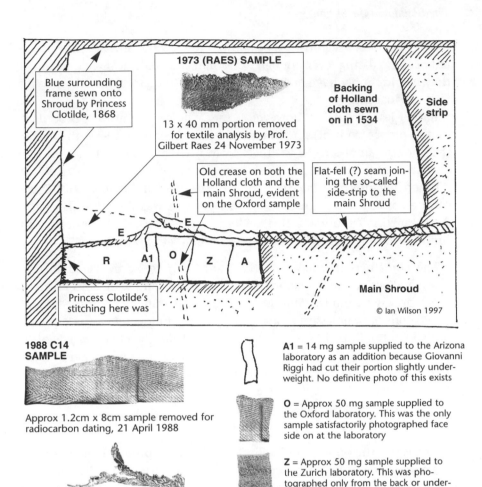

1973 (RAES) SAMPLE

Blue surrounding frame sewn onto Shroud by Princess Clotilde, 1868

13 x 40 mm portion removed for textile analysis by Prof. Gilbert Raes 24 November 1973

Backing of Holland cloth sewn on in 1534

Side strip

Old crease on both the Holland cloth and the main Shroud, evident on the Oxford sample

Flat-fell (?) seam joining the so-called side-strip to the main Shroud

E

E

R   A1   O   Z   A

Princess Clotilde's stitching here was

Main Shroud

© Ian Wilson 1997

1988 C14 SAMPLE

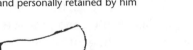

Approx 1.2cm x 8cm sample removed for radiocarbon dating, 21 April 1988

E = Edges trimmed away by Giovanni Riggi and personally retained by him

A1 = 14 mg sample supplied to the Arizona laboratory as an addition because Giovanni Riggi had cut their portion slightly underweight. No definitive photo of this exists

O = Approx 50 mg sample supplied to the Oxford laboratory. This was the only sample satisfactorily photographed face side on at the laboratory

Z = Approx 50 mg sample supplied to the Zurich laboratory. This was photographed only from the back or underside at the laboratory

A = Underweight 40 mg sample supplied to the Arizona laboratory. A definitive photograph exists of only a portion of this

R = Portion apparently retained unused and in Cardinal Saldarini's care

Fig 24   How the Shroud sample that Giovanni Riggi cut off on 21 April 1988 became apportioned

This plan not only shows the falsity of German writers Kersten and Gruber's claims that the samples received by the radiocarbon-dating laboratories could not fit the piece of Shroud cut away by Riggi, it also corrects Riggi's own original plan of the apportionment, in which he omitted to note his initial under-measure for Arizona. The samples are shown approximately actual size. The radiocarbon laboratories were each able to subdivide their individual portions into three or four smaller portions for individual radiocarbon-dating runs, exemplifying the very tiny amount of sample needed when using the accelerator mass spectrometry method.

for the laboratory scientists to be allowed to view the Shroud prior to the radiocarbon dating, even though in normal archaeological circumstances they would simply have had the samples sent to them, rather than going to the actual site.

Rather less acceptable, however, is that whereas the normal procedure in any proper 'control' situation would have been for at least the age of the control samples to be withheld from the dating laboratories, in this particular instance, and for reasons that have never been made clear, Dr Tite actually informed the laboratories of the dates of their controls. There can be absolutely no doubt about this, for this was the wording of the certificate that Tite and Cardinal Ballestrero gave to each laboratory's head simultaneous with their handing over of each set of samples:

> The containers labelled ... 1 ... 2 and ... 3 to be delivered to representatives of [named laboratory] contain one sample of cloth taken in our presence from the Shroud of Turin at 9.45 a.m., 21 April 1988 and two control samples from one or both of the following cloths supplied through the British Museum: *first-century cloth; eleventh-century* [cloth]. The identity of the samples put in the individual containers has been recorded in a special notebook that will be kept confidential until the measurements have been made.
>   [signed] Anastasio Ballestrero
>   Michael Tite[5]

Nor is this the only cause for disquiet. The 1986 protocol laid stress on the care which Mme Flury-Lemberg should exercise when choosing the location from which the samples for the radiocarbon dating should be taken. Yet despite all the years of apparent planning for the taking of the carbon-dating samples it was not until the very moment itself that Gonella and Riggi chose this location – after a very public, heated and protracted argument witnessed and attested by the entire contingent of bemused radiocarbon-dating scientists.

They could hardly have chosen anywhere much more unsuitable than they did (image areas excepted). For if we go back to the very first principles of radiocarbon dating, these include as fundamental that any sample should consist of purely the original organic matter (in the case of the Shroud, its once-living flax), in as unadulterated form as possible. As long ago as the 1960s Vera Barclay, then a doyenne of British Shroud research, was warned by two scientists of the Harwell radiocarbon-dating laboratory that the Shroud might be far from ideal from this point of view. As she was told by the laboratory's Dr J. P. Clarke: 'There appears to be some doubt as to whether the carbon content of the material has remained constant over the years. It would be an assumption of any dating that no carbon exchange had taken place by perhaps the addition of something at a date later than that of the fabrication of the Shroud.'[6]

Likewise Harwell's P. J. Anderson told her:

The history of the Shroud does not encourage one to put a great deal of reliance upon the validity of any C14 dating. The whole principle of the method depends upon the specimen not undergoing any exchange of carbon between its molecules and atmospheric dioxide, etc. The cellulose of the linen itself would be good from this point of view, but the effect of the fires and subsequent drenching with water ... and the possibility of contamination during early times, would, I think, make the results doubtful. Any microbiological action upon the Shroud (fungi, moulds, etc., which might arise from damp conditions) might have important effects upon the C14 content. This possibility could not be ruled out.

That such concerns have been far from eliminated by more modern methods is quite evident from a recent booklet by Dr Sheridan Bowman, Michael Tite's successor as Keeper of the British Museum's Research Laboratory, in which she lists the sorts of conservation and packing materials that archaeologists should avoid using when sending their samples for processing by a radiocarbon-dating laboratory: 'Many materials used for preserving or conserving samples may be impossible to remove subsequently: do not use glues, biocides ... [etc.] Many ordinary packing materials such as paper, cardboard, cotton wool and string contain carbon and are potential contaminants. Cigarette ash is also taboo.'[7]

It is worth reminding ourselves here of the variety of already listed carbon-containing materials with which the Shroud maintains daily contact, e.g. a sixteenth-century holland cloth, a nineteenth-century silk cover – quite aside from the innumerable candles that have been burnt before it, the water that was thrown over it at the time of the 1532 fire, and so on. And those are merely the events we know about.

But now we come to the decision that Gonella and Riggi arrived at after their argument: to take the sample in the form of one single sliver from the frontal image bottom corner closest to the side-strip [pl. 43a]. This must be regarded as misguided in the extreme. For yet another major cause of possible contamination of a radiocarbon-dating sample arises

191

from any excessive handling to which it may have been subjected at times distant from when it originated. And when we study the hundreds of depictions of the Shroud being held up before the crowds during past centuries, what do we see? In example after example [pls 43b & c, also 30a & 31a] a cleric's hand can be seen holding up the Shroud at, yes, the frontal image bottom corner closest to the side-strip. While it would be quite wrong to suggest that it was contamination from hundreds of sweaty hands at this corner which actually caused a 1300-year error in carbon dating it remains irrefutable that Gonella's and Riggi's choice of this location was ill considered. Also, while their wisest decision would have been to take several tiny samples from scattered areas, by opting for just this single site they ensured that any contamination error, however large or small, would be bound to be repeated by all three laboratories.

Equally ill considered, and the blame must be laid squarely at the door of Gonella, was that the three laboratories chosen should be ones using the same accelerator mass spectrometer method, rather than that at least one should use the stretched version of the Libby proportional counter method. Even Dr Walter McCrone, looking at the subject from the point of view of possible (to him) aberrant early dates being produced, remarked to me in a letter seven years[8] before the radiocarbon dating, that 'it would seem desirable if possible to obtain a date using these two different methods'. Since the Oxford, Arizona and Zurich laboratories are essentially clones of each other, any result obtained by one of them would inevitably be obtained by them all.

Although radiocarbon-dating laboratory scientists are notoriously chary of admitting it, carbon dating can produce results with errors considerably wider than their quoted margins, a fact well known to archaeologists. A prime example of this was Lindow Man, the well-preserved body of a sacrificial victim unearthed from a peatbog in Cheshire, England in 1984. Samples from this body were sent to three different British radiocarbon-dating laboratories: Harwell, which dated him to around the fifth century AD; Oxford, which dated him to around the first century AD, and the British Museum, which dated him to the third century BC.[9] Although each laboratory claimed its dating to be accurate to within a hundred years, in actuality their datings varied between each other by as much as 800 years, the discrepancy remaining unresolved to this day, with each institution insisting that its estimate is the most accurate.

Another example concerns ancient Egyptian Mummy No. 1770 in the collection of the Manchester Museum. When back in the late 1970s the noted Egyptologist Dr Rosalie David and colleagues scientifically unwrapped this mummy [pl. 42c] and sent samples of its body tissues and bandages off for carbon dating, the British Museum's carbon-dating laboratory produced the astonishing calculation that the bandages were 800 to 1000 years younger than the body they wrapped.[10] While one possible explanation could be that the mummy was re-wrapped 1000 years after its first burial, Dr David does not think so.

Archaeologists, who routinely call upon radiocarbon-dating laboratories' services, tend to shy from openly criticising the results they receive, even if they do not necessarily agree with some of them, but one who certainly has had no such qualms is Greece's Spyros Iakovidis, speaking at an international conference in 1989: 'In relation to the reliability of radiocarbon dating I would like to mention something which happened to me during my excavation at Gla [in Boeotia, Greece]. I sent to two different laboratories in two different parts of the world a certain amount of the same burnt grain. I got two readings differing by 2000 years, the archaeological dates being right in the middle. *I feel that this method is not exactly to be trusted.*'[11]

Nor are such examples isolated and anecdotal. In the same year of 1989 Britain's Science and Engineering Research Council commissioned a special inter-comparison trial for radiocarbon-dating laboratories in which altogether thirty-eight different laboratories took part, collectively representing both the conventional Libby method and the accelerator mass spectrometer one. Each laboratory was given artefacts of dates known to the organisers, but unknown to them. The shock finding of this totally scientific trial was that the laboratories' actual margins of error were *on average* two or three times greater than those that they quoted. Of the thirty-eight who participated, only seven produced results that the organisers of the trial considered totally satisfactory, with the laboratories using the new accelerator mass spectrometer technique faring particularly badly.[12] It is also a matter of record that the Oxford laboratory [pl. 42b], inevitably the highest profile of any, actually declined to take part. Yet this is the method that we are supposed to believe 'conclusively' proved the Shroud a mediaeval fake.

This is not to say that any of the possible sources of contamination that have been pointed out in this chapter were necessarily *the* reason why the Shroud radiocarbon dating erred by thirteen centuries, if indeed this was the case. As we will be learning later in this book, there is another possible source of error that even the science of 1988 would have been some way from anticipating.

Rather, the point of major concern is that the radiocarbon laboratory scientists, in their eagerness to present a copybook example of the accelerator mass spectrometer method's prowess before the world, seriously neglected to take due account of any way in which their findings might be wrong in respect of the Shroud. In the *Nature* report they described their findings as 'conclusive'. Professor Hall, in his post-dating lecture to the British Museum, most ebulliently derided any suggestion of how his laboratory's findings might be in some as yet undetermined way mistaken. And this even though neither he nor any of the other laboratory scientists could offer any properly thought-out explanation for how the Shroud image might have been made in the century they claimed it to be made.

Accordingly, while I would unhesitatingly defend the laboratories against the sorts of charges of which they have been accused by Bonnet-Eymard, Kersten, and Gruber and their confrères, altogether less defensible is the sheer hubris with which they have represented their carbon dating as in effect infallibly providing an arbiter for the issue of the Shroud's authencity, such that all other considerations may be dismissed as of no account. Anyone who is in the slightest doubt of this hubris needs only to read Professor Harry Gove's recently published book *Relic, Icon or Hoax? Carbon Dating the Turin Shroud*. As a highly detailed and accurate diary-type account of all the cut-and-thrust politicking leading up to the carbon dating and the announcement of its results, I cannot recommend it too highly. It is worthy of a Samuel Pepys. But it is also most illuminating regarding the radiocarbon scientists' overwhelming confidence that they alone possessed the key that would unlock the answer to the Shroud mystery. And of the Shroud itself, and the utterly valid question of how, if the carbon-dating method really is right, someone of the fourteenth century produced a fake that 'good', one looks in vain for the slightest light on this in Gove's book. Professor Hall said likewise that this question was of absolutely no interest to him and he would be giving no thought to it.

But the Shroud simply cannot be left in such limbo. The carbon-dating verdict was either right or it was wrong. And if it was right, just how *could* someone have produced something like it back in the fourteenth century?

Chapter 14

If the carbon dating is right, could the Shroud be the work of a mediaeval artist?

I f the radiocarbon-dating verdict of 1988 really is right, then we do not have to look far for historical clues concerning how the Shroud was faked. According to Bishop d'Arcis, writing closest of anyone to the radiocarbon-dating scientists' date for the Shroud, it was 'cunningly painted' just a generation before his time. As d'Arcis insisted, we should simply regard it as 'a work of human skill, and not miraculously wrought or bestowed'.

But what artistic 'cunning' and 'skill' would need to have been involved, purely from the point of view of the translation of the image to the 'canvas'?

As the STURP examination found, whatever constitutes what the eye sees as the 'body' image, whether this is iron-oxide pigment, as McCrone would contend, or some form of degradation of the Shroud's surface, as favoured by most of the STURP scientists, it is undeniably a mere 'surface' phenomenon, affecting purely the topmost fibres, with no apparent penetration to any depth. Whatever method may have been used for applying this 'surface phenomenon' to the cloth, it exhibits nothing of the directionality that artists normally cannot help betraying as they move their brush from one side to another when conventionally painting a canvas. And even if for the sake of argument we allow that some kind of 'paint' might have been used in this manner, not only has this to have been vanishingly lightly applied, it also has to have been both insoluble and thermally and chemically stable, since there is no evidence either of 'paint run' from the water used to douse the fire of 1532, or any kind of melting from this same fire and that of 1997. Likewise the STURP tests showed it firmly resistant to bleaching and other standard chemical agents. All this is in addition to the image being only properly meaningful when viewed in inverse, or negative light values, its medical, anatomical, historical and cultural accuracies.

Even so, can we at least try to conceive of an artist of some time around the 1350s who might have managed all this? One man who has certainly found no difficulty from this point of view is Dr Walter McCrone [pl. 44a] of Chicago who, as we have seen earlier, insists that the Shroud was painted by a mediaeval artist, essentially conventionally, using a pigment consisting of billions of minute particles of iron oxide in a medium of water and collagen.

According to McCrone the way that this 'talented' artist tackled his task was that he

> ... carefully studied the New Testament, sources of information on the crucifixion and other artists' paintings of Christ. He then thought about a shroud image in terms of a dark tomb. Instead of the usual portrait with normal light and shadow, he assumed that the image could only be produced by body contact with the cloth. He painted directly on the cloth to image the body-contact points (forehead, bridge of nose, cheekbones, moustache, beard, etc., over the entire body, front and back). This automatically creates a negative image; areas that normally catch available light and appear bright, like the bridge of the nose, would instead all be dark with a paint. However, those areas appear bright on a photographic negative. He decorated the body with blood-stains as required by the New Testament descriptions. These he rendered dark on the Shroud, hence they form a photographic positive image superimposed on the otherwise negative Shroud body image.[1]

Now if only it were as easy as McCrone makes it sound! While I readily acknowledge only the haziest understanding of microscopy, I do know at least something about how to paint a human figure, and as the professional artist Isabel Piczek has already insisted (and I can only agree with her), to create a figure accurately in reverse tones in the manner described by McCrone, particularly without any means of checking your work, is frankly impossible. None the less, determined to 'prove' his point, in the early 1980s McCrone actually asked a professional artist, Walter Sanford, to paint a 'Shroud' face using the technique and pigment that he specified. Yet although all Sanford had to do was to approximate the Shroud face tone for tone, his finished result [pl. 44b] simply does not bear serious comparison with the Shroud original. Even McCrone, who first of all produced it with all the enthusiasm of having solved the Shroud mystery, seems to have accepted that it hardly advances his cause and has quietly downgraded his references to it.

196

Similarly unconvincing have been McCrone's suggestions concerning the likely identity of the artist who might have painted the Shroud image so cunningly back in the fourteenth century. His first ploy was to quote the Victorian art collector Sir Charles Eastlake who, in his *Methods and Materials of Painting of the Great Schools and Masters*, remarked on certain fourteenth-century German and English techniques of painting with extreme transparency on cloth. In Eastlake's words: 'In the Treviso record, preserved by Guid' Antonio Zanetti, mention is made of a German mode of painting (in water-colours) on cloth. This branch of art seems to have been practised on a large scale in England during the fourteenth century, so as to attract the notice of foreigners ... after this linen is painted, its thinness is no more obscured than if it was not painted at all, as the colours have no body.'[2]

Promising though this might sound as indicating that someone back in the fourteenth century could have been capable of working in the Shroud manner, in actuality there are no known surviving examples of the works mentioned by Eastlake that might or might not prove McCrone's point.

Accordingly, McCrone has more recently turned to the rather better documented mediaeval fad for *grisaille* painting, that is, painting in monochrome, most commonly, as the name suggests, in different tones of grey. Although *grisaille* seems to have begun in stained glass, a most notable example being York Minster's famous thirteenth-century 'Five Sisters' window, it was specifically during the mid 1300s that *grisaille* painting on cloth became fashionable in France.

A particularly notable example of this is the Parement de Narbonne, so called after the French city in which it was found, which was painted on silk and has been authoritatively dated by art expert Millard Meiss to *c.* 1370–75.[3] Today preserved in the Louvre, Paris, it includes lively scenes of Jesus's scourging, his carrying of the cross to Golgotha, his undergoing crucifixion and his being laid in the tomb, this latter notably including the distinctive crossed-hands pose. And intriguingly in the crucifixion scene, the centurion, innovatively depicted facing away from the spectator, can be seen to have a long plaited pigtail hanging down his back, highly reminiscent of the unbound one on the Shroud's dorsal image.[4]

Furthermore in 1991, while vacationing with his wife in Provence, McCrone came across, in the Palace of the Popes at Avignon, an intriguing Christ Pantocrator fresco [pl. 44c] that had apparently been created in 1341 for Avignon's Cathedral of Notre-Dame des Doms. The painter of this was the Italian Simone Martini who lived *c.* 1284–1344 (therefore almost directly contemporary with Geoffrey de Charny and the prime period indicated by radiocarbon dating), but what particularly struck McCrone was the fact that, as in the case of the French *grisaille* paintings on cloth, Martini had painted in a simple monochrome, in this instance in a reddish colour. Careful study revealed this to be sinopia, a red-ochre pigment used for the preparatory drawings for a fresco and obtained from sinopite, an iron ore. While McCrone does not claim that it was necessarily Martini himself who created the Shroud, nevertheless he thinks that whoever did was fairly close, both in time and place. And a remark by art expert Millard Meiss deserves noting, that the 'immediate origins [of *grisaille* paintings] . . . remain undiscoverable today'.[5]

Even so, this is a very long way from demonstrating that the Shroud image really was the work of someone from this time. Technically proficient and talented though the Parement Master and Simone Martini undoubtedly were, their figure drawings are light-years removed from the Shroud image. Although they painted in a monochrome that can be construed as akin to this aspect of black-and-white photography, in every other way they followed all the conventions of mediaeval art. Their figures have totally conventional outlines and brushmarks. Neither their lighting nor their modelling has anything even remotely photographic about it. The crossed-hands pose in the Parement Entombment (there is another *grisaille* example on a bishop's mitre) merely reflects the artistic trend of the time, one whose antecedents may well even have been dictated by the Shroud's prior emergence in Lirey. And while the Parement Master did his best to be graphically realistic in showing blood flowing from Jesus's hands, feet and side, like everyone else of his time he had no idea of the principles of gravity. The blood that is to be seen coming from the hands and from the side totally lacks the kind of realism exhibited by the Shroud bloodflows.

When in early July 1988 I visited Professor Edward Hall at the Oxford laboratory, he told me that although his recent trip to Turin had not persuaded him of the Shroud's genuineness, even so, having taken the opportunity to examine its imprint carefully with a hand lens, he thought it very unlikely to be a painting. On hearing this, I quizzed him why he did not accept McCrone's findings and he told me very candidly that he was totally unimpressed by McCrone as a scientist and thought he relied far too much on subjective visual assessments from looking through a conventional microscope. Likewise, Dr Michael Tite expressed himself unconvinced by the McCrone mediaeval-painter hypothesis, inclining instead to the view that the Shroud had been made, albeit in the fourteenth century, by someone who used a genuinely crucified human body for his purpose.

Further undermining the force of McCrone's arguments has been the discrediting of the work which won him greatest recognition, his highly publicised debunking of Yale University's Vinland Map. Just as the Shroud purports to show Jesus's dead body, so the Vinland map purports to show the Viking discovery of North America before Columbus. And although when its existence was first publicised in 1965 its authenticity was attested by a trio of distinguished scholars that included R. A. Skelton, Super-intendent of the British Museum's Map Room,[6] when McCrone was invited to examine it in 1972 he quickly came to a quite different opinion.

Initially, McCrone's suspicions were aroused by his observing that whoever had drawn the map had first outlined its land areas in a yellow ink and had then carefully added a black line on top of this. Then, when he studied samples of the yellow ink under his microscope, he spotted among these a substance that he identified as anatase, a crystalline form of titanium dioxide only developed in 1920. This identification of the map as a modern forgery[7] directly led to my seeking his expertise in respect of the Shroud.

However, the map's original investigators remained far from convinced, as a result of which in 1985 it was flown to the University of California's Crocker Laboratory, where a promising new analysis technique called proton-induced X-ray analysis (or PIXE) was being developed. This deploys a powerful cyclotron to fire a harmless beam of protons through whatever object is being analysed, generating X-rays by which all elements present can be almost instantaneously identified and quantified without recourse to any analytical eyeball. And whereas all McCrone's micro-analytical deductions had necessarily been made from near-invisible scrapings that were not necessarily representative, PIXE was able to evaluate essentially the whole object.

When applied to the Vinland Map, it indeed proved a revelation. In 1987 Crocker's Dr Thomas Cahill announced in the scientific journal *Analytical Chemistry*[8] that he and his colleagues had found the Map to contain 5000 times less titanium dioxide than the amount that McCrone had claimed, and in fact no more than could readily be found in other mediaeval documents of unquestioned genuineness. Arguing that McCrone had been quite wrong to claim that titanium dioxide/anatase could not and did not predate 1920, Cahill showed that when PIXE was used to analyse the ink of an unquestionably genuine fifteenth-century Gutenburg-printed Bible, this too was found to have quantities of titanium dioxide, likewise a string of other authentic early documents dating from between the twelfth and fifteenth centuries.

As independently discovered by Jacqueline Olin of Washington's Smithsonian Institution, anatase is a by-product of the green vitoral used in the mediaeval ink-making process. It therefore cannot be used as an arbiter of date, as McCrone had supposed. Without specifically upholding the Vinland Map's authenticity Cahill was thereby able to conclude that McCrone's reasons for identifying it as a modern fake had been fundamentally flawed.

Although McCrone has protested with characteristic vigour, insisting PIXE to be unsuitable for objects like the Vinland Map and the Turin Shroud, and that his method is still best, it is Dr Cahill's findings that have carried the day with academia, such that R. A. Skelton and his colleagues' expensive original tome on the Map has recently been reissued by Yale University, accompanied by a new Introduction by the Smithsonian Institution's Dr Wilcomb Washbourn forthrightly declaring that those who have hitherto cried 'forgery' must now 'assume a defensive role and respond to those previously on the defensive'.[9] Quite independently, Brookhaven radiocarbon-dating laboratory head Dr Garman Harbottle, in personal correspondence to me shortly before the carbon dating, commented that 'They [the Crocker Laboratory] have demonstrated to my satisfaction that ... McCrone was off by a factor of 10,000'. If, then, such distinguished academic opinion has adjudged McCrone's analysis to have been in such error in respect of the Vinland Map, clearly his findings on the Shroud can be questioned too.

Even so, McCrone's theory of how the Shroud's image may have been conventionally painted by a fourteenth-century artist is merely one scenario. Another is that although the Shroud was the work of an artist, he was not necessarily of the fourteenth century, a period artistically too undeveloped for such genius. Thus when the Shroud was examined back in 1973 by the small group of experts appointed by Turin's Cardinal Pellegrino, the lone woman among them, Noemi Gabrielli, former Director of Piedmont's art galleries, remarked: 'If we consider the [Shroud's] stylistic characteristics we must admit that this is not the same Shroud which appeared for the first time in 1356, which belonged to Geoffrey de Charny and then became the property of the Dukes of Savoy. It would appear to be a later version by about 150 years, but still predating the fire of 1532.'[10]

Put simply, the Gabrielli theory is that some time in the late fifteenth–early sixteenth century someone of the Savoy family surreptitiously replaced an earlier unconvincing de Charny shroud for one that had been specially painted at that time by 'a great artist' whose identity she did not find it too difficult to guess. In her words: 'If we compare the Shroud with the face of Christ in *The Last Supper* we find a similarity in the technique and the spirituality'. Gabrielli meant, of course, Leonardo da Vinci, and if the Shroud really is a painting, as insisted by McCrone, then despite all the evidence that we have seen against this, Gabrielli's suggestion has at least to be treated seriously. While the 1532 fire marks indicate beyond reasonable doubt that the present-day Shroud is the same as that which survived that fire, this also being inferable from the poker holes on the Lierre copy of 1516, the possibility of some surreptitious earlier switch simply cannot be ruled out. And as I wrote back in 1986 of Leonardo's possible authorship of the Shroud:

> If any artist may be said to be equal to the Shroud's anatomical expertise, that artist must be Leonardo. As no one before him, Leonardo endlessly studied and dissected dead bodies, both animal and human ... He is one of the few artists who would quite automatically have gone to the trouble of studying the contact points a body might make on a cloth, calculating the effects of gravity on bloodflows and working out the exact fall of a scourge. He is one of the few artists who would have experimented with materials to produce the subtle iron-oxide gelatin medium identified by McCrone. He is the only artist before the nineteenth century to have used a *sfumato* or smoky style of painting with something of the outlineless quality of the Shroud. Above all, more than that of any other artist, only Leonardo's work exhibits significant parallels to some of the Shroud's most enigmatic features, such as the absence of apparent brush marks and of any obvious substance.[11]

Yet none of this is to say that Leonardo *was* the Shroud's artistic creator. It is to be remembered that the radiocarbon verdict dated the Shroud to well before Leonardo's birth, requiring that he would have to have obtained a genuinely old cloth for his purpose (acknowledgedly hardly impossible), in addition to all his other displays of brilliance. The Lirey pilgrim's medallion is evidence that something very like the Shroud as we know it today existed well before Leonardo was born, quite aside from evidence such as the poker holes on the Pray Manuscript of 1192. And despite the considerable quantities of Leonardo's notes and sketches that survive, including material that he quite deliberately kept secret during his lifetime, they contain absolutely nothing to indicate his having worked on anything like the Turin Shroud. Likewise there is no sign of his having had any connection with the Savoy family, even though his famous chalk self-portrait *is* now in the Turin Royal Library.

Yet even the Leonardo theory by no means exhausts the possibilities that the Shroud was produced by the hand of an artist. Another quite recent suggestion, conjured by University of Tennessee textile specialist Professor Randall R. Bresee and his colleague Emily A. Craig, is that it may have been produced by what may be best described as a 'burnishing' technique. In 1992 Emily Craig happened to attend a lecture given by Professor Bresee in which he specifically encouraged his audience to come up with ideas of how a mediaeval artist might have produced the Shroud image and this sent Craig's mind racing. Back at her home she tried a series of experiments which led her to believe she had solved how the Shroud's 'cunning' mediaeval painter must have worked.

According to her theory, first the artist painted the Shroud's body image life-size onto a piece of paper or vellum. At this stage he would have worked perfectly conventionally, using indeed the very same finely powdered iron-oxide-in-collagen binding medium as deduced by Dr McCrone. Then came the clever part. By placing his painted paper image face downwards onto an identically sized piece of linen and rubbing it vigorously with a wooden spoon from the non-image side, he burnished its mirror image onto the linen, somewhat in the manner of a brass rubbing. By simple application of heat he would then have been able to 'fix' this permanently, very much in the manner that xerox photocopies are produced.

Having developed their idea further, Bresee and Craig published their findings in the *Journal of Imaging Science and Technology*,[12] in January–February 1994 accompanying these with the claim that their technique had historical support, the mediaeval Italian artist Cennino Cennini, in his *Il Libro dell'Arte*, having spoken specifically of 'instruction for grinding pigment into powder, brushing charcoal with feathers and *burning* an image onto cloth'. They also included in their article photographs of the demonstration 'Shroud' face that they had painted onto newsprint [pl. 45a], the result they achieved by burnishing this onto a piece of linen [pl. 45b] and the photographic negative that can be derived from this [pl. 45c]. As they were able to claim, not without justification, their burnished image was a pale, surface phenomenon only, without any obvious sign of pigment or brushmarks, and resistant to the effects of heat and water, thereby readily corresponding to these seemingly so singular characteristics of the Shroud. As for the photographic negative, they described this as 'rich in three-dimensional detail'.

Their allusion to Cennino Cennini may be set aside without difficulty. His book, genuinely full of all manner of techniques used by mediaeval artists, actually contains nothing along the lines of the method they claim to have been used on the Shroud. They have simply read far more into a single phrase than its context justifies. As for their images, these are, it must be stressed, of a face only, and it must be for the reader to judge whether even by this very limited demonstration, lacking as it is in the wounds and so much else, they have achieved any truly convincing replication. Certainly to me their face on the cloth looks just what it is, a rather amateurishly hand-painted face that has been faintly transferred to a piece of linen, thereby offering a superficial resemblance to the Shroud, but that is all. It totally lacks the Shroud's photographic quality and any three-dimensional detail.

But while we are still considering the Shroud as the work of an artist, we should also take account of the idea that rather than using a paintbrush the mediaeval faker may cleverly have deployed some life-sized statue of Jesus in a manner so as to transfer its image to a piece of linen. Professor Hall, while generally shunning taking a serious interest in how the Shroud's image might have been made, told me during our July 1988 meeting in Oxford that the one idea he did favour was this so-called 'hot statue' theory. The simple principle behind this is that a forger heated a metal statue of Jesus, then quickly wrapped a length of plain linen around it, thereby scorching the 'body' image onto it rather in the manner of a branding iron. It is an idea that has circulated for some while, having been demonstrated as early as the 1970s by the English author Geoffrey Ashe,[13] who for his 'statue' simply heated a brass ornament (one used to decorate the trappings of horses) and applied it to a piece of linen he had dampened. Even though the effect, home-spun as it was, was far from totally convincing, it was actually rather more Shroud-like than anything we have seen from either McCrone or Craig and Bresee.

Even so the 'hot statue' theory suffers from the serious problem that it demands the existence, back in the fourteenth century, of a life-size, anatomically convincing and totally nude statue of a recumbent Jesus, made in metal, that someone managed to heat to just the right temperature and manipulate so that a fourteen-foot length of linen could be wrapped all round it. We must be careful not to rule out such a possibility completely, not least since a French chronicle called the *Chronicon de Melsa* (Meaux), written *c*. 1340, describes an abbey sculptor as having carved a very realistic crucifix by studying a nude model.[14] Furthermore, a surviving tomb sculpture of King Charles V,[15] successor of the King John the Good who was Geoffrey I de Charny's patron, exhibits a naturalism indicating a sculptor of undeniably high talent being active in France at precisely the period indicated by the Shroud radiocarbon dating and the d'Arcis memorandum.

None the less even if we could accept that a mediaeval sculptor had created such a statue, in doing so he would then have had to paint in the wounds – not with whole blood, but in the mode of bloodclot transfers – so realistically that they fooled dozens of twentieth-century doctors and pathologists. And this is aside from all his other accuracies and the evidence we have seen for the existence of something like our Shroud well before the Middle Ages. Further contradicting any such 'scorch' theory is the fact that the STURP team's ultraviolet fluorescence photography of 1978 revealed that whereas the cloth's scorches from the 1532 fire fluoresce red when irradiated with ultraviolet light, the body images do not. This argues strongly against the Shroud's body image having been created in some conventional scorch-like manner.

Accordingly, despite Bishop d'Arcis, and the best efforts of McCrone, Craig and Bresee and their ilk, there really is no hypothesis of creation by the hand of a cunning painter, at least one that has been advanced so far, that even begins satisfactorily to explain the image that we see on the Shroud. As already noted, even some of the radiocarbon-dating scientists readily concur with this.

Chapter 15

Could the Shroud be of someone specially crucified in the Middle Ages?

If we regard the radiocarbon dating of 1988 as having produced an accurate date, yet continue to be convinced by all the medical evidence that the Shroud's image is that of someone genuinely crucified in the manner of Jesus, then we are pushed towards one singularly upalatable possibility: that the man we see on the Shroud is some poor mediaeval unfortunate who was tailor-crucified and laid out in death in the deliberate semblance of the way Jesus was put to death. Professor Tite favours this and according to a recent article in London's *Sunday Telegraph*, so do many present-day scientists in the wake of the carbon dating.[1]

In fact, such a theory embodies within itself two quite distinct alternatives: one, that the crucifixion was performed upon some unknown mediaeval man, living or dead, with the specific intention of thereby creating the Shroud image; the other, that the same crucifixion was performed solely in order to execute this man, the image just happening to have been produced quite unexpectedly when he was buried, and its marketability as a 'Jesus shroud' then duly seized upon.

Were the first alternative to be true, then the Shroud might justly be described, in the words of one commentator, as 'an unspeakable product of barbarism contrived in the interests of ecclesiastical commerce'.[2] However, this is substantially the more difficult of the two alternatives and probably for this reason lacks any present-day proponent who has developed it in any properly fully fledged kind of way.

Yet what can hardly be denied is that the Middle Ages were a time of almost ghoulish interest in the physical details of Jesus's sufferings, exemplified not least by the psychosomatic phenomenon of stigmata assumed by St Francis of Assisi in 1224, to be followed by many an imitator, male and female, during the subsequent centuries. The *Dunstable Annals* record how in 1222, two years before St Francis's stigmatisation, a young Englishman was tried before the Council of Oxford for having 'made himself out to be Christ and ... perforated his hands and feet.'[3] Evident from other sources is that this young man had his hands and feet pierced, somewhat in the manner of ear-lobes for ear-rings, so that he could be publicly nailed to a cross as a source of fairground-style spectacle.

Also it was notably in the 1340s – i.e. within Geoffrey I de Charny's very lifetime – that the Flagellant movement broke out in Europe, taking the form of bands of young men marching from town to town stripped to the waist, lashing each other with whips of leather tipped with metal, evoking the manner of Jesus's scourging.

But with regard to the idea that someone of the Middle Ages deliberately used an actual dead body, specially murdered or otherwise, for the purpose of faking the Shroud, it needs to be stressed that the whole ethos of the time was against it. So paramount was the mediaeval concern for the dead being given a quick and decent burial that dissections for medical research purposes were almost completely banned. The papal bull 'De sepulturis', as issued by Pope Boniface VIII (1294–1303), specifically forbade all unauthorised human autopsies under penalty of excommunication and death at the stake. Although there was some isolated flouting of this, such as at Montpellier in France, where in 1340 a biennial anatomy class was authorised, allowing a surgeon to dissect a cadaver while a doctor of medicine lectured,[4] it simply beggars belief that anyone of the Middle Ages might have gone to the lengths and risks of killing someone for the purpose of making the Shroud, when they might have made a perfectly credible and marketable 'relic' by spilling a few drops of animal blood onto an old rag.

Even if you did indeed tailor-crucify some poor unfortunate, lay him out for death still covered in blood, then wrap a cloth round him, you would not get an image like that visible on the Shroud. As endless experiments during the last decades have shown, there are always serious distortions that arise when anyone attempts to make a Shroud-like image by this otherwise seemingly obvious means. This is because the Shroud's image is not a direct-contact one, at least with regard to the body imprint. If created by a body at all, it appears to derive from something that has emanated from the body and transferred itself to the cloth even where the latter was not in immediate contact.

So what of the alternative scenario, that the Shroud was perhaps the accidental by-product of someone who just happened to have been crucified during the Middle Ages? Besides the aforementioned difficulty over the transfer of the image, which applies equally to this version, another objection has long been that crucifixion was not practised in the Middle Ages, having been stamped out in the West in the first half of the fourth century as a result of a decree by the first Christian Roman emperor, Constantine the Great.

Yet while this is true, it is equally true that crucifixion was from time to time revived by Christianity's enemies, sometimes as a means of exhibiting contempt for all that Christianity stood for. This was certainly so in the case of the Japanese, who crucified a large delegation of Christian missionaries at Nagasaki in 1597.[5] The Mexican revolutionary Emiliano Zapata is said to have crucified hated landowners on telegraph poles, and Nazi officers during World War II reportedly crucified Jews in Dachau. Yet more recently, the Turks are said to have used crucifixion as a means of torturing some of their political prisoners.

Indeed it was hearing news of this latter, just after returning from holidaying in Turkey and shortly before the Shroud radiocarbon-dating verdict, which sparked off in British physician Dr Michael Straiton's mind an idea for how the Shroud's image might have been created without anyone necessarily ever having intended any fraudulence. Straiton, a Home Counties general medical practitioner, was – and continues to be – fully convinced that the Shroud's image is genuinely of someone crucified in the exact manner of Jesus. But as he reasoned in the light of the radiocarbon-dating verdict, might the person whom we see on the cloth have been not the historical Jesus, but just some hapless Crusader who was crucified by Turks or Saracens in deliberate mockery of Jesus's crucifixion?

As noted by Dr Straiton, while the radiocarbon-dating scientists claimed in the *Nature* report on their findings a ninety-five per cent confidence that the Shroud had been woven between 1260 and 1390, they also claimed a perfectly respectable sixty-eight per cent probability for the Shroud having originated in a much narrower range of years, between 1270 and 1290.

From Straiton's wide historical interests, he knew these years to be 'the exact period' in which the Crusaders had suffered particularly heavy losses during the last stages of their struggle to prevent the taking over of the Holy Land by the Seljuk Turks. Before 1277 the Crusaders' most formidable opponent had been the Sultan Baibars, who very nearly succeeded in killing by poison the English Prince Edward, later to become Edward I. Then on Baibars's death his successors pursued ever more ruthless policies of out-and-out war against the Crusaders. In 1285 they captured the

Hospitaller fortress of Margat. Four years later the port of Tripoli fell to them, whereupon they massacred everyone left inside.

Finally, in 1291 it was the turn of the Crusaders' last stronghold, Acre. Again, the Turks showed no mercy and, as proposed by Straiton, it was most likely some time in the course of these atrocities that the Shroud imprint was created on some unknown Crusader's burial cloth. According to the scenario envisaged by him:

> I propose that the Shroud, with perhaps others that have disappeared during the intervening centuries, is evidence of a monstrous barbaric joke of Seljuk Turk vengeance on the enemy they were finally exterminating from the Middle East. What would be more likely than that minds like these would think up a plan to destroy some of the enemy by carefully re-enacting in every detail the brutal death of the Divine Master they served, by crucifixion? One, or maybe a group of victims, would have been scourged, crowned with thorns, made to carry the cross, then nailed to it to be objects of ridicule and revenge. The ritual would be completed after the victim expired by piercing the side in the well-known manner, and then left to rot, to be devoured by roaming wild beasts. Later, removed possibly by sympathisers, [it would have been] interred and wrapped in simple locally made cloth, [and put] into one of the many long-plundered Roman tombs scattered in the area.
>
> Later the body or bodies would be discovered by peasants who recognised the value of the cloth to relic-hunters who would take them home to France with no idea of their provenance. What would be more natural than that such a cloth, bearing details exactly conforming to the gospel accounts of Christ's crucifixion, would be thought to be the burial-cloth of Christ himself? The thought that it was a product of a recent crucifixion action-replay would not even occur to them.[6]

As concluded by Dr Straiton: 'I suggest that the man in the Shroud is the "Unknown Soldier" of the Crusades – the victim of a carbon-copy crucifixion.'

Now however plausible Straiton's hypothesis might first appear, it fails to answer how the 'barbarian' Turks, who can hardly have been expected to have any detailed New Testament knowledge and whose only motive would have been to mock Christianity, could have been so clever as to have carried out such an exact re-enactment of Jesus's crucifixion, complete with implements that so far as can be judged were one hundred per cent historically authentic. Also, it is more than a little difficult to believe that this unknown Crusader, having suffered crucifixion, should then not have been left to the wild beasts, but have been given such a clearly swift and dignified burial by sympathetic strangers, a necessary corollary since, as we have seen earlier, the mode of enshrouding of the body was certainly not western. Not least, the theory almost completely fails to account for how this particular Crusader could have managed to leave such a detailed imprint of himself on the Shroud, when no other dead body throughout the entire span of human history seems to have done the same.

In fairness to Dr Straiton, he does paint a credible-sounding picture of the Crusader's 'badly bruised and scourged' body being left 'hanging in the sun for some time, covered in flies', thereupon producing exudations which, when the body was laid in the Shroud, might have created the imprints which we now see. Also, he has justifiably alluded to one modern-day Shroud-type phenomenon that is undeniably intriguing, the so-called Jospice Mattress. When in 1981 a West Indian died of cancer of the pancreas in a Jospice International hospice on the outskirts of Liverpool, to the astonishment of his carers he left an indelible partial imprint of himself, predominantly his hand, buttocks, arm, shoulders and jaw, on the synthetic mattress on which he had been lying [see detail, pl. 13a].

Yet enigmatic though this imprint remains in its own right, in the final analysis it cannot be regarded as sufficient of a parallel to the Shroud to suit Straiton's argument. The body features appear on it in the form of simple outlines and blocks of shadows. Even the lines of the hand can be seen. And there is nothing special to its photographic negative. Furthermore, Dr Straiton's theory necessarily demands that all the pre-1270s artistic and documentary indications of the existence of something very like our Shroud should be tossed aside as mere coincidence. While this is an opinion to which Straiton is obviously entitled, and he deserves our respect for it, the reader must make up his or her own mind whether it is fully justified in the light of all the evidence we have seen.

In short, the argument for some mediaeval person crucified in the semblance of Jesus happening to have left an imprint of himself as extraordinary as that on the Turin Shroud no more succeeds in satisfying all the evidence than does the idea of someone having just painted the image on.

But is there yet another alternative? That, far-fetched as it might sound, even back in the fourteenth century someone might have created the Shroud as none other than the world's first photograph...?

209

Chapter 16
Could the Shroud be the Work of a Mediaeval Photographer?

If the Shroud really does date from the fourteenth century, yet has neither been painted by a cunning artist, nor 'imprinted' using a real-life crucified human body, there does remain one further option: that someone even as long ago as the Middle Ages created it by some photographic means.

At first sight this may well seem the most improbable. After all, photography as we know it was not invented until well over four centuries after the very latest date ascribed to the Shroud by radiocarbon dating. And even then its development was a long-drawn-out process, beginning with Thomas Wedgwood's first use of light-sensitive chemicals to copy silhouette images in 1802, then Joseph Nicéphore Niépce's making of the first permanent pictures in 1814, then Louis Jacques Daguerre's introduction of his daguerreotype process in 1839, then Scott Archer's method using light-sensitive silver salts in a collodium film on a glass plate launched in 1851. And even after all that it took another thirty-three years before George Eastman managed to patent the first successful roll film.

Yet the Shroud's image is so strikingly photographic in its character, particularly from the point of view of what appears on the negative whenever it is photographed using black-and-white film, that the possibility has to be taken seriously that perhaps someone of earlier times may quite well have worked out very basic photographic means of producing it.

In the event, the first promulgation of this idea failed to do it justice, for all the media attention that its authors managed to attract. When in 1994 London journalist Lynn Picknett and accountant Clive Prince launched their book *Turin Shroud: In Whose Image? The Shocking Truth Unveiled*,[1] their 'shocking truth' was that photography should be added to the already impressive list of Leonardo da Vinci's inventions, the Shroud having been made by him as the world's first ever photograph. This information purportedly derived from a mysterious Italian called 'Giovanni', a high-ranking member of a secret society, the Priory of Sion (of *Holy Blood, Holy Grail* fame), which had been guarding the secret for centuries.

Although Giovanni's identity can never be revealed (I certainly do not know it), he apparently initially tried to make contact with me. Surprisingly, he failed in this endeavour (my home address has always been freely available to people seriously interested in the Shroud) and so he singled out Lynn Picknett, who had no known connection with, or serious interest in, the Shroud before the early 1990s, to reveal his society's hitherto closely guarded secret to the world. As Picknett and Prince summarise the extraordinary insights they learned from him:

> Leonardo faked the Shroud in 1492. It was a composite creation: he put the image of his own face on it together with the body of a genuinely crucified man. It was not a painting: It was a projected image 'fixed' on the cloth using chemicals and light: in other words it was a photographic technique. The Maestro faked it for two main reasons. First, because he had been commissioned to do it, by the Pope, Innocent VIII, as a cynical publicity exercise. But the reason he invested it with such concentration, daring and genius was that it represented for him the supreme opportunity to attack the basis of Christianity from within the Church itself (and perhaps he rather liked the idea of generations of pilgrims praying over his own image). He imbued it with subtle clues that, if understood, would be profoundly challenging to the Establishment.[2]

A 'healthily sceptical' Picknett and Prince duly discovered all this to be 'true' and, if one could encapsulate their hypothesis into a single sentence, this would have to be: 'intriguing idea; shame about the facts.' To support their theory of Leonardo having made the Shroud in 1492 they have repeatedly quoted me as having told Lynn Picknett, 'Yes, the Shroud did disappear around then.' With due deference to Ms Picknett's reporting skills, I have equally consistently insisted that I would never in my right senses have made this statement, as ought to be obvious from the chronologies of the Shroud set out both in my 1978 book and this present one.

For in my lengthy chronicling of the Shroud's two 'disappearances', the year 1492 most certainly does not figure and never has. In that year the Shroud's technical owner was, in fact, a two-and-a-half-year-old boy, Duke Charles II, the cloth's effective control thereby being in the hands of his widowed mother the Dowager Duchess Bianca, a very devout woman who personally exhibited the Shroud at Vercelli in 1494, and who would hardly have failed to notice had this been a different cloth from the one that she and her retinue had carried around during their travels in the preceding years.

Of Picknett's and Prince's argument that Leonardo used his own face for the Shroud, one can only wonder whether the notoriously vain 'Maestro', as they refer to him, arranged to have his face specially beaten up to match the man of the Shroud's injuries? Of their claim that the absence of wine on the table of his *Last Supper* shows Leonardo's anti-Christian leanings, the error of this can readily be seen in Gianpetrino's excellent early copy of this painting, currently on display at Magdalen College, Oxford, in which enough liberally charged wine tumblers for everyone present appear on the table [see detail, pl. 46d]. Despite the atrocious condition of Leonardo's original painting they can be distinguished readily enough even on this, Picknett's and Prince's mistake seemingly being due to the poor photographs they consulted. As for Pope Innocent VIII's commissioning the Shroud as a cynical publicity exercise, the very suggestion of this is ludicrous, given that the Shroud, of very low-grade credibility in that pope's time, was never even remotely under his control and, for any publicity, cynical or otherwise, he had far better things available to him in Rome.

In short Picknett's and Prince's Leonardo da Vinci arguments would deserve dismissal but for one potentially interesting element, the basic idea that someone at some early time, though certainly not Leonardo, may genuinely have created the Shroud by some as yet undetermined photographic means. And while Picknett and Prince made a valiant enough attempt to work this out (much experiment, first with a gargoyle, then with a white-painted bust, producing a passably photographic face, albeit retouched and with very obviously painted-on 'bloodstains', there is a far more satisfying Shroud replication, involving a whole body image free of Leonardo da Vinci associations, that has been achieved by Professor Nicholas Allen, dean of the Faculty of Art and Design at the Port Elizabeth Technikon, a technology university located in Port Elizabeth, South Africa.

Working quite independently of Picknett and Prince, Professor Allen had noted as one of the most fundamental of the American STURP team's findings that the Shroud's body image seemed not to be composed of any physical substance, such as an artist's pigment, but instead of some surface alteration to the Shroud's linen such as by the effect of light or other form of radiant energy. This raised in his mind the idea that it might have derived from some photography-related technology that people back in the Middle Ages could have had access to and known at least something about.

Accordingly in late 1988, prompted by the carbon-dating results (and thereby, before Picknett and Prince had even begun developing their ideas), Professor Allen began to apply himself to thinking out the sort of substances by which someone of the Middle Ages might have been able photographically to create the Shroud's image, even with the limited know-how of that time. After careful thought and experimentation, the substances that he alighted upon were rock crystal, silver salts and salts of ammonia, the latter as present, for example, in urine. However unpromising these may sound, the important thing about rock crystal, for instance, is that in photographic terms it is quartz, optical quality specimens of which can be perfectly suitable to serve as a camera lens. Likewise, silver salts such as silver nitrate and silver sulphate have all the necessary properties to behave as light-sensitive chemicals. As for salts of ammonia (scientifically, specifically ammonium hydroxide, but urine would serve), these can dissolve silver and thereby act, in effect, like a film fixative.

With regard to the knowledge of how to use such substances photographically, the Ancient Egyptians certainly used rock crystal – quartz, and later glass, for lenses, particularly for magnification purposes. But Professor Allen found even more pertinent the writings of a tenth–eleventh century Arab scholar, Ibn al-Haytham, whose book *Kitab al-manazir* was translated into Latin in the thirteenth century, stirring up very considerable mediaeval-European interest in optical matters and particularly in that prototype of the modern-day camera, the camera obscura.

As Professor Allen further discovered, besides their having a basic understanding of a camera, the more scientific-minded Arabs and Christians of the Middle Ages also had surprisingly advanced knowledge of the properties of the light-sensitive silver salts silver chloride and silver nitrate. The Arab writer Jabir ibn Haayan, for instance, wrote as early as the ninth century of how silver nitrate can be made by dissolving silver in *eau prime*, now better known to us as nitric acid. Exactly as in the case of Al-Haytham's writings, Ibn Haayan's were translated into Latin for western consumption under the title *De Inventione Ventatis* and attracted wide interest.

Having thus assembled in his mind the variety of materials that someone of the Middle Ages would have had available to him for what we would call photographic purposes, Professor Allen applied himself to how these

213

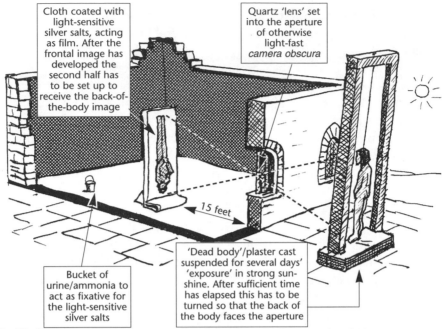

Cloth coated with light-sensitive silver salts, acting as film. After the frontal image has developed the second half has to be set up to receive the back-of-the-body image

Quartz 'lens' set into the aperture of otherwise light-fast *camera obscura*

15 feet

Bucket of urine/ammonia to act as fixative for the light-sensitive silver salts

'Dead body'/plaster cast suspended for several days' 'exposure' in strong sunshine. After sufficient time has elapsed this has to be turned so that the back of the body faces the aperture

Fig 25 How a mediaeval forger produced the Shroud 'photographically'?
Professor Nicholas Allen's reconstructed 'camera' for producing the Shroud image, using basic 'photographic' materials and know-how that would have been available in the Middle Ages. In effect the Shroud was the 'film' inside the camera obscura. (Based on a model by Professor Allen)

might practically be deployed for the obvious crucial test: the making of a truly convincing Shroud replica.

For this, Professor Allen's first task was to construct a camera obscura, in the form of a living-room-sized room (this is how the term 'camera' has its origin, from the Italian for a room), that he made completely light-fast with the exception of the aperture for the rock-crystal lens [see plan, fig. 25]. With this aperture initially closed, he brought into the room a cloth made to the same dimensions as the Shroud, and after setting it up some fifteen feet from the aperture and folding it once across its width (because he was making the image in two halves, first frontal, then dorsal), he then soaked it in the light-sensitive silver nitrate.

When this was dry, and with his 'camera' thus ready loaded with what was in effect an unexposed film, i.e. the 'Shroud', all that Professor Allen now needed was a suitable 'corpse'. For this he painstakingly made a perfect plaster cast [pl. 47a] from the naked body of a suitably bearded

214

male life model whom he had arranged in a pose corresponding as closely as possible to that of the man of the Shroud. He 'doctored' this cast to incorporate Shroud facial features such as a damaged nose and bruised cheek, etc., then once this was complete he suspended it in full sunshine fifteen feet in front of the aperture to his still darkened camera obscura.

The moment had now come for the camera obscura's aperture or shutter to be opened and the exposure made. As Professor Allen knew from earlier experiments, the distances that he had chosen for the cast to be from the aperture and likewise the 'shroud' meant that the image of the cast would be life-size as projected via the lens onto the cloth (on which it would be received upside down). All that was needed was sufficient time, in this instance several days, for the sun-charged reflection of the cast to imprint its 'negative' upon the cloth. To create a double, i.e. back-and-front imprint as on the Shroud, it was necessary to repeat the whole process, closing the 'shutter' on completion of the first 'exposure', then turning the cast round so that the back of the body faced the aperture, then turning the 'shroud' around so that its as yet unexposed half faced the aperture, then reopening the aperture for another few days.

As Professor Allen knew from his earlier experiments, after all this there would be a purplish-brown 'negative' of the cast on the cloth formed from reduced silver salts, which would be quickly ruined upon exposure to the light so long as the light-sensitive silver salts still remained active. Accordingly, this was where his third ingredient, the solution of ammonia salts, came into its own. After a washing of the 'Shroud' in this to remove all the silver salts the image was made fast, enabling it safely to be brought into the light of day.[3]

The result of this experiment, as produced and published by Professor Allen, bears some remarkable affinities to the image visible on the Turin Shroud. As the parallel characteristics have been listed by him:

   (i) a straw-yellow discoloration of the upper fibrils of the linen material
  (ii) the appearance of being photographic negatives which are only visually coherent at distances upwards of two metres
  (iii) no pigment, powder, dye or stain
  (iv) no directionality
   (v) thermal stability
  (vi) water stability
 (vii) relative chemical stability in that the author's test pieces are affected

215

by household bleach to the same degree as any other mild scorch on organic material is altered.[4]

Perhaps the most impressive of all such features, however, was the result when Professor Allen photographed his 'shroud' using black-and-white film and then viewed this in negative. Exactly as on the Shroud itself, there appeared the unmistakable naturalistic positive 'photograph' of a naked man laid out in death, convincingly three-dimensional and quite impossible to interpret as the work of an artist [pl. 47c]. After all the unconvincingness of earlier replications of the Shroud – by McCrone and Sanford, Craig and Bresee, Picknett and Prince, to name but a few, none of which even managed to get further than producing a face only – the Nicholas Allen version has to be taken seriously.

More than anyone else, whether for or against the Shroud's authenticity, Professor Allen has demonstrated that the Shroud's image (or at least its body image), is convincingly replicable. As he has forthrightly concluded:

It would seem ... that people in the late thirteenth or early fourteenth century were privy to a photographic technology which was previously thought to be unknown before the beginning of the nineteenth century. The implications that this has for the history of technology and the history of art cannot be underestimated, and far from condemning the Shroud of Turin as a mere mediaeval forgery or clever 'fake' we should strive to ensure that this remarkable and unique vestige of a lost mediaeval technology be carefully preserved for future analysis.[5]

Now it can also be said unreservedly of Professor Allen that more than anyone else before him he has demonstrated that the Shroud's image really is photographic in character. This is in fact something that those in favour of the Shroud's authenticity have been saying for years and is certainly bad news for Walter McCrone and others.

Rather more serious, however, from the pro-authenticity camp's point of view is that he has demonstrated that it *could* have been achieved with materials and knowledge readily available in the Middle Ages. And while I for one would not wish to question that this indeed *might* have been possible, this is still very far from accepting that this actually was how (and when) the Shroud's imprint came into being.

For Professor Allen himself has been more than a little hesitant with regard to certain details, not least whether, for the Shroud proper, the hypothetical mediaeval photographer used either an actual corpse or a

216

plaster cast of the same.[6] Among just some of the difficulties of the former method are that if an actual crucified human corpse really were suspended for 'several days' in full sunshine, then its likely condition after such a length of time, particularly in any climate with the required sufficiency of sunshine, boggles both the mind and the olfactory system. This is quite aside from the offence it would have caused to every mediaeval religious sensitivity. An actual corpse must therefore be considered most unlikely, given that rigor mortis would in any case never have held sufficiently long to create the impression of the figure lying flat. Also, had the body been genuinely crucified, its correspondingly convincing 'bloodstains' could hardly have become transferred to the Shroud over Professor Allen's required focal length of twice fifteen feet.

Yet some equally imponderable difficulties pertain to the other possible method, that the Shroud may have been made in the Middle Ages in the same way that Professor Allen created his replica, with a plaster cast made from a living (or possibly dead) male model. As we know from the mediaeval Italian artist Cennino Cennini's *Il Libro dell'Arte*, the technical means of making plaster casts from bodies had just about been worked out in the fourteenth century. If a living model were used, it was usual for straws to be stuffed into the nostrils to enable him or her to breathe while the plaster hardened. But making a really good cast would have been quite difficult enough in itself, without the highly elaborate subsequent procedures, necessarily demanding some prior experience of the basics of producing a photographic-type image, by which the 'Shroud' was then contrived according to Professor Allen's hypothesis.

Furthermore, it cannot be stressed enough that even in the unlikely event of someone of the Middle Ages having successfully mastered such an advanced degree of photographic expertise – only then to lose it again – this would have been directed solely to producing a 'negative' image that to any mediaeval observer could only have seemed most unconvincing. The so compelling hidden 'positive' photograph would still have been inaccessible to anyone, even the 'photographer' who created it, for another five hundred years.

As for the Shroud 'bloodstains', Professor Allen's plaster-cast theory, just like the 'cunning painting' theory, necessarily requires that these were no more than daubings-on for effect, despite all the attestations by pathologists and doctors of their medical convincingness. And this is again all quite aside from the historical evidence that something very like the Shroud really does seem to have existed well before the period that this amazing piece of forgery is supposed to have been performed.

Overall, then, and without in any way wishing to undermine Professor Allen's very fine achievement, there remain some major flaws to his, as well as to every other, hypothesis conceived so far concerning how the Shroud's image might have been contrived in the Middle Ages or later.

Which does not mean to say that the Shroud cannot have been made by some cunning artificer in the Middle Ages. For all we know, an all-embracing theory may yet emerge. But in the meantime it does at least justify us taking seriously that the radiocarbon dating *could* have been wrong. And looking therefore at some of the ways in which three very reputable radiocarbon-dating laboratories, despite the confidently quoted 'thousand trillion to one' odds against, just might have come up with a very seriously incorrect result.

Chapter 17

If the carbon dating is wrong,
how could that happen?

W e saw earlier how immediately following the announcement of the radiocarbon-dating results, the first reaction from some of the more die-hard Shroud enthusiasts was to claim that there must have been some kind of fraud on the part of those who had scientifically supervised the radiocarbon dating. As we have stressed, this sort of argument is as unworthy as it is misguided.

However, such are the pitfalls littering the path of Shroud investigation that even those who may affect to be serious scientists supportive of a first-century date may be very far from the friends of the subject that they represent themselves to be. A case in point is the Russian biochemist Dr Dmitri Kouznetsov and his only recently aired explanation for how the radiocarbon dating may have erred. For most who have an active interest in the Shroud, including myself, the first awareness of Dr Kouznetsov came in June 1993, when he appeared at a conference in Rome organised by the French Shroud group CIELT.[1] Polite, quiet-spoken and youthful-looking (despite a Genghis Khan-style moustache), Dr Kouznetsov styles himself as a director of Moscow's E. A. Sedov Biopolymer Research Laboratories and winner of a Lenin Prize. In his Rome talk[2] he explained how the radiocarbon-dating laboratories did not take into their calculations that linen has some special properties arising from its original manufacture from flax, during which the flax plant's proteins and lipids (i.e. waxes and fats) are driven out, thereby imparting to the remaining fibres a misleadingly higher radiocarbon content. Furthermore, if a linen textile has been subjected to unusually high temperatures, such as inevitably happened during the 1532 fire, then its radiocarbon content can be 'enriched', making it appear substantially younger than its true age when it is radiocarbon dated. Although Kouznetsov acknowledged he was unsure exactly why anything of this might occur, he suggested that one factor might well be some as yet imperfectly understood process of isotopic exchange. Very much the 'scoop' of the conference, he was seized upon by the Italian media as offering *the* answer to the radiocarbon dating. And such was his seemingly modest, understated manner than even the more reserved attendees quietly hoped that this might prove to be the case.

Indeed, from Dr Kouznetsov's initial behaviour during the succeeding months and years, there seemed perfectly reasonable justification for such optimism. My own first guarded reaction to him was to invite Professor Michael Tite to peruse the text of the paper that he had read in Rome. Tite's very affable response was that because the radiocarbon-dating laboratories had found a normal ratio of carbon 12 to carbon 13 in their Shroud samples, he seriously doubted that any enrichment of the kind argued by Kouznetsov could have happened to the Shroud's carbon 14. But no one expected Tite to go overboard to welcome anyone questioning the carbon dating on his own ground. And when Kouznetsov responded to Tite that it was perhaps the radiocarbon-dating scientists' definitions of 'normal' which needed to be revised, honours seemed just about even.

Generously supported and encouraged by STURP scientists such as Dr John Jackson, Kouznetsov thereupon very commendably went on to publish his findings in peer-reviewed American scientific journals, notably the *Journal of Archaeological Science*. In one particularly key paper in this, 'Effects of fires and biofraction of carbon isotopes on results of radiocarbon dating of old textiles: the Shroud of Turin', published in 1995,[3] he outlined how he had created in his laboratory as close as possible a simulation of the conditions of the fire of 1532 in which, as will be recalled, the heat in the Shroud's immediate surrounds was so intense that its silver casket melted irreparably.

Using samples of ancient linen, one of these a first-century fragment found at En Gedi in Israel, Kouznetsov described having 'cooked' these to 200 degrees Centigrade under controlled conditions, finding sufficient of what he called a 'fire-induced carboxylation', i.e. 'carbonization' of the textile cellulose', to have caused 'a significant error in the radiocarbon-dating results'. In the light of these findings he claimed that a major 're-evaluation' of the results that the radiocarbon-dating scientists had published in *Nature* was now needed.

With Kouznetsov having issued so fundamental a challenge, Professors Paul Damon, Douglas Donahue and their close colleague A. J. T. Jull of the Arizona laboratory duly set about formulating an appropriate answer on behalf of all three laboratories who had worked on the Shroud. In the very same issue of the *Journal of Archaeological Science* in which Kouznetsov published, they described having tried without success to reproduce the carboxylation effect that he claimed. Pointing out that the Russian and his colleagues had 'not had appropriate control experiments performed' and that they had carried out their measurements 'on an apparently untested piece of equipment with no reference to normal procedures of reproducibility, standards, control and blank samples', they went on:

> We have shown that even if the carbon displacements proposed during the heat treatment were correct, no significant change in the measured radiocarbon age of the linen would occur. We must conclude that the attack by Kouznetsov and his co-workers on measurements of the radiocarbon age of the Shroud of Turin, and on radiocarbon measurements on linen textiles in general, are unsubstantiated and incorrect. We further conclude that other aspects of the experiment are unverifiable and irreproducible.[4]

In a reply published in the regular newsletter of the British Society for the Turin Shroud, which had fully reported the Arizona laboratory's criticisms, Kouznetsov defended himself with what seemed characteristic vigour, charging the Arizona scientists with having used short cuts in their replications of his experiments and therefore not being able to make valid like-for-like comparisons. He also questioned some of the Arizona team's scientific calculations, quoting at them some very complex physics formulae with every apparent authority.

However, what Kouznetsov's response omitted to disclose was that the high-powered physics calculations which he had bandied about were not his own, but had been copied by him from a review of the Arizona findings written by STURP's Dr John Jackson, who had been looking to find some way of reconciling the two conflicting points of view. Neither acknowledging that this was Jackson's work, nor seeking his approval for its use, Kouznetsov blithely used the calculations as if they were of his own devising, not knowing that in fact they contained an error which Jackson had discovered and would have wanted to correct in the event of any publication. Furthermore, when Jackson, who had most generously hosted some six visits by Kouznetsov to the US, merely queried the Russian's aberrant behaviour, not a word of apology or explanation was forthcoming. All communication simply very abruptly ceased.

Meanwhile, yet more questionable behaviour on Kouznetsov's part was beginning to come to light, some of this involving myself. After he and I met for the first time in Rome he requested a copy of my original 1978 book on the Shroud, which I duly sent him. Shortly after his receiving this he said he hoped he might be able to get it published in Russian, news which I warmly welcomed, as I felt it could be of particular interest to Russian Christians because of their sustained revering of the cloth of Edessa long after its loss to the Orthodox Church when it disappeared from Constantinople in 1204.

In September 1995 Kouznetsov phoned me to say that he had already obtained thousands of advance orders for the book and that a translation was well in hand for publication in May 1996. All that he needed from me, and urgently, was a formal letter authorising him to handle everything pertaining to the Russian-language copyright, a nicety which a bureau-cratic printer in St Petersburg had demanded. As Russia was a 'very poor country' he asked if I would accept just a two per cent royalty and include a note to this effect in the letter.

Shortly after my compliantly writing and faxing the requested letter all communication ceased, which initially raised no alarm bells, as contact had never been more than spasmodic and I knew him to be often away from Moscow for several months at a time. But then in the March of 1996 I learned to my astonishment that he had been hawking my letter among various Americans, asking them to finance my book's Russian-language edition in return for guaranteed large profits. Sums running into tens of thousands of dollars had apparently changed hands. My suspicions duly roused, I immediately tried contacting him to ask him to explain himself only, like John Jackson, to meet a wall of silence. The American financiers, at first incredulous of my concerns for them, initially received bland reassurances from Kouznetsov. But when no Russian translation appeared on the due date they met with the same silence, along with a complete absence of any returns from their 'investments'. And that silence and lack of return has continued to the very time of writing.

Accordingly, while the reader must form his or her own conclusions concerning the above, it may be appreciated that I have some very good reasons indeed for the utmost scepticism towards Kouznetsov's scientific claims, for all that I and others might 'like' to believe them. No one has yet been able to replicate Kouznetsov's experiment showing that heating an ancient piece of linen inside a closed container could seriously alter the linen's radiocarbon content. And I would concur totally with the radiocarbon-dating laboratory scientists' opinions that in all probability they never will.

But as it happens, Kouznetsov has not been the only individual to advance a serious scientific case for how the radiocarbon dating could have been wrong. At the very same Rome conference at which he surfaced in June 1993 there was another newcomer, whose paper 'Biogenic Varnish and the Shroud of Turin' sounded so unpromising that to my own subsequent chagrin I did not attend it. This was the University of Texas's Dr Leoncio Garza-Valdès [pl. 48b], already briefly mentioned in earlier chapters, whose near-professional hobbies have long been microbiology and archaeology, in particular as applied to ancient Mayan artefacts. He has had several specialist papers on this topic published in international scientific journals and by a round-about route this led him to the Shroud. For in 1983 Garza-Valdès was told by two New York art connoisseurs that a purportedly ancient Mayan carving he owned, the 'Itzamna Tun', was a worthless modern fake, obvious to them from its shiny, varnish-like coating. The connoisseurs even offered to buy the 'Itzamna', and another similar item for a special collection of such 'fakes' that they were assembling.

Fortunately Garza-Valdès declined their offer and decided to make a careful analysis of the coating, discovering to his satisfaction that it was not composed of any type of man-made varnish, whatever period the 'Itzamna' might have been made. Instead it was a completely natural bioplastic material that had accumulated from the symbiotic activity of millions of bluey green bacteria and pink-pigmented fungi building up into a hard casing somewhat in the manner of a coral reef.

As Garza-Valdès was aware, if the 'Itzamna' were genuine it would have been used in a special ritual in which the Mayan king anointed it with his own blood and, on noting patches of brownish detritus in the 'Itzamna's' crevices, he took scrapings of these and had them analysed, finding them indeed positive for blood and for human DNA. When he sent samples to Arizona's radiocarbon-dating laboratory, he learned that they dated to *c.* AD 400, thereby conclusively overturning the dismissal of the carving as a modern fake by the two New York 'connoisseurs'.

Even so, the puzzle about this date was that it was some six centuries later than the particular Mayan period suggested by the carving's artistic style and it was here that Dr Garza-Valdès's bioplastic coating discovery came into its own. Because the coating's steady accumulation had covered all surfaces of the carving and, like plaque on teeth, is virtually invisible unless its presence is revealed by a disclosing medium, the Arizona laboratory had completely unwittingly dated this coating along with the blood. The combined result therefore made the carving seem several centuries younger than it actually was.

And as Dr Garza-Valdès further discovered, such a bioplastic coating was not just peculiar to this one artefact. Something similar had been found on other antiquities which he was able to study for comparison purposes, including a Mayan chert drill from Guatemala; a late Mayan chest ornament made of jasper, also from Guatemala; an ancient Mexican carved bone used for blood-letting; even a gold pendant from Colombia.

The key question, therefore, was whether the Shroud's linen has such a coating. In April 1993 Dr Garza-Valdès travelled with his own portable microscope to Turin, where Giovanni Riggi allowed him to study some of the pieces of the Shroud that he trimmed off from the sample provided for the carbon-dating laboratories (fig. 24). He has described his reactions on his first studying them: 'As soon as I looked at a segment in the microscope, I knew it was heavily contaminated. I knew that what had been radiocarbon dated was a mixture of linen and bacteria and fungi and bioplastic coating that had grown on the fibres for centuries.'[5]

Dr Garza-Valdès was able to return to San Antonio with tiny portions of the sample. With some help from Professor Stephen Mattingly, head of Microbiology at the University of Texas's San Antonio campus, he went on to make a very full and thorough study of this coating and what needs to be emphasised immediately is that the coating really is there. In his Rome talk and subsequent presentations to scientific audiences he has shown slides and diagrams that reveal it as a tube of varying thickness surrounding the Shroud fibres [fig. 24 & pl. 48c] reminiscent of the protective plastic casing around electrical wiring.

In early September 1994 Professor Harry Gove accepted Garza-Valdès's invitation to an informal Round Table at the University of Texas San Antonio campus at which he was enabled, along with the others present, to study under the microscope several Shroud threads with this coating. He subsequently expressed himself, in his own words, thoroughly 'convinced of the general validity of Garza-Valdès's findings – [that] there was some sort of "halo" or bioplastic coating around some of the threads'.[6]

Now as Professor Gove would wish me immediately to make clear, this is very far from him saying that he accepts that such a coating either could or does seriously invalidate the Shroud radiocarbon dating. He has simply very graciously and even-handedly acknowledged that the coating is not

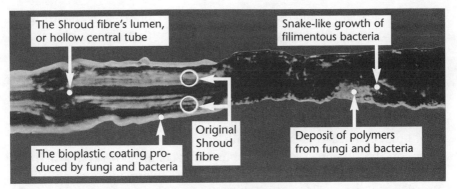

The Shroud fibre's lumen, or hollow central tube

Snake-like growth of filimentous bacteria

The bioplastic coating produced by fungi and bacteria

Original Shroud fibre

Deposit of polymers from fungi and bacteria

Fig 26 Cross-section of a Shroud fibre, based on a high-magnification photograph, showing the bioplastic coating identified by Dr Garza Valdès
Using a microtome, an instrument used to cut microscopic samples, and he and his co-researchers have been able to show a typical disposition of the bioplastic coating on a Shroud fibre, also the accretion of other bacteria and fungi, as indicated above. (Based on an original microphotograph by Dr Garza-Valdès)

a figment of Garza-Valdès's imagination. It can genuinely be seen by even the most independent-minded of observers. Instead, the crucial issue is the extent to which it might or might not affect any radiocarbon-dating reading.

An important factor is that the micro-organisms from which the coating has been formed not only contain carbon, they are rich in it, and thereby in carbon 14. This was one of several points regarding Dr Garza-Valdès's argument on which I consulted Dr Thomas Loy of the University of Queensland's Centre for Molecular and Cellular Biology for independent verification. The coating apparently necessarily has a very high proportion of 'young' carbon 14 for the very good reason that many of the bacteria and fungi are still alive. As Dr Garza-Valdès explained to my wife and me when we visited him in San Antonio in August 1996, he was able to demonstrate this by putting some of his Shroud samples into a culture medium, with quite spectacular results. In his own words: 'What happens is that the bacteria reproduce like crazy for a period of two weeks. So this is the proof that the bacteria are alive. And I have the cultures showing the speed that they grow with the deposit of the plastic. So no one can say that there is no contaminant. No way.'[7]

Now one major objection that has been raised by Dr Walter McCrone is that if there were any coating of this kind on the Shroud fibres (which he has disputed), this would be bound to have been removed by the stringent pre-treatment cleaning processes that all radiocarbon-dating laboratories routinely use specifically to remove any contaminants and impurities which might interfere with their results.

In the case of the Shroud, it is conveniently on record that all three of the participating laboratories used as cleaning agent the same formulation of hydrochloric acid and sodium hydroxide (caustic soda), thereby enabling Dr Garza-Valdès specifically to replicate this and to observe its effect on Shroud fibres bearing the bioplastic coating. He says: 'When you clean these with hydrochloric acid and sodium hydroxide not simply with the concentration used by the radiocarbon laboratories but with six times the strength of that used in 1988, you don't do a single thing to the bacteria and the bioplastic coating. The only thing that you do is to dissolve part of the cellulose from the flax, so that you are going to make bigger the contaminant in relation to the cellulose of the flax.'[8]

Another particularly forceful objection raised by Dr McCrone and others is that in order to affect the radiocarbon dating so substantially that a true first-century date became a false fourteenth-century one, the thickness of the coating would have to be very considerable. As calculated by McCrone, this 'would require that the linen be coated with two-thirds of its own weight'[9] of modern material. Professor Hall, in his 1989 lecture to the British Museum Society, had similarly calculated that something of the order of a sixty per cent contamination would be required to skew the dating, and although he knew nothing of Dr Garza-Valdès's coating at that time, he ridiculed the idea that anything more than the tiniest fraction of modern material might have been left on the Shroud sample his laboratory worked on.

As it happens, the figure of sixty per cent is one which Dr Garza-Valdès accepts without qualm, since he claims that varying amounts up to this proportion are indeed present on some of the Shroud fibres. He has been able to show the thickness using a special stain, base carmine, which becomes absorbed by the cellulose of the linen fibres, but not by the bioplastic coating. This process clearly reveals the coating's presence in the form of what Professor Gove described as a 'halo' when seen in cross-section. In the wake of his examination of the Shroud samples at San Antonio, Gove reportedly actually accepted that this halo was present up to a proportion of fifty-seven per cent,[10] though he subsequently retracted this statement.

Complicating the issue, as Dr Garza-Valdès acknowledges, is that on any artefact, including our Shroud, the coating's thickness may vary considerably from one part to another, with bacterial growth being inevitably greatest where there has been the greatest handling. In the case of the Shroud, this only makes yet more questionable Gonella's and Riggi's selection of the corner site for the taking of the radiocarbon-dating sample. Cumulatively literally hundreds of sweaty hands would have clutched this corner to hold up the cloth at expositions over the centuries [pls 43b & c], thereby unwittingly creating here and at its opposite end the maximum bacterial build-up of any areas on the cloth.

Inevitably the greatest difficulty, however, concerns why, if the Shroud's fibres do indeed have so substantial a coating, this has failed hitherto to be noticed either by the STURP scientists in the course of their examination of the Shroud in 1978, or by Dr McCrone in his microanalytical work, or by the radiocarbon-dating scientists, during their preliminary examinations of their samples prior to carrying out the radiocarbon dating in 1988. This was a point put to me particularly forcefully by Dr McCrone: 'I have had and observed very closely, over sixty tape samples from the Shroud on which there were, by extrapolation from half a dozen tapes, more than 100,000 linen fibers. The only coating that I found on any of those fibres was a paint layer made up of red ochre or vermilion and collagen tempera.'[11]

To this, Dr Garza-Valdès has totally calmly and reasonedly responded that unless you knew the coating was there, you simply would not see it, or be aware of its presence. Since it resembles a clear plastic, you would look through it without seeing it, very much in the manner of a pane of glass. In his own words: 'This is why many people have looked with the microscope and have missed the deposit and said the fibres are clean. A few years ago they could not have understood how the Mayans gave that beautiful polish to the ancient jades. No one could understand the technology they used to give that beautiful lustre. But the Mayans didn't do it. It was the bacteria that deposited this acrylic on the ancient surfaces.'

Now the importance of these remarks in relation to the Shroud's earlier noted surprisingly clean-looking appearance cannot be emphasised enough. As recorded by Professor Gove in his book on the Shroud radiocarbon dating, the Zurich radiocarbon-dating laboratory's Dr Willi Wölfli specifically noted this cleanness of the Shroud sample that he received. And in my own case, forcefully recalled to mind was one of my profoundest surprises on first seeing the Shroud back in November 1973. As I remarked in my first book on the Shroud, published in 1978: 'The linen, although ivory-coloured with age, was still surprisingly clean-looking, *even to the extent of a damask-like surface sheen.*'[12]

So could this same 'clean', clear surface sheen have been the reason why no one, looking at Shroud samples through the microscope, saw any coating – because of its clear plastic quality? This was another point which I specifically checked with the University of Queensland's Dr Thomas Loy, to receive from him the firm assurance that unless anyone possessing modern-day microbiological knowledge happened specifically to be looking for such a coating, it could all too easily be missed. In fact, even Dr Garza-Valdès was only able to reveal its presence by the use of an amido black stain, precisely the same stain which McCrone used to show up what he interpreted as a gelatin painting medium. So could McCrone's 'gelatin' be one and the same as Garza-Valdès's 'bioplastic coating'? Conceivably, exactly as in the case of the Vinland Map, McCrone may have made the right observations, but had drawn the wrong interpretations.

What cannot be emphasised enough is that if Dr Garza-Valdès's findings are valid (and at the time of writing they have yet to be fully developed and published for proper independent scrutiny), their ramifications range far beyond just the Shroud. As he himself has stressed: 'Every single ancient artefact has a covering of the bacteria or bioplastic coating. It is not a thing peculiar to the Shroud.'[13]

In which regard, and confirming that this is no mere pseudo-scientific quackery, one person to have taken a very serious interest indeed in these ideas is the already mentioned world-respected Egyptologist Dr Rosalie David of the Manchester Museum. As may be recalled, during her intensive examination of the Manchester collection's Egyptian mummy no. 1770, Dr David had been puzzled by the British Museum radiocarbon-dating laboratory's finding that this mummy's bandages purportedly dated 800 to 1000 years younger than its body.[14] Although it could not be completely ruled out that the mummy had been re-wrapped 1000 years after its first interment, she did not think this likely.

Accordingly, this and other aberrant radiocarbon-dating findings, particularly pertaining to linen, led her to suspect that there might be some as yet unrecognised contaminant to such wrappings that made them seem very substantially younger than they really were. However, she had no real idea what this contaminant might be until she heard of Dr Garza-Valdès's bioplastic coating.

Such was her interest that when, in January 1996, Dr Garza-Valdès invited her to give a paper at an Archaeomicrobiology Symposium in San

Antonio, she accepted with alacrity, her visit providing an opportunity for them to discuss the extent to which the coating might skew radio-carbon dates. Together they set up a special project to check on the dating differentials between other mummy bodies and their wrappings, their first essay in this, arranged in collaboration with Professor Harry Gove, being to radiocarbon date some bone collagen and linen wrappings from the mummy of an ibis, a bird sacred to the ancient Egyptians and therefore very commonly mummified by them. One of their reasons for this choice was that, unlike in the case of a human mummy, an ibis is much less likely to have been re-wrapped in antiquity, thereby eliminating this particular reason for a dating discrepancy.

At the time that this book was being finalised for publication the results of this experiment were published in the form of a specialist scientific paper jointly authored by Professor Harry Gove, Dr Rosalie David and Dr Garza-Valdès, together with Dr Garza-Valdès's colleague at the University of Texas Health Center, Professor Stephen Mattingly.[15] From this paper we learn that after taking cloth, bone and tissue samples from the chosen ibis at the Texas Science Health Center, Dr David hand-carried these to the radiocarbon-dating laboratory at Tucson, Arizona, one of the three which had worked on samples from the Shroud. There the Arizona team cleaned the cloth samples, employing the very same pre-treatment procedure they had used for the Shroud. They then carbon dated these along with the samples from the bird's body, the expectation obviously being that both the mummy and its wrappings ought to be very similar in date.

However, the results were that whereas an averaging of the bone and tissue samples from the ibis showed this bird to have died some time between 829 and 795 BC, an averaging of its wrappings showed that the flax of which these were composed had 'died' some time between 384 and 170 BC. Exactly as Dr David had discovered in the case of her Mummy 1770, there was a very significant discrepancy, an average of 550 years, between the dating of the mummy's linen wrappings and the mummy itself. And this despite the laboratory's claimed accuracies of its results being an average of sixty-five years. Notably, in each case it was the linen which appeared substantially the younger. Furthermore, as Dr Garza-Valdès was able to observe under the microscope, the ibis wrappings would have spent most of their life undisturbed in Egypt's dry climate and did not have the same thickness of coating that the Shroud had accumulated during its repeated handlings over the centuries. Yet still the discrepancy was of a significant proportion.

As may be expected, in the light of such findings the radiocarbon-dating laboratories have now begun to shift their ground. Despite the fact that Professor Harry Gove, co-inventor of their carbon-dating method, was one of the experiment's very architects, they have suggested that an ibis mummy might not have been the best choice for this. As pointed out by Arizona's Donahue and Jull, both among the twenty-one signatories of the *Nature* report which declared the Shroud proven to be mediaeval, if this particular ibis had been raised on a diet of seafood from the Mediterranean then a 'marine correction' would need to be applied, since food of marine origin can contain 'old carbon'.[16] This is carbon depleted in carbon 14, which can make any creature that eats it seem older than its true age.

Unfortunately, given that 'Danny the mummy', as Garza-Valdès affectionately calls the ibis, quite definitely lived well over 2000 years before the age of radio tracking devices, no one can be exactly sure where he obtained his sustenance. None the less, as pointed out by Dr David in what is clearly her contribution to the report:

> ... it is likely it [the ibis] came either from Sakkara (south of Cairo), some 150 miles from the Mediterranean, or perhaps Hermopolis (the cult-centre of the god Thoth whose cult-animal was the Ibis), which is on the Nile in Middle Egypt, some 250 miles from the Mediterranean. Such ibises were probably bred and reared in captivity at these sites. Pilgrims to the local temple would purchase them and they would be mummified at the site as an offering to the god and buried nearby in vast underground galleries. It is most unlikely that they would have been fed on a diet of seafood from the Mediterranean (or for that matter from the Red Sea some 100 miles away) because of the distances involved rather than from the other suitable food sources readily available in the vicinity. Furthermore the delta carbon 13 for the collagen was about − 21 per mil and for the wrapping − 26.5 per mil. Both are quite different from the value of zero expected for marine samples. *It is thus highly probable that no marine correction is required for the radiocarbon date of the ibis collagen* [my italics].[17]

As the report goes on to acknowledge, the very fact that some portion of Danny the ibis's diet 'probably involved food whose carbon content came not from the carbon dioxide in the air, but from that in fresh or brackish water' opens the possibility that its carbon-14 ratio was lower than it would have been had it been a land-based animal. However, given that the same argument might well be applied to the conditions in which flax is grown and retted, this is effectively self-cancelling. The only way forward, as Gove, Mattingly, David and Garza-Valdès acknowledge in their conclusion, is for the experiment to be repeated, this time perhaps using samples from a mummified bull, another animal sacred to the ancient Egyptians of which surviving examples are common.

So clearly no one should as yet regard all this as having proven Garza-Valdès's argument for how the Shroud dating may have been so seriously skewed. None the less, might one be forgiven for suggesting that the radiocarbon laboratories' so confident odds of 'one in a thousand trillion' against their being wrong are beginning to look just a little overstated.

Chapter 18

Conclusion: The blood and the Shroud: examining your own heart on the matter

One point greatly favouring Dr Garza-Valdès's explanation of how the Shroud carbon dating may have produced the wrong result is that it requires absolutely no violation of science's natural laws. Assuming that the bioplastic coating exists (and as we have seen, even Professor Harry Gove acknowledges that it is there), it has to be about as natural as the Great Barrier Reef of Australia that lies just a few hours north of me as I type these words – and of a very similar, constantly forming character, albeit on a very different scale. This is why, whether or not Dr Garza-Valdès is eventually found to be right, he has to be taken seriously, as Professor Gove and other distinguished scientists are commendably doing. And if he is right then, the Shroud aside, there is a whole hitherto unrecognised possible source of error that will need to be taken into account in all future radiocarbon-dating tests, one which will enable the method deservedly to become more trustworthy than can be justified at the present time.

But what if Dr Garza-Valdès is found to be wrong? Would that mean the end of all arguments for how the Shroud carbon dating might have been in error?

Not necessarily. Another argument, also advanced by some high-level scientists, has been that if there were anything thermonuclear to the circumstance by which the crucified body image was created on the Shroud, then this in itself, by adding to the cloth's low-level radioactivity levels, could have made the Shroud appear younger than its true age. A letter from Dr Thomas J. Phillips of Harvard University's High Energy Physics Laboratory, published in the very same issue of *Nature* which carried the formal report of the radiocarbon-dating findings, commented:

> If the Shroud of Turin is in fact the burial-cloth of Christ … then according to the Bible it was present at a unique physical event: the

232

resurrection of a dead body. Unfortunately this event is not accessible to direct scientific scrutiny, but ... the body ... may have radiated neutrons, which would have irradiated the Shroud and changed some of the nuclei to different isotopes by neutron capture. In particular some carbon 14 would have been generated from carbon 13. If we assume that the Shroud is 1950 years old and that the neutrons were emitted thermally, then an integrated flux of 2×10^{16} neutron cm^{-2} would have converted enough carbon 13 to carbon 14 to give an apparent carbon-dated age of 670 years [i.e. fourteenth century].[1]

A similar view has been expressed by the pioneering British nuclear physicist Dr Kitty Little, now retired from her career at the UK's Atomic Energy Research Establishment at Harwell, Oxfordshire. She has recalled an experiment that she conducted back in the 1950s in which she irradiated a range of fibres, including several different cellulose ones, in a research reactor called BEPO: 'At the time BEPO was being run at only three MW, so that the temperatures were in the range 70° to 90° centigrade. This meant that I was obtaining radiation effects without the complication of heat effects.'

Little observed the fibres to change with only relatively low-grade heat to the very same colour reported of the Shroud image, something of which at that time she had no knowledge. In her own words: '[The] cellulose fibres turned to the straw-yellow colour that has been described for the image of the Shroud...'

Even more interesting, however, was that the very same radiation particles which produced this effect were necessarily also accompanied by neutron emission. And as she has explained, this would inevitably have resulted 'in the formation of extra carbon 14 on the sheet, the whole of it', this extra carbon tending quite categorically and specifically '... to make the apparent age of the fabric appear more recent than it really is...'[2]

This explanation, proposed completely independently of each other by Drs Phillips and Little, potentially accounts both for how the radiocarbon dating could have erred and for how the crucified body image could have been formed on the cloth, all in one neat single package. It is also a view to which I can hardly object, given that twenty years ago, when I wrote my 1978 book, I specifically suggested the image came to be formed by some such nuclear-type blinding flash from the body. As I then hypothesised: 'In the darkness of the Jerusalem tomb the dead body of Jesus lay, unwashed, covered in blood, on a stone slab. Suddenly there is a burst of mysterious power from it. In that instant the blood dematerialises, dissolved perhaps by the flash, while its image and that of the body becomes indelibly fused onto the cloth, preserving for posterity a literal "snapshot" of the Resurrection.'[3]

The great difficulty in such a hypothesis, whether it comes from me or from a trained scientist, is that it demands that 2000 years ago something far beyond the normal order happened to the body of Jesus as it lay in apparent death. That something of this kind indeed happened has of course been claimed by Christian believers throughout those 2000 years. But the honest agnostic can understandably only throw up his hands in horror at what he must instinctively reject as scientific heresy, calling, as it does, for the occurrence of a 'miracle'. As Dr Robert Hedges of the Oxford radiocarbon-dating laboratory commented, back in 1989, on Dr Thomas Phillips's arguments: 'If a supernatural explanation is to be proposed, it seems pointless to make any scientific measurement on the Shroud at all.'[4]

So what are we to make of the Shroud mystery? Surely, despite all the arguments advanced earlier in this book, we are too rationalist to accept belief in miracles? Surely we ought to be able to cast the Shroud from our minds as too good to be true, as something that simply *must* have been forged? Surely the 'safe', sensible, rational option must be to accept the verdict of the three radiocarbon-dating laboratories that some cunning forger simply faked the Shroud's image some time between 1260 and 1390? Mustn't it?

After some thirty years of actively grappling with the subject I almost envy this position, and if we want a role model of one man who, ostensibly at least, has been totally comfortable with it, it is the American Episcopalian priest Revd David Sox. While he was working as a teacher at the American School in London in 1977, Sox helped found Britain's Society for the Turin Shroud. As a result of his energy and enthusiasm he became the Society's first General Secretary and his well-informed book on the Shroud, *File on the Shroud*, published in 1978, although well balanced, obviously favoured authenticity.

Then, on his learning in 1980 of Dr McCrone's iron-oxide findings, Sox swiftly wrote *The Image on the Shroud*, clearly having made up his mind that the Shroud must be a fake. And when the radiocarbon-dating results were announced on 13 October 1988, it was he who was quickest to bring out a slim volume, *The Shroud Unmasked: Uncovering the Greatest Forgery of All Time*, its very title leaving no doubt about his opinions.

So why does Sox believe the Shroud to be a forgery? In his *Unmasked* he has conveniently listed his main reasons, aside from McCrone and the radiocarbon dating:

(1) *'no record of the Shroud's existence until 1356'* – This has hopefully been addressed reasonably thoroughly in our chapters 10 to 12.

(2) *'the bloodstains have remained red'* – 'Quite aside from Dr Alan Adler's argument, we have heard ancient blood specialist Dr Thomas Loy confirm that blood many thousands of years old can remain bright red in certain cases of traumatic death.

(3) *there are signs of artistic modesty* – As we have already shown, the crossed-hands pose can be found among both ancient and mediaeval burials. This is no indication of the hand of an artist.

(4) *'does not conform to Jewish burial practice'* – The Jewish academic Victor Tunkel has shown that the Shroud unexpectedly *does* conform to how a crucified Jew would have been buried in the time of Jesus.

(5) *twill linen ... not yet found in archaeological investigations in Palestine* – As we have learned, the twill weave was known in Jesus's time, there simply being no known surviving examples in linen.

Sox's objections to the Shroud's authenticity, therefore, can hardly be considered overwhelming, and we have answered them in the course of this book. As for the fundamental questions for anyone adopting the forgery hypothesis – for example: 'Who forged such an extraordinary image?' 'How did he do so without betraying any obvious sign of his artifice?' 'How did he manage to get so much right medically, historically and culturally?' – if you ask yourself whether Sox, or any of the other current detractors, from McCrone and Hall to Picknett and Prince, has yet offered any genuinely satisfying answers, the response has to be no.

Indeed, if anyone had come up with a convincing solution as to how and by whom the Shroud was forged, they would inevitably have created a consensus around which everyone sceptical on the matter would rally. Yet so far this has not even begun to happen. Realistically, to date there has been only one genuinely satisfying, albeit still only partial, replication of the Shroud's image, that by Professor Nicholas Allen. And that demands so much ingenuity and advanced photographic knowledge on the part of someone of the Middle Ages that it may actually represent rather better evidence for the Shroud's authenticity than for its forgery.

Yet I would be less than honest if I tried to argue that the opposite or pro-authenticity viewpoint is any more rational, free of difficulties and unified than the camp of the detractors. After all, as I have never ever tried to downplay, it absolutely beggars belief that the cloth in which Jesus was wrapped in the tomb should have survived to our time. Even more demanding upon human credulity is that it should have been imprinted with a photograph of him in all his wounds. Rationally, dead bodies do not normally leave imprints of themselves on their burial wrappings. And I would be the first to concur that radiocarbon dating is a useful and well-tried archaeological tool that is normally reasonably reliable.

But this is only the half of it. In tune with this book's title it would be no exaggeration to say that the subject of the Shroud has never been more 'bloodied' and in serious disarray than at this present time. As I type these words the Shroud itself, as a physical object, is almost literally 'in hiding'. Because of continuing mystery surrounding the identity and motives of those who perpetrated the incendiary attack on its chapel, its current whereabouts are being kept secret, possibly up to the very time of the expositions, and I am no more 'in the know' about them than anyone else. Of the normally calm, quiet, cloistered world in which the cloth has been kept during the past four centuries – the High Altar end of the cathedral where the bullet-proof display case was so recently erected; the Royal Chapel with the Bertola altar that was the Shroud's normal 'permanent' home; and the adjoining rooms of the Royal Palace where I had my viewing in 1973 and STURP conducted their testing work in 1978 – all these, as the world now knows, have been very seriously damaged as a result of the fire of April 1997 [fig. 27]. Although at the time of writing the most intense efforts are in hand to get them back to some sort of presentability in time for the expositions of 1998 and 2000, the anticipation is that repairs to the very badly damaged chapel will take until into the next century.

No less disarray surrounds the Shroud as a subject, for reasons that in this instance can hardly be blamed upon the recent fire. As will have been obvious from some of the comments expressed earlier in this book, much of the scientific-testing work which the STURP team carried out on the Shroud in 1978 was less than ideal, even by the standards of that time, let alone that of the radically advanced techniques that could be applied today. In the run-up to the radiocarbon dating of 1988 several serious programmes of scientific enquiry, including one from Britain, were for-mulated with the idea of these being conducted alongside the sampling for radiocarbon dating, so that at least some of the deficiencies of 1978 could be remedied.

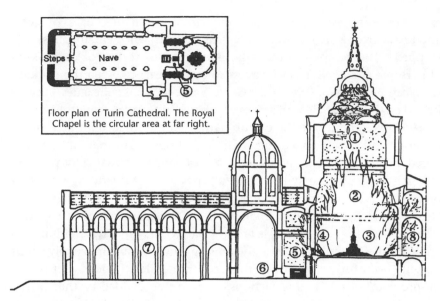

Floor plan of Turin Cathedral. The Royal Chapel is the circular area at far right.

1. Guarino Guarini's 17th-century dome. Possible danger of collapse

2. Royal Chapel. Central and high portions of the walls' marble cladding badly disfigured by intense heat

3. Bertola's 17th-century altar of the Shroud. More intact than at first feared thanks to protective scaffolding, but still needing restoration work

4. Ornate glass screen enabling Shroud altar to be viewed from the Cathedral. Totally destroyed by the fire

5. Bullet-proof glass display case made in 1993. Smashed by fireman Mario Trematore in order to rescue Shroud casket

6. Cathedral high altar. The Shroud's new display case lay immediately behind this

7. Cathedral nave. With the exception of the effects of water and smoke, the Cathedral proper largely escaped serious fire or structural damage. The Shroud was rushed through the nave to safety

8. Royal Palace. Extensive damage to the upper floor corridor and rooms immediately adjoining the Royal Chapel. 60% of the valuable 18th- and 19th-century works of art in these areas destroyed

Fig 27 Turin Cathedral: the fire damage of April 1997
Sectional view of Turin Cathedral and the Royal Chapel, showing the areas most seriously affected by the fire of 11 April 1997. (Based on sectional view reproduced in *Sindon* December 1993, p. 67)

In the event, when no other significant testing work was allowed following the appointment of the three radiocarbon-dating laboratories to carry out the Shroud carbon dating, all the other carefully prepared programmes had to be abandoned as so much waste paper. The only potential

237

exception was whatever might be done with those small samples of blood and textile over which Giovanni Riggi, as the man who actually physically snipped off the samples for the carbon-dating laboratories, took some kind of personal charge. But as we have also earlier learned, even the work on these samples, as pioneered by Dr Garza-Valdès and his colleagues, became halted by Cardinal Saldarini's ruling that anything taken from the Shroud in 1988 over and above the carbon-dating samples had no official authorisation and should be returned to him. Although Cardinal Saldarini has urged everyone 'to be patient until a clear and systematically planned research programme may be arranged', the result of his ruling is that all ongoing research, including lines of further enquiry that might conclusively overturn the radiocarbon verdict of 1988, are indefinitely frozen.

As for the camp of the people around the world who have continued to argue for the Shroud's authenticity (among whom I must inevitably count myself), even this is hardly one to be recommended, divided as it is into umpteen often quarrelling factions every bit as divided as that of the Shroud's detractors. Although country after country has its Shroud group, many of these include people with wild ideas and most are in some kind of strife.

Thus Italy has its 'Centro Internazionale di Sindonologia' in Turin and 'Collegamento pro Sindone' in Rome, neither of which particularly sees eye to eye with the other. America's STURP group largely disintegrated because of internal quarrels and was formally wound up in 1996. Although this has recently been replaced by a new group, AMSTAR, there are at least five others dotted around the United States, none exactly flourishing or in harmony with the others. In Europe Spain has its Centro Español de Sindonologia, France its very Gallic Centre International d'Études sur le Linceul de Turin, and Britain its British Society for the Turin Shroud. And despite this latter being an inoffensive, genuinely non-partisan society that makes no attempt to promote itself, even it has had its problems, in the early 1990s suffering an extraordinary 'infiltrate, discredit and destroy' attack from the 'Leonardo da Vinci theory' authors Picknett and Prince.

We should not be amazed at any of this. Both in his life and his way of death Jesus himself was no stranger to strife. And even after his death his disciples heatedly quarrelled among themselves and had to endure suffering, ridicule and worse from those violently opposed to all that they stood for.

But in the face of all this the bemused bystander may well be minded to ask: why should I be at all interested in such a strife-ridden subject?

1203 'The shroud in which Our Lord had been wrapped ... every Friday raised itself upright, so that one could see the figure of Our Lord on it' (French Crusader Robert de Clari, writing of the 'marvels' he saw in Constantinople). Did the Byzantines have a device for making the Shroud appear to rise from its casket?

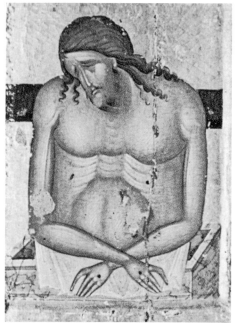

33a. (above) Italian sculptor Giovanni Pisano's depiction of angels with linen cloth of which a Shroud-like half-figure of Jesus is imprinted, *c.*1310. Originally created for the pulpit of the Cathedral of Pisa.

33b. (right) 14th century Byzantine example of Christ with crossed hands (known as the Man of Sorrows in the West, and King of Glory in the East) rising from the tomb. This theme recurring in both European and Byzantine art from at least as early as the late 12th century/early 13th century, seems to have been closely linked to the Grail concept of an image of the crucified Christ rising from a casket.

34a. Fresco of *c*.1225 depicting Jesus being taken down from the cross, from the Chapel of the Holy Sepulchre, Winchester Cathedral. Note just to the left of the cross the figure holding up a large 'shroud' clearly intended to go over the head and down to the feet in the manner of that of Turin.

34b. *c*.1100 Shroud-like 'crossed hands' style depiction of Jesus in death, from a Byzantine ivory in the collection of the Victoria & Albert Museum, London.

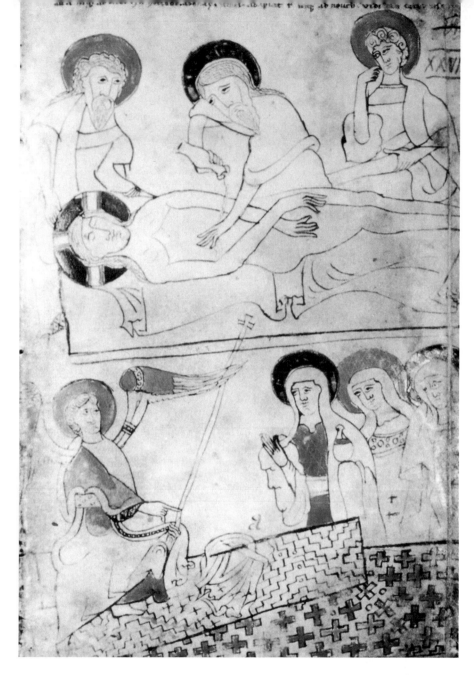

35a. *c.*1192 Entombment scene from the Hungarian Pray manuscript, reliably dated 1192–5, showing unmistakably Shroud-like figure of Christ. Note the four fingers and no thumbs, also the distinctive bloodstain on the forehead.

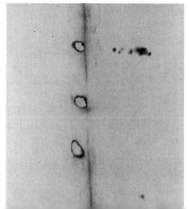

35b. One of the four groups of so-called 'poker hole' burn damage on the Shroud, damage known to have predated the 1532 fire. A tiny group of similar holes appear on the shroud depicted in the Pray manuscript above, also on the sarcophagus lid.

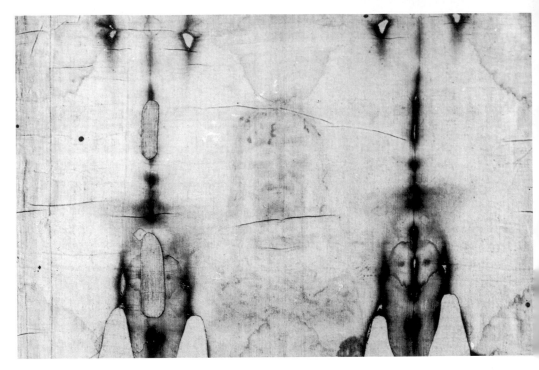

36a. The facial area of the Shroud, natural appearance.

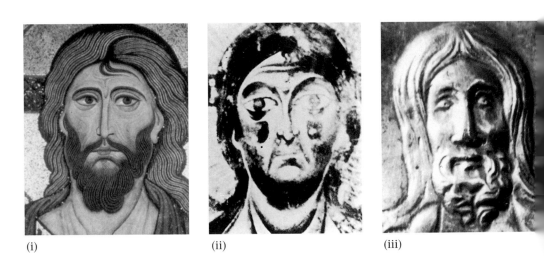

(i) (ii) (iii)

36b. Typical seemingly Shroud-inspired Christ likenesses from Byzantine art of the 12th- back to the 6th-centuries:

  (i) *c.*1200 Christ Pantocrator, Cefalú, Sicily.

 (ii) *c.*1000 Christ Pantocrator, San Angelo in Formis, Italy.

(iii) *c.*600 Christ Pantocrator, medallion portrait on silver vase found at Homs, Syri

37a. *c.*1100 One of the earliest-known direct artistic depictions of the cloth of Edessa, from a fresco above an arch in the Sakli or 'Hidden' Church in the Goreme region of central Turkey.

37b. Artist's copy of the cloth of Edessa, fresco, end of 12th-century, from the Church of the Archangel Michael, Kato Lefkara, Cyprus.

37c. 12th-century copy of the cloth of Edessa from the Church of Spas, Nereditsa, Russia. This is no longer extant. Note on these copies the striking affinity to the equivalent area on the Shroud opposite.

38a. *c.*692 Christ portrait on a gold solidus of the Byzantine emperor Justinian II (685-695; 705-711 AD), the first known coinage to feature Christ's portrait. This example is thought to date from around the year 692, and bears a particularly close affinity to the Shroud face opposite.

38b. *c.*600 Christ Pantocrator. Icon from the Monastery of St. Catherine, Mount Sinai.

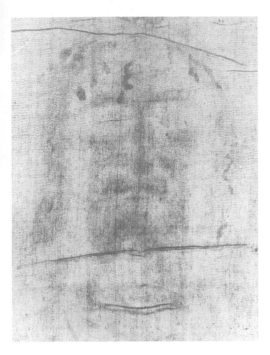

39a. The Shroud face. 39 b. Plan of some of the more distinctive of the 'Vignon' markings: (1) Two strands of hair (2) Transverse streak across forehead (3) Topless 'square' between eyebrows (4) 'V' shape at bridge of nose (5) Raised right eyebrow (6) Heavily accentuated, 'owlish' eyes (7) Accentuated left cheek (8) Accentuated right cheek (9) Enlarged left nostril (10) Accentuated line between nose and upper lip (11) Heavy line under lower lip (12) Hairless area between lower lip and beard (13) Forked beard (14) Transverse line across throat (15) Left sidelock of hair longer than right.

39c. c.700 Christ Pantocrator from the Ponziano catacomb Rome. Note the distinctive topless square between the eyebrows corresponding to an identical feature on the Shroud.

39d. c.1100 Christ Pantocrator, also exhibiting Vignon markings, e.g. the 'V' shaped triangle at the bridge of the nose, and a stylised version of the topless square. Mosaic from the dome of the Church of Christ Pantocrator, Church of Daphni, near Athens.

40a. Urfa, the former Edessa, as it looks today. Once it was world-famous for its beautiful Christian churches, all totally obliterated and replaced by Islamic mosques such as that of Halil Rahman seen here.

40b. The 6th-century discovery of the cloth of Edessa hidden in a niche above a gate of the city, from a Byzantine icon.

41a. Coin of Lucius Aelius Abgar VIII of Edessa (177–212). Was he the first monarch in all history to display the Christian cross on his tiara, the Edessan symbol of his monarchy?

41b. American historian Professor Dan Scavone. He argues that confusion over the word 'Britio' (a transliteration of the Syriac word 'birtha', denoting Edessa's citadel) generated the idea that Joseph of Arimathea, the procurer of Jesus's Shroud, took the Grail to Britain, when the real original story was of the Shroud being taken to Edessa.

41c. The 'Britio' or citadel of Edessa, on which Christianity was preached to Edessa's citizens, and on which Abgar VIII built a palace, as it looks today.

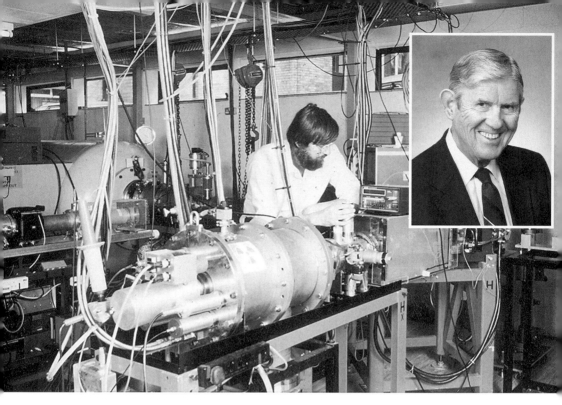

42b. The Oxford radiocarbon-dating laboratory where a snippet from the Shroud was radiocarbon-dated to *c*.1325.

42a. (inset) American nuclear physicist Professor Harry Gove, the prime inventor of the carbo‑ dating method used for the Shro‑ who claims odds of a thousand trillion to one against the Shro‑ being of 1st century date.

42c. Manchester Museum Egyptologist Dr. Rosalie David working on the autopsy of an Egyptian mummy. She became puzzled by instances of the linen wrappings of such mummies sometimes being given radio-carbon-dates up to a thousand years 'younger' than that for the body which they had covered.

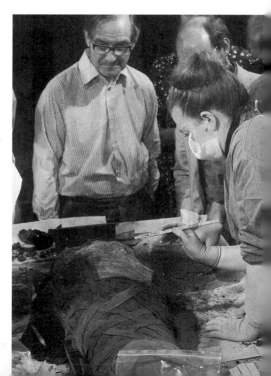

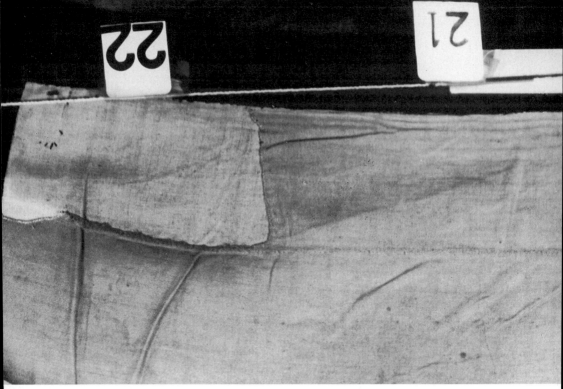

43a. (above) The corner of the Shroud from which the sample was taken for radio-carbon-dating with details of the same corner repeatedly being held up by churchmen at Shroud expositions back through the centuries (b-c below). The fact that this was a very commonly-handled part of the Shroud, with consequent high risk of bacterial build-up, made its choice for the radiocarbon-dating samples particularly inadvisable.

43b. (left) c.1690 Detail of engraving of exposition of the Shroud in Turin (see 30b, above).

43c. 1578. Detail of engraving of exposition of the Shroud on its arrival in Turin.

Did a mediaeval forger paint the image onto the Shroud? The theory of Chicago microscopist Dr. Walter McCrone (44a below).

44b. Conventional 'mediaeval artist' replication of the Shroud face by Chicago professional artist the late Walter Sanford, following McCrone's formula for how the Shroud image was painted.

44c. Monochromatic painting of Christ Pantocrator at Avignon by Simone Martini, created *c*.1341 and suggested by Dr. Walter McCrone as produced using a similar artistic technique to that used for the Shroud.

Did a mediaeval forger burnish the image onto the Shroud? The theory of University of Tennessee researchers Professor Randall Bresee and Emily Craig:

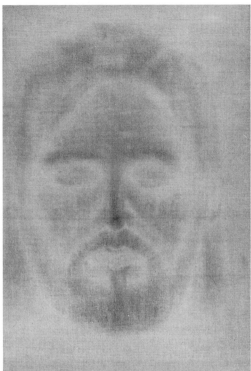

45a. Stage one: A face is conventionally painted on paper.

45b. (above right) Stage two: By placing the painted paper face downwards on a cloth of the same size, and vigorously rubbing its non-painted side with a wooden spoon, a Shroud-like reversed face is transferred to the cloth.

45c. (right) Stage three: Photographic negative of (b). According to Craig and Bresee, this is but one of several ways by which this 'burnishing technique' replicates many of the characteristics of the Shroud image.

Did Leonardo da Vinci produce the Shroud photographically?

46a. According to London journalist Lynn Picknett and partner Clive Prince, back in 1492 Leonardo da Vinci specially invented a primitive form of photography in order to create the Shroud image, using a dead body and his own face (left) as models.

46b. Two of several tumblers liberally charged with wine on the table of Leonardo's *Last Supper*, as clearly depicted in Gianpetrino's much better preserved early copy of this, currently hanging in the chapel of Magdalen College, Oxford. This directly contradicts one of the Picknett-Prince prime arguments that Leonardo da Vinci faked the Shroud as a mark of his intense hatred of Christianity.

How a mediaeval forger produced the Shroud photographically?
The theory of South African art professor Nicholas Allen:

47a. The suspended plaster cast which Professor Allen used as his model

47b. Professor Nicholas Allen. He believes the Shroud could have been produced from materials and know-how available in the Middle Ages.

47c. Negative of the cloth on which Professor Allen produced a replication of the Shroud's whole frontal image, using mediaval know-how and materials. More convincing than all the rest of the Shroud 'replications' put together, this at least corroborates the Shroud image's character as a photograph rather than a painting.

How radiocarbon-dating may have seriously mis-dated the Shroud?
The theory of American microbiologist Dr. Leoncio Garza-Valdés:

48b. Dr. Leoncio Garza-Valdés (left) at his microscope. He wondered whether a similar bioplastic coating might have radically falsified the so-confident '1260–1390' radiocarbon-date attributed to the Shroud.

48a. The 'fake' that was not a fake. The Mayan carving known as the Itzamna Tun. A bacterial build-up, forming a shiny bioplastic coating, caused 'experts' seriously to mis-date this.

48c. Photomicrograph of a Shroud thread cut transversally, showing the fibres encased in a bioplastic material built up by millions of bacterial micro-organisms in the manner of a coral reef. According to Dr.Garza-Valdés, the proportion of this still living material relative to pure Shroud linen could readily account for a 1300 year error.

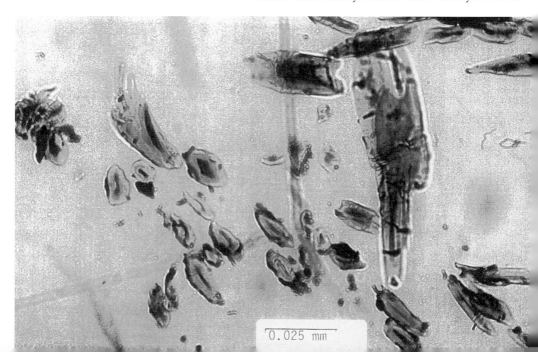

0.025 mm

Can the Shroud be worth all this 'blood'? After all, it is no more than a time-scarred piece of cloth that you can hardly beat anyone over the head with. So why should I give it even a second thought, let alone all the years of time that some of these 'enthusiasts' have devoted to it? At the end of the day, does it really matter to anyone whether it is genuine or a forgery?

The infinitely tantalising feature of the Shroud is that it freely allows these thoughts and more. After all, it *is* just a mute piece of cloth. It cannot answer you back. However you choose to react to it is purely up to you. And, thankfully, despite all the different quarrelling groups, there is no actual cult behind it.

But if you are a thinking person, ultimately you do have to decide in your own mind whether you believe the Shroud to be just a mediaeval fake – in the words of the American writer John Walsh 'one of the most ingenious, most unbelievable products of the human mind and hand on record'[5] or 'the most awesome and instructive relic of Jesus Christ in existence', imprinted with a 2000-year-old photograph of him as he lay in death. Those are the two stark alternatives that the Shroud presents, and although it was some thirty-five years ago that Walsh penned those words they remain every bit as valid today.

And you can play around as much as you like with all the evidence from chemistry, physics, history, archaeology and so much more, the testings for blood, for radioactive carbon and so on. But the issue comes down to what does that image on the photographic negative that so perplexed its discoverer Secondo Pia just a century ago say to your mind – or, even more pertinently, to your heart? Does it arouse in your blood the feeling that here is the very man who, in some still unimaginable way, broke the bounds of death as his blood-soaked corpse lay in a Jerusalem tomb 2000 years ago? Or does it leave you as cold as his body, by all normal logic, ought to have been?

One of the very heavy responsibilities carried by a writer is that your words can sometimes touch in the profoundest of ways people whom you have never met. Only recently I learned of the effect upon one Englishwoman, some twenty years ago, of the lines from my book *The Turin Shroud* that I quoted earlier in this chapter. These were the lines hypothesising how the entombed body of Jesus may perhaps have dematerialised as a result of 'a burst of mysterious power' from it, a burst that at one and the same time flashed onto the Shroud 'a literal "snapshot" of the Resurrection'.

The Englishwoman in question was Margaret Hebblethwaite, who on her own admission had been educated into the modernist Bishop-of-Durham-type way of thinking that any historical truth to Jesus and his Resurrection is completely unimportant. She has described her reactions to my words in an article she wrote for the Catholic journal, *The Tablet*, only a few days after the Turin Cathedral fire:

> I will never forget the hot and cold feelings of shock and even fear – like the Gospel women – when I read those lines. So did the resurrection really happen, historically, bodily, after all? Was the Shroud the enduring evidence not just of what Jesus looked like, and of the pains he bore, but of his resurrection from the dead?
>
> There was also a second strand of amazement, which was amazement at my own amazement, for my very emotions gave the lie to my theories. If possible evidence of Jesus's bodily resurrection made me tingle with disbelieving joy and terrified faith, then I could no longer maintain that historical facts made no difference. Faith in Jesus Christ is built on the fact that God's son *did* live, die and rise for us, and not just on the belief that he could have done. I now believed in the bodily resurrection *not because the Shroud proved it* [my italics], but because that kind of faith simply feels different and stronger, and it was no use my pretending that it could feel the same.[6]

Now to the best of my recollection I have never met or corresponded with Margaret Hebblethwaite, but I have news for her. Her words sent equally as much of a chill and thrill through to the innermost core of my being as mine clearly did to hers. Except in each case, of course, as I am sure she would acknowledge, it was not our individual ever inadequate struggles for the right words to express ourselves which was important. *It was what our words had opened our hearts to*. For as Margaret Hebblethwaite went on to say: 'When the news of the carbon dating came through I did not much mind: the Shroud had already fulfilled its purpose for me.'

While on the face of it that sentence might sound almost callous, the late Fr Peter Rinaldi, an Italian-born Catholic priest whom many in America regarded as 'Mr Shroud' and to whom I owe directly my viewing of the Shroud in 1973, expressed very similar sentiments in the wake of the carbon-dating result. He wrote that what troubled him was not his own reactions to the news, but what effect it might have on others with '. . . an exaggerated notion . . . of the importance of the Shroud in the scheme of our Christian faith. When lecturing on the Shroud, I often reminded my listeners that for us Christians, it is the Lord that matters, not the Shroud.

If the Shroud does have a meaning, it is because it speaks to us of his sufferings as no other image does. But at best the Shroud is only a sign of our faith and hope in Christ. He and he alone is our greatest and dearest possession.'[7]

Such is the paradox in those words that it is all too easy for those of dissident opinion to misinterpret them, as has in fact happened. In the wake of Fr Rinaldi's death in February 1993, Dr Walter McCrone, in his recent book *Judgement Day for the Shroud*, has chosen to quote this passage as evidence that even Fr Rinaldi must have lost his faith in the Shroud's authenticity in the wake of the carbon dating.

Well, despite my respect for Dr McCrone, I can only say that as in his other highly publicised judgements, he simply could not be more wrong. I knew Fr Rinaldi as a most dear and close friend to the very end of his life, five years after he wrote those words, and all that he was saying, as he said consistently throughout, is that at the end of the day it is indeed not the Shroud itself that is important. Instead, far, far more important – as the pragmatic Margaret Hebblethwaite so poignantly learned from within herself – are those intangible emotions to which, whatever its own material origins, the Shroud opens our hearts.

So what of the hearts of other hard-nosed scientists? Although Professor Harry Gove, as we have learned from earlier in this book, is very far from being a 'true believer' in the Shroud, he is an admirable, honest man who freely acknowledges in his book that his own assistant, Shirley Brignall, from whom he won a pair of cowboy boots in a bet over the Shroud carbon-dating result, told him in all seriousness that 'even now her heart still tells her it is Christ's shroud'. He even comes very close in his book to admitting that he feels the same, despite what his instruments told him. As for Walter McCrone, anyone who reads his *Judgement Day for the Turin Shroud* may be astounded by the amount of space that he, as the strictly no-nonsense expert in microscopy, has devoted to quoting verbatim from Fr Rinaldi's letters in all their pastoral detail. So as I have directly suggested to him, could it be that there is something – or someone – crying to be let out even in his heart?

But the most crucial question of all is: what about you, dear reader? Throughout your reading of this book and in particular your viewing of the photographs on its pages, has the man of the Shroud said anything to you? Has anything been fired in your blood?

Only you can know the *honest* answer to that one.

Author's Postscript
The DNA of God?

At the time of this book going to press, February 1998, Turin Cathedral is just about to re-open its doors after repairs from the fire. It is understood that the Shroud expositions of April to June will definitely be held there, even though the High Altar end will remain blocked off because of damage behind it.

Otherwise, most developments reported in the press during the run-up to the Expositions do not seem to contribute significantly to any greater understanding of the Shroud mystery. For instance, the American psychiatrist Dr Alan Whanger, supported by the highly respected Israeli botanist Dr Avinoam Danin, has identified the images of twenty-eight different species of flowers in the Shroud, all but one of which grow within a few miles of Jerusalem. Also, according to researchers at an optical laboratory in Paris, all around the face of the man of the Shroud there are words written in ancient Latin and Greek, including 'Jesus' and 'Nazareth'. While there can be absolutely no doubting the sincerity of those who make these claims, the great danger of such arguments is that researchers may 'see' merely what their minds trick them into thinking is there.

Another development, reported only in the local press, without its Shroud links yet realized, concerns Dr Dmitri Kouznetsov. In December 1997 the *New Times* of Connecticut reported his arrest on charges of attempted larceny and forgery, for trying to pass stolen cheques. At the time of writing he is being held awaiting trial.

Altogether development holding serious promise concerns Dr Garza-Valdès, and his discovery of the bioplastic coating, as described in Chapter 17. In September 1997 Dr Garza-Valdès and his publishers Doubleday sought my help on a book that he was writing, and as a result of this I visited him a second time in San Antonio, accompanied by my wife Judith. On this occasion we were actually shown the bioplastic coating under the microscope. It seemed quite obvious to me that this was indeed one and the same as that puzzling 'surface sheen' that I had noted on my first firsthand examination of the Shroud nearly a quarter of a century before.

During this same visit I was also able to interview Professor Stephen Mattingly, head of the Texas University microbiology department that had 'hosted' Dr Garza-Valdès's researches. Although no 'Shroudie', Professor Mattingly told me matter-of-factly that he regarded it as only a matter of time before the radiocarbon-dating scientists would have to accept that its presence invalidated the results that they arrived at in 1988. During this same visit I also spoke on the telephone to Professor Gove, who gave me to understand that despite his 'thousand trillion to one' pronouncements, the main obstacle to greater acceptance of Dr Garza-Valdès's findings now actually lies not so much with himself, but with face-saving concerns on the part of the three laboratories who worked on the Shroud samples in 1988.

As we went on to discuss, a very necessary preliminary to any possible retraction of the 1988 claimed proof of the Shroud's medieval date has to be the development of a reliable method of eliminating bioplastic coating from any ancient sample. Such a method, involving the breaking-down of cellulose into glucose, I learned from Professor Mattingly, is actually already available. Now the immediate need is for it to be properly tested on ordinary ancient linen samples, such as anomalously dated Egyptian mummy wrappings, before it can be applied to the Shroud. Clearly if such samples were to exhibit significantly older radiocarbon dates once they had the bioplastic coating eliminated, then the door would be wide open for the method to be applied to the Shroud. In this regard we may recall that a snippet of the sample taken for carbon dating was held back in 1988, and is understood to be in Cardinal Saldarini's safekeeping. Even with the treatment to eliminate the bioplastic coating this would probably contain sufficient carbon for Arizona, Oxford and Zurich to do a full re-run of their original dating.

But however promising all this might look for such a re-run to be done in the near future, and for Dr Garza-Valdès's findings to be fully recognised, a sticking point lies with Dr Garza-Valdès himself, and the obduracy he has maintained following Cardinal Saldarini's letter of 31 July 1996, formally notifying him that because the Cardinal had not sanctioned Riggi's supplying him with Shroud samples, the findings he has drawn from them cannot be recognised.

During my visit of September 1997 I studied Saldarini's letter, and what impressed me was the care which he had taken to explain why he could come to no other ruling. He pointed out that because he had not been consulted, he had not even any guarantee that Riggi's samples came from the Shroud. I sympathise too his concerns regarding what he had learned from sensationalised media reports about the testing of 'blood' samples in a DNA laboratory. To me, therefore, the diplomatic approach would have been for him to seek an early audience with the Cardinal. He could then have explained that he had acted in good faith, and that because the samples he received had borne Cardinal Ballestrero's seal (and had been photographed with it *in situ*) there could be no doubt of their genuineness. The other point of importance was to explain that the matter of the DNA had been much over-blown in the press reports; the only available finding, although of major importance, was that the Shroud 'blood' was indeed blood, and that of a human male. Given such an approach, there is every reason to believe that the characteristically genial Cardinal Saldarini might have revised his earlier declaration of Dr Garza's findings as invalid, and given him the fullest backing for the re-run of the carbon dating earlier outlined.

In the event, however, Dr Garza-Valdès responded to Cardinal Scaldarini's letter by sending a copy of a papal secretary's run-of-the-mill letter giving the Pope's blessings on his work, saying it was all the authority he needed. He is also going ahead with the publication of his book under the title *The DNA of God*, a title that, catchy as it may sound (and I should know, as it inadvertently originated via me), is not only irrelevant to the main thrust of his findings, but also can only be offensive to the very people whose cooperation he most needs.

The situation is an almost unbelievable Catch-22, but that is how it stands as at the end of January 1998. And how it will all ultimately be resolved is anyone's guess . . .

Notes and References

Introduction

1. Shroud of Turin Research Project.
2. Ian Wilson, *The Shroud of Turin*, New York, Doubleday, 1978; also published in the UK the same year by Gollancz under the title *The Turin Shroud*.
3. Paris, Bibliothèque Nationale, Collection de Champagne, vol. 154, folio 138.
4. As translated from the Latin by the Revd Herbert Thurston SJ, and published in his article 'The Holy Shroud and the Verdict of History', *The Month*, CI (1903), pp. 17–29.
5. Michael Sheridan and Phil Reeves, the *Independent*, Friday, 14 October 1988.
6. Ibid.
7. P. E. Damon et al., 'Radiocarbon dating of the shroud of Turin', *Nature*, vol. 337, no. 6208, 16 February 1989, pp. 611–15.
8. Christopher Knight and Robert Lomas, *The Hiram Key: Pharaohs, Freemasons and the Discovery of the Secret Scrolls of Jesus*, London, Century, 1996. The authors claim the Shroud image 'perfectly matches' the 'known image of the last Grand Master of the Knights Templar', in support of which they include in their illustrations a line drawing that might certainly be construed to bear a reasonable resemblance to the man of the Shroud. But where does this 'known image' come from? In the book's list of sources this is simply quoted as from the authors' own collection. In fact, there is no known authoritative contemporary or near-contemporary image of Jacques de Molay, and their line drawing bears all the hallmarks of being from some nineteenth-century illustrator's imagination of what de Molay *might* have looked like.
9. Harry Gove, *Relic, Icon or Hoax?*, Bristol and Philadelphia, Institute of Physics Publishing, 1996, p. 264.

Chapter 1

1. Had Pia successfully taken his photograph on the first day of the expositions, as he attempted, then he would have been able to do so without glass intervening. But after this opening day protective glass was placed over the Shroud at the insistence of the Princess Clotilde of Savoy.

2. Quoted in *Amateur Photographer*, 8 March 1967.
3. Schwortz makes this statement in the Introduction to his web site on the Internet, http://www.shroud.com.
4. Quoted on *Everyman* programme screened on BBC 1, 15 October 1995.
5. Isabel Piczek, 'Why the Shroud of Turin Could Not Have Been the Work of a "Clever" Artist', publication for private circulation, Los Angeles, 1989.
6. See Frederick T. Zugibe, *The Cross and the Shroud. A Medical Examiner Investigates the Crucifixion*, New York, Angelus, 1982, p. 108.
7. For an excellent account of these, with accompanying illustrations, see Luigi Fossati SDB, 'Copies of the Shroud Part I' and 'Copies of the Shroud Parts II and III' in *Shroud Spectrum*, issues no. 12 (September 1984) and 13 (December 1984) respectively. *Shroud Spectrum* is published by the Indiana Center for Shroud Studies, 1252 N Jackson Branch Ridge Road, Nashville, Indiana 47448, USA.
8. Correspondence with the author.
9. Dr Alan Whanger, Duke University Medical Center, Durham, North Carolina, press release, 29 March 1994.

Chapter 2
1. See David Buckton (ed.), *Treasures of Byzantine Art and Culture*, London, British Museum, 1994, exhibit no. 112.
2. Information kindly supplied by Robin Bootle, producer of the QED programme *Riddle of the Shroud*, transmitted BBC 2, 17 October 1988.
3. Article by the author in the *Observer* Colour Magazine, 31 January 1988.
4. Paris, Bibliothèque Nationale, Nouv. acq.lat.3093, p. 155, reproduced in Millard Meiss, *French Painting in the Time of Jean de Berry: The Late Fourteenth Century and the Patronage of the Duke*, London, Phaidon, 1967, p. 35.
5. Whenever right or left is referred to in the context of the man of the Shroud, this is based on an actual body having been laid in the Shroud to produce the imprint, the Shroud itself being a true negative, with light and shade reversed, and the Pia–Enrie photographic negative, suitably left-to-right reversed, providing a true 'photograph'. We therefore refer to the true body's left or right.
6. See in particular Dr Sebastiano Rodante, 'The Coronation of Thorns in the Light of the Shroud', *Shroud Spectrum* 1, 1982, pp. 4–24.
7. Lynn Picknett and Clive Prince, *Turin Shroud: In Whose Image? The Shocking Truth Unveiled*, London, Bloomsbury, 1994, pl. 7 of the plates between pp. 148 and 149.
8. For full translation of Paleotto's remarks, see Dorothy Crispino, 'Perceptions of an Antecessor', *Shroud Spectrum International* 23, June 1987, pp. 16–21.
9. Dr Pierre Barbet, *The Passion of Our Lord Jesus Christ*, trans. the Earl of Wicklow, Dublin, Clonmore & Reynolds, 1954.

10. Anthony F. Sava, 'The wounds of Christ', *Catholic Biblical Quarterly* 16, 1957, p. 440.
11. Frederick T. Zugibe, *The Cross and the Shroud*, op. cit.
12. See Gertrud Schiller, *Iconography of Christian Art*, vol. II, London, Lund Humphries, 1972, pl. 494.
13. Ibid., pl. 696.
14. Ibid., pl. 777.
15. Source missing.
16. 'On the middle of the body one notices the vestiges of an iron chain which bound him so tightly to the column that it appears all blood ...' From Dorothy Crispino's excellent translation of the official report of the Poor Clare nuns who repaired the Shroud, 'The Report of the Poor Clare Nuns, Chambéry, 1534', *Shroud Spectrum* 2, March 1982, p. 25.
17. Quoted in Reginald W. Rhein, Jr, 'The Shroud of Turin: Medical Examiners Disagree', *Medical World News* 21, no. 26, 22 December 1980, p. 50.
18. Gilbert R. Lavoie, Bonnie B. Lavoie, Revd Vincent J. Donovan, John S. Ballas, 'Blood on the Shroud of Turin: Part II', *Shroud Spectrum International* 8, September 1983, pp. 2–10.

Chapter 3

1. See, for instance, the results of the University of California's Constitution Research Project, as reported in Britain's *Sunday Times* magazine, 13 October 1968. Although this project found that the rate of growth is quickening, i.e. in many countries young people are taller than comparable like-aged groups were a generation ago, it also found that the height of men in America increased by less than a quarter of an inch between 1875 and 1960. It also noted that there is no evidence that average present-day maximum heights of Europeans are greater than those in comparable populations of 100 or even 1500 years ago.
2. Nicu Haas, 'Anthropological Observations on the Skeletal Remains from Giv'at ha-Mivtar', *Israel Exploration Journal*, vol. 20, nos 1–2, 1970.
3. H. Gressman 'Fetschrifte' for K. Budde, appendix to the *Zeitschrift für die alttestamentliche Wisenschaft* 34, 1920, pp. 60–68.
4. H. Daniel-Rops, *Daily Life in Palestine in the Time of Christ*, London, Weidenfeld & Nicolson, 1962.
5. Matthew 27:26; Mark 15:15; and John 19:1.
6. John 19:34.
7. J. R. Cole in *Current Anthropology*, vol. 24, no. 3, June 1983, p. 296.
8. m.Sanh 6:4; y.Hag 77d–78a; y.Sanh 23. I am indebted to James H. Charlesworth (see next note) for these references. He in his turn quotes indebtedness to Baumgarten, *Studies in Qumran Law*, p. 176.
9. 11QTemple 64.6–13, quoted in James H. Charlesworth, *Jesus and the Dead*

Sea Scrolls, New York, London, etc., Doubleday 1992. It should be noted that the very same phrase, 'hanged upon a tree' was also used by St Peter, specifically of the crucifixion of Jesus, in the speech he gave in the house of the centurion Cornelius, as quoted in Acts 10:39.

10. Josephus, *Antiquities* 17, 295.
11. Josephus, *The Jewish War* 5, 449–51.
12. Ibid., book 7, trans. G. A. Williamson, Harmondsworth, Penguin, 1981, pp. 389–90.
13. John 20:25.
14. The name means Hill of the Divide.
15. N. Haas, 'Anthropological Observations on the Skeletal Remains from Giv'at ha-Mivtar', *Israel Exploration Journal*, vol. 20, nos 1–2, 1970, pp. 38–59.
16. Eugenia L. Nitowski, *The Field and Laboratory Report of the Environmental Study of the Shroud in Jerusalem*, Salt Lake City, Carmelite Monastery, 1986, p. 101.
17. In his original letter Dr Webster spoke here directly of 'Jesus', which in the present context I have altered to preserve neutrality of identification.
18. Letter from Dr Victor Webster to the author, sent 4 August 1978.

Chapter 4
1. Victor Tunkel, lecture 'A Jewish View of the Shroud' to the British Society for the Turin Shroud, 12 May 1983.
2. Solomon Gansfried, *Code of Jewish Law* (*Kitzur Shulchan Aruch*), trans. Hyman E. Goldin, New York, Hebrew Publishing Company, 1927, vol. IV, Ch. CXCVII. Laws relating to Purification (Tahara) nos 9 & 10 (pp. 99–100).
3. Personal correspondence with Victor Tunkel, 1983.
4. John 20:6. Jerusalem Bible translation.
5. See Fr Robert A. Wild, 'The Shroud of Turin – Probably the Work of a 14th-Century Artist or Forger', *Biblical Archaeology Review*, March–April 1984; also David Sox, *The Shroud Unmasked*, Basingstoke, Lamp Press, 1988, p. 71.
6. See photo from travel book of the nineteenth century as reproduced in *Shroud Spectrum International* 13, December 1984, pp. 46–7.
7. See, for example, the reconstruction of the burial of an early Briton whose log coffin and shroud were found at Quernmore, Lancaster in 1973, in Jean Glover, 'The Conservation of Medieval and Later Shrouds from Burials in North West England', *Archaeological Textiles*, Occasional Papers No. 10, United Kingdom Institute for Conservation of Historic and Artistic Works, 1990, p. 49.
8. Roland de Vaux OP, 'Fouille au Khirbet Qumran', *Revue Biblique*, vol. 60, 1953, pp. 83–106, esp. p. 102 & pl. V.
9. See, for example, Milard Meiss, *French Painting in the Time of Jean de Berry: The Boucicaut Master*, London, Phaidon, 1968, pls 143, 152, 154, 156, 157, 158 and 162.

10. John 19:40.
11. See examples in Kurt Weitzmann, 'The Origin of the Threnos', *De Artibus Opuscula XL Essays in Honour of Erwin Panofsky*, (ed.) Millard Meiss, New York University Press, 1961, figs 2, 3, 6, etc.
12. *The Rohan Book of Hours, Bibliothèque Nationale, Paris*, Introduction by Millard Meiss, London, Thames & Hudson, 1973, pls 71 & 73.
13. See Jean Glover, 'The Conservation of Mediaeval and Later Shrouds from Burials in North West England', *Archaeological Textiles*, op. cit., pp. 51–4.

Chapter 5

1. 1969, 1973, 1978, 1988, 1992 and 1997 (the last to check its condition after the fire).
2. For an English translation, see Dorothy Crispino, *Shroud Spectrum* 2, March 1982, pp. 19–27.
3. The poker theory is my own and, if correct, suggests some 'trial by fire' test to which people of the early Middle Ages were rather partial. But others have disagreed with this, some suggesting that the damage occurred when some triple-branched candlestick was accidentally knocked over, though to me the centrality of the holes to the folding arrangement suggests something rather more deliberate.
4. A fragment recently discovered by University of Chicago archaeologists excavating at Çayönü in south-eastern Turkey is reliably thought to date back to 7000 BC. See Heather Routledge, 'Oldest Cloth', *Archaeology*, 1994, p. 20.
5. See photograph reproduced in John Tyrer, 'Looking at the Shroud as a Textile', *Shroud Spectrum International* 6, March 1983, p. 38.
6. D. De Jonghe and M. Tavernier, 'Les damasses de la Proche-Antiquité' in *Bulletin du Centre International d'Étude des Textiles Anciens*, no. 47/8, Lyon, 1978, p. 14; 'Les damassés de Palmyre', ibid., no. 54, Lyon, 1981, p. 20.
7. This is a matter which, for instance, I discussed particularly with Dr John Peter Wild, Senior Lecturer in Archaeology, Manchester University and author of *Textiles in Archaeology*, Shire Archaeology, 1988.
8. Donald King, 'A Parallel for the Linen of the Turin Shroud', CIETA Bulletin 67, 1989, pp. 25–6.
9. John Tyrer, 'The Textile Said to be Similar in Weave to the Shroud', *British Society for the Turin Shroud Newsletter* 27 December 1990/January 1991, pp. 11–13.
10. Gabriel Vial, 'Le Linceul de Turin – Étude Technique', *Bulletin du Centre International d'Étude des Textiles Anciens*, no. 67, Lyon, 1989, pp. 11–24.
11. Gilbert Raes, letter to the author, 23 May 1974.
12. R. Pfister, *Nouveaux textiles de Palmyre*, Les Editions d'Art et d'Histoire, Paris, 1937, p. 40; Yigael Yadin, *The Finds from the Bar-Kokhba Period in 'The Cave*

of Letters', Israel Exploration Society, Jerusalem, 1963, p. 252; and G. M. Crowfoot, *Discoveries in the Judaean Desert II*, Oxford, Clarendon Press, 1961, p. 59. I owe these references to Gabriel Vial, op. cit. above, note 6.

13. From the Tarkan [?] dynasty, this has 140 warp and 50 weft threads to the inch, the approximate Shroud equivalents being 97 warp and 62 weft.
14. Elisabeth Crowfoot, letter to the author, 19 September 1977.
15. Donald M. Smith, 'Textiles and Spain', *Shroud Spectrum International* 35–6, June–September 1990.
16. Isaac Chilo, a pilgrim visiting Jerusalem in 1334, wrote, 'We next pass Ramleh … Among [the Jews] there I found a man from Cordoba, and another from Toledo: both of them men of wealth and position. They have cotton factories.' *Jewish Travellers in the Middle Ages*, Dover, 1987. I owe the quote to Dorothy Crispino's article 'Qutn', *Shroud Spectrum* 35–6, June–September 1990, p. 22.
17. Giovanni Riggi, *Rapporto Sindone (1978–87)*, 3M edition, Milan, 1988, p. 61, trans. John D'Arcy, private publication, pp. 66–7.
18. Personal correspondence with Bill Mottern, 8 February 1982.

Chapter 6
1. Dr Pierre Barbet, *The Passion of our Lord Jesus Christ*, trans. the Earl of Wicklow, op. cit., p. 23.
2. Ian Wilson, *The Turin Shroud*, op. cit., p. 9.
3. Robert Wilcox, *Shroud*, London, Corgi, 1978, p. 39.
4. It is worth noting here that on the morning of Saturday, 24 November 1973 I observed the Shroud as it hung in subdued interior daylight, unilluminated by any artificial lighting. Although I was not able to see it in extreme close-up on this occasion, the colour seemed to be more 'brownish', thereby corresponding to Pierre Barbet's description.
5. See my *The Mysterious Shroud*, New York, Doubleday, 1986, pls 11 & 12.
6. For my first letter to Dr McCrone, and his reply, see his *Judgement Day for the Turin Shroud*, Chicago, Microscope Publications, 1996, pp. 48–51.
7. This was diplomatically disastrous because Turin's Cardinal Ballestrero, having to deal with a communist local government technically having charge of all ex-King Umberto's Taurinese possessions, assumed personal 'hands-on' charge of the Shroud and rejected any 'authorisations' by Umberto as a matter of policy.
8. From a photocopy of McCrone's handwritten notes from his 'Shroud research notebook', kindly sent by him to me in the course of our long personal correspondence. In fact I note that McCrone has also reproduced these in his book *Judgement Day for the Turin Shroud*, received only as this present book was nearing completion. I find the notes puzzling; they have the

unmistakable air of being written, from the very outset, with an 'audience' in mind.

9. Walter McCrone, 'Microscopical Study of the Turin "Shroud" in *Newsletter of Analytical Chemistry Division of American Chemical Society*, Spring 1989.
10. This was to the British Society for the Turin Shroud, on 11 September 1980.
11. From an interview McCrone gave to American journalist, published in the Chicago *Sun-Times*, 24 October 1981.
12. Ray Rogers quoted in David Sox, *The Shroud Unmasked*, op. cit., pp. 67–8.
13. From comments written on the relevant photograph reproduced in my book *The Evidence of the Shroud*.
14. Walter McCrone, 'Microscopical Study of the Turin Shroud' IV, *The Microscope...*
15. Letter to the author from Dr Plesters, 29 July 1982. This is quoted in my book *The Mysterious Shroud*, pp. 127–8.
16. Allan A. Mills, 'Image formation on the Shroud of Turin: the reactive oxygen intermediates hypothesis', *Interdisciplinary Science Reviews*, vol. 20, no. 4, December 1995, pp. 319–26.

Chapter 7

1. This quotation derives from Lalaing's *Voyage de l'archiduc Philippe-le-Beau*, as quoted in Ulysse Chevalier's *Étude critique sur l'origine du S. Suaire de Lirey–Chambéry–Turin*, Paris, A. Picard, 1900, pièce justificative DD.
2. From a photocopy of the handwritten original kindly supplied to me by Dr McCrone in the course of correspondence.
3. T. W. Case, *The Shroud of Turin and the C-14 Dating Fiasco*, Cincinnati, White Horse, 1996, p. 53.
4. Isabel Piczek, 'The Shroud According to the Professional Arts', privately circulated manuscript, p. 14.
5. Gilbert R. Lavoie, Bonnie B. Lavoie, Revd Vincent J. Donovan, John S. Ballas, 'Blood on the Shroud of Turin: Part II', *Shroud Spectrum International* 8, September 1983, pp. 2–10.
6. Alan D. Adler, 'The Origin and Nature of Blood on the Turin Shroud' in *Turin Shroud – Image of Christ* (ed.) William Meacham, Hong Kong, 1987, p. 59.
7. Remark made as an annotation in the course of our personal correspondence.
8. Pierluigi Baima-Bollone, Mario Jorio & Anna Lucia Massaro, 'Identification of the Group of the Traces of Human Blood on the Shroud', *Shroud Spectrum International* 6, March 1983, pp. 3–6.
9. From an article by journalist Luciano Regulo published in the August 1995 issue of the Italian journal *Chi*.
10. Ray Leonard, *The Legacy of the Shroud*, 1988.
11. Letter of Cardinal Saldarini to Garza-Valdès, Protocol no. 200.41/96, sent 31 July 1996.

Chapter 8

1. Dr John Heller, *Report on the Shroud of Turin*, Boston, Houghton Mifflin, 1983, p. 112.
2. There were at least three women as active members of the STURP team proper, also attendant wives. Poor Clare nuns have also been present as helpers.
3. The dimensions are 4.40 × 1m.
4. Domenico Leone, *El Santo Sudario en España*, Barcelona, Biblioteca Sindoniana, 1959, pp. 47–56.
5. From a report to British film producer David Rolfe, January 1977.
6. From information given to Paul Maloney of the American Shroud group ASSIST by Professor Luigi Gonella during their meeting, 21 November 1987.
7. Joe Nickell, 'Pollens on the "Shroud": A Study in Deception', *Skeptical Inquirer*, vol. 18, Summer 1994, pp. 379–85.
8. Association of Scientists and Scholars International for the Shroud of Turin.
9. Paul Maloney, 'The Current Status of Pollen Research and Prospects for the Future', a paper given at the Paris 'Symposium Scientifique International sur le Linceul de Turin', 7–8 September 1989, p. 10 of Maloney's unpublished manuscript.
10. Dr Oliver Rackham, letter to John Ray of Selwyn College, Cambridge, 19 October 1996.
11. This manuscript has apparently been translated into English by Dr Anna M. Ottolenghi of Durham, North Carolina, under the title 'A Contribution to the Study of the Problem of the Authenticity of the Shroud based on Microscopic traces', but no copy has yet been seen by this author. According to Maloney's summary of this manuscript, in it Frei states 'that he made his survey of the tapes and circled the pollen he found. Then when he was ready to make a mount of each pollen he cut a T-shaped incision into the tape, dissolved the adhesive with toluol and very carefully lifted the grain of pollen out with a small wire loop. But this must have seemed a very unsatisfactory method of manipulating the grains and ensuring that they were not lost during transport from the tape to the slide. Hence Dr Frei invented a very special technique using triangles of sticky tape. He would dip the point of the triangle into the incision and retrieve the pollen grain on the tip or edge of the triangle and then lay this down on a microscope slide. He would then put a drop of mounting medium on the slide and place control pollen with this and finish off the mount with a cover slip. This way he could compare the pollen on the triangular shape with the controls.' From Maloney, 'The Current Status of Pollen Research ...', op. cit., p. 7.
12. For typical Horowitz specialist publications relating to pollen analysis, see his 'Climatic and Vegetational Developments in North-eastern Israel during Upper Pleistocene–Holocene Times' in *Pollen et Spores* 13, 1971, pp. 255–78;

also 'Preliminary Palynological Indications as to the Climate of Israel during the last 6000 Years', *Palaeorient* 2, 1974, pp. 407–14.

13. From private correspondence between Paul Maloney and Horowitz and Danin, as referred to in Maloney's article, 'The Current Status of Pollen Research and Prospects for the Future', kindly made available to the author.

14. Joseph A. Kohlbeck and Eugenia L. Nitowski, 'New Evidence May Explain Image on Shroud of Turin', *Biblical Archaeology Review*, July–August 1986, p. 23.

Chapter 9

1. See L. Fossati, 'L'Ostensione del 1842', *Collegamento Pro Sindone*, November–December 1992, pp. 24–5.

2. Archives of the Department of the Aube, 9 G4, quoted in Ulysse Chevalier, *Étude Critique sur l'origine du Saint Suaire de Lirey–Chambéry–Turin*, Paris, Picard 1900, pièce justicative Q.

3. This is a purely arbitrary numbering to distinguish him from his father, Geoffrey I, of whom there will be discussion to follow.

4. For the full English translation of this memorandum, as translated by the Revd Herbert Thurston, see my own *The Turin Shroud*, op. cit., Appendix B.

5. This is an appeal by Geoffrey I's wife Jeanne de Vergy for grants formerly made to her husband Geoffrey I to be made in favour of Geoffrey II, described as *'en bas âgé'*.

Chapter 10

1. The manuscript reference is MS 487, folio 123. The definitive modern-day edition of this text was prepared by Philippe Lauer, *La conquête de Constantinople*, Paris, Classiques français du moyen âge, 40, 1924, reprinted 1956. A useful translation into English is that by Edgar H. McNeal, *The Conquest of Constantinople, translated from the Old French*, Columbia University Records of Civilisation 23, New York, 1936.

2. The word Robert employs is *sydoines*, a variant of *sindon*, the word used for Jesus's shroud in the Greek text of the New Testament.

3. As has been stressed by Canadian-born professor of Old French literature at the University of California, Dr Peter Dembowski: 'The French word *figure* acquired the meaning 'face' only in the era of the *précieux*. Before *c.* 1650 *figure* meant what it signified in Latin, i.e. 'figure', 'outline', 'form' etc. This fact is common knowledge to all students of Old French language: see for example Walther von Wartburg, *Französisches Etymologisches Wörterbuch*, vol. III, p. 521.' From Dembowski, 'Sindon in the Old French Chronicle of Robert de Clari', *Shroud Spectrum International* 2, March 1982, p. 16.

4. This was the response from genealogist and heraldry specialist Noel Currer-Briggs, when I enquired whether the fact that Jeanne de Vergy's shield

appears on the right-hand side of the medallion suggested that Geoffrey was dead, and she was the prime mover in the expositions: 'It is true that the dexter side in heraldry is more important, but only when two or more arms are quartered together ... On the Lirey medallion the arms of Charny and Vergy are not quartered, but each shown separately, with Charny on the left and Vergy on the right. Perversely in heraldry, sinister and dexter mean left and right as seen from behind the shield, not as the observer sees it, so when the shield was carried across the knight's chest to protect him, his right side was protected by the dexter side of the shield, and his left by the sinister. So far from the medallion telling us that Geoffrey was dead, it tells us that he was very much alive when the medallion was made, and that his wife was equally involved as himself' [letter to the author, 22 June 1992].

Subsequent to Noel Currer-Briggs's letter, I made a separate enquiry to the College of Arms, London. The current Garter Principal King of Arms, P. Ll. Gwynn-Jones, kindly informed me in a letter of 5 September 1998: 'Whilst I think it likely that Geoffrey de Charny was alive at the time of the making of the medallion, I do not feel this should be taken as a certainty. There would have been nothing to prevent his widow from depicting her late husband's Arms should she have wished to do so. I fear there must therefore be an element of doubt.'

5. Stephen Murray, *Building Troyes Cathedral*, Indianapolis, 1987, pp. 16ff.
6. Froissart, *Chronicles*, trans. Geoffrey Brereton, Harmondsworth, Penguin, 1968, p. 129.
7. Richard W. Kaeuper and Elspeth Kennedy, *The Book of Chivalry of Geoffroi de Charny*, Philadelphia, University of Philadelphia Press, 1996.
8. From Maurice Keen's summary of Geoffrey de Charny's principles in his book *Chivalry*, New Haven, Yale, 1984, p. 14.
9. Richard Kaeuper and Elspeth Kennedy, *The Book of Chivalry of Geoffroi de Charny: Text, Context and Translation*, op. cit., pp. 3–4.
10. The sampling at Templecombe was carried out by Dr John Gowlett of the Oxford radiocarbon-dating laboratory on 20 November 1986 and was personally witnessed by me. The following Easter a television documentary *A Head of Time*, including a report of the carbon dating results, was shown on TSW, an independent television station serving Plymouth and the South-West.
11. Some render this individual's surname as 'de Charnay' in deference to which I did so in my 1978 book. But there was no standardisation of spellings in the thirteenth–fourteenth centuries, as a result of which different renderings have no real bearing on the issue of whether the two de Charnys were or were not related to each other.
12. Malcolm Barber, 'The Templars and the Turin Shroud', *Catholic Historical Review*, April 1982, republished in *Shroud Spectrum International*, March 1983, pp. 16–34.

13. 'Remember, Lord, the soul of your servant Milutin Ures.'
14. Preserved in the Galleria Sabauda, Turin, and reproduced in my 1978 book *The Turin Shroud* immediately opposite p. 50. At that time this aquatint was widely attributed to Clovio, but is now more reliably attributed to G. B. della Rovere, whose family is specifically known to have enjoyed Savoy family patronage.
15. See Louis M. La Favia, *The Man of Sorrows: Its Origin and Development in Trecento Florentine Painting*, Rome, Edizioni 'Sanguis', 1980.
16. It is worth noting that two angels or angel-like beings are described associated with the Grail in some of the Grail stories; likewise two angels frequently accompany the body of Jesus as depicted on *epitaphioi*.
17. Reproduced in Hans Belting, *The Image and its Public in the Middle Ages, Form and Function in Early Paintings of the Passion*, trans. Mark Batusis and Raymond Meyer, New York, Caratzas, 1990, p. 125.
18. Ibid, p. 124.
19. For two representative sample quotes from these stories, see Geoffrey Ashe's chapter on the Grail in his book *King Arthur's Avalon*, London, Collins, 1957, pp. 265–8.
20. Gervase of Tilbury, *Otia Imperialia*, III, from *Scriptores rerum brunsvicensium*, (ed.) G. Liebnitz, Hanover, 1707, I, pp. 966–7.

Chapter 11

1. Ordericus Vitalis, *Historia ecclesiastica*, part III, book IX, 8, 'De gestis Balduini Edessae principatum obtinet'.
2. The use of the plural for shroud (in the original it is *sindones*) is of no special significance; in fact, Robert de Clari did the same, using the word *sydoines*.
3. It is so named after its eighteenth-century discoverer Georgius Pray.
4. Jérôme Lejeune, 'Étude topologique des Suaires de Turin, de Lier et de Pray', *L'Identification Scientifique de l'Homme du Linceul Jésus de Nazareth: Actes de Symposium Scientifique International, Rome 1993* (ed.) A. A. Upinsky, Paris, CIELT, François-Xavier de Guibert, 1995, p. 107, translation by the author.
5. Hans Belting, *The Image and its Public*, op. cit., p. 122 (fig. 75).
6. For an excellent account of this, see Steven Runciman, *The Emperor Romanus Lecapenus and his Reign*, Cambridge University Press, 1963, p. 145.
7. See, for instance, J. B. Segal, *Edessa, 'The Blessed City'*, Oxford, Claredon, 1970, p. 216.
8. Averil Cameron, 'The Sceptic and the Shroud', Inaugural Lecture, Department of Classics and History, King's College, London, 29 April 1980.
9. Sir Steven Runciman, 'Some Remarks on the Image of Edessa', *Cambridge Historical Journal* III, 1929–31, p. 244.
10. Quoted without source, and therefore presumably from personal correspondence with Sir Steven (whom he met and befriended), in David Sox,

File on the Shroud, London, Coronet/Hodder & Stoughton, 1978, p. 55.

11. Often referred to under its Latin name, the *Narratio de Imagine Edessena*, the original Greek text can be found in J. P. Migne, *Patrologia Cursus Completus, Series Graeca*, Paris, 1857–66, vol. CXIII, cols 423–54. For a translation into English, by Bernard Slater and boys of Bradford Grammar School, assisted by the Revd John Jackson, see my *The Turin Shroud*, op. cit., p. 235ff.

12. Luke 22:44.

13. In my book *Holy Faces, Secret Places* I have devoted considerable attention to these 'holy faces', also the famous 'Veronica' of Rome, all of which I consider to have originated as copies of the Shroud face, then acquired their own cult status. Here, however, I have merely mentioned these in order not to over-complicate the argument.

14. See in particular André Grabar, 'La Sainte Face de Laon et le Mandylion dans l'art orthodoxe', *Seminarium Kondakovianum*, Prague, 1935 for images from before World War II. The present condition of the Serbian frescos is unknown. That of Spas Nereditsa has definitely been destroyed.

15. For an account of Zaninotto's research, and further development of this, see A. M. Dubarle, 'L'homèlie de Grégoire le Référendaire' in *Actes du Symposium de Rome*, op. cit., p. 51.

16. John Jackson, 'Fold marks as a Historical Record of the Turin Shroud', *Shroud Spectrum* 11, 1984, pp. 6–29.

17. John Jackson, 'New Evidence that the Turin Shroud was the Mandylion', *Actes du Symposium de Rome*, op. cit., pp. 301ff.

18. For original text, see the *Codex vaticanus syriacus* 95, folios 49–50. For French translation and discussion of date, see André Grabar, 'Une hymme Syriaque sur l'architecture de la Cathédrale d'Edesse' from *L'art de la fin de l'antiquité et du moyen âge*, Collège de France Fondation Schlumberger pour des études Byzantines, 1968.

19. See James D. Breckenridge, 'The Numismatic Iconography of Justinian II', *Numismatic Notes & Monographs no. 144*, New York, American Numismatic Society, 1954.

20. Alan Whanger, 'Polarized Overlay Technique; A New Image Comparison Method and Its Applications', *Applied Optics* 24, no. 16, 15 March 1985, pp. 766–72.

21. Paul Vignon, *Le Saint Suaire devant la science, l'archéologie, l'histoire, l'iconographie, la logique*, Paris, Masson, 1939.

Chapter 12

1. After this year the Emperor Justinian initiated some major rebuilding of Edessa's walls and gates during which, as I suggested in my 1978 book, the true discovery of the cloth might have taken place.

2. See *The Doctrine of Addai the Apostle*, trans. G. Phillips, 1876.

3. See Luke 10:1.
4. As has been pointed out by J. B. Segal in his book *Edessa The Blessed City*, mixed into the *Doctrine* story also seems to have been a story of the conversion to Judaism of Queen Helena of Adiabene, as recounted by the Jewish historian Josephus (*c.* 37–*c.* 100).
5. A particularly fine specimen, worn by the short-reigned Abgar X (240–42), can also be seen on a Roman coin depicting him being received by the Emperor Gordian III.
6. Eusebius rendered this name as 'Thaddaeus'.
7. Eusebius, *History of the Church*, trans. G. A. Williamson, Harmondsworth, Penguin, 1965, p. 66.
8. For an excellent account of this, see ... Ethelbert Stauffer, *Christ and the Caesars*, London, SCM Press, 1955.
9. On the emergence of frontality in Parthian art, specifically around the first-century period, see Malcolm A. R. Colledge, *The Parthians*, New York, Praeger, 1967, pp. 150ff. Several Edessan examples of frontality can be seen among the illustrations in Segal's book on Edessa (see note 4 above).
10. See J. B. Segal, *Edessa The Blessed City*, op. cit., for detailed background on the fate of the bones of Addai and Abgar.
11. I owe the details of Professor Scavone's theory to a paper 'Joseph of Arimathea and the Edessa Icon' presented by him at a Symposium held at Mount Saint Alphonsus, Esopus, New York State, 24–5 August 1996, also much private correspondence.
12. This has been translated into German in Adolph Harnack, 'Ein in georgischer Sprache überliefertes Apokryphon des Josef von Arimathia' in *Sitzungsberichte der Königlich preussischen Akademie der Wissenschaften*, vol. 17, 1901, pp. 920–31.
13. Translation by Professor Scavone.
14. Bede, *A History of the English Church and People*, trans. Leo Sherley-Price, Harmondsworth, Penguin, 1955, p. 42.
15. Adolf Harnack, 'Der Brief des britischen Königs Lucius an den Papst Eleutherus', *Sitzungberichte der Königlich preussischen Akademie der Wissenschaften*, 26, 1904, pp. 909–16.
16. For example, see the gateway of Hatra, as reconstructed in London's British Museum.

Chapter 13

1. Harry E. Gove, *Relic, Icon or Hoax? Carbon Dating the Turin Shroud*, Bristol and Philadelphia, Institute of Physics Publishing, 1996, p. 303.
2. Pierluigi Baima-Bollone, 'Why Hasn't the Shroud Been Dated with the Carbon-14 Test?', *Stampa Sera*, Turin, 17 September 1979, as quoted and translated in Sox, *The Shroud Unmasked*, op. cit., p. 82.

3. Harry Gove, *Archaeometry* 31, 2, 1989, p. 35.
4. Harry E. Gove, *Relic, Icon or Hoax?*, op. cit., p. 264.
5. Quoted in David Sox, *The Shroud Unmasked*, op. cit., p. 136.
6. Communication by Vera Barclay in *Sindon*, December 1961, p. 36.
7. Sheridan Bowman, *Radiocarbon Dating*, London, British Museum Publications, 1990, p. 56.
8. Walter McCrone, letter to the author dated 21 April 1981.
9. *Current Archaeology*, August 1986.
10. Baima-Bollone, 'Why Hasn't the Shroud Been Dated with the Carbon-14 Test?' op. cit., as quoted and translated in Sox, *The Shroud Unmasked*.
11. *Thera and the Aegean World*, International conference on the Island of Thera, 1989, III. Proceedings of the Third International Congress, Santorini, Greece, 3–9 September 1989, vol. 3 (Chronology), 1990, p. 240.
12. Andy Coghlan, 'Unexpected errors affect dating techniques', *New Scientist*, 30 September 1989, p. 26.

Chapter 14

1. Walter McCrone, 'The Shroud of Turin: Blood or Artist's Pigment?', *Accts. Chem. Res.*, vol. 23, no. 3, 1990, p. 82.
2. Charles Eastlake, *Methods and Materials of Painting of the Great Schools and Masters*, London, Longman, Brown, Green & Longman, 1857, repr. Dover 1969, pp. 95–6.
3. Millard Meiss, *French Painting in the Time of Jean de Berry: The Late Fourteenth Century and the Patronage of the Duke*, text volume, London, Phaidon, 1967, pp. 99–107.
4. McCrone in his recent book *Judgement Day for the Turin Shroud*, received only when my own book was all but complete, does not in fact even mention the Parement Master and in general presents a poorer art-historical case for his own hypothesis than is represented here. I am indebted to Mr D. Aldred of Norwich, a specialist on mediaeval glass painting, for having first drawn the Parement Master to my attention.
5. Meiss, op. cit., p. 102.
6. R. A. Skelton, T. E. Marston, G. D. Painter, *The Vinland Map and The Tartar Relation*, New Haven (Connecticut), Yale University Press, 1965.
7. W. C. McCrone, 'Chemical Analytical Study of the Vinland Map', Report to Yale University Library, Yale University, New Haven (Connecticut), 1974.
8. T. A. Cahill, R. N. Schwab, B. H., Kusko, R. A. Eldred, G. Möller, D. Dutschke and D. L. Wick, 'The Vinland Map, Revisited: New Compositional Evidence on its Inks and Parchment', *Analytical Chemistry*, 15 March 1987, 59, pp. 829–33.
9. Quoted in John Noble Wilford's article 'Disputed Map Held Genuine After All', *New York Times*, 13 February 1996.

10. Noemi Gabrielli, report in *La S. Sindone*, published as supplement to the *Revista Diocesana Torinese*, January 1976.
11. Ian Wilson, *The Evidence of the Shroud*, London, O'Mara, 1986, p. 69.
12. Emily A. Craig and Randall R. Bresee, 'Image Formation and the Shroud of Turin', *Journal of Imaging Science and Technology*, January–February 1994.
13. Geoffrey Ashe, 'What Sort of Picture', *Sindon*, 1966, pp. 15–19.
14. The relevant passage reads; '*et hominem nudum coram se stantem prospexit secundum cuius formosam imaginem crucifixum ipsum aptius decoraret*', *Chronicon* 3, 35, quoted in Herbert Thurston, 'The Holy Shroud as a Scientific Problem', *The Month*, 101, 1903, p. 175.
15. See Millard Meiss, op. cit., illustrations volume, pl. 591.

Chapter 15

1. *Sunday Telegraph*, 28 January 1996. Although the article appeared under the name of Robert Matthews, the paper's Science Correspondent, who was reporting on a scientific paper on the Shroud written by Leicester University's Dr Allan Mills, a *Telegraph* sub-editor, acting without Matthews's knowledge or approval, added this concluding sentence: 'Like most scientists, Dr Mills supports the 1989 theory that the image was formed by the body of a dying Crusader tortured and crucified in a mockery of his religion by the Saracens.' In fact, Dr Mills does not support this theory, but it would be a reasonable guess at the view of many present-day scientists persuaded of the radiocarbon dating's accuracy.
2. See Joseph Marino OSB, article in *Fidelity*, p. 43.
3. *Annals of Dunstable*, Rolls Series, (ed.) Luard, p. 76.
4. Barbara Tuchman, *A Distant Mirror*, Harmondsworth, Penguin, 1979, p. 105.
5. Dr Tarquinio Ladu, 'La Crocifissione dei Santi Paolo Miki S. J. e Pietro Battista Blasquez, OFM, e Compagni, Martiri in Giappone nel 1597', *Sindon* (new series), quad.n.5–6, December 1993, pp. 35–44.
6. Dr Michael Straiton, 'The Man of the Shroud: A Crucified Crusader?', Lecture to the British Society for the Turin Shroud, 13 April 1989. Also published in *Catholic Medical Quarterly*.

Chapter 16

1. Lynn Picknett and Clive Prince, *Turin Shroud: In Whose Image? The Shocking Truth Unveiled*, op. cit.
2. Picknett and Prince, op. cit., p. 68.
3. As Professor Allen has pointed out on checking this passage, 'technically when the image is first formed (i.e. employing the reduced silver salt), two images are in fact produced simultaneously. The one is already permanent, being a chemically induced scorch on the linen fibrils (the by-product, if you like, of the more visible, reduced silver image). The other is the reduced

silver image overlaying the "scorch" or oxidised image. On treatment with ammonium hydroxide the reduced silver image is stripped away, leaving only the "scorch" record behind.'

4. Nicholas Allen, 'Verification of the Nature and Causes of the Photo-negative Images on the Shroud of Lirey–Chambéry–Turin', *De Arte* [Journal of the Department of Art History and Fine Arts, University of South Africa], April 1995, p. 31.

5. Ibid, p. 34.

6. As Professor Allen has pointed out on kindly checking this chapter, it should not be construed that he has neglected to give this much careful thought. He writes: 'I have considered possibilities ranging from life casts to preserved bodies to frozen corpses. Indeed the whole success of the process depends critically on two factors, viz: (a) the duration of the exposure; and (b) the stability of the subject (i.e. cadaver, sculpture, etc.). I believe the image on the Shroud indicates a degree of naturalism that is normally associated with a fresh corpse. I believe this because the apparent bruising and "torn beard" feature of the image are just a bit too detailed to be casually reproduced by a body cast or to be successfully maintained by preservation techniques (other than freezing). For this reason I presently advocate that the persons who produced this image *most probably* used a fresh corpse and a speedy exposure rate *or* a frozen–chilled corpse and a speedy–moderate exposure rate (possibly in the Venetian Alps). These considerations are not reflected in your following argument [Professor Allen's emphasis].'

Chapter 17

1. Centre International d'Études sur le Linceul de Turin.

2. Andrei A. Ivanov and Dmitri A. Kouznetsov, 'Biophysical correction to the old textile radiocarbon-dating results', *L'Identification Scientifique de l'Homme du Linceul . . .*, op. cit., pp. 229–35.

3. Dmitri A. Kouznetsov, Andrei A. Ivanov and Pavel R. Veletsky, 'Effects of fires and biofraction of carbon isotopes on results of radiocarbon dating of old textiles: The Shroud of Turin', *Journal of Archaeological Science*, vol. 22, 1995.

4. A. J. T. Jull, D. J. Donahue and P. E. Damon, 'Factors affecting the apparent radiocarbon age of textiles: a comment on effects of fires and biofractionation of carbon isotopes on results of radiocarbon dating of old textiles: the Shroud of Turin' by D. A. Kouznetsov et al. in *Journal of Archaeological Science* 1 (1996), pp. 157–60.

5. As quoted in an article by Jim Barrett, 'Science and the Shroud: Microbiology meets archaeology in a renewed quest for answers', *The Mission*, Journal of the University of Texas Health and Science Center, San Antonio, Spring 1996.

6. Professor Harry Gove, letter to the author as published in the British Society

for the Turin Shroud's Newsletter No. 40, May 1995, pp. 20–22.
7. Tape-recording of interview with Dr Garza-Valdès made in San Antonio, Texas, the evening of Wednesday, 28 August 1996.
8. Tape-recording of Dr Garza-Valdès, op. cit.
9. Letter to the author, 17 January 1995.
10. Dan Scavone, Letter to the Editor, British Society for the Turin Shroud Newsletter no. 41, September 1995, p. 21.
11. Ibid.
12. Ian Wilson, *The Turin Shroud*, op. cit. p. 8.
13. Tape-recording of Dr Garza-Valdès, op. cit.
14. Rosalie David, *Mysteries of the Mummies: The story of the Manchester University investigation*, London, Cassell, 1978.
15. H. E. Gove, S. J. Mattingly, A. R. David, L. A. Garza-Valdès, 'A problematic source of organic contamination of linen', in *Nuclear Instruments and Methods in Physics Research – Section B*, Amsterdam, Elsevier, 1997, pp. 504–7.
16. Private communication, cited in Gove, Mattingly, David and Garza-Valdès, op. cit., note 7.
17. Gove, Mattingly et al., op. cit., p. 506.

Chapter 18
1. Thomas J. Phillips, Letter to the Editor, *Nature*, 16 February 1989.
2. Dr Kitty Little, 'The Holy Shroud of Turin and the Mystery of the Resurrection', *Christian Order*, April 1994, p. 226. An interesting further remark made by Dr Little in this same article is that, besides altering a radiocarbon-dating reading, any such radiation could also have had a preservative effect on the Shroud, accounting for its remarkable intactness: 'The effects of radiation on cellulose fibres vary considerably according to the molecular structure of the fibre ... With good quality material, although higher doses degrade it, lower doses act to enhance its stability and resistance to degradation – and it has been reported that the linen of the Shroud is in very good condition. This would be in accord with the rich Joseph of Arimathea buying the best available.'
3. Ian Wilson, *The Turin Shroud*, op. cit., p. 211.
4. Robert Hedges, Letter to the Editor, *Nature*, 16 February 1989.
5. John Walsh, *The Shroud*, New York, Random House, 1963.
6. Margaret Hebblethwaite, 'The Shroud and my faith', *The Tablet*, 19 April 1997.
7. 'Dear Friends' round robin sent from Turin to various recipients, including Dr McCrone and myself, October 1988.

from the time of Christ to the present day
(with historical background and partly reconstructed,
as based on the Shroud's identification with the
cloth of Edessa to 1204)

The Shroud in Jerusalem?

30   Likeliest year of the crucifixion of Jesus, known to have taken place during Pontius Pilate's governorship of Judaea (AD 27–36).

Friday, 7 April [?]. Likeliest date of Jesus's death, which would have happened on the Jewish 13 Nisan. According to the Christian gospels, the wealthy Joseph of Arimathea, a secret follower of Jesus, asks Pilate's permission to take charge of Jesus's crucified body, purchases a clean *sindon*, wraps the body in this and lays it in his own stone-hewn tomb.

Sunday, 9 April [?]. According to the Gospel of John, the disciples Peter and John, on visiting the tomb that morning, find the body gone, but the burial wrappings left behind. John describes in particular what he calls a *sudarion* 'rolled up and in a place by itself'. This may have been our Shroud.

The Shroud goes to Edessa?

According to later tradition, possibly in this very same year a disciple of Jesus called Thaddaeus or Addai travels from Jerusalem to Edessa (today Urfa, in eastern Turkey) at the invitation of the city's ruler Abgar V, with whom Jesus had purportedly been in correspondence. All accounts describe Thaddaeus/Addai healing Abgar of a disease and converting at least a proportion of Edessan citizens to Christianity. According to some versions, however, he also brings with him a **cloth miraculously imprinted with Jesus's likeness**, which later variants will describe in Shroud-like terms as bearing the full imprint of Jesus's body. This cloth we will call '**the cloth of Edessa**'.

50   Death of Abgar V to be succeeded by his eldest son Ma'nu V bar Abgar.

57   Death of Ma'nu V, to be succeeded by his brother Ma'nu VI. According to the tradition associated with the cloth of Edessa, it would have been this 'rebellious' son of Abgar who reverted to paganism and

persecuted the early Christians, possibly to extinction. These would appear to have hidden the Christ-imprinted cloth inside a niche above one of the city's gates as a desperate measure to ensure its long-term safety. **We now enter a long period of obvious ignorance concerning this cloth's whereabouts.**

The Shroud's first period of disappearance, hidden above one of Edessa's gates?

177   In Edessa, accession of Lucius Aelius Septimius Megas Abgar VIII (177–212), a ruler for whom there is some direct historical evidence of both pro-Roman and pro-Christian sympathies.

180   In Rome accession of the Emperor Commodus, known to have been well disposed to Christianity because of his Christian wife Marcia. Edessa's copper coinage now begins to feature Commodus on the obverse and Lucius Abgar's portrait, with what looks to be a Christian cross on his tiara, on the reverse, Abgar VIII thereby being the first known monarch in all history publicly to display this Christian symbol on his regalia.

c. 190   The Church father Clement of Alexandria (*c.* 150–216), listing the burial places of Jesus's disciples in the fifth book of his *Outlines*, records that Thaddaeus/Addai's was with that of Thomas 'in the Britio of the Edessans'. According to American historian Professor Scavone, this 'Britio' was Edessa's *birtha*, or citadel, still a major landmark of the city.

192   Commodus falls victim to conspiracy, his successor, after a period of strife, being the Emperor Severus, with no known Christian sympathies. Edessa's coinage now features Lucius Abgar sometimes with a plain tiara, sometimes with pagan symbols mixed with the occasional cross-like device – as if it was felt prudent not to be too overt about any Christian affiliations.

201   November. According to the Chronicle of Edessa, Edessa suffers disastrous flooding, killing 2000 citizens. The 'church of the Christians' is described as damaged in this, strongly reinforcing the likelihood of Lucius Abgar's ready tolerance of Christianity.

205   According to the Chronicle of Edessa, Abgar orders construction work on the *birtha*, or citadel, in this year.

212   Death of Lucius Abgar, to be succeeded by Abgar IX, whom the Romans swiftly seize and depose. The cross disappears from the tiara on Edessan coinage and within four years Edessa becomes a Roman military colonia.

303   Flood at Edessa. In Rome the Emperor Diocletian orders the destruction of Christian scriptures and churches, and the abolition of Christian worship.

313	With the accession of Constantine the Great as the first Christian Roman emperor, Christianity becomes officially tolerated throughout the entire Roman Empire. In Edessa, the city's first official bishop, Cona, orders the construction of a cathedral.
325	The Church historian Eusebius of Caesarea (260–339) writing in his *History of the Church*, includes a detailed account of the story of Jesus and Abgar exchanging messages. Eusebius insists that he has seen the original documents of these in Edessa's Record Office, 'embracing early history and also the events of Abgar's time. This record is found preserved from then till now.' He says he has transcribed the documents from the original Syriac, but he makes no mention of any cloth with Jesus's likeness.
c. 375–90	Composition of the *Doctrine of Addai* in Edessa, based on earlier versions of the Abgar story, but incorporating several interpolations, including a story of Abgar's legate Hannan painting Jesus's portrait 'with choice paints'. This seems to be a garbled memory of some kind of likeness of Jesus having once been brought to Edessa.
?383	Visit to Edessa by the highly observant Spanish nun 'Egeria', as part of a major pilgrimage to the Holy Land, Asia Minor, Egypt and Constantinople. The bishop of the time shows her round, pointing out to her statues of Abgar and his son, and quoting to her the alleged letter from Jesus to Abgar. But she is not told of anything else answering the description of the cloth of Edessa.
413	Flood at Edessa.
492	Beginning of pontificate of Pope Gelasius (to 496). The so-called Gelasian Decree attributed to him relegates the purported Abgar correspondence with Jesus among the writings dismissed as apocryphal. From this point on, the Abgar story is firmly rejected by Western Christendom, though it is equally firmly retained in the East.
494	The remains of Edessa's first evangelist Thaddaeus/Addai are transferred to Edessa's Church of St John the Baptist (described by Arab geographers as 'in the middle of the city' along with 'the church of the Mother of God').
pre-500	Georgian manuscript says Joseph of Arimathea collected the blood of Jesus in the linen cloth that wrapped his body: 'But I [Joseph] climbed Holy Golgotha, where the Lord's cross stood, and collected in a headband and a large sheet the precious blood that had flowed from his holy side.' This seems to indicate an awareness that Jesus's shroud was stained with his blood. This same tradition also seems to be a forerunner of the Grail story.
502	Edessa's walls are repaired and the city gates stopped up with stone. This is a possible date of the Shroud's discovery as the cloth of Edessa.

503	Persian attack on Edessa is repulsed, the defenders claiming, 'Christ stands before our city.'
507	The chronicle of Joshua the Stylite is completed, with no mention of the cloth of Edessa.
521	Jacob of Serug, prolific Edessan writer, dies without referring to the cloth of Edessa.
525	Major flood at Edessa. One third of the population (30,000) die. Some of the finest buildings are destroyed, including the cathedral. Shortly after, the Byzantine Emperor Justinian orders reconstruction work, to include a magnificent new cathedral and rebuilding of the city walls. Possibly it was at this time that where the early Christians had hidden the Edessa cloth was opened up **and the cloth found**.
c. 530	In Rome a copyist of the *Book of the Popes* inserts under Pope Eleutherus that a king of Britain called Lucius had asked this pope to send Christian missionaries. This is thought to have been a confusion with King Lucius Abgar VIII of Edessa, a contemporary of Pope Eleutherus, residing in the Britio/*birtha* of Edessa.

As the cloth of Edessa, the Shroud re-emerges as a historical object?

544	Unsuccessful siege of Edessa by the Persian Chosroes Nirshirvan. The contemporary and very secular historian Procopius of Caesarea, in describing this, makes no mention of any cloth likeness of Christ saving the city, attributing it instead to the defenders' courage and resourcefulness. However, according to Evagrius, writing his *Ecclesiastical History* just over a generation later, the Persian attack was repulsed by 'the divinely wrought likeness [*theoteukon eikona*] which human hands have not made'. When all seemed lost, the bishop had discovered the hiding-place of this, ostensibly as a result of a vision. One of the earliest references to the Edessa cloth as a historical object, this specifically describes the likeness as not of human handiwork, thereby corresponding to one of the prime attributes of the Turin Shroud.
569	A Syriac hymn praising the beauty of Edessa's new cathedral likens its marble to 'the image not the work of [human] hands'. This and the Evagrius chronicle thereby represent the earliest reports of the Edessa cloth as an extant historical object, both agreeing that its Christ likeness is not by the hand of an artist.
before 600	*Acts of Thaddaeus*, a version of the story of Edessa's evangelisation written no later than this time, describes Jesus wiping his face on a *tetradiplon*, a cloth 'doubled in four', and leaving his image on this, which again suggests the Edessa cloth was of substantial length,

necessitating its folding.

639   Edessa falls relatively peaceably to the Moslems. Nestorian, Mon-
        ophysite and Orthodox Christian denominations are represented
        in the city at this time, and the city's new masters accord them
        toleration.

c. 692 Byzantine Emperor Justinian II issues gold coins bearing portrait of
        Christ Enthroned, the first ever proper likeness of Jesus to appear on
        any coin. Thought to be based on the Edessa cloth, the likeness
        exhibits striking similarities to the face on the Turin Shroud.

723   For the next 120 years both the Byzantine and the Moslem empires
        suffer outbreaks of 'iconoclasm' in which countless icons and artis-
        tically created images of Jesus are destroyed. But the cloth of Edessa,
        because its imprint is obviously not artistically created, survives.

c. 730 In a treatise condemning Iconoclasm, John of Damascus (?675–749)
        remarks of the Edessa cloth, 'A certain tale is told how that when
        Abgar was king of Edessa he sent a portrait painter to paint a likeness
        of the Lord. And when the painter could not paint because of the
        brightness which shone from his countenance, the Lord himself put
        a *himation* over himself, imprinted his likeness on this and sent it to
        Abgar to satisfy his desire.' A *himation*, the standard outer garment
        for the Greeks of antiquity, was usually at least three metres long
        and two metres wide.

c. 750 In England the Venerable Bede, writing his *History of the English
        Church and People*, inadvertently repeats the mistake made 200 years
        earlier in the *Book of the Popes* concerning the purportedly 'British'
        King Lucius, in reality Lucius Abgar VIII of Edessa.

787   Leo, Lector of Constantinople, says at the Council of Nicaea that he
        visited Edessa and saw 'the holy image made without hands revered
        and adored by the faithful'.

943   Spring. The elderly Byzantine Emperor Romanus, who has usurped
        the throne from the rightful heir Constantine Porphyrogenitus,
        sends an army to Edessa to negotiate with the Moslems for possession
        of the Edessa cloth imprinted with Jesus's likeness. Romanus's
        general, Curcuas, makes the unprecedented promise that providing
        the cloth is safely handed over to him he will not harm Edessa, but
        instead guarantee it perpetual immunity from attack, pay 12,000
        pieces of silver and release 200 Moslem prisoners. After protracted
        deliberations the Moslem authorities agree and a bishop who has
        travelled with the Byzantine army enters Edessa to receive the cloth
        on the emperor's behalf. Although there are attempts by Edessa's
        Christians to hand over mere copies, the bishop is eventually satisfied
        that he has the original and travels with it across Anatolia back to

Constantinople.

As the cloth of Edessa, the Shroud moves to Constantinople?

944   15 August (Feast of the Assumption of the Virgin Mary). The cloth of Edessa arrives in Constantinople, preliminarily resting at the church of St Mary at Blachernae, the home of the Virgin's robe, where it is viewed by members of the imperial family. Reportedly the artistically inclined Constantine Porphyrogenitus readily discerns the cloth's imprint, but Romanus's two sons Stephen and Constantine find it difficult to distinguish. Taken by galley to the Imperial Palace it is placed overnight in the chapel of the Pharos.

16 August. The cloth is carried around the walls of Constantinople in its casket, then taken to Hagia Sophia, where it is placed on the 'throne of mercy'. On this occasion Gregory, archdeacon of Hagia Sophia, delivers a sermon in which he imparts that it bears not only 'the drops of sweat from the agony [in Gethsemane] which flowed from [Christ's] face like drops of blood' but also 'blood and water [*haima kai hudor*] from his very side'. This indicates (i) that there was more to the imprint on the cloth of Edessa than just a face; and (ii) that **the imprint included blood of the Passion and must thereby have been created after Jesus was taken down from the cross, i.e. precisely corresponding to the Turin Shroud**.

c. 945   27 January. Constantine Porphyrogenitus takes over power as as rightful emperor and shortly after issues gold coins bearing an impressive and very Shroud-like Christ 'Rex Regnantium' (King of Kings) portrait that some numismatists specifically argue to have been inspired by the recently arrived cloth of Edessa. From this point Byzantine coins with this type of likeness of Jesus show his halo decorated with three pellets on each bar, possibly deriving from the so-called 'poker holes' on the Shroud (historically unrecorded damage which may have been sustained during the iconoclastic period). Under Emperor Constantine's direction an official history of the Edessa cloth, the *Narratio De Imagine Edessena* is written. This authoritatively describes the imprint as 'a moist secretion without pigment or the painter's art', and elsewhere it remarks that the likeness was 'due to sweat, not pigments'. It also gives two alternative explanations for how the imprint may have been formed: the first, from Jesus washing himself; the second, from when sweat dropped from Jesus 'like drops of blood' in the Garden of Gethsemane (Luke 22:44).

958   In a letter sent to encourage his troops in Asia Minor, Constantine Porphyrogenitus writes that to give them added strength he is

sending them water consecrated by its contact with holy relics: 'undefiled and ancient signs of the Passion of Christ, our true Lord; the precious wood ... the God-bearing shroud [*sindon*] and other signs of his undefiled Passion'. The first known documentary reference to a shroud of Jesus being in Constantinople, this is inexplicable unless the Edessa cloth and the cloth we now know as the Turin Shroud were one and the same.

959   Death of Constantine Porphyrogenitus. Some time before this he has the original rock of the Holy Sepulchre in Jerusalem covered with a marble facing with three circular openings through which pilgrims could view the rock. These are strikingly evocative of the three 'poker' holes on the Shroud, and may indicate a historical connection.

965   In England, former Glastonbury monk St Ethelwold of Winchester
(–75)   (908–84) writes a liturgical play, the *Concordia Regularis*, featuring the *sudary* (another word for shroud) being held up in the face of the clergy to demonstrate that Christ is risen from the dead.

968   Byzantine Emperor Nicephoros Phocas orders the *keramion*, the tile reputedly discovered with the cloth of Edessa, to be transferred from Hierapolis to Constantinople.

977   A group of refugee Greek monks, led by Sergius, metropolitan of Damascus, set up a cult of St Alexis in Rome's near-abandoned Church of St Boniface. According to their version, the young Alexis was attracted to become a beggar at Edessa by hearing of its cloth bearing Jesus's imprint. Their *Vita Alexius* describes the imprint as 'an image of our Lord Jesus Christ made without human hand on a *sindon* [the same word used in the gospels for Jesus's shroud]'. According to another Latin text, Lat.Cod. Monac.Aug.S.Ulr.111:

> [Alexis came] to the city of Edessa,
> In which there was preserved a *blood-stained* image of the Lord
> Not made by hands, but treated decorously as to the face.

c. 990   First literary occurrence of the name 'Mandylion' for the cloth of Edessa, in a biography of the ascetic Paul of Mt Latros. In this the author says that Paul, without ever leaving Mount Latros, was granted a miraculous vision of 'the likeness of Christ not made by hands, which is commonly called "the holy Mandylion"'.

1011   23 November (the Feast of St Clement). In Rome, Pope Sergius IV (1009–12) consecrates an altar in John VII's chapel, dedicated to the *sudarium*. This seems to be the first reference to the existence of Rome's Veronica which, like the cloth of Edessa, was purported to bear an imprint of Jesus's face. As suggested by subsequent artists' copies of the Veronica this was a facsimile of the facial area of the cloth of Edessa/Shroud specially made for Rome shortly before the Roman and Eastern Orthodox Churches went their separate ways.

1036   The cloth of Edessa is recorded as being carried in procession in Constantinople.

1054   Rome's Cardinal Humbert da Silva excommunicates the Eastern Orthodox Church. He expresses particular shock at the Eastern custom of depicting Jesus dead on the cross.

1058   Christian Arab writer Abu Nasr Yahya states that he saw the cloth of Edessa in Hagia Sophia, Constantinople.

1063   A Menologion with the story of Abgar, now preserved in Moscow, is created.

1078   Seljuk Turks capture Jerusalem, taking over the holy places and thereby sparking off the Crusades.

c. 1100   Created no later than around this time is a Byzantine ivory, now in the Victoria and Albert Museum, depicting Jesus laid out on a large cloth in exactly the manner of the Shroud [pl. 34b]. Also of this same period is the so-called Stroganoff reliquary in St Petersburg, with a similar scene of Christ laid out in death inscribed 'Christ lies in death, manifesting God'.

c. 1130   A Western sermon of this date, borrowing from a discourse by Pope Stephen II in 769, describes the cloth of Edessa as representing Jesus's entire body: 'On this cloth, wonderful as it is to see or even hear such a thing, the glorious features of [Jesus's] face, and the majestic form of his whole body have been supernaturally transferred, that for those who never had the opportunity to see his earthly appearance, they can do so thanks to the way this has been imprinted onto the linen.' This therefore explicitly describes the cloth of Edessa as bearing the imprint of Jesus's entire body.

c. 1130   Ordericus Vitalis [1075–1143?], an English-born monk of St Evroult, Normandy, writes in his highly respected *Ecclesiastical History*: 'Abgar reigned as toparch of Edessa. To him the Lord Jesus sent ... a most precious cloth, with which he wiped the sweat from his face and on which shone the Saviour's features, miraculously produced. This displayed to those who gazed upon it the likeness and proportions of the body of the Lord.'

1144   Edessa falls to Turkish Moslems. Although the bodies of Abgar and Addai are thrown out of their coffins in the Church of St John the Baptist and their bones scattered, these are retrieved and deposited in the Church of St Theodore.

1146   After a temporary Crusader recapture, Edessa is again taken by the Turks, this time with huge bloodshed. The whole city is ruthlessly ransacked, its churches reduced to rubble and from this time on it becomes a wholly Moslem city, with all traces of its former Christianity ruthlessly obliterated.

1147   Count Henry of Champagne visits Constantinople and is royally received by the Emperor Manuel I Comnenus (1143–80). It is from Count Henry's Champagne that a generation or so later surface the Grail stories of a very mysterious image of the crucified Jesus being seen at a special Mass.

1149   15 July. In Jerusalem, dedication of the Crusader Church of the Holy Sepulchre, built on the reputed site of the tomb of Jesus. In this same year there occurs the first known example – on a bronze baptismal font at Tirlemont in Belgium – of the feet of Jesus being portrayed as being transfixed by a single nail, as the Shroud seems to indicate. This mode gradually spreads, to become the norm in the Western church.

c. 1150   English pilgrim to Constantinople describes among its relics a gold container '*capsula (aurea)* in which is the *mantile* which, applied to the Lord's face, retained the image of his face'. The same pilgrim also itemises a '*sudarium* which was over his head'.

1171   Chronicler William of Tyre (*c.* 1130–*c.* 85), accompanying a state visit to the Emperor Manuel I Comnenus in Constantinople, describes being very privilegedly shown 'the most precious evidences of the passion of our Lord Jesus Christ' including 'the cross, nails, lance, sponge, reed, crown of thorns, *sindon* and sandals'.

c. 1180   Composition of *Conte del Graal* or *Perceval* by Chrétien de Troyes, a poet of Champagne, for Philip, Count of Flanders. For Chrétien the *graal* was quite definitely not a chalice, despite later misunderstandings.

1190   In Constantinople an anonymously drawn-up inventory lists among the city's relics (1) 'part of the linens [*linteaminum*] in which the crucified body of Christ was wrapped'; (2) the *sindon*; (3) 'the towel sent to King Abgar of Edessa by the Lord, on which the Lord, by his own doing is transfigured as an image.'

c. 1192   Artist illuminating the Pray manuscript of Budapest [pl. 35a] depicts Jesus laid out naked in death, with hands crossed in the manner depicted on the Shroud, and laid out on a cloth clearly envisaged as double body length and going over the head. In this same year occurs the first surviving appearance in art, at Kurbinovo (on the Greece–Serbia border), of the *Melismos*. Strongly evocative of the Grail stories, this is a eucharistic scene in which the body of the infant Jesus and that of a very Shroud-like dead Jesus covered in his crucifixion wounds become interchangeable.

late 12th *c.* According to an anonymous Icelandic list of the relics at

	Constantinople: 'In Constantinople in certain ancient palaces is the piece of writing that our Lord himself wrote with his own hands, a spear and nails, crown of thorns, mantle, scourge, goblet, tunic, footwear, a stone which was under the Lord's head in the tomb, and winding sheets with a sweat cloth and the blood of Christ.'
1201	Nicholas Mesarites, overseer of the relic collection in the Great Palace at Constantinople, lists as included in this the 'burial *sindons* [*entaphioi sindones*] of Christ'. He authoritatively describes these as 'of linen ... of cheap and easy-to-find material, still smelling of myrrh, and defying destruction, since they wrapped the uncircumscribed, fragrant with myrrh, naked body after the Passion'. He adds, 'In this place He [Jesus] rises again, and the sudarium and the burial sindons are the proof.' In the same document Nicholas also mentions a towel *'cheiromanteion'* with a 'protoypal' image of Jesus on it 'as if by some art of drawing not wrought by hand'.
1202	Commencement of the Fourth Crusade, intended to call in on Constantinople to restore to power a recently deposed Byzantine emperor. This is accompanied by Gautier de Montbéliard, thought to have been the patron of the Grail author Robert de Boron.
1203	17 July. The Crusaders manage to breach Constantinople's walls, causing the emperor who has usurped the Byzantine throne to flee. They release from prison the deposed former emperor, reinstate him, call a halt to the fighting and then temporarily become tourists-guests in Constantinople, while they wait for payment for their services. During this period, in which Constantinople's citizens grow increasingly to dislike the heavily armed Westerners moving among them, Robert de Clari, a Crusader from Picardy, describes seeing in the Church of St Mary at Blachernae 'the *sydoines* in which our Lord had been wrapped' adding, 'on every Friday this raised itself upright [*se drechoit tous drois* – *'se dressait tout droit'*] so that one could see the figure of our Lord on it.' This appears to be a description of the cloth of Edessa, alias the Turin Shroud, being made to rise up from its casket by some rather typically Byzantine piece of gadgetry.
1204	12 April. Angry at not having been paid, and with Constantinople's walls again firmly shut against them, the Crusaders of the Fourth Crusade attack and successfully capture Constantinople for the second time. This time the city is violently looted and ransacked. Troops of Boniface, Marquis de Montferrat, occupy the area of the Blachernae church. Although Garnier de Trainel, Bishop of Troyes, lists and safeguards all relics found in the Imperial Chapel, his list does not appear to include either the cloth of Edessa, or Robert de Clari's *sydoine* (if this was a separate object). This seems corroborated

by Robert de Clari's specific remarks of the *sydoine*: 'Neither Greek nor Frenchman knew what became of this shroud when the city was taken.' The keramion tile likewise is never heard of again. If the cloth of Edessa was one and the same as the Turin Shroud, we are therefore faced with a second and much more mysterious period of disappearance.

The Shroud's second period of disappearance, whereabouts unknown

1205   1 August. Theodore, brother of Michael Angelus, Despot of the Epirus region of Greece remaining under Byzantine control, writes in his brother's name to Pope Innocent III in Rome complaining of the looting of Christian relics that had occurred following the Crusader sack of Constantinople the previous year: 'The Venetians partitioned the treasures of gold, silver and ivory while the French did the same with relics of the same and the most sacred of all, the linen in which our Lord Jesus was wrapped after his death and before his resurrection. We know that the sacred objects are preserved by their predators in Venice, in France and in other places, the sacred linen in Athens.' This could be interpreted to mean that the Shroud went to Athens, which came under the control of the French Crusader Otho de la Roche, who according to some genealogies was ancestor of Geoffrey I de Charny's wife Jeanne de Vergy. But since the document exists only in a secondary copy, its authenticity is not beyond question.

1209   Division among the Crusaders of the Morea district of Greece. As his portion Crusader Hugh de Lille de Charpigny, an ancestor of Geoffrey I de Charny's brother Dreux's wife, receives the barony of La Vostice, today the small port of Egion.

c. 1210   Composition of Bavarian knight Wolfram von Eschenbach's Grail story *Parzival*. In this we find the Grail castle of Munsalvaesche guarded by Templars. At around this same time also, composition of the Grail story *Perlesvaus*, probably written by a chaplain to some noble household in north France/Belgium. In this the Grail is the vessel used to collect Christ's blood and Gawain is featured as seeing its great secret: a chalice, changing to a child and then to the crucified Christ, in the manner of the *Melismos*. Also, early in the story King Arthur is described at mass, in which it seemed that the hermit conducting this: '... was holding in his arms a man, bleeding from his side ... [and from] his hands and feet, and crowned with thorns ... then ... he thought he saw the man's body change [again] into the shape of the child.'

273

c. 1211   Relating specifically the story of the cloth of Edessa, the chronicler Gervase of Tilbury writes in his *Otia Imperialia*: 'The story is passed down from archives of ancient authority that the Lord prostrated himself with his entire body on whitest linen and so by divine power there was impressed on the linen a most beautiful imprint of not only the face but the entire body [*toto corpore*] of the Lord.'

c. 1220   Major redecoration, after only forty years, of the frescos in the Holy Sepulchre chapel, Winchester Cathedral. The revised deposition scene shows a helper holding up a large shroud clearly intended to go over the head and down to the feet in the manner of that of Turin.

1225   Otho de la Roche, the Crusader responsible for Athens where Theodore Angelus said the Shroud had been taken (see entry for 1205), becomes Preceptor of the Knights Templar.

1247   Last Latin Byzantine Emperor Baldwin II, by a so-called Golden Bull, cedes a list of relics, including the crown of thorns, to his cousin Louis IX of France. The list includes 'part of the *sudarium* which wrapped his [Christ's] body in the tomb'.

1306   Death of Geoffrey I de Charny's mother Margaret de Joinville no later than this year. This is therefore a *terminus ante quem* for the date of the Shroud-owning Geoffrey de Charny's birth. In this same year the Templar Grand Master Jacques de Molay travels from Cyprus to Paris to answer charges against his Order, including rumours that its higher echelons have been secretly worshipping some kind of bearded head.

1307   Friday, 13 October. On the orders of King Philippe the Fair of France all Templars in France, including Jacques de Molay, are arrested at dawn. Whatever the source of these 'bearded head' rumours, this is not found.

1309   Avignon becomes the seat of the papacy for the next seventy-eight years, with French popes pursuing a French foreign policy.

1313   Louis of Burgundy leads a successful protective expedition to the Morea in Greece, in which Geoffrey I de Charny's elder brother Dreux, who takes part, is rewarded by being given the hand in marriage of Agnes de Charpigny, heiress–granddaughter of the Crusader Hugh de Charpigny who had received the Morea barony of La Vostice.

1314   19 March. In Paris Jacques de Molay together with the Templar Master of Normandy, Geoffrey de Charny, are brought out for sentencing to life imprisonment. They protest their innocence, claiming that confessions they made to misdeeds had been extracted under torture. That same night they are burnt at the stake. This Geoffrey may possibly have been a relative of the Shroud-owning Geoffrey I de Charny of just a generation later.

c. 1321   In Serbia, creation of the 'Epitaphios' of King Uros Milutin Uros II, a liturgical embroidery bearing an image of Jesus laid out in death strikingly reminiscent of the Shroud.

1325   Death of Dreux de Charny no later than this year.

1337   Start of the Hundred Years War. First historical emergence of first known Shroud owner Geoffrey I de Charny, described at this time as a *bachelier* (a knight who has not yet acquired a fief by marriage or inheritance), taking part in the wars of Languedoc and Guyenne under Raoul de Brienne, High Constable of France.

1340   Geoffrey I de Charny is recorded as among the 'flower of chivalry' who successfully defend Tournai against the army of England's Edward III.

1341   Geoffrey I de Charny is recorded as at Angers, preparing to accompany the Duke of Normandy on a campaign against the English in Brittany.

1342   30 September. Geoffrey I de Charny is recorded commanding the first line of attacking cavalry at the battle of Morlaix, Brittany. The attack fails with the loss of fifty leading knights and Geoffrey is taken prisoner by Richard Talbot, who takes him to his principal residence, Goodrich Castle, Herefordshire. A subsequent letter patent refers to Geoffrey returning to France 'to find the money for his ransom'. Although there is some confusion about dates, the ransom seems to have been quickly paid since by the end of this same year Geoffrey is recorded commanding the rearguard of an army being led against the English near Vannes (also in Brittany). This action has to have been before 19 January 1343 since that day the French and English agree to a three-year truce.

1343   13 June. King Philip VI grants Geoffrey I de Charny a rent of 120 livres for the creation of a church and chapter at Lirey.

1345   Geoffrey takes part in a Crusade under the command of of Humbert II, Dauphin of Vienne, which sails from Marseilles. His subsequent poem the *Livre Charny*, which includes a description of the hardships of a knight's voyage overseas, seems to reflect his seasickness on this voyage and he is named among the beneficiaries of Humbert's estate apparently as a reward for his services.

1336   2 August. Clearly having returned to France, and been promoted to the rank of *chevalier*, Geoffrey is recorded as taking part in the siege of Aiguillon in south-western France.

        Winter. Geoffrey is recorded defending the town of Béthune against the Flemish.

1347   July. At Sangatte, near Calais, Geoffrey de Charny is among the French delegation which tries, in vain, to persuade England's King Edward III to lift his siege of Calais, which the French know they cannot relieve militarily. Shortly after the failure of the negotiations Calais's starving citizens surrender. According to some sources, it is in this same year that Geoffrey is named *porte-oriflamme*, bearer of France's sacred royal battle-standard. For this, bareheaded and on his knees in the presence of his king and other worthies, he would have had to take the following traditional oath: 'You swear and promise on the precious, sacred body of Jesus Christ present here ... that you will loyally in person hold and keep the *oriflamme* ... and not abandon it for fear of death or whatever else may happen ...'

1348   In the January of this year Geoffrey joins the council of King Philip VI and in the October is granted by the king a house in Paris's rue Petit Marais. Throughout this same year the Black Death rages across Europe, causing widespread deaths, and it is possibly during this epidemic that Geoffrey loses his first wife, Jeanne de Toucy, whose actual date of death is unknown. Also in this year Geoffrey is named governor of St Omer, with all the military powers of the king.

1349   3 January. Geoffrey confirms a donation of land yielding 140 livres annually that will pay the salaries and expenses of the canons who will take charge of the Lirey church in which the Shroud will be exhibited.

     17 January. Geoffrey de Charny is recorded at the Abbey of Lis, near Melun, in council with King Philip VI, the Archbishop of Rouen, the Archbishop of Laon, the Abbot of Corbie and others.

     16 April. Geoffrey de Charny writes to Pope Clement VI reporting his intention to build a church at Lirey, to be staffed by five canons and a prebendary. He requests that Guillaume de Baserne de Toucy, uncle to Jeanne de Toucy, be one the canons. This is granted but not taken up because of Geoffrey's subsequent imprisonment (see entry for 1350).

     19 April. Philip VI grants to Geoffrey de Charny and his heirs an income of 5500 livres to be paid from the first forfeitures which might occur in the seneschalties of Toulouse, Beaucaire and Carcassonne. This is in lieu of his previous lifelong annuity of 1000 livres payable from Philip's treasury. The advantage of this for Geoffrey is that the income will benefit his heirs, a crucial clue that he now had heirs. We may therefore infer reasonably that the birth of his son (to be known as Geoffrey II de Charny) had been quite recent.

     26 April. Geoffrey sends another petition to Clement VI.

     Later this same year, while based at St Omer, Geoffrey plans the recapture of Calais from the English. He secretly negotiates with Aimery of Pavia, a Lombard serving with the English as captain of Calais's citadel, that in return for a bribe of 20,000 écus Pavia will let the French into the city.

31 December. At dead of night Geoffrey de Charny arrives with Pavia's bribe and a fighting force, unsuspecting that Pavia has been acting as a double agent and has already informed King Edward III of the ruse. As a result, Edward III has secretly reinforced the garrison at Calais and attired in plain armour under the banner of Walter Mauny, he personally ambushes the force led by Geoffrey. After a fierce skirmish, in which Geoffrey receives a head wound, the French are routed and Geoffrey is taken prisoner a second time.

1350 1 January. After being treated with exemplary chivalry by Edward III Geoffrey is again shipped to England for a spell of imprisonment. In this same year King Philip VI dies, to be succeeded by Geoffrey's commander John II (the Good).

In Rome, Holy Year celebrations are held from Christmas to Easter, attracting more than a million pilgrims, for whom the highlight is showings of the Veronica at St Peter's every Sunday and every Feast day, attracting such dense crowds that fatalities from suffocation and trampling are not uncommon.

1351 31 July. Geoffrey is freed from imprisonment for a handsome ransom of 12,000 gold écus paid by King John the Good.

September. Geoffrey attends the negotiations prolonging the Anglo–French truce. Shortly after this he makes a surprise night raid upon the castle of his betrayer, Aimery of Pavia, taking him back to his base at St Omer and decapitating him as a traitor to the sworn word.

1352 6 January. Geoffrey de Charny is made a member of King John the Good's newly formed Order of the Star, a religious military brotherhood formulated along the lines of the Knights Templar and Knights of the Round Table.

1353 June. Geoffrey de Charny obtains an annual rent of 140 livres from King John the Good of France for his foundation of the church at Lirey. According to a notice in the church as rebuilt in the sixteenth century, this church was 'of wood ... very small and insubstantial, awaiting more fortunate times...'

1 July. The church of Lirey is formally founded, staffed by four canons and a dean.

1354 Geoffrey de Charny renews his petition of five years previously for the collegiate status of the church of Lirey, this time to the new incumbent at Avignon, Antipope Innocent VI. In the same year

Henri of Poitiers is transferred to the see of Troyes, and will take charge of the city as its captain and governor.

3 August. Antipope Innocent VI grants indulgences to pilgrims visiting the collegiate church at Lirey. In this same year Philipe de Joinville, husband of Geoffrey's niece Guillemette de Charny (heiress of the La Vostice barony in Greece), moves back to France.

The Shroud's reappearance - in tiny Lirey, near Troyes

1355   According to the 'd'Arcis Memorandum', written in 1389, the first known expositions of the Shroud are held in Lirey at around this time. Large crowds of pilgrims are attracted and special souvenir medallions struck for these, as indicated by the unique surviving example in the Cluny Museum, Paris. But Bishop Henri refuses to believe the Shroud could be genuine, claims it to be the work of an artist and orders the expositions to be stopped. The Shroud is then hidden away for thirty-four years.

20 February. Geoffrey de Charny gives receipt as lord of Savoisy and Montfort, fiefs which he received on taking the Vermandois, a region to the north of Paris around Noyon.

25 June. Geoffrey de Charny is definitely named *porte-oriflamme* – bearer of the French sacred battle-standard.

1356   Saturday, 28 May. At Aix, formal ratification by Bishop Henri of Poitiers, of Geoffrey de Charny's letters instituting the collegiate church of Lirey. On this occasion, and seemingly in complete contradiction of Bishop d'Arcis's allegations of thirty-four years later, Geoffrey is warmly praised by Henri, who says 'we praise, ratify and approve the said letters in all their parts', and speaks of 'ourselves wishing to develop as much as possible a cult of this nature'. Henri also mentions 'the said knight's [i.e. Geoffrey's] sentiments of devotion, which he has hitherto manifested for the divine cult, and which he manifests ever more daily'.

July–August. Geoffrey de Charny is described as taking part in the siege of Breteuil. As a clear indication of him still being very much in royal favour, he is given another Paris house close to the royal palace, also a 'country' residence at Ville-l'Evêque, then just outside the walls of Paris. Both houses had been confiscated from the queen's treasurer, who had defected to the king of Navarre.

19 September. Geoffrey de Charny dies a hero's death at the battle of Poitiers, during a last stand against the English in which, with the *oriflamme* battle-standard in his hands, he valiantly defends his king with his own body. He is given a hasty burial in a nearby Franciscan friary. While King John is taken into captivity, his nineteen-year-old

son Charles, who had been fighting alongside, escapes the field to become Regent.

November. Geoffrey's second wife, the now widowed Jeanne de Vergy, successfully appeals to Regent Charles for grants formerly made to Geoffrey to be made in favour of their son (Geoffrey II), who is described as still a minor.

1357   5 June. Twelve bishops of the pontifical court at Avignon grant indulgences to all who visit the church of St Mary of Lirey and its relics. The conditions for granting the indulgences include prayers for the souls of 'the lord Geoffrey de Charny, knight . . . and the lady Jeanne de Toucy, this same Geoffrey's wife'.

1358   Marauding bands of English seize Bishop Henri of Poitiers's château at Aix-en-Othe and attempt to capture Troyes. To add to the disorder, the Jacquerie uprising breaks out, in which a large band of French brigands terrorise much of France. At Lirey Simon Fratris takes over as dean, the former dean, Robert de Caillac, having died. It may well have been at this time that Jeanne de Vergy leaves Lirey.

1364   King John the Good dies in London, to be succeeded by his former Regent son, who now becomes King Charles V.

1366   In a census return completed by his mother and stepfather, Geoffrey II de Charny is described as an *'escuyer, moindre d'aage'*, that is, a squire who had not yet reached the age of majority.

1367   Aymon of Geneva is described as lord of Lirey from around this time. This confirms that he has married Jeanne de Vergy some time before this date.

1370   Charles V arranges for Geoffrey I de Charny to be reburied, at royal expense, as befits a hero, in the recently founded and richly endowed Abbey of the Celestines, Paris, joining there the heart of King John the Good.

25 August. Death of Bishop Henri of Poitiers.

1375   Royal commissioners report Troyes as a city in decline, due to the citizens' inability to meet the heavy taxes being imposed to pay ransoms and fund national defence.

In this same year Geoffrey II de Charny is appointed *bailli* for Caux.

1378   20 September. Robert of Geneva, a relative of Jeanne de Vergy's new husband Aymon, is elected pope under the name Clement VII by cardinals opposed to Urban VI. The papacy becomes split between Avignon and Rome.

1380   Death of Charles V and accession of Charles VI, under the charge of his uncles the *ducs* of Berry and Burgundy. English troops attack Troyes, but are unable to take it.

1382   21 November. The French defeat the Flemish at the battle of Roose-beke. Geoffrey II de Charny, serving under the Duc de Burgundy, is praised by France's young King Charles VI for his part in this.

1388   Death of Aymon of Geneva, thereby widowing Jeanne de Vergy for a second time. Shortly after this Jeanne institutes in the church of Geneva an anniversary for Aymon's soul, indicating that she was definitely still alive at this time.

In this same year her son Geoffrey II de Charny is promoted to the larger baillieship of Mantes.

1389   4 August. A letter signed in Paris by Charles VI of France orders the *bailli* of Troyes to seize the Shroud at the ecclesiastical college of Blessed Mary of Lirey in Champagne, in the diocese of Troyes. This letter states that the Bishop of Troyes (known to be Pierre d'Arcis) has asserted that 'in the collegial church of Blessed Mary in Lirey, a certain hand-made and artificially depicted cloth was kept, bearing the figure or likeness of, and in commemoration of, the holy *sudarium* in which the most precious body of our Lord Jesus Christ the Saviour was wrapped after his holy Passion. And although the faithful are in danger of idolatry, the knight Geoffrey II has himself displayed or caused to be displayed the cloth with full ceremony as if it was the true *sudarium Christi* and he has not ceased, though we have tried to impede this practice. And so we command you, *Bailli*, to get the cloth and bring it to me, so that I might relocate it in another church in Troyes and place it under honest custody.'

15 August. Report by Jean de Venderesse, lord of Marfontainnes and *bailli* of Troyes, concerning his going to the Lirey church on the Feast of the Assumption. 'We went to the church at Lirey and by virtue of the Royal papers asked that the cloth be delivered to us by command of the King. The Dean responded that he could not give it to us because it was sealed in a treasury where vestments, relics, precious books [records] were kept, and locked with several keys. He had only one key. My procurer was for breaking in, but the Dean opposed this saying the cloth was not there. We placed our seal on the treasury door, left a guard and went to dinner. That evening the Dean again said the cloth was not there and requested that we remove our seal. Then he said that the other key resided with the people of the lord of Lirey. We said we would continue to keep a seal on the treasury until the other key should arrive. The Dean replied that he did not know when the keeper of the lord's key might come. We said we would wait until the next day; but when the Dean with all his canons filed an official appeal we did not proceed further in the matter.' An appendage to this document names Lirey's dean as

Nicole Martin and his canons as Jean Boygney, Jacques Coardot and Thiebaut Goutey.

5 September. King's first serjeant reports to *bailli* of Troyes that he has gone to Lirey and informed Dean Nicole Martin and his canons that the cloth is now 'verbally put into the hands of our lord the king'. This decision has also been conveyed to Jacquemon de Monfort, a squire of the de Charny household, for passing on to his master.

30 October. Charles VI and his uncles (with Geoffrey de Charny II very likely part of the Duc de Burgundy's entourage), attend Antipope Clement VII's court at Avignon for eight days of festivities and conferences.

(Late) Bishop Pierre de'Arcis of Troyes appeals to Antipope Clement VII concerning the exhibiting of the Shroud at Lirey. He describes the cloth as bearing the double imprint of a crucified man and that it is being claimed as the true Shroud in which Jesus's body was wrapped, attracting crowds of pilgrims, but according to his information it was discovered to be the work of an artist.

Christmas. Collapse of the nave of Bishop d'Arcis's cathedral at Troyes, apparently because of the failure of one of the enclosing arches of its clerestory. Shortly after, the rose window of the north transept falls out.

1390　　January. In Troyes an emergency team of some thirty labourers are recruited to clear away the fallen timber and stone rubble from the partial collapse of the cathedral.

6 January. Clement VII writes to Bishop d'Arcis, ordering him to keep silent on the Shroud, under threat of excommunication. On this same date Clement writes a letter to Geoffrey II de Charny apparently restating the conditions under which expositions could be allowed. Again on this same day, Clement writes a letter to other relevant individuals, asking them to ensure that his orders are obeyed.

June. Papal bull grants new indulgences to those who visit St Mary of Lirey and its relics.

1398　　22 May. Death of Geoffrey II de Charny. He is buried at the Cistercian abbey of Froidmont, near Beauvais, his tomb decorated with his effigy as a knight in armour.

1400　　Geoffrey II de Charny's daughter Margaret marries Jean de Baufremont.

1408　　Beginning of building of what would become Sainte Chapelle at Chambéry, initiated by Amadeus VIII of Savoy, and dedicated to the Mother of God, to St Paul and St Maurice.

1415　　Jean de Baufremont, first husband of Geoffrey II de Charny's daughter Margaret, is killed at Agincourt.

1416   Amadeus VIII, who is busy establishing direct rule over the Savoy-ards' scattered domains in Piedmont (to which he adds Vercelli), is created first Duke of Savoy by the Emperor Sigismund.

1418   8 June. The widowed Margaret de Charny marries Humbert of Vil-lersexel, Count de la Roche, Lord of St Hippolyte sur Doubs.

     6 July. Due to danger from marauding bands, the Lirey canons hand over the Shroud to Humbert for safe-keeping. A voucher receipt describes the Shroud as 'a cloth on which is the figure or rep-resentation of the Shroud of our Lord Jesus Christ'. Humbert keeps it in his castle of Montfort near Montbard.

     Later the Shroud is kept at St Hippolyte sur Doubs, in the chapel called des Buessarts. According to seventeenth-century chroniclers annual expositions of the Shroud are held at this time in a meadow on the banks of the River Doubs called the Pré du Seigneur.

1434   Duke Amadeus VIII of Savoy, esteemed as a generous prince and a 'Solomon of his Age' resigns his dukedom and retires to a priory. His son, Louis, who will in two decades receive the Shroud, becomes Louis I Duke of Savoy.

1438   Death of Humbert de la Roche, husband of Margaret de Charny.

1439   After a revolt against Pope Eugenius IV ex-Duke Amadeus, being considered as possessing the right qualities to resolve the crisis in the Church, is elected Pope Felix V.

1443   8 May. Dean and canons of Lirey petition Margaret de Charny to return the Shroud to them. Margaret de Charny's deposition states that the Shroud was *'conquis par feu messire Geoffroy de Charny'*.

     9 May. Judgement of the Parlement of Dôle on the dispute between the Lirey canons and Margaret de Charny.

1447   18 July. The Court of Besançon gives judgement on the case of Margaret de Charny v. the Lirey canons.

1448–9   6 July. Archives of Mons (folio 24) record Margaret de Charny (as Mme de la Roche) having in her care 'what is called the Holy Shroud our Our Lord' and entering Mons where she orders French wine.

1449   Benedictine chronicler Cornelius Zantiflet records Margaret de Charny exhibiting the Shroud in this year at Chimay in the diocese of Liège, Belgium. According to Zantiflet, clearly sceptical about the Shroud's authenticity, it was 'a certain sheet on which the shape of the body of our Lord Jesus Christ has been skilfully painted, with remarkable artistry, showing the outlines of all the limbs, and with feet, hands and side stained with blood-red, as if they had recently suffered stigmata and wounds'.

1452   13 September. Margaret de Charny shows the Shroud at Germolles (near Mâcon) in a public exposition at the Castle.

1453   22 March. Margaret de Charny, at Geneva, receives from Duke Louis I of Savoy the castle of Varambon and revenues of the estate of Miribel near Lyon in return for 'valuable services'. These services are thought to have been the bequest of the Shroud.

The Shroud becomes the property of the Dukes of Savoy, initially with no fixed abode

1457   Margaret de Charny is threatened with excommunication if she does not return the Shroud to the Lirey canons.

            30 May. Letter of excommunication sent.

1459   Margaret de Charny's half-brother Charles de Noyers negotiates compensation to the Lirey canons for their loss of the Shroud, which they specifically recognise they will not now recover. The excommunication is lifted.

1460   7 October. Margaret de Charny dies, leaving her Lirey lands to her cousin and godson Antoine-Guerry des Essars.

1464   6 February. By an accord drawn up in Paris, Duke Louis I of Savoy agrees to pay the Lirey canons an annual rent, to be drawn from the revenues of the castle of Gaillard, near Geneva, as compensation for their loss of the Shroud. (This is the first surviving document to record the Shroud as having become Savoy property, and clearly shows the Lirey Shroud and that subsequently owned by the Savoy family to be one and the same.) The accord specifically notes that the Shroud had been given to the church of Lirey by Geoffrey de Charny, lord of Savoisy and Lirey, and that it had then been transferred to Duke Louis by Margaret de Charny.

1465   Duke Louis I dies at Lyon. Just over two decades later a chronicle of Savoy will record his acquisition of the Shroud at his greatest achievement. Louis is succeeded by his son Duke Amadeus IX, an inactive but devout prince who shares with his wife Duchess Yolande of France a particular devotion to the Shroud. Amadeus is said in 1502 to have instituted the cult of the Shroud in the Sainte Chapelle at Chambéry and Yolande to have founded Chambéry's Poor Clares convent.

1467   21 April. Pope Paul II elevates status of the Chambéry chapel to a collegiate church.

            In this same year, appointment of the Franciscan Francesco della Rovere (the future Pope Sixtus IV) as Cardinal. In his treatise 'The Blood of Christ' della Rovere has written of the Lirey–Chambéry Shroud: 'On this shroud we see the image of Jesus Christ traced in his very blood.'

1471   Beginning of second phase of construction of what will subsequently be known as the Sainte Chapelle at Chambéry.

20 September. Shroud transferred from Chambéry to Vercelli.

1472   Death of Duke Amadeus IX.

Philibert I ('The Hunter') of Savoy succeeds his father at the age of six. Although his mother, Dowager Duchess Yolande, assumes the role of regent during his minority, this is contested by Louis XI and the Duke of Burgundy (her brother).

1473   14 May. Two delegates from the canons of Lirey press Regent Yolande for eight years' arrears in the promised rent, or, in place of this, the return of the Shroud to them. The same petition is made to Louis IX, who responds by sending letters to the *baillis* of Sens, Troyes and Chaumont.

2 July. The Shroud is transferred from Vercelli to Turin.

5 October. The Shroud is transferred from Turin to Ivrea.

1474   18 July. The Shroud is transferred from Ivrea to Moncalieri.

25 August. The Shroud is transferred from Moncalieri to Ivrea.

1475   5 October. The Shroud is transferred across the Alps from Ivrea back to Chambéry.

1477–8   The Shroud is at Susa–Avigliano–Rivoli.

1478   20 March (Good Friday). The Shroud is exhibited at Pinerolo.

1482   A warrant is issued on behalf of the Lirey canons that the Dowager Duchess of Savoy should observe the agreement made by her late husband. In this same year Duke Philibert I of Savoy, now about sixteen years old, dies in a hunting accident. He is succeeded by his fourteen-year-old brother Charles, who becomes Duke Charles I, inheriting also through his maternal aunt the empty title of King of Cyprus and Jerusalem.

1483   Death of King Louis XI of France and succession of Charles VIII.

On 6 June this year Jean Renguis and Georges Carrelet, respectively chaplain and sacristan of the Sainte Chapelle at Chambéry, draw up an inventory in which the Shroud is described as 'enveloped in a red silk drape, and kept in a case covered with crimson velours, decorated with silver-gilt nails, and locked with a golden key'.

1485   Duke Charles I of Savoy marries Blanche de Montferrat, daughter and sole heir of the Marquis of Saluzzo. She will subsequently become known as Bianca of Savoy. This same year the French painter Jean Colombe adds to a Book of Hours that Duchess Bianca had inherited a very Shroud-like miniature of the risen Christ accompanied by the arms and portraits of Duke Charles and Duchess Bianca. The Shroud is at this time regularly carried around with the Savoys as their Court journeys from castle to castle, e.g. on 2 June of this year the clerk Jean Renguis, who would seem to have had special charge of the

Shroud, is recorded as being paid 2 écus 'in recompense for two journeys which he made from Turin to Savigliano carrying the Shroud'.

1488   Easter Sunday. The Shroud is exhibited at Savigliano.

A Passion play known as the *Passion de Semur* is written in this year, probably at Semur-en-Auxois in Burgundy, that includes what modern-day mediaevalist Lynette Muir describes as 'an explicit and undeniable reference to the [former] Lirey Shroud'. In the scene of the Marys visiting the tomb on Easter Day, the second Mary says, 'There is nothing but the Shroud', followed by Mary Magdalen exclaiming, 'See the trace of the wound'. This is then followed a little later by a stage direction requiring that Mary Magdalen 'shall take the Shroud "sudorem" and display it thus'.

1490   Death of Duke Charles I of Savoy at the age of twenty-three, leaving daughter and seven-month-old son.

1494   Good Friday. Dowager Duchess Bianca of Savoy exhibits the Shroud at Vercelli in the presence of Rupis, secretary to the Duke of Mantua. According to Rupis's report to the Duke: 'A sudarium was exhibited, that is, a sheet in which the body of our Lord was wrapped before being laid in the tomb, and on which his image can be seen outlined with blood – both front and back – and it looks as though blood is still issuing.'

1496   Death of the now seven-year-old Duke Charles II of Savoy. He is succeeded by his fifty-eight-year-old granduncle Philip II, Count of Bresse, husband of Claudine de Bresse de Bretagne.

1497   Death of Duke Philip II of Savoy, and succession by his seventeen-year-old son Philibert II ('the Handsome').

1498   An inventory detailing the Shroud when at Turin in this year describes its case as 'a coffer covered with crimson velours, with silver gilt roses, and the sides silver and the Holy Shroud inside wrapped in a cloth of red silk'.

1501   Duke Philibert II of Savoy, now twenty-one, marries young widow Margaret of Austria.

The Savoys move the Shroud 'permanently' to Chambéry

1502   11 June. At the behest of Duchess of Savoy Margaret of Austria, the Shroud is no longer moved around with the Savoys during their travels, but given a permanent home in the Sainte Chapelle, Chambéry. Duke Philibert and other notables, together with nearly all the local clergy, attend the ceremony of translation during which the Shroud is solemnly conveyed in its silver-gilt case from Chambéry's Franciscan church to the Royal Chapel. The Shroud is displayed on the Chapel's High Altar, then put back in its case and deposited behind the High Altar, in a special cavity hollowed out of the wall. For maximum security this cavity is protected by an iron grille with four locks, each opened by separate keys, two of which are held by the Duke.

1503   14 April (Good Friday). Exposition of the Shroud on an altar at Bourg-en-Bresse, to which it has been specially brought from Chambéry, in honour of Archduke Philip the Handsome, grand-master of Flanders, on his return from a journey to Spain. Savoy courtier Antoine de Lalaing, an eyewitness of the occasion, describes three bishops showing the Shroud to the public, then remarks: '[The Shroud] is, I believe, the most devotional and contemplative thing on earth. It is the rich "sydoine" and noble Shroud bought by Joseph of Arimathea. One sees it clearly bloody with the most precious blood of Jesus our Redeemer . . . One sees imprinted all his most sacred body . . .' Lalaing also adds that the Shroud's authenticity has been confirmed by its having been tried by fire, boiled in oil, laundered many times 'but it was not possible to efface or remove the imprint and image'.

1504   10 September. Death of Philibert II of Savoy, aged twenty-four, from drinking too much iced wine after hunting, thereby widowing Margaret of Austria, who had loved him passionately, for the second time in her mere twenty-two years. Philibert is succeeded by his 'learned, just and virtuous' eighteen-year-old brother, who becomes Duke Charles III.

16 September. Just six days after Philibert's death Margaret of Austria instals herself at Bourg-en-Bresse and begins work on a special cult of remembrance of her dead husband at Brou, chosen because in 1480 Dowager Duchess Claudine had made an as yet unfulfilled vow to found a monastery at Brou if her husband Philip recovered from an accident (which he had).

1505   5 May. By a special treaty Margaret relinquishes custody of the Shroud to her mother-in-law, Dowager Duchess Claudine. Claudine, who is said to have prayed every day before the Shroud, temporarily keeps it with her, it is thought, in her castle of Bylliat en Michaille, on the banks of the River Rhône. From here she invites Margaret to 'come and see the Holy Shroud' to preserve her from the epidemic then raging in the locality. Meanwhile Duke Charles III and his mother have petitioned Pope Julius II to approve the text of an Office and Mass in honour of the Shroud which has been compiled by Dominican Father Antonio Pennet, the Duke's confessor.

1506   21 April. Thanks to the intermediacy of Cardinal Louis de Gorrevod, Pope Julius II is persuaded to institute a Feast of the Holy Shroud, with proper Mass and Office. This is assigned to 4 May the day after the feast assigned to the finding of the True Cross. Initially this Feast is just for Chambéry, intended as the Shroud's permanent home.

9 May. Papal Bull is issued formally approving Mass of the Shroud, which includes the words: 'Almighty, eternal God ... you have left us the Holy Shroud on which his image is imprinted ...' The Shroud is returned to the chapel in Chambéry.

1507   Dowager Duchess of Savoy Margaret of Austria becomes regent in the Netherlands and sets up a Court there, but is thought to have kept a copy of the Shroud with her, since an inventory of her goods, made when she moves from Mechelen (Malines) to Brussels in 1523, includes 'The picture of the Holy Shroud of Our Lord made on cloth'. This may be the copy today preserved in the Church of St Gommaire at Lierre, Belgium [pl. 8b].

1508   20 February. Margaret of Austria draws up her will, in which she gives to her beloved church of Brou, among other relics, a snippet of the Shroud.

Under the direction of John Huart, dean of Lirey, work begins in this year on the rebuilding in stone of Geoffrey de Charny's wooden church at Lirey, now fallen into disrepair. This will take another eighteen years.

1509   Margaret of Austria commissions one of the best goldsmiths in her court, Lievin van Latham, to create a magnificent new casket for the Shroud, at a cost of more than 12,000 gold écus. This is brought from Flanders to Chambéry by one of Margaret's closest advisers, Laurent de Gorrevod. The Shroud's installation in this new casket takes place on 10 August, before the Sainte Chapelle's grand altar, in the presence of many dignitaries. In one of his letters Gorrevod writes of the occasion: 'I have brought the casket of the Holy Shroud to Chambery, and it was considered to be very fair and rich ... and now as many people or more come to see the said casket as they do the Holy Shroud.'

1511   Private exposition of the Shroud for Anne of Brittany, Queen of France, and for Cardinal Francesco of Aragon. A major programme of embellishment of Chambéry's Sainte Chapelle is commenced. From contemporary descriptions, this includes the provision of stained glass, Flemish sculpture, marble tombs of the princesses of Savoy, rich draperies, ornamentation from Cyprus, reliquaries studded with precious stones, etc. Expositions of the Shroud take place each 4 May.

1514   17 October. Pope Leo X extends the Feast of the Holy Shroud throughout Savoy.

287

1516   15 June. Dressed as a monk, King Francis I of France arrives in Chambéry to venerate the Shroud, having journeyed on foot from Lyon to give thanks after his victory at the battle of Marignac.

    The copy of the Shroud preserved in the Church of St Gommaire at Lierre, Belgium (see entry for 1507), is dated to this year. This clearly shows marks of damage to the Shroud – triple holes visible to this day – that must have been made on some unrecorded occasion prior to this year.

1517   Don Antonio de Beatis, companion to the cardinal archbishop of Aragon, writes of the Shroud in his diary for this year: 'This winding sheet, sindon or sudarion is about five and a half spans high and only a little longer than the imprint, which is double – a front and a rear impression. These images of the most glorious body are impressed and shaded in the most precious blood of Christ and show most distinctly the marks of the scourging, of the cords about the hands, of the crown on the head, of the wounds to the hands and the feet, and especially of the wound in the most holy side, as well as various drops of blood spilled outside the most sacred image – all in a manner that would strike terror and reverence into Turks, let alone Christians.'

1518   28 October. Shroud exhibited at Chambéry in honour of the Cardinal of Aragon. This is conducted from the castle walls, in order for the Shroud to be better viewed by the crowds of pilgrims. Antoine de Lalaing describes the Shroud bloodstains as 'clear as if they had been made today'.

1521   Duke Charles III of Savoy marries Beatrice, daughter of King Emanuel of Portugal and they make a pilgrimage from Vercelli to Chambéry to venerate the Shroud. The Shroud is exhibited at Chambéry for benefit of Dom Edmé, abbot of Clairvaux. Carried by three bishops, it is shown on the castle walls and then for privileged observers hung over the High Altar of the Sainte Chapelle, Chambéry.

1522   The choir of the Sainte Chapelle at Chambéry is decorated with a stained-glass window depicting the Shroud, created by Jean del'Arpe.

1523   First properly documented reference to the existence of a purported Holy Shroud at Besançon. On 18 March the chapter of St Etienne cathedral send to Dijon to enquire how the Easter mystery is being performed there, as they wish to present a similar performance. On 27 March the chapter make a formal decision that 'the shroud' which they have apparently acquired as a result of their enquiry, should be secured in a chest with three locks and three keys. At Easter the Mystery Play of the Resurrection, which had fallen into disuse, comes to be reinstated, centring on this. In time this shroud comes to be regarded as of equal authenticity to the Lirey–Chambéry one, theoretically having been used to wrap the body of Christ after it had been washed. In this same year a Chapel of the Holy Shroud is founded in Lausanne.

1525   Notice is posted in the church at Lirey, giving a lengthy but not overly accurate account of the Shroud's history. This notes that 'the big strong *armoires* where the Holy Shroud was housed and carefully guarded are still here'.

1532   4 December. A major fire breaks out in the Sainte Chapelle, Chambéry. Because the grille covering the cavity where the Shroud is kept has four locks, with keys kept by different dignitaries, not all of whom are immediately available, blacksmith Guillaume Pussod is summoned to prise open the grille. By the time he succeeds the Shroud's magnificent casket–reliquary has already been irreparably melted by the heat. When this is opened up the Shroud folded inside is found to be already partly on fire from a drop of molten silver that has fallen on one corner. This is quickly doused with water. Most of the Chapel's fine decoration, including Jean del'Arpe's stained glass of the Shroud, suffers destruction during this same conflagration.

1533   The Shroud is not exhibited at Chambéry, giving rise to rumours that it was destroyed in the chapel fire.

1534   April. Pope Clement VII sends his envoy Cardinal Louis de Gorrevod to make an official recognition of the Shroud and to have it repaired.

Wednesday, 15 April. Gorrevod and the Duke of Savoy give notice to the local Poor Clares convent that they are to make repairs to the Shroud.

16 April, 8 a.m. Borne by Cardinal Gorrevod, the Shroud is carried in procession to the Poor Clares convent. After it has been laid on the convent church's altar, it is taken to a specially prepared table set up in the choir, upon which the repair work is to be carried out. With the cloth laid out on this table, Gorrevod asks the assembled notables present, who include three bishops and ten noblemen, to testify that the cloth before them is the same as that they knew before the fire. According to the Cardinal, 'It is the same sheet as we ourselves before the fire have many times held in our hands, seen, touched and shown to the people.' Asked by Gorrevod to choose the nuns to do the mending, the convent's Mother Superior, Louis de Vargin, nominates herself and three others.

The nuns deputed to do the sewing are given absolution and after dinner an embroiderer brings a wooden frame for stretching the holland cloth onto which the Shroud is to be sewn. Watched by a large crowd kept back only by the locked grille of the choir, the Poor Clares stitch the Shroud onto the holland cloth and sew patches over the unsightliest of the damage. As the Shroud is described by the Mother Superior, Louise de Vargin: 'We saw ... traces of a face all plummeted and bruised with blows ... We noticed at the left side of the forehead a drop larger than the others, and longer; it winds in a wave ... the cheeks, swollen and disfigured, show well enough that they had been cruelly struck, particularly the right ... And we saw a long trace which went down onto the neck, which made us think he was bound by an iron chain ... the wound of the divine side seems large enough to receive three fingers, surrounded by a bloodstain of four fingers, narrowing at the bottom, and about half a foot long. On the other part of this Holy Shroud, representing the back of the body of our Saviour, can be seen the nape of the head pierced by long, big thorns, which are so numerous that one can see by that that the crown was made like a hat ... the shoulders are entirely torn and brayed with whip lashes, which spread all over. The blood drops appear as large as marjoram leaves ... on the middle of the body one notices the vestiges of an iron chain which bound him so tightly to the column that it appears all blood [this seems to be the spillage of blood from the lance-wound, but which, because of its chain-like appearance, the Poor Clare nuns and others of earlier centuries, including the artist of the Lirey medallion, seem to have interpreted as a chain] ... on looking through the underside of the Shroud, when it was stretched on the Holland cloth or on the loom, we saw the wounds as if we had looked through a glass.'

2 May. After completion of the repairs, the Shroud is rolled around a roller with a sheet of red silk, then covered in cloth of gold, then returned to the Savoys' castle in Chambéry.

1535 Savoy is invaded by French troops. Duke Charles III and his family abandon Chambéry and the Shroud is taken to Piedmont, passing through the Lanzo valley via Bessans, Averoles, Ceres and Lanzo. A fresco of an exposition of the Shroud, probably by Bernardo Rossignolo, is painted for the church of Voragno at Ceres.

4 May. The Shroud is exhibited in Turin.

22 May. The Besançon shroud is exhibited before a crowd of 30,000 pilgrims.

1536 7 May. The Shroud is exhibited in Milan. Indicative of the rumours that it had been destroyed in the fire, Rabelais's *Gargantua* published in France in this year includes a scene in which soldiers sacking a monastery vineyard call upon various saints and relics: 'Some made a vow to St James, others to the Holy Shroud of Chambéry, but it caught fire three months later so that not a single scrap [*brin*] could be saved; others to Cadouyn...'

1537   The Shroud is taken for safety to Vercelli because of the French invasions.

        29 March. The Shroud is exhibited from the tower of Bellanda, Nice.

1540   The Shroud is at Aosta.

1543   Duke Charles III brings the Shroud back to Vercelli, to be kept in the treasury of St Eusebius Cathedral.

1545   The Shroud is privately displayed for Maria of Aragon.

1552   In Russia, Ivan the Terrible, fighting the battle of Kazan, carries a copy of the cloth of Edessa as his battle-standard, inscribed, 'May you preserve your creatures from the enemy's wiles'. He dedicates to the cloth of Edessa the first Christian church built at Kazan.

1553   18 November. French troops sack Vercelli and six of their soldiers enter the cathedral looking for the Shroud, which the canon, Antoine-Claude Costa, has presciently hidden in his house.

        Accession in this year of Duke Emmanuel-Philibert of Savoy, who will greatly enhance Savoy's prosperity.

1559   Following the treaty of Câteau-Cambrésis in this year, thirty-year-old Duke Emmanuel-Philibert repossesses his territories and marries Margaret de Valois. A miniature in Duchess Margaret's prayer book, thought to have been painted for her marriage, shows the Shroud held up by three bishops. This exhibits the so-called poker-holes, but not the damage sustained as a result of the fire of 1532. Dorsally the body of Jesus is shown naked, though frontally there is an indication of a loincloth. This seems to be the last depiction showing the actuality of nakedness in the Shroud image before the implementation of the prudish policies of the Counter-Reformation Pope Paul IV.

1560   Showing of the Shroud from balcony at Vercelli.

1561   Early June. The Shroud is brought back to Chambéry and deposited in the Church of St Mary the Egyptian, in the Franciscan convent.

        4 June. The Shroud is taken in procession to the Sainte Chapelle, Chambéry, accompanied by four trumpeters, torches, etc.

        15 and 17 August. Showings of the Shroud from the walls of the city and in the piazza of the castello, the first for more than a quarter of a century.

1563   Duke Emmanuel-Philibert definitively fixes Turin as the capital of his dominions, thereby relegating Chambéry to the outskirts.

1566   Showing of the Shroud for the benefit of the new Duchess of Savoy, from Nemours. The father of St Francis of Sales is present. The Shroud is described as kept in an iron box at this time, because of the destruction of its casket in 1532.

21 July. The Shroud is privately shown at Annecy. St Francis de Sales's mother kneels before it, praying for a son. Francis is born the following year.

1568   June. Making of the Shroud copies of Gaudalupe (in the Spanish archdiocese of Toledo) and Navarrete (in the diocese of Logrono). The Italian inscription of the Guadalupe example reads: 'At the request of Signor Francesco Ibarra this picture was made as closely as possible to the precious relic which reposes in the Holy Chapel of the Castle of Chambéry and was laid upon it in June 1568.' The Navarrete copy's inscription is almost identical, but in favour of Signor Diego Gonzales.

1571   Commissioning of two copies by Pope Pius V, one of these now identifiable as the copy of Alcoy, Archdiocese of Valencia, Spain. This particular example was given by Pope Pius V to Don Juan of Austria, who gave it to the Holy Sepulchre Convent in Alcoy in 1574.

The Shroud is moved permanently to Turin

1578   Hearing that the saintly Cardinal Charles Borromeo (1538–84) has decided to walk from Milan to Chambéry to give thanks to the Shroud following the release of Milan from the plague, Duke Emmanuel-Philibert orders the Shroud to be brought to Turin, ostensibly to save Borromeo the journey over the Alps.

14 September. The Shroud arrives in Turin, heralded by a gun salute from the local artillery. It will never again return to Chambéry.

Friday, 10 October. Private showing of the Shroud for Charles Borromeo and his companions. Upon removal of its black silk coverlet, the cloth is stretched out on a large table for this viewing.

Sunday, 12 October. The Shroud is carried in procession from the Cathedral to the Piazza del Castello where, with Borromeo, Vercelli's cardinal, the archbishops of Turin and Savoy, and six other bishops officiating, it is shown on a large platform before a crowd estimated at 40,000.

14 October. After forty hours' devotions, a second procession brings the Shroud to the piazza for a second showing.

15 October. Second private showing of the Shroud for the close circle of Charles Borromeo. Cusano describes the Shroud as 'testimony to its own authenticity'.

A special print, also a medal showing Duke Emmanuel-Philibert on one side and the Shroud on the other, being held aloft by a kneeling angel, commemorate the Shroud events of this year.

1580   Death of Duke Emmanuel-Philibert of Savoy. He is succeeded by Duke Charles-Emmanuel I, to become known as 'the Great'.

1582	12 April. Pope Gregory XIII extends the Feast of the Holy Shroud throughout the entire dominions of the Duke of Savoy.
	13, 14 and 15 June. Showings of the Shroud on the occasion of a fresh pilgrimage by Cardinal Charles Borromeo to Turin, with Cardinal Gabriele Paleotto and his cousin Alfonso as other participants. These showings are recorded on a rare print preserved in the Ufficio Manoscritti e Rari of Turin's Biblioteca Civica. Paleotto subsequently recorded: 'It is worth considering the fact that the sacrosanct Shroud is of linen; one notices that the material of origin is quite coarse. Length 12 feet, width 3 feet.'
1587	A *tempietto* standing on four tall columns is erected in the Turin Cathedral presbytery as a housing for the Shroud.
1598	Publication of *Esplicatone del Sacro Lenzuolo ove fu involto il Signore* ('Account of the Holy Shroud which wrapped Our Lord'), by Alfonso Paleotto, the cousin of Cardinal Gabriele Paleotto. This indicates Paleotto's recognition, from his direct observation of the Shroud in 1582, that the nail wounds were in the wrists, rather than the palms of the hands. He writes: 'it appears on the Holy Shroud that the [nail] wound is seen at the joint between the arm and the hand, the part anatomists call the carpus, leaving the backs of the hands without wounds.'
1604	4 May. Showing of the Shroud in the presence of Duke Charles-Emmanuel I and his Court.
1605	25 March. Church of the Most Holy Shroud is dedicated in Rome.
1606	14 February. Private showing of the Shroud to Silvestro da Assisi-Bini, father general of the Capuchin order, an offshoot of the Franciscans.
	9 May. Public showing of the Shroud in Turin, the crowd swelled by 40,000 foreign visitors.
	Towards the end of this year Girolamo della Rovere, from a Piedmontese family of artists, obtains from Duke Charles-Emmanuel I licence, for himself and his sons, to make reproductions and related depictions of the Shroud image and to sell these throughout Savoy.
1607	Reference in the Turin State building accounts to four columns in black marble being supplied by a stone cutter 'in conformity with the design of Court Carlo di Castellamonte for the Chapel of the Holy Shroud'. This is the first indication of an intention to construct a special chapel for the Shroud in Turin.
1608	The thirtieth anniversary of the Shroud's arrival in Turin. A print issued to mark the occasion is preserved in London's British Museum.
1613	4 May. Exposition of the Shroud at which St Francis de Sales, as bishop of Geneva, is one of the three bishops who holds the cloth up before the populace. He will describe the Shroud as 'our standard of salvation'.

1620	The Shroud is shown in the Turin castle piazza to mark the marriage of Prince Victor Amadeus with Christine of France. A life-size copy is made for Torres de Alameda, Spain.
	A missal with a scene of Jesus being laid in the Shroud is made, preserved today in the Royal Library of Turin. This is thought to derive from the workshop of Girolamo della Rovere.
1623	May. Copy of the Shroud is made for the church in Logroño, northern Spain. Latin documents in the cathedral, written 4, 5 and 12 May, describe this copy as having been put in contact with the original.
1624	Exposition of the Shroud. Maria Maddalena, Grand Duchess of Austria, asks for copy to be made. She gives it to the Dominican nuns of Rome. This will go, 300 years later, to the Dominican nuns of the convent of Our Lady of the Rosary, in Summit, New Jersey, USA.
	In Antwerp, publication of I. I. Chifflet's *De Linteis Sepulchralibus Christi Servatoris Crisis Historica*, a history of the burial linens of Christ. He writes that he regards the Turin Shroud as having wrapped the body of Jesus '*ante pollincturam*', that is, before the performing of the full burial rites, thus enabling him to recognise the Besançon Shroud as also authentic.
1626	A Shroud copy is made for the monastery of the Augustinian Oblates in Rome in this year.
1630	Turin's escaping the worst of a widespread plague in this year is attributed to the Shroud's 'protection'.
	Death of Duke Charles-Emmanuel I, to be succeeded by his popular and highly respected son Victor Amadeus I.
1633	16 June. Public showing of the Shroud in the Castle Piazza, Turin.
1634	Shroud copy made for Moncalieri in the Archdiocese of Turin.
1635	4 May. Public showing of the Shroud in the Castle Piazza.
1637	Death of Duke Victor Amadeus I, to be succeeded by his young son, who becomes Duke Charles-Emmanuel II.
1639	Private showing of the Shroud at Turin for St Jeanne Françoise de Chantal, founder of the Order of the Visitation. This takes place in the Duke's residence, now known as the Palazzo Madama.
1640	The Shroud is shown as an expression of thanks for Turin's release from plague. A painted copy of the Shroud for the Hospital Church, Castillo de Garcimunoz, Spain, is described as 'taken from the original' at this time.
1642	Solemn showing of the Shroud to mark the conclusion of peace between the princes of Savoy, in the presence of Christine of France, Dowager Duchess of Savoy, her young son Duke Charles-Emmanuel II and the Princes Maurice and Thomas of Savoy.

1643	Copy of the Shroud that is the property of the Count Lovgera di Castiglione is made.
1644	Copies of the Shroud are made that are today preserved in (1) the Basilica San Sebastiano, Acireale, Catania, Italy; and (2) the Capuchin nuns' convent of Madonna del Suffragio, Turin.
1646	A copy of the Shroud in the Cathedral of St Peter, Bologna, Italy, is dated to this year. Executed in tempera on linen cloth, this is attributed to the Princess Francesa Maria, daughter of Duke Charles-Emmanuel I. According to her biography, 'She took delight in making faithful copies [of the Shroud] with her own hands, presenting them then to eminent personages or to pious sodalities.' Another copy of the Shroud, in the cathedral at Bitonto, Bari, Italy, dates to this year, also one in the church of St Catherine, Fabriano, Ancona, Italy and another in the Ursuline convent, Quebec. This latter is inscribed, 'Taken from the original in Turin'.
1647	4 May. When the Shroud is shown in the cathedral on this date, some of the enormous crowd die of suffocation.
1650	9 December. Exhibition of the Shroud in the piazza of the Royal Palace, on the occasion of the marriage of Princess Erichetta Adelaide, sister of Duke Charles-Emanuel II to the son of the Elector of Bavaria. An engraving of this occasion shows the piazza packed with pilgrims and soldiers. A surviving copy of the Shroud, only recently rediscovered in Turin, is dated to this year.
1654	Shroud copy is made for La Cuesta, Spain.
1655	4 May. La Cuesta's parish archives state that a Carmelite priest placed their copy in contact with the original in Turin on this date.
1657	5 June. Issuing of official warrant authorising developed plans by Swiss-Italian architect Bernardino Quadri for a Chapel of the Holy Shroud, raised high above the level of the cathedral presbytery and connected directly through to the royal apartments in the adjoining Royal Palace.
1663	16–17 May. Exposition of the Shroud in the cathedral of Turin is delayed from the normal 4 May to coincide with the wedding of Duke Charles-Emmanuel II of Savoy with Francesca d'Orleans, this wedding in its turn having been postponed because of the death of the Duchess of Parma. The copy of the Shroud preserved in St Paul's Church, Rabat, Malta is placed in contact with the Shroud at this time.
1664	Duke Charles-Emmanuel II assumes personal control of Savoy upon the death of his mother, Christine of France.
1665	Showing of the Shroud in the Royal Chapel, in the presence of Archbishop Michele Beggiano.

14 May (Feast of the Ascension). The Shroud shown in public before huge crowd, held up by seven bishops.

1666   24 March. Private showing of the Shroud for Duke Maximilian of Bavaria.

4 May. Public showing of the Shroud, conducted by the Archbishop of Turin and four bishops.

1667   4 May. Public showing of the Shroud, with ambassador Morosini of Venice in attendance.

1668   19 May. Guarino Guarini is appointed ducal engineer for the construction of the Chapel of the Holy Shroud, Turin Cathedral.

1670   18 November. Congregation of Indulgences grants plenary indulgence 'not for venerating the Shroud as the true shroud of Christ, but rather for meditating on his passion, especially his death and burial' – a tacit acknowledgement that the Shroud's authenticity is not beyond dispute.

1675   Death of Duke Charles-Emmanuel II and accession of Victor Amadeus II.

1678   Shroud copy is made for the church of St Maurice at Imperia, on the Ligurian coast between Nice and Genoa.

1694   The Shroud is formally deposited in a specially designed 'sepulchre' high up in the wedding-cake-tiered altar, designed by Antonio Bertola, constructed at the centre of the new Chapel of the Holy Shroud. For this occasion it is given a new black lining cloth by the Blessed Sebastian Valfré, who also adds patches where those of the Poor Clares were becoming inadequate.

1697   A copy of the Shroud is made by Giovanni Battista Fantino. This is now in a Carmelite monastery in Savona, Italy.

1703   An engraving of this year shows an exposition of the Shroud in front of the Bertola altar in the new Chapel of the Holy Shroud.

1706   12 April. The Shroud is exhibited in Turin.

1722   4 May. Showing of the Shroud in Turin.

3 June. Another showing.

1730   Beginning of the long reign of Duke Charles-Emmanuel III.

1736   21 September. The Shroud is exhibited in Turin.

1737   1 April. Marriage of Charles-Emmanuel III (whose titles include King of Sardinia), with Princess Elizabeth Teresa of Lorraine.

4 May. Public showing of the Shroud to mark the royal marriage, commemorated by print showing vast crowd in front of the Royal Palace, as the Shroud is displayed from a balcony.

1750   29 June. Showing of the Shroud, presided over by Cardinal Delle Lanze, to celebrate the marriage of Prince Victor Amadeus (III) with Maria Antonia de Bourbon, Infanta of Spain.

1758	Death of the very scholarly Pope Benedict XIV (Prosper Lambertini), who had written of the Shroud: 'The Holy Shroud, that outstanding relic, is preserved at Turin. Popes Paul II (1464–71); Sixtus IV (1471–84); Julius II (1503–13) and Clement VII (1523–34) all bear witness that this is the same in which our Lord was wrapped.'
1769	16 June. Private showing of the Shroud for Emperor Joseph II of Hapsburg-Lorraine. The Shroud is then displayed from the balcony of the Royal Chapel for large crowd gathered in the cathedral below.
1773	Death of Duke Charles-Emmanuel III.
1775	Beginning of reign of Duke Victor Amadeus III.
	5 October. The marriage of Piedmont Prince Charles-Emmanuel (IV) with Princess Marie Clotilde of France is marked by a showing of the Shroud with same ceremonial as used in 1750.
1778	The genealogist Guichenon describes the Shroud as a 'preservative against all kinds of accidents'.
1792	Revolutionaries of the French Revolution break into the French royal relic collection in the Sainte Chapelle, Paris. The chapel's 'fragment du S. Suaire' is destroyed, along with its 'sainte toelle' and other objects with possible Shroud links.
1796	Accession of Charles-Emmanuel IV as Duke of Savoy.
1798	9 December. Forced to leave Turin and withdraw to Sardinia, Charles-Emmanuel IV venerates the Shroud with the rest of the royal family before their departure.
1804	13 November. Private showing of the Shroud for the visit to Turin of Pope Pius VII, *en route* from Rome to Paris at the command of Napoleon, who has insisted that he be crowned by none other than the pope. Pius reportedly kneels to venerate the cloth, and kisses it 'with tender devotion'. Seven cardinals, eight bishops and many other notables are present.
1814	20 May. Solemn showing of the Shroud to mark the return of the royal family, in the person of Victor Emmanuel I. This is the first full public showing of the Shroud since 1775.
1815	21 May. Pope Pius VII's second presiding over an exposition of the Shroud, this time marking his return to Italy after Napoleon's defeat. He personally displays it from the balcony of the Palazzo Madama. On the Shroud being returned to its casket the latter is sealed with the papal and royal seals.
1822	4 January. Showing of the Shroud to mark the start of the reign of Charles Felix, following the abdication of his brother Victor Emmanuel I. This is held out first in the Royal Chapel, in the presence of the royal family, then displayed from the Chapel balustrade for the benefit of the ordinary populace in the cathedral below.

1842   4 May. Showing of the Shroud to mark the marriage of Crown Prince Victor Emmanuel (II) with Maria Adelaide, Archduchess of Austria. The making of a daguerreotype of the Shroud on this occasion is considered but rejected. Among the crowds is Don Bosco, founder of the Salesian order, then only twenty-seven.

1868   24–7 April. During the brief archbishopric of Alessandro Riccardi dei Conti di Netro, one marked by exceptional pastoral care, the Shroud is shown in this year to mark the marriage of Prince Umberto of Savoy with Princess Margaret. Instead of a brief holding up of the cloth in the cathedral or from a balcony of the Palazzo Madama, as had happened in 1815 and 1842, the Shroud is properly displayed on a board on the cathedral High Altar for four days. Don Bosco again attends, accompanied by boys from his Oratory.

        28 April. Working on her knees, the twenty-five-year-old Princess Clotilde of Savoy (1843–1911), daughter of Victor Emmanuel II and wife of Prince Gerolamo Napoleon, changes the Shroud's former lining cloth of black silk that had been sewn on by the Blessed Sebastian Valfré back in 1694, replacing it with one of crimson taffeta which is sewn the length of one side. An official record of this, with a sample of the former black silk lining, is preserved in Turin. On this same occasion Princess Clotilde removes a thread that 110 years later will be considered, and rejected, for radiocarbon dating. On the same date the Shroud is '*scrupulosamente*' measured by Monsignor Gastaldi, then bishop of Aluzzo, and later archbishop of Turin, and found (wrongly) to be 410 cm × 140 cm.

1898   25 May. Beginning of eight-day exposition of the Shroud on the occasion of Italy's fiftieth anniversary as a kingdom ruled by the House of Savoy. Because Gastaldi measured the Shroud incorrectly in 1868, the case in which it is displayed is made too short and too wide. To compensate for his miscalculation of the length, both ends of the cloth are therefore folded under. Secondo Pia takes two trial photographs of the Shroud using short exposures which reproduce poorly because of uneven lighting. Although the Shroud is displayed on this day without glass, for the rest of the exposition protective plate glass is ordered at the insistence of Princess Clotilde.

        28 May. Second, official photographing of the Shroud by Secondo Pia, this time with two large plates, one exposed for fourteen minutes, the second for twelve minutes, also several smaller plates. Turin Cathedral's head of security, Lieutenant Felice Fino, and Father Salaro, both keen amateur photographers, also take photographs.

        Midnight. Pia begins developing the negatives, discovering that the image becomes 'photographic' when the light values are reversed.

2 June. The Shroud is returned to its casket in the Royal Chapel.

13 June. First press account of Pia's discovery in Genoa's *Il Cittadino*.

14 June. The story of Pia's discovery is told in the national newspaper, *Corriere Nazionale*.

15 June. The story of Pia's discovery is told in Rome's *Osservatore Romano*.

Christmas. The British photographic magazine *Photogram* publishes a large reproduction of Pia's photograph.

1900   Canon Ulysse Chevalier's *Etude critique sur l'origine du Saint Suaire de Lirey–Chambéry–Turin* is published in Paris, detailing the d'Arcis memorandum and other mediaeval documents indicating the Shroud's fraudulence.

1902   Monday, 21 April (afternoon). Agnostic anatomy professor Yves Delage presents a paper on the Shroud to the Academy of Sciences, Paris, arguing for the Shroud's medical and general scientific convincingness, and stating his opinion that it genuinely wrapped the body of Christ.

(Evening) Secretary for the physics section of the Academy, Marcelin Berthelot, inventor of thermo-chemistry and a militant atheist, orders Delage to rewrite his paper (for publication in the *Comptes rendus de l'Académie des Sciences*) so that it treats only on the vaporography of zinc and makes no allusion to the Shroud or to Christ.

23 April. Paris edition of *New York Herald* carries headline, 'Photographs of Christ's Body found by science'.

27 April. Paris edition of *New York Herald* carries headline, 'Scientists Denounce Turin's Holy Shroud. M. Leopold Delisle tells Academy of Inscriptions "the claim has not been proved"'.

1903   Canon Ulysse Chevalier alleges that the Vatican's Congregation of Rites had privately condemned the Shroud in a report to Pope Leo XIII.

1918   Alarmed by the danger of air raids from the world war then raging, King Victor Emmanuel III orders the Shroud to be put in a place of safety, on condition that it does not leave the Royal Palace. A secret underground chamber is specially constructed two floors below ground level in the south-east side of Turin's Royal Palace, with not even the contractors told its purpose. On the floor of this chamber is set a large strongbox with a complex combination lock. On 6 May the casket of the Shroud is removed from the Royal Chapel (in which it has lain undisturbed since 1898), wrapped in a thick blanket of asbestos, put in a chest made of tin plate, hermetically sealed with cold solder, then carried down to the secret chamber, where it is solemnly locked inside the strongbox. Prayers are recited, after which the chamber's heavy entrance doors are locked.

1931   Cardinal Fossati, archbishop of Turin has an audience with Pope Pius XI. He is told, 'Be entirely at ease. We speak now as a scientist and not as Pope. We have made a personal study of the Holy Shroud and are convinced of its authenticity. Objections have been raised but they do not hold water.'

3–24 May. The Shroud is exhibited on the occasion of the marriage of Prince Umberto of Piedmont, later to become Umberto II of Savoy, to Princess Maria José of Belgium. Cardinal Fossati officiates. Two million visitors flock to Turin for this occasion.

21 May. Professional photographer Giuseppe Enrie photographs the Shroud in three sections.

Friday, 22 May. Erie, Vignon and others spend the night in vigil before the Shroud.

23 May. Enrie takes three pictures of the Shroud face, one life-size; also a detail of the shoulders and back, and a seven-fold enlargement of the wound in the wrist. The photography takes place in the presence of the now seventy-six-year-old Secondo Pia and scientists of the French Academy.

In this same year and the following one, Dr Pierre Barbet conducts experiments on cadavers to reconstruct the Passion of Jesus as exhibited in the Shroud's bloodstains and wound marks.

1933   24 September–15 October. At the request of Pope Pius XI the Shroud is exhibited as part of the celebrations for Holy Year. The young Salesian priest Fr Peter Rinaldi, fluent in French and English, as well as Italian, acts as interpreter. On the final day, 15 October, the Shroud is held out in daylight on the steps of the cathedral where Dr Pierre Barbet views it from a distance of less than a yard. He writes: 'I saw that all the images of the wounds were of a colour quite different from that of the rest of the body, and this colour was that of dried blood which had sunk into the stuff. There was, thus, more than the brown stains on the Shroud reproducing the outline of the corpse. The blood itself had coloured the stuff by direct contact. It is difficult for one unversed in painting to define the exact colour, but the foundation was red ("mauve carmine" said M. Vignon, who had a fine sense of colour), diluted more or less according to the wounds.'

1935   January. Publication of Dr Pierre Barbet's brochure *Les Cinq Plaies du Christ*.

1938   Publication of Paul Vignon's *Le Saint Suaire de Turin devant la science, l'archéologie, l'histoire, l'iconographie, la logique*, by far the most definitive book on the Shroud published up to that time.

1939   First Congress on Shroud Studies held in Turin, with some twenty papers presented.

September. Following the outbreak of the Second World War the Shroud is secretly taken for safety to the Benedictine Abbey of Montevergine, in the province of Avellino, north-east of Naples. There are brief stops in Rome and Naples on its journey.

25 September. The Shroud arrives at the Abbey. Only the prior, the vicar general and two of the monks are entrusted with the knowledge of what they are protecting.

1946   June. The Italian people vote for a republic, ending the rule of Umberto II of Savoy, the Shroud's legal owner.

28 October. The Shroud is exhibited to the monks of Montevergine prior to its post-war return to Turin. It is laid on a table in the abbey's reception hall, but strict orders are given that no one should directly touch it.

The Shroud returns to Turin and its traditional housing in the Royal Chapel. However, with the fall of the monarchy, and because the Chapel is part of the now state-owned Royal Palace, the Shroud is technically on Italian state territory.

1950   International Sindonological Congress held, as part of Holy Year celebrations, at the Palazzo della Cancelleria, Rome. Pope Pius XII sends telegram of benediction.

1954   Holy Week. British war hero, Group Captain Leonard Cheshire VC, having become inspired by the Shroud face while recuperating from tuberculosis, uses bus to tour Britain with an exhibition of Shroud photographs.

1955   Easter. Group Captain Cheshire publishes articles on the Shroud in the British *Picture Post* and *Daily Sketch*.

11 May. Cheshire receives letter from Mrs Veronica Woollam of Gloucester, asking if her ten-year-old daughter Josephine, crippled with osteomyelitis in the hip and leg, 'could be blessed with the relic of the Holy Shroud'. Unable to travel by air because of his lungs, Cheshire takes Josephine and her mother by train, first to Portugal, for ex-King Umberto's permission, then to Turin in the hope of her being healed via the Shroud. The Shroud is taken out of its casket, its seals are broken and Josephine is allowed to put her hand in beneath the silk covering. But it is not unrolled. Although there is no immediate change in Josephine's condition, she later recovers to lead a normal life, though she will die young.

1959   18 December. Formation of the Centro Internazionale di Sindonologia, the Turin International Centre for the Turin Shroud.

1960   British Shroud enthusiast Vera Barclay writes to scientists at the

	Atomic Energy Research Establishment, Harwell, regarding the viability of radiocarbon dating the Shroud. Dr F. J. P. Clarke and P. J. Anderson respond, expressing serious doubts.
1961	17 December. Death of Dr Pierre Barbet.
1969	16–18 June. On the orders of Turin's Cardinal Michele Pellegrino, the Shroud is secretly taken out of its casket for its state of preservation to be studied by a team of experts. These examine, photograph and discuss for three days, but do no direct testing. During this same period, and with the Shroud hung vertically for the purpose, Giovanni Battista Judica-Cordiglia takes the first ever Shroud photo in colour, also fresh black-and-white ones, and ones by Woods light.
1972	1 October. Attempt to set fire to the Shroud on the part of an unknown individual who breaks into the Royal Chapel after climbing over the palace roof. The Shroud survives unscathed due to an asbestos protection within its altar shrine.
1973	4 October. Dr Max Frei and others, assembled in Turin's Hall of the Swiss and with the Shroud apparently in a frame before them, notarise as authentic the Shroud photographs taken by Giovanni Battista Judica-Cordiglia. Although it is not stated, the Shroud would seem to have been brought out on this occasion as a test-run/frame fitting for the TV exposition of six or seven weeks later.

Thursday, 22 November. The Shroud is displayed in the Hall of the Swiss, within Turin's Royal Palace, in preparation for its first ever television showing. International journalists and some serious researchers on the subject, including Britain's David Willis and Fr Maurus Green, are allowed to view the Shroud directly during this time.

23 November (9.15–9.45 p.m.). The Shroud is shown for the first time ever on television, in colour, and with a filmed introduction by Pope Paul VI.

24 November. The Shroud is secretly examined by a new Commission of experts, brought together by Cardinal Pellegrino. On this occasion Professor Gilbert Raes takes from one edge of the Shroud's frontal end one 40-×-13mm sample, also from the side-strip one 40-×-10mm portion, together with one 13 mm warp thread and one 12 mm weft thread. Dr Max Frei is among the other specialists present, and is allowed to take twelve samples of surface dust from the Shroud's extreme frontal end, using adhesive tape to remove these. The Shroud is then returned to its casket the same evening.

1976	19 February. In the USA, at the Sandia Laboratories, Dr John Jackson and Bill Mottern view for the first time the Shroud's three-dimensional image via a VP8 Image Analyzer.

April. Release of Report of the Turin Scientific Commission, with the first public information of the pollen findings of Dr Max Frei, who claims that the Shroud's dust includes pollens from some plants that are exclusive to Israel and to Turkey, suggesting that the Shroud must at one time have been exposed to the air in these countries.

1977   23–4 March. First US Conference of Research on the Shroud, at the Ramada Inn, Albuquerque, New Mexico, attended by Frs Rinaldi and Otterbein, Revd. David Sox, Dr John Robinson, film-maker David Rolfe and many members of what would become the STURP team.

May. First experimental use, at Rochester University, New York State, USA, of the accelerator mass spectrometry method of radio-carbon dating, by which very much smaller samples can be dated than had previously been thought possible. This is the method that will be used to date the Shroud. One of the leading pioneers of this method is Rochester University's Professor Harry Gove.

24 June. Revd. David Sox, General Secretary of the newly formed British Society for the Turin Shroud, writes to Professor Harry Gove of Rochester, following an article in *Time* magazine about the new radiocarbon-dating technique.

16–17 September. A Symposium on the Shroud is held at the Anglican Institute of Christian Studies, London, with Drs Jackson, Jumper, Frei and McCrone among the speakers, also Frs Rinaldi and Otterbein, Monsignor Ricci and Don Coero-Borga.

1978   20 January. Anastasio Ballestrero, the new archbishop of Turin, announces that the Shroud is to be publicly exhibited from 27 August to 8 October of this year, with an International Congress on the last two days.

3–4 June. In Colorado Springs, USA, John and Eric Jackson's group of scientists meet for a conference to plan their scientific testing of the Shroud.

6 August. Sudden death of Pope Paul VI, who had expected to visit Turin to view the Shroud during the period of the expositions, one of his only two out-of-Rome engagements pencilled in for the autumn. Convening of conclave to elect the next Pope.

26 August. With admirable simplicity and non-commercialism – in order to avoid any cause for criticism from Turin's communist administration – the Shroud is exhibited at inaugural Mass on the first day of a six-week-long period of expositions, the first since 1933. In the very same hour of the inaugural Mass, Cardinal Luciani of Venice is proclaimed Pope in Rome, becoming Pope John Paul I, to live just thirty-three days more.

1 September. Among the pilgrims who view the Shroud on this

day is Karol, Cardinal Woytywa of Poland, shortly to become Pope John Paul II.

2–3 September. In Lebanon, Connecticut, Dr John Jackson's group of scientists, at this time calling themselves the United States Conference of Research on the Shroud of Turin, meet to finalise their plans, following Turin having agreed to a twenty-four-hour-test period on 9 October.

28 September. Death of Pope John Paul I. While Cardinal of Venice, he had planned to visit the Shroud on 21 September and was rumoured to have been intending a quiet private visit before the close of the expositions.

Early October. *En route* to Turin to take part in Second International Symposium on the Shroud, Professor Harry Gove stops off in Oxford to inform Hall of Oxford about the possibility of radiocarbon dating the Shroud. Although Hall does not yet have an AMS facility, he expresses himself and his colleagues very enthusiastic to 'get in on the act'.

7–8 October. Second International Symposium on the Shroud is held at the Istituto Bancario San Paolo, Turin, at which Gove's new method is announced.

8 October. The Shroud is removed from public display and taken to the Hall of Visiting Princes within Turin's Royal Palace for a five-day period of examination, photography and sample taking by John Jackson's group of scientists from the USA. They now call themselves the Shroud of Turin Research Project (STURP). Dr Max Frei, Giovanni Riggi, Professor Pierluigi Baima-Bollone and others carry out independent own research programmes alongside. During this time the Shroud is lengthily submitted to intense photographic floodlighting, to X-rays and to ultraviolet light. Dozens of pieces of sticky tape are pressed onto its surface and removed. The bottom edge (at the foot of the frontal image) is unstitched and apparatus inserted underneath. On the night of 9 October Baima-Bollone obtains sample of Shroud bloodstain by mechanically disentangling warp and weft threads in the area of the 'small of the black' bloodstain on the Shroud's dorsal image.

Friday, 13 October. STURP complete their scientific work during the evening of this day. The Shroud is returned to its casket the following morning.

En route back to New Mexico Dr Ray Rogers stops off in Chicago and hand-delivers to Dr Walter McCrone's laboratory thirty-two of the sticky-tape samples taken from the Shroud.

25 December. Dr Walter McCrone begins examination of image

samples from the Shroud.

1979   February. Gove and colleagues write to Archbishop Ballestrero of Turin formally offering to radiocarbon date the Shroud using their new method.

24–5 March. STURP holds its 'First Data Analysis Workshop' on the Shroud, in Santa Barbara, California. According to their preliminary findings the image shows no evidence of the hand of an artist; the body image appears to be some form of scorch; and the blood image was probably present before the body image. But Walter McCrone claims he has found evidence of an artist.

1980   13 April. On a visit to Turin Pope John Paul II has a private showing of the Shroud and kisses the cloth's hem.

11 September. Dr Walter McCrone lectures to the British Society for the Turin Shroud in London, again claiming the Shroud to be the work of a mediaeval artist who painted in iron oxide, using a very dilute tempera binding medium. British journalist Peter Jennings unauthorisedly publishes the news.

1981   9 March. Death from cancer of the pancreas of West Indian patient Les at a Jospice International hospice at Thornton, near Liverpool. An imprint with some resemblance to the Shroud is left on the cover of the mattress of the bed in which Les died.

Spring. Dr John Jackson and Larry Schwalbe of STURP, together with Luigi Gonella, and Frs Otterbein and Rinaldi visit ex-King Umberto II of Savoy in Cascais, Portugal, to report on the 1978 testing.

Wednesday, 13 May. John Jackson, Fr Adam Otterbein and other STURP representatives are in St Peter's Square awaiting an audience with Pope John Paul II to report to him on the 1978 testing when the Pope is shot by Turkish gunman Mehmet Ali Agca.

December. STURP inform the Turin authorities that the Arizona, Brookhaven, Oxford and Rochester laboratories have all agreed to participate in a radiocarbon dating of the Shroud.

1982   July. The British Museum Trustees agree that their Keeper of Scientific Services should act as supervisor of any project to demonstrate satisfactory carbon dating of textiles, prior to any dating of the Shroud. AERE Harwell and the Zurich AMS facility are added to the list of laboratories willing to participate in any radiocarbon dating of the Shroud.

1983   14 January. Death of Dr Max Frei, leaving unfinished the book he was writing on his pollen findings. His estate, with all his Shroud materials, passes to his widow Gertrud and their son Ulrich.

18 March. Death of ex-King Umberto II in Cascais. The Shroud's

formal owner, his will discloses that he has bequeathed the Shroud to the Pope and his successors, with the proviso that the cloth stays in Turin.

1984   16 October. Dr John Jackson and Tom D'Muhala present Cardinal Ballestrero with proposals for further scientific work on the Shroud.

1985   1 June. At a meeting in Trondheim, Norway, Dr Tite and Richard Burleigh of the British Museum, London, release the results of an inter-comparison experiment conducted between six radiocarbon-dating laboratories, some using the old proportional counter method, others the new AMS method pioneered by Dr Harry Gove. One of the samples was a 4000-year-old Egyptian mummy wrapping for which one of the laboratories, Zurich, produced a 1000-year error due to faulty pre-treatment. Despite this gaffe, the experiment is seen as opening the way for a radiocarbon dating of the Shroud. Dr Harry Gove sets in motion plans for a meeting of the six laboratories and the British Museum to agree on a working procedure for the Shroud dating. It is suggested that the Pontifical Academy of Sciences be contacted.

August. The idea is submitted to Professor Carlos Chagas, President of the Pontifical Academy of Sciences, Rome.

October. Professor Gove meets with Professor Chagas in New York to discuss the holding of a workship of all parties interested to radiocarbon date the Shroud.

November. Professor Chagas intimates that there will soon be a meeting to discuss the dating of the Shroud.

1986   January. Paul Maloney of the US Shroud group ASSIST receives from Dr Max Frei's widow two copies of Frei's unpublished manuscript, together with five of the sticky-tape samples he took in 1978.

February. Gove meets with Turin's Professor Gonella in New York, who insists that the proposed radiocarbon-dating workshop be held in Turin.

16 February. Shroud Conference at Elizabethtown College, Elizabethtown, Pennsylvania, at which some of Max Frei's pollen samples are examined by the attendees, who include Walter McCrone. McCrone almost immediately confirms observing pollen.

April. Professor Chagas sends out invitations for the workshop meeting to take place in Turin on 9–11 June. Chagas has revealed this to the British journalist Peter Jennings, who publishes the story, precipitating heated feelings concerning this disclosure.

16 May. The Pontifical Academy of Sciences send cable postponing the meeting to discuss the carbon dating of the Shroud.

27 May. Dr Harry Gove, with Professor Hall of Oxford and British

Museum Director Sir David Wilson as co-signatories, cables Cardinals Casaroli and Ballestrero, angrily protesting at the postponement and warning that several institutions may withdraw.

29 September–1 October. Representatives of several radiocarbon-dating laboratories at last meet in Turin, under Chagas's chairmanship, to discuss the best 'protocol' for radiocarbon dating the Shroud. A protocol is drawn up for seven laboratories (five AMS, two small counter) to take part, the AMS facility at Gif-sur-Yvette, France, having been added to the list. This is then submitted to both the Pope and the Cardinal of Turin.

6 October. News of the meeting is released to the world's press.

1987   A year of deteriorating relations between Gove of Rochester and Professor Luigi Gonella.

27 April. The Turin paper *La Stampa* publicly quotes Professor Gonella as saying that only two or three laboratories would be involved in the testing.

1 July. Representatives of the seven laboratories write letter to Cardinal Ballestrero advising: 'As participants in the workshop who devoted considerable effort to achieve our goal we would be irresponsible if we were not to advise you that this fundamental modification in the proposed procedures may lead to failure.'

10 October. Cardinal Ballestrero of Turin writes to the seven radiocarbon laboratories informing them that on the advice of his scientific adviser, Professor Gonella, it is only three of their number, the Oxford, Arizona and Zurich laboratories, who have been chosen to perform the testing. Ballestrero's letter states that 'experience in the field of archaeological radiocarbon dating' was a criterion. The cardinal also advises that certain other details of the 1986 protocol have been scrapped, including any further involvement of the Potifical Academy of Sciences in the exercise, also the participation of Swiss textile expert Mme Flury-Lemberg who, it had been intended, would actually physically remove the samples from the Shroud. Dr Tite is named as the appointed supervisor for certification of the samples.

November. The directors of the three chosen laboratories warn Cardinal Ballestrero: 'As you are aware, there are many critics in the world who will scrutinise these measurements in great detail. The abandonment of the original protocol and the decision to proceed with only three laboratories will certainly enhance the skepticism of these critics.' The chosen three declare themselves 'hesitant to proceed' and request the matter be given 'further consideration'.

1988   13 January. The Turin newspaper *La Stampa* discloses that Professor Gove and Dr Harbottle have written an open letter to the Pope, also to *Nature* and the director of the British Museum, deploring the rejection of the seven-laboratory protocol. They claim that the Pope has been 'badly advised' and 'that he is making a mistake if he approves a limited or reduced version of the research whose outcome will be, to say the least, questionable'.

15 January. In a press release Gove and Harbottle remark that it is interesting that the archbishop stated 'experience in the field of archaeological radiocarbon dating' to have been a criterion, bearing in mind that 'the Harwell laboratory, left out, has had more experience than the three chosen laboratories put together'. They also point out that the Zurich laboratory, though highly competent, 'was the ... one with the 1000-year error in the earlier inter-comparison'. They conclude, 'The Archbishop's plan, disregarding the protocol, does not seem capable of producing a result that will meet the test of credibility and scientific rigour' and that 'it is probably better to do nothing than to proceed with a scaled-down experiment'.

15 January. At a press conference at Columbia University Gove reiterates: 'We feel it's extraordinarily bad advice the cardinal is being given by his science adviser [i.e. Professor Gonella] ... He's a man nobody [in the scientific community] ever heard of.'

Professor Gonella declines to explain the reasons for his choice of laboratories, terming it a private matter. Although the three chosen laboratories express reservations, Gonella threatens to use the Italian Pisa and Udine laboratories in their place if they refuse to co-operate.

22 January. Professor Gonella and leading representatives of the Oxford, Arizona and Zurich laboratories meet in the Board Room of the British Museum, London, to discuss the best procedures to be adopted. News of this meeting is released the same evening.

February. Dr Tite tries unsuccessfully to find control samples of weave identical to the Shroud.

25 March. Professor Gove writes to the Pope outlining all that has transpired and appealing to him to persuade Cardinal Ballestrero to revert to the original protocol. His letter is ignored.

Wednesday, 13 April. Professor Paul Damon holds an 'open house' for journalists at his Arizona radiocarbon-dating laboratory to show them where and how the work on the Shroud samples will be done.

Thursday, 21 April. At 4.30 a.m. a security guard working in the Turin Royal Palace is startled to find lights on in the Shroud Chapel. On investigating, he discovers two cathedral canons perched with a ladder on the chapel altar, with another senior clergyman supervising from below. Because of concern to avoid intrusion by the press, no one had warned the guard that the Shroud was to be brought out that day. At 5 a.m. the Shroud is secretly taken out of its casket. At 6.30 a.m. Dr Tite and the representatives of the three laboratories assemble at the cathedral, only to be told that there has been a political hitch and the project cannot proceed. Four officials from the Turin city government are at the chapel entrance claiming that the Royal Chapel is on Italian State premises and that no official permission has been obtained for the Shroud to be removed from this. The impasse is resolved by the officials' inclusion as witnesses. In the cathedral sacristy the Shroud is unrolled and shown to assembled representatives of the three chosen radiocarbon-dating laboratories. Professor Testore of Turin Polytechnic, Gonella's choice as textile expert in place of Mme Flury-Lemberg, reportedly asks 'What's that brown patch?' of the wound in the side. Riggi and Gonella reportedly spend two hours arguing about the exact location on the Shroud from which the sample should be taken. In the event it is Riggi who seems in charge of the operation and, with a video-camera recording his every move (he will later sell copies to international media and others), at 9.45 a.m. he cuts a sliver from one edge and divides this into two, then divides one of these halves into three. In a separate room (the Sala Capitolare), and now unrecorded by any camera, the Cardinal and Dr Tite place these three latter samples in sealed canisters, for the respective laboratories to take away with them. At 1 p.m. the sample taking for carbon-dating purposes is formally completed and the laboratory representatives depart. During the afternoon, and in the presence of some twenty witnesses, Riggi takes blood samples from the lower part of the crown-of-thorns bloodstains on the Shroud's dorsal image. According to Riggi's own subsequent account, he received the cardinal's permission to take for himself both these 'blood' samples and the portion of the Shroud he cut away but which was superfluous to the needs of the carbon-dating laboratories. These samples he will deposit in a bank vault. At 8.30 p.m. the Shroud is returned to its casket.

Friday, 22 April. The news of the taking of the samples is released to the world's press.

Sunday, 24 April. Safely arrived back in Tucson, Damon and Donahue of the Arizona laboratory informally open the samples, immediately recognising the characteristic weave of the Shroud on opening sample A1. A photograph taken on this occasion shows this sample to have been in two parts.

Monday, 25 April. Formal opening of the Arizona samples, with Damon and Donahue now joined by Toolin and Jull.

Early May. The Arizona laboratory begins work on its Shroud

sample and accompanying controls.

6 May, 9.50 a.m. In the presence of Professor Harry Gove, who has been invited to be present, the Shroud sample is run through the Arizona system. With the calibration applied, the date arrived at is AD 1350.

8 June. The Arizona laboratory completes its work on the Shroud.

Week commencing 4 July. Having delayed because of technical adjustments to their radiocarbon-dating unit, the Oxford laboratory begins its pre-treatment of its Shroud sample and controls.

15 July. At the Hotel Thalwiler Hof, Thalwil, Switzerland, Dr Max Frei's entire collection of twenty-eight sticky-tape Shroud samples is formally handed over to the American Shroud group ASSIST.

Friday, 22 July. Dr Michael Tite of the British Museum receives the Zurich laboratory's radiocarbon-dating findings.

23 July. Shroud Meeting at the Academy of Natural Science, Philadelphia, in which Dr Max Frei's sticky-tape samples, as just brought over from Europe, are formally and collectively studied by Dr Walter McCrone, Dr Alan Adler and others, under the auspices of the US Shroud group ASSIST. This reveals that, in addition to pollens and fabric particles, the tapes bear a surprising proportion of plant parts and floral debris, suggesting that actual flowers were laid on the Shroud at some time during its history.

Wednesday, 27 July. The Oxford laboratory commences its first run of its Shroud sample and controls.

8 August. The Oxford laboratory completes its Shroud work.

26 August. The London *Evening Standard* carries banner headlines declaring the Shroud to be a fake made in 1350. The source, Cambridge librarian Dr Stephen Luckett, has no known previous connection with the Shroud, or with the carbon-dating work, but in this article declares scientific laboratories 'leaky institutions'. The story is picked up around the world.

Mid-September. The London *Sunday Times* receives an advance copy of the Revd David Sox's book *The Shroud Unmasked: Uncovering the Greatest Forgery of all Time*. This reveals that Sox already knows the radiocarbon-dating results.

18 September. Without quoting its source, *The Sunday Times* publishes a front-page story headlined: 'Official: The Turin Shroud is a Fake'. Professor Hall and Dr Tite firmly deny any responsibility for this story.

Thursday, 13 October. At press conferences held in Turin and at the British Museum, London, it is announced that the Shroud dates between AD 1260 and 1390. Newspaper headlines around the world immediately brand the Shroud a fake and declare that the Catholic Church has accepted this result.

15 October. Official launch of the Revd David Sox's book *The Shroud Unmasked*.

Thursday, 17 November. Dr Michael Tite gives lecture to the British Society for the Turin Shroud on his radiocarbon-dating work.

1989   Wednesday, 15 February. In a £5-a-ticket talk at the Logan Hall, Institute of Education, 20 Bedford Way, London, Professor Hall lectures to the British Museum Society on 'The Turin Shroud: A Lesson in Self-Persuasion'. He very forcefully declares anyone continuing to regard the Shroud as genuine a 'Flat Earther' and 'onto a loser'.

16 February. Publication, in the prestigious scientific journal *Nature*, of the official results of the Shroud radiocarbon dating. This has twenty-one signatories. It declares that the results 'provide conclusive evidence that the linen of the Shroud of Turin is mediaeval'.

19 March (Palm Sunday). Retirement of Cardinal Ballestrero as archbishop of Turin, to be succeeded by Giovanni Saldarini, formerly of the Milan archdiocese. Cardinal Ballestrero temporarily remains official custodian of the Shroud.

24 March (Good Friday). A press release to the UK press announces that forty-five businessmen and 'rich friends' have donated £1 million to create a chair of archaeological sciences at Oxford to perpetuate the radiocarbon-dating laboratory created by Professor Edward Hall. The first incumbent is to be the British Museum's Dr Michael Tite.

28 April. Interviewed by journalists during a plane journey forming part of the papal visit to Africa, Pope John Paul II guardedly speaks of the Shroud as an authentic relic, while insisting that 'the Church has never pronounced on the matter'.

6–7 May. International Shroud Symposium held in Bologna.

4 June. Death, in unclear circumstances, of University of Arizona physicist Timothy W. Linick, one of the authors of the *Nature* report on the Shroud radiocarbon dating.

7–8 September. Shroud Symposium organised by the French Shroud group CIELT is held in Paris. The speakers include Professor Michael Tite.

30 September. *New Scientist* reports findings of scientific workshop at East Kilbride that 'the margin of error with radiocarbon dating ... may be two or three times as great as practitioners of the technique have claimed'.

1990   9 March–2 September. London's British Museum holds exhibition entitled 'Fake. The Art of Deception'. This includes a life-sized transparency of the Turin Shroud.

4 May. During celebration of the Feast of the Holy Shroud in the Royal Chapel, Turin (reputedly, shortly after the words '*Ita missa est*'), several chunks of stone crash to the floor from the roof ninety-eight feet above. These are due to shifts on the part of exterior sustaining arches. The chapel is closed and a temporary canopy erected over its altar.

18 September. A Vatican press conference announces the transfer 'of the position as Pontifical Custodian for the conservation and cult of the Holy Shroud to His Excellency Monsignor Giovanni Saldarini, Archbishop of Turin'. The new custodian's responsibilities are expressly stated to be conservation and cult.

1992   28 April. Death of John Tyrer, a British textile expert with a strong belief in the Shroud's authenticity.

Monday, 7 September. The Shroud brought out for examination in the sacristy of Turin Cathedral before five textile experts: England's Sheila Landi; Switzerland's Mechthild Flury-Lemberg; the USA's Jeanette M. Cardamone; and Italy's Silvio Diana and Gian Luigi. Optical observation only is permitted and no samples are taken. The Shroud is re-sealed in its casket.

1993   24 February (Ash Wednesday). Because of the repairs to the Royal Chapel, the Shroud, without being taken out of its casket, is removed from its normal shrine in the Royal Chapel and transferred to a specially designed but temporary plate-glass display case behind the High Altar, in the main body of Turin Cathedral. In poor health, Fr Peter Rinaldi has flown from the States to be present at this transfer, but collapses and is taken to a Turin hospital.

28 February. Death of Fr Peter Rinaldi.

15 April. American paediatrician Dr Leoncio Garza-Valdès, a respected amateur microbiologist, gives a paper on 'Lichenothelia varnish' to the Society for American Archaeology annual meeting at St Louis, Missouri.

May. Dr Garza-Valdès examines Riggi's Shroud sample in Turin.

10–12 June. Shroud Symposium, organised by CIELT, held at the Domus Mariae conference centre, on the outskirts of Rome. Among the speakers are Dr Leoncio Garza-Valdès, who suggests that 'Lichenothelia varnish, or bioplastic coating, on the Shroud may have falsified the Shroud radiocarbon dating'. Russian Dr Dmitri Kouznetsov is another of the speakers.

In this same year the official charter of STURP, the team who worked on the Shroud in 1978, is formally dissolved by the Secretary of State for the State of Connecticut.

1994   12 February. Conference on the Shroud held at the University of Southern Indiana, Evansville, at which paediatrician Dr Leoncio Garza-Valdès again conveys his findings concerning a bioplastic coating on the Shroud's fibres falsifying the radiocarbon dating.

2–3 September. Round Table at the University of Texas San Antonio Health Science Center, attended by Professor Harry Gove, during which Gove views Shroud threads under the microscope and acknowledges that these certainly seem to have a substantial bioplastic coating.

1995   14–23 February. John and Rebecca Jackson lecture on the Shroud in Russia.

5 September. In a broadcast on Italian television, Cardinal Saldarini announces that fresh expositions of the Shroud are to be held in 1998 and 2000.

September. Cardinal Saldarini issues statement declaring unauthorised any Shroud samples in circulation other than those taken with official permission for the tests of 1978. He remarks that 'if such material exists ... the Holy See has not given its permission to anybody to keep it and do what they want with it' and he requests those concerned to give the piece back to the Holy See. This statement seems clearly to be directed at the samples taken by Giovanni Riggi in April 1988, portions from which were procured in all good faith by Dr Garza-Valdès.

1997   11 April. Shortly after 11 p.m. fire breaks out in Turin's Royal Chapel, quickly threatening the Shroud's bullet-proof display case. Fireman Mario Trematore uses a sledge-hammer to break open this case and the Shroud, in its traditional casket, is taken temporarily to Cardinal Saldarini's residence. Signs of arson are found in the environs of the Royal Chapel, the walls of which are very badly damaged, likewise the whole High Altar end of the cathedral and the part of the Royal Palace directly adjoining the chapel.

14 April. In the presence of the Cardinal and several invited specialists, including Mme Flury-Lemberg, Professor Baima-Bollone and Dr Rosalia Piazza of Rome's Istituto Centrale del Restauro, the Shroud is brought out from its casket and its condition carefully examined. It is found to have been completely unaffected by the fire. It is taken to an undisclosed place of safety.

11–4 May. International Symposium on the Shroud held in Nice, France.

1998   18 April–4 June. Scheduled date of expositions of the Shroud to commemorate the centenary of the discovery by Secondo Pia of its hidden negative.

313

Bibliography

[It should be noted that *Sindon* is published by the Centro Internazionale di Sindonologia, Via S. Domenico, 10122 Turin; *Shroud Spectrum International* (currently inactive), by the Indiana Center for Shroud Studies, R3, Box 557, Nashville, Indiana 47448, USA]

Adler, Alan D., 'The Origin and nature of Blood on the Turin Shroud,' in *Turin Shroud – Image of Christ?*, (ed.) William Meacham, Hong Kong, 1987

Alexander, Jonathan and Paul Binski (eds), *Age of Chivalry: Art in Plantagenet England 1200–1400*, London, Royal Academy of Arts/Weidenfeld & Nicolson, 1987

Allen, Nicholas P., 'Verification of the Nature and Causes of the Photo-negative Images on the Shroud of Lirey–Chambéry–Turin, *De Arte* 51, Pretoria, UNISA, 1995

Ashe, Geoffrey, 'What Sort of Picture', *Sindon* 1966, pp. 15–19

Babinet, Robert, 'La profession de foi des derniers templiers', *La Pensée Catholique* 281, March–April 1996

Baima-Bollone, P., M. Jorio, A. L. Massaro, 'Identification of the Group of the Traces of Human Blood on the Shroud', *Shroud Spectrum International* 6, March 1983, pp. 3–6

Barber, Malcolm, 'The Templars and the Turin Shroud', *Catholic Historical Review*, April 1982, republished in *Shroud Spectrum International*, March 1983, pp. 16–34

Barbet, Pierre, *The Passion of Our Lord Jesus Christ*, trans. Earl of Wicklow, Dublin, Clonmore & Reynolds, 1954

Bede, *A History of the English Church and People*, trans. Leo Sherley-Price, Harmondsworth, Penguin, 1955

Berard, Aram, S. J., (ed.), *History, Science, Theology and the Shroud*, Proceedings of a Symposium at St Louis Missouri, 22–3 June 1991, Amarillo (Texas), 1992

Belting, Hans, *The Image and its Public in the Middle Ages, Form and Function in Early Paintings of the Passion*, trans. Mark Bartusis and Raymond Meyer, New Rochelle, New York, Aristide D. Caratzas, 1990

Bibliography

Blanchet, A., 'L'influence artistique de Constantine Porphyrogenète,' Pagkarpeia, *Mélanges Grégoire: Annales de l'Institut de Philologie et d'Histoire Orientales et Slaves* IX, 1949

Bowman, Sheridan, *Radiocarbon Dating*, London, British Museum Publications, 1990

Breckenridge, James D., 'The Numismatic Iconography of Justinian II', *144*, New York, American Numismatic Society, 1954

Buckton, David (ed.), *Treasures of Byzantine Art and Culture*, London, British Museum, 1994

Buttigieg, Br Michael, 'The Shroud of Turin and the Shroud of Rabat', offprint, Can. J. Azzopardi (ed.) *St Paul's Grotto, Church and Museum at Rabat, Malta*, Malta, Progress Press, 1990

Cahill, T. A., R. N. Schwab, B. H. Kusko, R. A. Eldred, G. Möller, D. Dutschke, D. L. Wick, 'The Vinland Map, Revisited: New Compositional Evidence on its Inks and Parchment', *Analytical Chemistry*, 15 March 1987, 59, pp. 829–33

Cameron, Averil, *The Sceptic and the Shroud. An Inaugural Lecture in the Departments of Classics and History delivered at King's College London on 19 April 1980*, London, 1980

Case, T. W., *The Shroud of Turin and the C-14 Dating Fiasco*, Cincinnati, White Horse, 1996

Cauwenberghe, André van, 'The 1902 Concealment', *Shroud Spectrum* 41, pp. 13 ff

Cennino Cennini, *The Craftsman's Handbook 'Il Libro dell'Arte'*, trans. D. V. Thompson Jr, New York, Dover, 1933

Charlesworth, James H. with others, *Jesus and the Dead Sea Scrolls*, New York, London, etc., Doubleday, 1992

Cherpillod, André, *Le Suaire de Truin, L'Impossible Objet*, Courgenard, self-published, 1996

Chevalier, Ulysse, *Étude Critique sur l'origine du Saint Suaire de Lirey–Chambéry–Turin*, Paris, Picard, 1900

Chifflet, Jean-Jacques, *De Linteis sepulchralibus Christi servatoris, crisis historica*, Paris, 1624

——*Hiérothonie de Jésus-Christ, ou Discours des Saints Suaires de Notre Seigneur*, trans. from Chifflet's Latin by A. Duchesne, Paris, 1631

Coghlan, Andy, 'Unexpected errors affect dating techniques', *New Scientist*, 30 September 1989

Cohen, Kathleen, *Metamorphosis of a Death Symbol: The Transi Tomb in the Late Middle Ages and the Renaissance*, Berkeley, University of California Press, 1973

Contini, Gianfranco, *L'opera completa di Simone Martini*, Milan, Rizzoli, 1970

Craig, Emily A. and Randall R. Bresee, 'Image Formation and the Shroud of Turin', *Journal of Imaging Science and Technology*, vol. 34, no. 1, January–February 1994

Crispino, Dorothy, 'Perceptions of an Antecessor', *Shroud Spectrum International* 23 June 1987, pp. 16–21

——'The Letter of Agostino Cusano', *Shroud Spectrum* 26, March 1988, pp. 12–17

——'The Charny Genealogy', *Shroud Spectrum International* 27, December 1990, p. 19

Damon, P. E. et al., 'Radiocarbon dating of the shroud of Turin', *Nature*, vol. 337, no. 6208, 16 February 1989, pp. 611–15

Daniel-Rops, H., *Daily Life in Palestine in the Time of Christ*, London, Weidenfeld & Nicolson, 1962

David, Rosalie, *Mysteries of the Mummies: The Story of the Manchester University Investigation*, London, Cassell, 1978

Drews, Robert, *In Search of the Shroud of Turin*, New Jersey, Roman & Allanheld, 1984

Dubarle, Père A. M., *Histoire ancienne du Linceul de Turin jusqu'au xiie siècle*, Paris, OEIL, 1985

——'La Première Captivité de Geoffroi de Charny et l'acquisition du Linceul', *Montre-nous Ton Visage*, no. 8, pp. 6–18

——'L'homèlie de Grégoire le Référendaire' in *Actes du Symposium de Rome*, op. cit., p. 51

Eastlake, Charles, *Methods and Materials of Painting of the Great Schools and Masters*, London, Longman, Brown, Green & Longman, 1857, repr. Dover, 1969

Eusebius, *History of the Church*, trans. G. A. Williamson, Harmondsworth, Penguin, 1965

Fossati, L., 'L'Ostensione del 1842', *Collegamento Pro Sindone*, November–December 1992, pp. 24–5

Froissart, *Chronicles*, trans. Geoffrey Brereton, Harmondsworth, Penguin, 1968

Gabrielli, Noemi, report in *La S. Sindone*, published as supplement to the *Rivista Diocesana Torinese*, January 1976

Gansfried, S., *Code of Jewish Law (Kitzur Shulchan Aruch)*, trans. Hyman E. Goldin, vol. IV, Ch. CXCVII, New York, Hebrew Publishing Company, 1927

Gervase of Tilbury, *Otia Imperialia* III, from *Scriptores rerum brunsvicensium*, (ed.) G. Liebnitz, Hanover, 1707

Glover, J., 'The Conservation of Mediaeval and Later Shrouds from Burials in North West England', *Archaeological Textiles*, Occasional Papers No. 10, United Kingdom Institute for Conservation of Historic and Artistic Works, 1990, pp. 49ff

Gove, Harry E., *Relic, Icon or Hoax: Carbon dating the Turin shroud*, Bristol and Philadelphia, Institute of Physics Publishing, 1996

——and S. J. Mattingly, A. R. David, L. A. Garza-Valdès, 'A Problematic Source of Organic Contamination of Linen', *Nuclear Instruments and Methods in Physics Research* [in press]

Grabar, André, 'La Sainte Face de Laon et le Mandylion dans l'art orthodoxe',

Seminarium Kondakovianum, Prague, 1935

Haas, Nicu, 'Anthropological Observations on the Skeletal Remains from Giv'at ha-Mivtar', *Israel Exploration Journal*, vol. 20, nos 1–2, 1970

Heller, John, *Report on the Shroud of Turin*, Boston, Houghton Mifflin, 1983

Jackson, John, 'Foldmarks as a Historical Record of the Turin Shroud', *Shroud Spectrum* 11, 1984, pp. 6–29

——'New Evidence that the Turin Shroud was the Mandylion', *Actes du Symposium de Rome*, op. cit., pp. 301ff

Jones, Mark (ed.), *Fake? The Art of Deception*, London, British Museum, 1990

Josephus, *The Jewish War*, trans. G. A. Williamson, Harmondsworth, Penguin, 1981

Jumper, E. J., A. D. Adler, J. P. Jackson, S. F. Pellicori, J. H. Heller, J. R. Druzik, 'A comprehensive examination of the various stains and images on the Shroud of Turin', in J. B. Lambert (ed.), *Archaeological Chemistry III, Advances in Chemistry Series*, no. 205, American Chemical Society, pp. 446–76

Kaeuper, Richard and Elspeth Kennedy, *The Book of Chivalry of Geoffroi de Charny: Text, Context and Translation*, Philadelphia, University of Philadelphia Press, 1996

Keen, Maurice, *Chivalry*, Newhaven, Yale University Press, 1984

Kersten, Holger and Elmar Gruber, *The Jesus Conspiracy: the Turin Shroud and the Truth about the Resurrection*. Shaftesbury (Dorset), Element, 1994

Kingsbury, Paul, 'Material Witness: Professor Robert Drews unravels the Shroud of Turin's mute testimony', *Vanderbilt Alumnus*, Summer 1984

Kohlbeck, Joseph A. and Eugenia L. Nitowski, 'New Evidence May Explain Image on Shroud of Turin', *Biblical Archaeology Review*, July–August 1986, pp. 23–4

La Favia, Louis M., *The Man of Sorrows: Its Origin and Development in Tracento Florentine Painting*, Rome, Edizioni 'Sanguis', 1980

Laureau, E., 'Le Saint-Suaire de Turin à Mont-Saint-Jean', *Almanach de Mont-Saint-Jean Missery* (Côte d'Or), 1910

Lavoie, Gilbert R. and B. Bonnie, Revd Donovan, J. Vincent, John S. Ballas, 'Blood on the Shroud of Turin: Part II' *Shroud Spectrum International* 8, September 1983, pp. 2–10

Leone, Domenico, *El Santo Sudario en España*, Barcelona, Biblioteca Sindoniana, 1959

Longnon, Jean and Raymond Cazelles, *Les Très Riches Heures du Duc de Berry, Musée Condé, Chantilly*, London, Thames & Hudson, 1969

W. C. McCrone, 'Light-Microscopical Study of the Turin Shroud' III, *The Microscope* 29, 1981, pp. 19–38

——and C. Skirius, 'Light-Microscopical Study of the Turin Shroud' I & II, *The Microscope* 28, 1980, pp. 1–13

——'Microscopical Study of the Turin "Shroud" in *Newsletter of Analytical Chemistry Division of American Chemical Society*, Spring 1989

——'Microscopical Study of the Turin Shroud' IV, *The Microscope* (publication date not known)

——'Chemical Analytical Study of the Vinland Map', Report to Yale University Library, Yale University, New Haven (Connecticut), 1974

McNeal, Edgar H., *The Conquest of Constantinople, translated from the Old French*, Columbia University Records of Civilization 23, New York, 1936

Meacham, William, 'The Authentication of the Turin Shroud: An Issue in Archaeological Epistemology', *Current Anthropology*, vol. 24, no. 3, June 1983, pp. 283–311

——(ed.), *Turin Shroud – Image of Christ, Proceedings of a Symposium held in Hong Kong March 1986*, Turin Shroud Photographic Exhibition Organising Committee, Hong Kong, March 1987

Meek, H. A., *Guarino Guarini and his Architecture*, New Haven, Yale University Press, 1988

Meiss, Millard, *French Painting in the Time of Jean de Berry: The Late Fourteenth Century and the Patronage of the Duke*, London, Phaidon, 1967

Migne, J. P., *Patrologia Cursus Completus, Series Latina*, Paris, 1844–55

——*Series Graeca*, Paris, 1857–66

Miller, V. D. and S. F. Pellicori, 'Ultraviolet fluorescence photography of the Shroud of Turin', *Journal of Biological Photography*, vol. 49, no. 3, July 1981, pp. 71–85

Mills, Allan A., 'Image Formation on the Shroud of Turin: the reactive oxidation intermediates hypothesis', *Interdisciplinary Science Reviews*, vol. 20, no. 4, December 1995, pp. 319–27

Moretto, Gino, *Sindone, La Guida*, Turin, Editrice Elle di Ci, 1996

Muir, Lynette R., 'The Holy Shroud in Medieval Literature', *Sindon*, December 1982, pp. 23–36

Murray, Stephen, *Building Troyes Cathedral: The Late Gothic Campaigns*, Indianapolis, Indiana University Press, 1987

Nelson, Jan A., 'The Holy Mandylion of Edessa and the Legend of Saint Alexis', *Medieval Studies in Honor of Robert White Linker*, Editorial Castalia, 1973, p. 155–61

Nickell, Joe, *Inquest on the Shroud of Turin*, New York, Prometheus, 1983

——'Pollens on the "Shroud": A Study in Deception', *Skeptical Inquirer*, vol. 18, Summer 1994, pp. 379–85

Nitowski, Eugenia L., *The Field and Laboratory Report of the Environmental Study of the Shroud in Jerusalem*, Salt Lake City, Carmelite Monastery, 1986

Perret, M., 'Essai sur l'histoire du S. Suaire du XIVe au XIVe siècle', *Mémoires de l'Académie des Sciences, Belles Lettres et Arts de Savoie*, IV, 4IV, 1960, pp. 49–121

Petrosillo, Orazio and Emanuela Marinelli, *The Enigma of the Shroud: A Challenge to Science*, trans. from the Italian by Louis J. Scerri, Malta, Publishers Enterprises Group, 1996

Picknett, Lynn and Clive Prince, *Turin Shroud: In Whose Image? The Shocking Truth Unveiled*, London, Bloomsbury, 1994

Piczek, Isabel, *Why the Shroud of Turin Could not have been the Work of a Clever Artist*, Los Angeles, private publication, 1989

——*The Shroud of Turin According to the Professional Arts. Why it cannot be a painting*, private publication, 1991

Rhein, Reginald W. Jr, 'The Shroud of Turin: Medical Examiners Disagree', *Medical World News* 21, no. 26, 22 December 1980, p. 50

Riggi, Giovanni, *Rapporto Sindone (1978–87)*, 3M edition, Milan, 1988 (also trans. into English by John D'Arcy, private publication)

Rodante, Sebastiano, 'The Coronation of Thorns in the Light of the Shroud', *Shroud Spectrum* 1, 1982, pp. 4–24

Rohan Book of Hours, The, Bibliothèque Nationale, Paris, Introduction by Millard Meiss, London, Thames & Hudson, 1973

Runciman, Steven, 'Some Remarks on the Image of Edessa', *Cambridge Historical Journal* III, 1929–31

——*The Emperor Romanus Lecapenus and his Reign*, Cambridge University Press, 1963

——*A History of the Crusades*, 3 vols, Harmondsworth, Peregrine, 1965

Sava, Anthony F., 'The wounds of Christ', *Catholic Biblical Quarterly* 16, 1957

Scavone, Daniel C., 'The Shroud of Turin in Constantinople: The Documentary Evidence', *Daidalikon; Studies in Memory of Raymond V. Schroder, S. J.*, (ed.) Raymond F. Sutton, Jr, Wauconda (Illl.), Bolchazy-Carducci, 1989

——'The Turin Shroud from 1200 to 1400', *Alpha to Omega: Studies in Honor of George John Szemler on his Sixty-Fifth Birthday*, (ed.) W. J. Cherf, Chicago, Ares, 1993

Schiller, Gertrud, *Iconography of Christian Art*, vol. II, London, Lund Humphries, 1972

Segal, J. B., *Edessa The Blessed City*, Oxford, Clarendon, 1970

Sinclair, T. A., *Eastern Turkey: An Architectural and Archaeological Survey*, vol. IV, London, Pindar, 1990

Skelton, R. A., T. E. Marston, G. D. Painter, *The Vinland Map and the Tartar Relation*, New Haven (Connecticut), Yale University Press, 1965

Sox, Revd David, *File on the Shroud*, London, Coronet/Hodder & Stoughton, 1978

——*The Image on the Shroud: Is the Turin Shroud a Forgery?*, London, Unwin Hyman, 1981

——*The Shroud Unmasked: Uncovering the Greatest Forgery of all Time*, Basingstoke, Lamp, 1988

Stauffer, Ethelbert, *Christ and the Caesars*, London, SCM Press, 1955

Stevenson, Kenneth E. and Gary R. Habermas, *Verdict on the Shroud*, Ann Arbor, Servant, 1981

Taylor, Michael, *A Critical Edition of Geoffroy de Charny's Livre Charny and the*

Demandes pour la Joute, les Tournois et la Guerre, University of North Carolina at Chapel Hill, 1977

Teil, Joseph du, *Autour de Saint-Suaire de Lirey*, 1902

Thurston, Herbert, 'The Holy Shroud as a Scientific Problem', *The Month* 101, 1903

Tuchman, Barbara, *A Distant Mirror*, Harmondsworth, Penguin, 1979

Upinsky, A. A. (ed.), *L'Identification Scientifique de l'Homme du Linceul Jésus de Nazareth: Actes de Symposium Scientifique International, Rome 1993*, Paris, CIELT, François-Xavier de Guibert, 1995

Vial, Gabriel, 'The Shroud of Turin: A Technical Study', *Shroud Spectrum International* 38–9, March–June 1991, pp. 7–20

Vignon, Paul, *Le Saint Suaire devant la science, l'archéologie, l'histoire, l'iconographie, la logique*, Paris, Masson, 1939

Volckringer, Jean, *The Holy Shroud: Science Confronts the Imprints*, trans. Victoria Harper, Manly, Runciman, 1991

Walsh, John, *The Shroud*, New York, Random House, 1963

Weitzmann, Kurt, 'A Constantinopolitan Lectionary', *Studies in Art and Literature for Bella da Costa Greene*, (ed.) Dorothy Winer, Princeton, Princeton University Press, 1954

——'The Origin of the Threnos', *De Artibus Opuscula XL Essays in Honor of Erwin Panofsky*, (ed.) Millard Meiss, New York University Press, 1961

Whanger, Alan, 'Polarized Overlay Technique; A New Image Comparison Method and Its Applications', *Applied Optics* 24, no. 16, 15 March 1985, pp. 766–72

Wilcox, Robert, *Shroud*, London, Corgi, 1978

Wild, Robert A., 'The Shroud of Turin – Probably the work of a 14th-century artist or forger', *Biblical Archaeology Review*, March–April 1984

Wilson, Ian, *The Turin Shroud*, London, Gollancz, 1978

——*The Evidence of the Shroud*, London, O'Mara, 1986

——*Holy Faces, Secret Places*, London, Doubleday, 1991

Zaccone, Gian Maria, 'La Fotografia della Sindone del 1898: Recenti Scoperte e Confereme nell'Archivio Pia', *Sindon*, new series, III, 3 December 1991, pp. 69–94

Zaninotto, Gino, *Jehohanan, Cruciario di Gerusalemme Contemporaneo di Gesu*, Rome, 1986

Zias, J. and E. Sekeles, 'The Crucified Man from Giv'at ha-Mivtar; A Reapprasial', *Israel Exploration Journal* 35, 1985, pp. 22–7

Zugibe, Frederick T., *The Cross and the Shroud. A Medical Examiner Investigates the Crucifixion*, New York, Angelus, 1982, p. 108

INDEX

Abbey du Paraclet, 130
Abelard, Peter, 130
Abgar V (Ukkama), King of Edessa, 144, 161, 162, 164–5, 166, 169, 172, 174, 263, 265, 270
Abgar VIII (Lucius Aelius), King of Edessa, 165, 166–9, 172, 173–6, 264, 266, 267; fig. 22, pl. 41a
Abgar IX, King of Edessa, 264
Abu Nasr Yahya, 270
accelerator mass spectrometry (AMS), 5–6, 180–1, 185, 192, 193, 194, 303
Acireale, 295
Acre, 208
Acts of Thaddaeus, 266
Addai, 164–5, 169, 172, 173–6, 263, 264, 265, 270
Adler, Dr Alan, 80–1, 82, 83, 87–9, 90, 92, 96, 97, 235, 310; pl. 27c
Agca, Mehmet Ali, 305
Aggai, 165, 169
Alcoy, 292
Alexander Jannaeus, 43
Alexis, St, 269
Allen, Professor Nicholas, 10, 212–18, 235; pl. 47
Amadeus VIII, Duke of Savoy, 281, 282
Amadeus IX, Duke of Savoy, 283, 284
ammonia salts, 213, 215
AMSTAR, 238
Analytical Chemistry, 199
Ananias, 166
anatase, 199, 200
Anatolia, 100, 148, 267
Anderson, P.J., 191, 302
Anne of Brittany, Queen of France, 287
Anne of Cyprus, Duchess of Savoy, 118
Annecy, 292
Anselme, Père, 133
Aosta, 116, 291
Arabs, 71, 213

aragonite, 105–7; fig. 11
Archer, Scott, 210
Arcis, Pierre d', Bishop of Troyes, 7, 17, 20, 74, 79, 83, 111, 120, 121–2, 126, 127, 128–9, 195, 204, 278, 280, 281; pl. 3a
Arizona University, 6, 181, 183, 185, 187, 192, 220–1, 224, 229, 243, 309–10
Arpe, Jean del', 288, 289
Arthur, King, 169–71, 172, 273
Ashe, Geoffrey, 203
Assisi-Bini, Silvestro da, 293
ASSIST, 101–3, 104, 306, 310
Athens, 273, 274
Atomic Energy Research Establishment, 233, 302
Avigliano, 284
Avignon, 128, 197, 274
Aymon of Geneva, 279, 280

bacteria, bioplastic coating, 84, 223–30, 232; fig. 26, pl. 48
Baden, Dr Michael, 39
Baibars, Sultan, 207
Baima-Bollone, Professor Pierluigi, 89, 304, 313
Baldwin II, Emperor, 274
Ballestrero, Cardinal Anastasio, 5, 8, 90, 93, 183–4, 187, 190, 244, 303, 305, 306, 307, 308, 311
Barbero, Fr Francesco, 2
Barbet, Dr Pierre, 26, 35, 37, 50, 74, 86, 300, 302
Barclay, Vera, 190–1, 301–2
Baroque art, 36
Baufremont, Jean de, 281–2
Beatis, Don Antonio de, 288
Beatrice, Duchess of Savoy, 288
Becket, St Thomas à, 127
Bede, Venerable, 171, 172, 267
Beggiano, Archbishop Michele, 296
Belgrade, 137, 139
Benedict XIV, Pope, 297

323